## Additional Praise for *The Right Moment*

Voted a "Book World Rave" by *The Washington Post* and a "Choice Selection" by *The Chicago Tribune*.

"The story of [Reagan's] rise is ably told by Matthew Dallek in his well-researched chronicle of Reagan's extraordinary run for the California governorship in 1966, a victory nearly as total as Goldwater's loss. By crushing the incumbent Edmund 'Pat' Brown, a star of the Democratic Party's liberal wing, Reagan rescued Goldwaterism and made it the dominant force in the modern GOP...and in the politics of the past thirty-five years."

—Sam Tanenhaus, *The New Republic*

"*The Right Moment*...is an inspiration for me right now. I'm running for governor, just as Reagan did, but I also appreciate the book's spirit of hope and the example of how somebody can reach inside himself."

—2002 California GOP gubernatorial candidate,
Bill Simon, *National Review Online*

"Dallek is masterful at providing the telling detail.... [His] thorough account provides the raw material for an explanation of Reagan's political success."

—*The American Prospect*

"In this briskly readable, insightful...study, Dallek (who has been a columnist for *Slate* and a contributor to the *Atlantic Monthly*, *Salon*, and other publications) argues with some justification that the California election was a watershed event.... Dallek's even-handed, incisive critique will compel both liberals and conservatives to rethink their strategies."

—*Publishers Weekly*

"*The Right Moment* may be the seminal work on Reagan's first gubernatorial campaign.... Dallek grasps the long-term importance of those early Reagan years and understands that Reagan personally was a vital, irreplaceable force within that period, and thus far beyond as well. This book...will help shape the historical view of Ronald Reagan."

—*The American Enterprise Online*

"By zeroing in on this half-forgotten episode of Reagan's career, Dallek shows how the consequences of one election can reverberate throughout the years.... Readers will be drawn to *The Right Moment* for its detailed chronicle of how Reagan got his start in politics."

—*Amazon.com*

"Exhaustively researched in primary sources, *The Right Moment* nevertheless moves at a breathtaking pace. Ours is a golden age of political biography and reportage, and with this stunning debut Matthew Dallek joins the front ranks of practitioners. In the 1966 gubernatorial contest between Ronald Reagan and Edmund G. (Pat) Brown, long-standing alliances collapsed and the politics of the nation itself veered in a new and post-New Deal direction. Here at once is the inside story and the national significance of what happened that summer and fall in volatile California."

—Dr. Kevin Starr, State Librarian of California and author
of *The Americans and the California Dream* series

# THE RIGHT MOMENT

*Ronald Reagan's First Victory and the Decisive Turning Point in American Politics*

MATTHEW DALLEK

OXFORD
UNIVERSITY PRESS

Oxford New York
Auckland Bangkok Buenos Aires
Cape Town Chennai Dar es Salaam Delhi Hong Kong
Istanbul Karachi Kolkata Kuala Lumpur Madrid
Melbourne Mexico City
Mumbai Nairobi São Paulo Shanghai
Taipei Tokyo Toronto



First published by The Free Press,
A Division of Simon & Schuster Inc., 2000
1230 Avenue of the Americas, New York, New York 10020

Published as an Oxford University Press paperback, 2004
198 Madison Avenue, New York, New York 10016

www.oup.com



Library of Congress Cataloging-in-Publication Data

Dallek, Matthew, 1969-
The right moment : Ronald Reagan's first victory and the decisive turning point in American politics / Matthew Dallek.
p. cm.
Originally published: New York : Free Press, c2000.
With a new afterword.
Includes bibliographical references and index.
ISBN 0-19-517407-0 (pbk.)
1. California—Politics and government—1951–
2. Governors—California—Election.
3. Reagan, Ronald.
4. Brown, Edmund G. (Edmund Gerald), 1905–
5. United States—Politics and government—1945–1989—Case studies.
I. Title.

F866.2 .D35 2004
973.92'092dc22 2003026282

1 3 5 7 9 8 6 4 2

*Printed in the United States of America on acid-free paper*

To my parents, Robert and Geraldine

and

to my sister, Rebecca

# *Contents*

*INTRODUCTION*: The Critical Years *ix*

ONE The Giant Killer *1*
TWO The Anticommunist *25*
THREE "Are You Now, or Have You Ever Been, a *Liberal*?" *42*
FOUR "Run Ronnie Run" *62*
FIVE "You've Got to Get Those Kids Out of There" *81*
SIX "A Bunch of Kooks" *103*
SEVEN "Charcoal Alleys" *128*
EIGHT The George Wallace of California *150*
NINE The Search for Order *173*
TEN Prairie Fire *212*

*EPILOGUE* *240*
*AFTERWORD* *243*
*NOTES* *255*
*ACKNOWLEDGMENTS* *285*
*INDEX* *289*

# *Introduction*

## *The Critical Years*

RONALD REAGAN redefined politics like no one since Franklin Roosevelt. His impact is so encompassing, so lasting, that pundits have even coined a phrase for it: the "Reagan revolution." There is widespread agreement on the meaning of that revolution: Reagan convinced us that government was not the solution, it was the problem. Taxes were too high, social programs were counterproductive, regulations were stifling entrepreneurial energy, and the United States was failing to prosecute the cold war in a vigorous manner. Two issues lay at the heart of the revolution: economics and foreign policy. It began in 1980. It continues to this day.

In truth the Reagan revolution began in 1966, and it was not primarily about economics or foreign policy. Reagan's stunning, out-of-nowhere victory in the California governor's race against two-term incumbent and Democratic giant Pat Brown marked the arrival of the Right in postwar American politics. Reagan's leadership of that movement is perhaps his most enduring legacy. It is also a story that has never been properly told.

In the mid-1960s revolution was in the air. Leaders of the New Left spoke of revolt against the Establishment; leaders of the Far Right echoed them in talk of toppling the liberal order. Media images were filled with violence: frightened National Guardsmen brandished fixed bayonets in Watts, where burned-out buildings lay in ruin; angry activists marched on military bases; protests erupted against segregated hotels and businesses; students turned out by the thousands to fight for free speech on campus; anticommunist leaders held rallies and workshops to teach people how to defend their homes and schools against the red menace. This was a time of stark contrasts, nowhere more so than in California. The much-discussed New Left activists of the '60s were offset by an equally impassioned group on the other side. For every organizer from Students for a Democratic Society (SDS) there was a John Birch activist; for every civil rights marcher there was an anticommunist rally-goer; for every antiwar protester there were several more who sympathized with American aims in Vietnam.

Ronald Reagan's race against Pat Brown—the real Reagan revolution—began as a debate about retaking control of a society in chaos. What Ronald Reagan stood for above all was law and order.

Reagan and Brown clashed on every issue, major and minor, of the day. Understanding the collapse of the liberal order and the rise of the conservative movement requires understanding how Reagan and Brown, during the several years leading up to 1966, came to embrace such bitterly opposed visions of government and society.

Reagan was a card-carrying conservative, Brown a proud liberal. For Reagan, opposing communism was paramount. For Brown, anticommunism was but one issue in foreign affairs and a nonissue at home. Reagan saw the welfare-state policies of recent decades as a slippery slope toward socialism. Brown viewed governmental programs as the best way to achieve a "great society." Reagan denounced moral decline on campus; Brown thanked God for the spectacle of students protesting. Brown seized an opportunity to lead the civil rights movement into the new frontier of fair housing; Reagan believed that even the 1964 Civil Rights Act was unconstitutional. Faced with urban riots, Brown looked to government to help eradicate poverty; Reagan vowed zero tolerance for criminals.

Prior to 1966, Reagan's views on all of these questions were considered extreme, not least by Brown and his followers. In 1962, Reagan was indeed part of a marginal movement; in 1964, Barry Goldwater led the movement in a national election, but suffered a stinging defeat. Reagan could not possibly have beaten Brown prior to 1966; only civil rights, Berkeley, Watts, and Vietnam made it possible. It was Reagan's promise to arrest moral decline that won him a million-vote victory over the popular incumbent, who had beaten Richard Nixon in 1962 and seemed destined to usher in California's progressive future.

Tomes have been written about Reagan, chronicling the dominant events of his life and career. They detail his early years in Illinois, exploits as an athlete, rise to fame in radio and film, and of course his two terms in the White House. Former aides have produced a stream of memoirs, and biographers have examined the main features of his presidency, from his victory over Jimmy Carter to his supply-side economic program to his role in Iran-Contra. Yet even the biographers rarely spend more than one or two chapters discussing his rise as a politician in the early and mid-1960s. Reagan's official biographer, Edmund Morris, passes over the 1966 election in a few short pages, his narrator explaining that he was not in California at the time.

Politics is about ideas, but it is also about the people who champion those ideas. How Ronald Reagan and Pat Brown came to embody two utterly contrasting sets of ideas is a fascinating story of two men who mirrored each other in many ways. Each came from a troubled home with a father who struggled with alcoholism. Each had his own conversion, Brown from Republican to New Deal Democrat, Reagan from New Deal Democrat to anticommunist Republican. Each became a pioneer in his political party: Brown was only the second Democrat to win statewide office in California in the twentieth century, and he was the leading voice of liberalism in the state. Reagan made the conservative movement legitimate for the first time, both in California and later in the nation.

In 1966 these two titans faced off in a battle of worldviews. Law and order was the hinge on which an era turned, yet the particular strategies involved were crucial. For the first time, the conservative movement was able to distance itself from the anticommunist fringe. For the first time, the conservatives learned how to push the right buttons on key issues, from race and riots to war and crime. Reagan successfully linked the liberal social programs of the '60s with disorder in the streets, and offered an alternative vision of what government should and should not do. The Reagan revolution would prove so lasting because the formulas developed in the heat of the moment—pro–social order, pro–individual liberty, anti–government meddling—had a lasting appeal. Americans, like most people, crave peace and prosperity. The Reagan revolution has come to be associated with the free market. Yet at its origins, and perhaps still today, it is equally about social order.

# THE RIGHT MOMENT

ONE

# THE GIANT KILLER

> The election reaffirms our conviction that the people of California are resolved to move forward with courage and confidence. Offered reaction by the radical right, the voters emphatically declined. Offered government by retreat, the people preferred progress. Clearly then, our duty is to bring to California the forward force of responsible liberalism.
>
> —PAT BROWN, Inaugural Address, 1959

MOST AMERICANS KNOW that at one point in his life Ronald Reagan was a staunch Democratic supporter of Franklin Roosevelt and the New Deal. Most do not know that Pat Brown started life as a Republican. One irony of their confrontation is that both men wound up standing for ideas that they once eschewed. Reagan would change his politics during the early years of the cold war, at a time of terrible anticommunist tension. Brown would change his at a similar moment of national peril, during the Depression and New Deal—a decade before Reagan's political crucible.

In 1934 the Great Depression cut a wide swath of misery through California, and San Francisco lay squarely in its path. A rough-and-tumble blue-collar town teeming with burly shipyard workers, tattooed stevedores, and seedy waterfront pubs, San Francisco was a city on the verge of revolt. Approximately 50,000 working-class Irish immigrants resided in uneasy proximity to growing numbers of Italian, German, and Chinese immigrants, a poor and increasingly desperate population living in tightly packed boardinghouses and makeshift apartment buildings. In the late spring, as labor unrest swept the United States, thousands of disgruntled longshoremen went on strike, shutting down the city's ports and fueling talk of a general walkout. Newspapers blared headlines about an impending urban implosion while printing pictures of helmeted soldiers with gas masks covering their faces standing in battle formation ready to cut a bloody path through "anyone foolish enough to defy this and other heavily-armed outfits."[1]

From the twelfth floor of the Russ Office Building on Montgomery Street in downtown San Francisco, a young lawyer named Edmund Gerald "Pat" Brown thought hard about the deteriorating economic situation. It was not something he did of necessity. A successful attorney with a firm footing in the city's legal community, Brown had a growing family, a sound professional career ahead of him, and strong ties to the Republican political machine in San Francisco. Most of his friends and family were members of the Republican party, and Brown had throughout his adult life subscribed to the Republican belief that the American economic system was the best in the world. Those who failed to succeed in it were corrupt, lazy, or both.

But as the Depression crept its way across California, it also began to whittle away at Brown's long-standing assumptions about the political parties and the ideologies that undergirded them. The labor struggles and street demonstrations and social discord concerned Brown. Sympathetic to those who had been hardest hit by the economic slump, worried about violence in the streets, Brown had been seriously reconsidering his Republican party affiliation since 1931. That year, Matthew Tobriner, a fiery young labor lawyer working down the hall, decided to abandon Herbert Hoover and the big business Republicans and embrace the party of Franklin Roosevelt. Tobriner had lost faith in the ability of Hoover to deal with the economy, and, eager to convince his less prescient friends of the error of their ways, he began telling Brown to open his eyes. The Republicans, Tobriner chided, represented the nation's business tycoons and corporate behemoths, and its vaunted standard-bearers—Calvin Coolidge, Warren Harding, and Herbert Hoover—had failed to stem the misery. They had done nothing to help American farmers whose fields lay barren through no fault of their own; had done nothing for the small entrepreneurs and manual laborers who played by the rules but ended up barely making ends meet. Franklin Roosevelt and the Democratic party were stepping into the political breach, taking responsibility for the American masses, doing for the man on the street what the uncaring and callous GOP would not.

Brown spent a good deal of time thinking about Tobriner's arguments, and he allowed that some of those arguments made sense. But Brown was torn: He recalled his own personal success, and reasoned that if he could make his way out of poverty and build a successful law practice, anyone could. Tobriner kept urging Brown to sever his ties to the Republican party, and for the next two years the men engaged in heated debates. One time Tobriner reached into his back pocket and pulled out a copy of *The New Republic* and asked his friend to read it. Brown returned to his office and did so, but he remained unconvinced.

The Republicans, he thought after putting down the liberal rag, would return to power as soon as the American economy rebounded.

Yet the American economy did not recover, and Tobriner continued in his hard-charging ways: He railed against tycoons and even began quoting the liberal newspaper columnist Walter Lippmann on the crumbling of the old order. "The only real question among intelligent people," Tobriner quoted Lippmann as saying, "is how business methods are to be altered, not whether they are to be altered. For no one unafflicted with invincible ignorance desires to preserve our economic system in its existing form." In 1934 Brown finally concluded that Lippmann and Tobriner were right: The Republicans represented the wealthy few; Democrats stood for the average working man. One morning that year, with farm prices at record lows and 20 million Americans out of work, Brown walked into the men's room on the twelfth floor of the Russ Office Building and told Tobriner that he had decided to become a Democrat. Tobriner responded with a whoop and a shout.[2]

Brown's switch was not unusual. Like many young men of his generation, Brown had decided that the GOP program, as he said years later, amounted to a set of outmoded economic notions and "an appeal for human selfishness." Brown also had come to admire Franklin Roosevelt, the new president whose fireside radio chats and promises of federally funded relief and recovery encouraged millions of Americans in these years. But Brown had another reason for bolting the Republicans—he wanted a career in politics. Although he had never held elected office, by 1934 Brown had his sights firmly set high. He realized, as had so many aspiring politicians in this era, that a shift in the American political order was underway, that the New Deal offered a popular political program that might help a budding politician such as Brown realize his ambitions. To be sure, Roosevelt's reform agenda dovetailed nicely with Brown's burgeoning activist leanings; it also offered him a way to get ahead in the one field that by the mid-1930s really mattered to him.[3]

BROWN'S BELIEFS and aspirations, the ones that would convince him to become a Democrat and make him one of the leading liberal politicians of the 1960s, sprang from a variety of eclectic and unlikely sources: the seedy card parlors and gambling dens south of San Francisco's Market Street; the Catholic church that his parents shunned; the literary lectures, fiery political rallies, and subdued libraries to which his mother dragged him; and the crush of economic hard times. Brown's political and moral tenets evolved slowly, imperceptibly at times, forged in family crises and world events. They also had deep roots in the immigrant West. Brown's mother Ida Shuckman was a first generation German Protestant who arrived in San Francisco in 1896, while his father, Edmund Joseph Brown, was a burly Irish-Catholic blade. The young couple shared an immigrant background but precious little else. He was an entrepreneur on the rise and a handsome charmer with a gift for blarney; she, a self-taught matron with an insatiable appetite for knowledge. Edmund enjoyed whiskey and craps; Ida loved books and lectures. He was fleshy, with wide and searching eyes and a fading shock of sandy-brown hair; she, rail thin, her neck so lithe it made her look like an eighteenth-century aristocrat. He cut deals and ran scams; she studied the Bible and attended lectures about deep and serious subjects.

They produced four children. The first, Edmund Gerald, arrived on April 21, 1905, a pudgy baby with big brown eyes who in his early years inherited his mother's passion for ideas, literature, and politics. Ida herself was an unusual woman for her time. Exceptionally bright and keenly interested in the larger world of political affairs, she had learned to read by the age of three, could quote from the classics by five, and was an ardent admirer of Jack London and Robert Louis Stevenson. She tried to inculcate her first child with a similar knowledge and interest in the outside world. When Brown was a child, Ida often dragged him and his brother Harold to packed political rallies and highbrow lectures by Mark Twain or other turn-of-the-century literary lions. She took Pat to see Governor Hiram Johnson speak at Dreamland Auditorium as he stumped for a United States Senate seat. She brought him to polling booths on election day, where the future governor would watch in awe as local officials tallied election returns. She encouraged him to campaign on behalf of a neighborhood grocery man running for the San Francisco Board of Supervisors, and she also, according to some rumors that would later take hold, brought her eldest to radical labor parades sponsored by the International Workers of the World—the Wobblies.[4]

Brown's father, Edmund Joseph, also shaped his son's view of the world, but in a much different way. A boisterous charmer and enterprising businessman, Edmund Senior passed on to Brown his considerable gift for gab and instilled in his namesake a strong desire to live clean, work hard, and avoid a life of poverty. In the years before Brown's birth, Edmund was an ambitious youth who after holding a series of low-paying, back-breaking jobs (horsecar conductor, laundry wagon driver) decided that the best way to get ahead in turn-of-the-century San Francisco was to start his own business. Hungry for his own slice of the bustling local economy, as a young man Edmund rented a cigar shop on Market Street and then used the profits from that store to acquire a handful of risky enterprises. In short order, Edmund purchased a photography studio, a penny arcade, a Market Street movie theater, and a novelty store where tourists could shop for trinkets. In the late 1900s, in the wake of the great earthquake of 1906, Edmund's businesses turned a substantial profit: American sailors on weekend shore leave began flocking to his photography studio, where they would have their pictures taken; tourists descended in droves on his trinkets shop, and local residents went in large numbers to the theater to catch the latest film. By 1910 Edmund had become a well-known fixture in the city's downtown, sporting derby hats and tailored suits while standing outside his business establishments and wooing customers into the store. Edmund earned enough money to purchase a three-flat house in the city's Western Addition, a new middle-class neighborhood on the outskirts of the city. But Edmund's good fortune and business success would prove short-lived. A heavy drinker and chronic gambler, Edmund spent many of his evenings holed up in one of the city's backroom gambling parlors, where he would sip bourbon, shoot craps, and play five-card draw (stud was illegal) against the hard-drinking, gamble-happy men who frequented such places. In 1912, a new theater outfitted with a brass band opened across the street from Edmund's, luring away his customers, forcing him to close shop. He made the mistake of trying to recoup his mounting losses by making a series of bets with bookies around town, and soon found himself plunged deeper into debt and mired in poverty. The family nest egg gone, in 1912 Edmund decided to put his two boys, ages 7 and 5, to work.[5]

From the first, Pat proved himself a hard worker and able breadwinner with a knack for deal making, corner cutting, and sales. He began his working life as a newspaper boy who trudged through the streets of San Francisco on Sunday mornings yelling "Chronicle! Examiner!" Later he worked as an usher at the Edison Theater, sold sodas at the fights, snapped pictures of tourists and sailors at his father's photography studio, attended to customers in his father's novelty store, and peddled holiday cards at Christmas time. Pat was a deft salesman and enterprising young businessman who sometimes hiked soda prices arbitrarily, concocted elaborate ruses to sell more Christmas cards, and raked in hundreds of dollars while gambling against boys his own age. Early on, Brown was determined to avoid his father's fate. Although he at first enjoyed hustling and swindling others out of their money, Brown developed an aversion toward the gaming life, with its floating craps games, swindlers, and loan sharks. Brown sometimes worked in his father's store while his father gathered with friends around a big table upstairs and gambled. Brown hated to see his father lose money and believed that Edmund's fast lifestyle and loose morals had contributed to the family's financial woes.[6]

Eager for a different existence, Brown plunged into his school work. A solid student, Brown above all was a rambunctious and popular youth with a flair for extracurricular activities and student politics. In elementary school he became a star soccer player, and after giving a rousing four-minute speech in the seventh grade in support of World War I liberty bonds in which he quoted the Revolutionary War hero, Patrick Henry ("Give me liberty or give me death," Brown shouted to classmates), he earned the nickname that would remain with him throughout his life. Brown cut an awkward figure in high school, weighing only ninety-five pounds, a spindly prepubescent who blossomed late. What he lacked in size he made up for in enthusiasm. Spirited and active in many of the school's extracurricular activities, Brown beat out an opponent for yell leader, starred on the hundred-pound basketball team, served as president of the camera and rowing clubs and the debating society, and helped organize the Nocturnes, a half-Jewish, half-Gentile fraternity known for its religious tolerance, private clubroom (well-furnished but no food), and raucous parties. Donning snappy, white flannel trousers and red jerseys with white megaphones emblazoned across the chest, Brown prided himself on being the most innovative and best-dressed cheerleader, and he enjoyed showering his team with confetti and balloons and whooping and yelling during sporting contests.[7]

After graduating from high school, when his family was unable to afford college, Pat accepted a job as a doorman at his father's cigar store. His duties included minding the shop and regulating the flow of traffic into his father's nightly game of five-card draw; for his hard work Brown received a hefty salary of $150 a month. He further boosted his income by running his own dice game at the front of the cigar store (often netting $200 a month in winnings). Quickly souring on the worlds of business and gambling and, eager to find work that would challenge his intellect and engage his ebullient personality, Brown decided to enroll in law school.[8]

The San Francisco College of Law was not the University of California at Berkeley, where many of Brown's fraternity friends had enrolled, but to Brown it represented a means to a better life, and he was determined to make the most of it. Working days, attending classes at night, and operating on the vague assumption that as a lawyer he would be able to make a good living and help out others, Brown worked grueling fifteen-hour days, a schedule that would become a hallmark of his later political career. A photograph from these years shows Brown sitting at a lawyer's table in the middle of what appears to be moot court, fast asleep, his head slumped over his briefcase, law tomes piled high in front of him. But Brown enjoyed the law and relished the furious pace. He became a top student in his class during his third year of law school, and after graduating he found a job working as an assistant to Milton Schmitt, a well-known blind attorney in the city who immediately took Brown under his wing. On cable cars that clacked their way over the hills of San Francisco, Brown skimmed his law books while Schmitt droned on about pending cases; during trial Brown helped his boss select juries and often read from court cases to bolster Schmitt's arguments.

Brown passed the bar in 1927, and after Schmitt was committed to a mental institution (he had begun comparing himself to Jesus Christ and babbling about making Brown a millionaire), Brown inherited his boss's practice and quickly established himself as a formidable lawyer in his own right. He was a jack-of-all-trades litigator who handled personal injury cases to divorces to bankruptcy cases (a lucrative area of the law during the Depression) to pro bono criminal defense work. In 1929 he eloped ("to save money," according to his wife) with his high school sweetheart Bernice Layne, the daughter of San Francisco Police Captain Arthur Layne. Children soon followed, and it seemed that Brown, although not yet twenty-five, had achieved the prize that had eluded his parents: a stable home and work life.[9]

But he wanted more. While he took a measure of satisfaction from helping clients and trying cases, Brown believed that there was only one career that would satisfy both his ambitions for fame and his yearning to perform good works. In high school Brown had run for class secretary and won, but he did not enjoy sitting in the back of the auditorium and being a note-taker, and he vowed that in the future he would seek out bigger offices that befit his talents. When he reached law school, Brown used to fantasize about being elected district attorney of San Francisco, assuring himself that someday he would be the chief law enforcement man in his city. Thus it was not entirely unexpected when Brown ran for the California State Assembly as a Calvin Coolidge Republican in 1928.[10]

Brown did not give much thought to the campaign or to the consequences of running for office, nor did he spend a great deal of time contemplating his party ties or political credos. Brown was a Republican, period. The party of Coolidge and Hoover dominated the machine politics of San Francisco, and virtually everyone Brown knew, from his father to his friends, belonged to and voted for the GOP. The party maintained such a viselike grip on local affairs, in fact, that a young man with political aspirations would have had to have been either dense or unusually brazen to side with the Democrats in the 1920s. Brown was neither; intensely driven, eager for the spotlight, and interested in public service, yes, but holding few firm political convictions. He considered politics a sport—a contest of men and wills in which what mattered was winning elections. When he did, on rare occasions, think about the beliefs and ideologies that undergirded the two major American parties, the GOP with its free market ideas made the most sense.

His campaign for a state assembly seat was doomed from the start. With only $500 to spend, and with Tom Finn, the Republican boss of San Francisco, backing Brown's opponent, the result was embarrassing. Brown received only 500 votes.

He would not run for political office again for eleven years, but politics would remain for the rest of his life near the surface of his thoughts and perhaps his one great passion in life. He began spending almost all of his free time frequenting local civic clubs and societies, cultivating potential political contacts, and attending campaign rallies and other political events. After switching to the Democrats in 1934, he won a seat on the San Francisco Democratic Central Committee and stuffed envelopes and gave speeches in support of Upton Sinclair, a utopian socialist and muckraking novelist who was running for governor that year on a promise to "End Poverty in California." Walloped at the polls, Sinclair imparted to Brown a simple lesson about American politics: One could not rail against the system and hope to win.[11]

From his first days as a Democrat, Brown blended the politics of urban reform with an intense interest in campaigns and political strategizing. Pragmatic, cautious, and attuned to the mood of voters and constituents, he believed strongly that men in public life possessed terrific power to accomplish good deeds and improve the lives of the people they served. Brown considered public service a noble endeavor, a wonderful way to spend one's life, and while he enjoyed the more grubby aspects of American politics—giving speeches, attending rallies, shaking hands, accosting voters on street corners—he believed above all that public officials either perpetuated the status quo and enriched and served themselves and their cronies, or performed good works, enacted needed reform measures, and left a lasting mark for the better on their communities and their cities. This was a stark approach to politics and governing, but Brown had good cause for embracing such a diametric view of the political process.

San Francisco in the 1930s was a city awash in corruption: illegal gambling parlors dotted the downtown district, small-time thieves committed robberies at will, corrupt policemen accepted bribes and kickbacks from criminal defense attorneys, and abortion mills and whorehouses abounded. Run for the most part by old-time machine politicians and a district attorney who turned a blind eye to crime, the city did little to improve itself. Brown believed that a program of municipal reform was just what was needed and his own personal ticket to a career in politics.

In the aftermath of the Sinclair campaign Brown plunged with verve into the politics of municipal reform. With the help of old friends and like-minded reformers, he created the New Guard, a nonpartisan organization committed to "bring[ing] about honesty and effectiveness in local government." Bylaws, however, prevented the New Guard from endorsing candidates for public office, and the organization proved impotent and soon disbanded. In 1935, after reading a series of articles about a group in Seattle called the New Order of Cincinnatus, Brown wrote a letter to Ralph Potts, the group's leader, in which he asked for permission to organize a Cincinnatus branch in San Francisco. Under Brown's leadership, the group blossomed quickly. Armed with scores of brash young men eager to extirpate corruption from the urban scene, the Order demanded that candidates file a statement of their assets and then place that statement in a safety deposit box. It also mounted a formidable campaign against incumbents on the San Francisco Board of Supervisors, holding press conferences, endorsing a rival slate of candidates, and adopting the campaign slogan "Skip the First Five," a reference to the supervisors in office. The campaign succeeded in ousting four of the board's five incumbents. The organization was exactly what Brown had been looking for, a "lively fighting" group composed of idealistic men committed to stamping out vice. Flush with his first real taste of political success, convinced that urban reform was a winning program that would prove popular with voters, Brown decided in early 1939 to challenge Matthew Brady, the long-time district attorney of San Francisco.[12]

Brown had been trying for some time to win a political appointment with either the mayor's office or the state administration in Sacramento. But his requests had been repeatedly rebuffed and he quickly concluded that if he wanted a career in politics he would have to strike out on his own. The district attorney's office seemed the perfect place for him to begin. Brady was a plodding attorney notorious for his do-nothing approach to police graft and lackadaisical attitudes toward law enforcement in general. Although Brown had never held elected office, and he realized his chances against the long-time incumbent were slim, Brown believed that Brady made a choice political target. Brown entered the campaign with great ardor; ringing doorbells and campaigning nonstop, he stumped everywhere in the city. He promised to transform San Francisco into a respectable city free of crime and criminals. Brown was easily beaten, but he made a respectable showing in a race he knew would be a trial run.[13]

Brown yearned for another shot at Brady, and almost immediately after the votes had been tallied from the 1939 campaign he began laying the groundwork for another race. Brown did not abandon his law practice, but he was growing bored with it. As the American nation found itself embroiled in World War II, Brown stayed home but felt guilty about doing so while men were fighting and dying overseas. Convinced that it was his duty to serve the public in some capacity, Brown also believed that he had a religious obligation to perform good works and lift up his fellow men.

In 1938 Brown had become a devout Catholic; his immersion in the church would shape for years to come his approach to politics and governing. In his younger years Brown had shown little feeling toward organized religion; his father was a Catholic, his mother a Protestant, and his parents feuded constantly about the role of religion in their household. Edmund wanted his boys to attend Mass on Sundays and Catholic schools during the week; Ida, however, felt a large dose of contempt toward the Catholic priests with their strict sermonizing, and she refused to send her children to parochial school. The battles grew rancorous and eventually contributed to Edmund and Ida's divorce. Brown reacted with bitter feelings toward organized churchgoing of all kinds. But in 1938 he experienced a kind of religious awakening. That year a fellow Democrat invited him to a religious retreat in the Santa Cruz Mountains. His curiosity piqued, Brown agreed to spend a weekend listening to the Catholic priests and reacquainting himself with his father's religion. Expecting to hear priests pontificating about purgatory and everlasting damnation, Brown, much to his surprise, found the sermons moving orations about the power of God's love. Brown listened intently as the priests argued that no matter how much material success a person acquired, there was always something more in life for which to strive: joining with God after death. Unexpectedly enthralled, he began to read Walter Lippmann on humanism and Carl Adam on Catholicism. He organized a bible study class for friends, and slowly his agnosticism gave way to a deeply felt devotion to God, Catholicism, and a commitment to carrying out God's work on earth.[14]

That work, for Brown, would continue to be found in politics. For the second race against Brady, Brown secured endorsements from two of San Francisco's most powerful dailies. The campaign would prove one of the most bruising of Brown's life. Reluctant to be tarred as a three-time loser, Brown launched a hard-hitting, exceedingly effective assault. When Brady accused the underworld of bankrolling Brown's campaign, Brown argued that his opponent was an incompetent law enforcement officer and a stupid man who himself had close ties to the bookies and abortionists in the city. Brown told voters that Brady had failed to stop the illegal card games and stamp out the city's lucrative gambling parlors, and he also blasted him for being a lazy lawyer who refused to do anything about police graft. Brady was an artful dodger, Brown complained, a do-nothing D.A. Campaigning eighteen hours a day, shaking hands with slaughterhouse workers, stumping at the produce and flower markets, giving speeches virtually every night, Brown worked himself to exhaustion. But he was armed with scores of supporters, a catchy rallying cry ("Crack down on crime, elect Brown this time"), and a compelling welter of negative information about his foe. On election day he finally achieved a victory.[15]

The district attorney's office that Brown inherited was a shambles, with few typewriters; part-time employees who wrote legal briefs and other court documents out by long hand; desk drawers bulging with paperwork; an oversized antique canvas-covered ledger as the docket for upcoming cases; and deputy district attorneys who often ran their own practices on the side. The city's entire legal system, in fact, resembled nothing so much as a bad joke: During trial, prisoners often found themselves locked in cage-like structures more appropriate for animals in a zoo. Brady's deputies had often personally handled bail money. Police and not attorneys often decided which charges to bring against criminals, and the city's more wily defense attorneys often kept their clients from jail with police payoffs and other well-placed bribes. Thomas Lynch, who would become Brown's top assistant in the office, had a simple description of the district attorney's office under Brady: "the most colossal disaster I've run into."[16]

Taking District Attorney Earl Warren in Oakland as his model, Brown embraced a slew of reforms. To be sure, he was not a radical eager to uproot the entire legal system in the city, and he was not above rewarding his supporters with political appointments and other plums. But Brown embarked on a systematic reform program that he believed would enjoy strong support from his constituents. He hired honest lawyers as his top deputies, warned police not to engage in corrupt activities, put a stop to the practice of police officers bringing indictments against criminals, and cracked down on abortionists, bookies, pornographers, and other leading members of the San Francisco underworld. Styling himself as a "mean little bastard" determined to crack down on crime, Brown even went so far as to close down his father's gambling parlor. As his reforms bore fruit and arrest rates began to soar, so too did Brown's reputation.[17]

The district attorney's office was only the start. In 1946, Brown decided to run for attorney general of the state of California. Running again as a law-and-order tough against a man Brown depicted as corrupt, Brown lost to the Los Angeles district attorney, Fred Howser, but proved himself a gregarious personality and a popular figure with a bright career ahead of him. Four years later, in 1950, Brown ran again and won. Feeding negative stories to the press linking Fred Howser to a bribery scandal, Brown succeeded in pressuring him to step down and retire from public life altogether. Promising voters that he would crack down on both crime and communists, Brown sailed to victory over a much weaker opponent and quickly went to work establishing himself as a no-nonsense attorney general who defended civil liberties, criticized state loyalty oaths and the red-baiting tactics of Joe McCarthy, and worked above all to root out official corruption in Sacramento. Allying himself with the popular Republican former governor Earl Warren, Brown considered running for that job in 1954 but ultimately decided that he could not defeat incumbent Goodwin "Goody" Knight. "My job as attorney general is not yet complete," Brown told disappointed Democrats at a state party convention in 1953. "My first three years must not be sacrificed for personal advancement. . . . Organized crime in California has been smashed. The network of gamblers and narcotics peddlers has been warned: 'Stay out of our state—there is no room for you here.' "[18]

Presiding over an office of 115 lawyers and bureaucrats, Brown's second term as attorney general looked much like his first. He worked to secure oil money owed the state, sued pornographic magazines, lambasted the sorry condition of state mental hospitals, and prosecuted corrupt assemblymen and California mafia dons. The sole Democrat to hold statewide office, Brown was easily the most popular and by far the best-known Democrat in California in the mid-1950s. Many in the party considered him their best chance of breaking the decades-long Republican stranglehold on the governorship, and activists and party leaders alike looked forward with great anticipation to the campaign season of 1958. Brown had been thinking for many years about running for governor; as district attorney he used to stand at his office window, longingly staring out at the San Francisco ferry building, and confess to Thomas Lynch, his longtime deputy, "You know, Tom, I can almost see Sacramento from here."[19]

But as the reality of the 1958 campaign approached, Brown harbored mixed feelings. No longer the brash upstart willing to take on all challengers no matter what the odds, in 1957 Brown again believed that if he ran for governor he would likely lose to Goody Knight, a relatively popular figure. The GOP controlled many of the major newspapers in California, and Brown would have to overcome a half-century history of Democratic futility in state gubernatorial campaigns. Now middle-aged, Attorney General Brown had a great deal at stake in any campaign for high office: He earned a nice salary and could likely continue for many years in a high-profile job that he found reasonably fulfilling. His wife Bernice and son Jerry were urging him to run for U.S. senator, because in Washington Brown would have more time for his family (Bernice's reason) and have an opportunity to shape world affairs (Jerry's reason). Somewhat worn down from two decades of nonstop politicking, Brown spent much of the year 1957 weighing his options. In late July, he even went so far as to tell a reporter from the *San Francisco Chronicle* that he was considering quitting politics and returning to private life.[20]

The admission that the most powerful Democratic leader in the state might bolt the political fray provoked a heated response from party faithful. Fred Dutton, Brown's top aide in the attorney general's office, chastised Brown for his comments, and using an old automatic typewriter at the United Auto Workers office in San Francisco, wrote a letter that he later mailed to the top 3,000 Democrats in the state. "We're approaching the next gubernatorial campaign," Dutton wrote party activists. "Who do you think the candidate should be? Do you think Pat Brown should run?" Upon receiving hundreds of responses to his query, most of which were favorably disposed toward Brown, Dutton promptly bundled up the letters and forwarded them to his boss, who was vacationing in Hawaii.[21]

In the end, what ultimately convinced him to run was the entry into the campaign of the senior United States senator from California, William Knowland. In a bizarre and complicated turn of events, Knowland announced that he was leaving the United States Senate, where he held great power as the minority leader, and returning to California to run for governor. Warning Knight that he would cut off most of his financial backing if he tried running for reelection, Knowland succeeded in pressuring the incumbent out of the contest and clearing a path for himself to his party's nomination. Knowland was a successful but plodding politician often derided as the "Senator from Formosa" for his fierce devotion to the anticommunist regime in Taiwan. Over the course of his long career Knowland evinced little interest in state politics; he had spent most of his political life feeling passionate about the titanic struggle between the Soviet-dominated Eastern bloc and the democratic and enlightened West. Political observers in California belittled Knowland's decision, arguing that he was simply trying to position himself better to campaign for president and speculating about Knowland's romantic life and troubled relations with his wife, Evelyn. Dutton wrote Brown excitedly from the East Coast: "The Knight-Knowland-Calif. political situation has gotten considerable coverage in Chicago, Detroit and NY. . . . The whole nation obviously seems to be zeroed in on our state. It's really a great opportunity!"[22]

Brown seized it quickly. In late August, three weeks after Knowland's announcement, Brown announced that he had decided to become a candidate for governor. Blasting his likely Republican opponent as a "reactionary who views the state's highest office only as a pawn in presidential power politics," Brown plunged into the 1958 gubernatorial contest with great passion. Mounting a centrist campaign designed to take advantage of Knowland's reputation as a right-wing firebrand, Brown worked hard to convince voters that he was a competent political leader well versed in state issues and a man who would govern in the bipartisan spirit of Earl Warren and Goody Knight. Cultivating his image as a moderate reformer, Brown brought into the campaign a host of prominent academics, lawyers, and businessmen, and they in turn produced a bevy of political position papers and helped put together a modest eight-point political program. The program included a promise by Brown that as governor he would work to abolish cross filing by voters, establish a Fair Employment Practices Committee (many states in the country already had one), reorganize government to make it more efficient, create a state department of economic development, provide government assistance to small businesses, appoint a "public defender of the consumer interest," solve classroom and teacher shortages, and accept "personal responsibility" for the adoption of a long overdue state water program. Calling his program by the relatively tame moniker of "responsible liberalism," Brown mostly hewed to the middle of the road and worked hard not to appear rash, indecisive, or a liberal ideologue eager to alter the face of California life once he was elected and in power.[23]

Brown reminded voters that Knowland had endorsed the unpopular right-to-work measure on the state ballot that year and he also drubbed the senator as an arrogant dullard who had wreaked havoc on his party simply because he wanted to be president. During the campaign, Knowland made a series of intemperate remarks and adopted any number of ill-conceived policy positions, and for the most part he came across to voters as the very man Pat Brown was warning them about—a right-wing radical unfit for the statehouse. Antagonizing labor leaders and union rank-and-file in the process, Knowland accused the United Auto Workers of harboring left-wing radicals and attacked Brown as an effete liberal who was in sympathy with the cause of communism. In the final days of the campaign Knowland's wife Evelyn mailed an incendiary letter to Republican leaders in the state in which she accused Knight of being "a tool of the labor bosses" and also vilified "'Patsy' Brown" as a puppet of organized labor.[24]

During his lengthy political career, Brown occasionally told the story of how as a young and aspiring politician in San Francisco he had spent years trying to win an election or a political appointment only to have his advances rebuffed; no one, Brown joked, recognized just how great a person and politician he really was. On November 4, 1958, the people of the state of California recognized Brown's greatness, handing him a stunning million-vote victory over his nationally known Republican political opponent. Trouncing a man who only a year earlier many had considered a serious contender for the presidency, and winning an election that made him only the second Democrat of the century to sit in the governor's chair, Brown achieved what by virtually all measures of the day was a sweeping electoral and political triumph. Brown's victory margin was enormous, and Democrats across the state rode his coattails into office. For the first time since 1878, Democrats in California would control both the state assembly and the state senate, marking a seismic shift in the political order that generated national media coverage and high expectations for the future from Democratic activists around the state.

Yet in the last days of 1958, even in the wake of this smashing election victory, it remained unclear what Brown would try to accomplish as governor. Brown had a long and illustrious record as a public servant, but in his previous political incarnations the governor-elect had dealt almost exclusively with legal and judicial matters; he possessed no experience in the legislative arena, had never in his life put together a legislative agenda, nor had he ever confronted the dizzying array of social and political issues that were sure to confront him now. Brown continued to invoke Hiram Johnson and Earl Warren, but how such admiration translated into a political program was anyone's guess. Johnson had made his mark on the state in the early 1900s, enacting a series of far-reaching reforms that affected the ballot and voting systems, and ferreting out corruption in Sacramento at a time when political kickbacks and payoffs were routine if troubling parts of the political process. Warren, in power during the 1940s and early 1950s, had worked to improve the public infrastructure in the state, had mobilized California to fight the Nazis and the Japanese during World War II (and as part of that, had agreed to intern in prison camps California residents and American citizens of Japanese descent), and at the same time had defended American civil liberties against conservative anticommunists eager to impose on government officials state loyalty oaths.

Pat Brown faced few of the same issues. He had run what by most reckonings was a bland campaign, proposing a slew of modest policy reforms but failing to articulate a larger vision of where he would take the state or what he considered the role of government in society. Brown had earned a reputation as a reliable vote-getter and tenacious fund-raiser but had not been a particularly brilliant orator or awe-inspiring statesman. He lacked the heroic aura of a President Dwight Eisenhower, possessed none of the good looks and dashing charm of a John F. Kennedy, and he sometimes shied from sticky political controversies and other such thorny situations. Brown had not served in the military, had failed to play a role in the national struggle against communism, and he also had had trouble making up his mind about important political matters. In short, there was little in Brown's earlier career that suggested a visionary in the rough.

But on January 5, 1959, before a joint session of the state legislature and a statewide television audience, Brown suggested that the conventional wisdom about his moderate, go-slow leanings might be wrong. On that day the newly installed governor delivered one of the more memorable inaugural addresses in state history, mapping his vision for California's future and giving voice to the reform currents that seemed to be gathering momentum in the state. Brown remained rather vague about which bills and programs he planned to champion in the legislature, but he made clear that his would be a bold and forward-thinking administration not afraid to wield the power at its disposal to help the citizens of the state: "Last November, a free people called for a new vision for California," Brown told a gallery of California legislators, family, friends, and state dignitaries. "We begin today the solemn duty and high privilege of translating that vision into public policy and into law. The election reaffirms our conviction that the people of California are resolved to move forward with courage and confidence. Offered reaction by the radical right, the voters emphatically declined. Offered government by retreat, the people preferred progress. Clearly then, our duty is to bring to California the forward force of responsible liberalism."[25]

Invoking the great progressive American governors of the twentieth century—Theodore and Franklin Roosevelt of New York; Woodrow Wilson of New Jersey; Robert La Follette of Wisconsin; and Johnson and Warren, Brown promised to strive in the spirit of these progressive giants and match the accomplishments of their administrations. Employing soaring rhetoric and an almost utopian vision of California's future, Brown promised constituents that his program of political and social reform would "liberate our human resources and demonstrate the renewed vigor of American society. . . . Let us recall the warning of the Bible that where there is no vision, the people perish," Brown said toward the end of his inaugural address. "I propose that we [go to work] on a wide range of long-term problems. . . . Providence seems intent on making us a great people in a great state. This destiny of greatness requires of us our best laws and fairest administration. . . . May we pray to God that our virtues grow with California and be durable, and that our vision for California be liberal and responsible."[26]

Not long after taking office Brown announced that his top priority would be to make government more efficient. The state deficit was skyrocketing, Brown said, the bureaucracy was running amok, and what the state really needed was to reduce expenditures and husband its resources. Whether or not this was visionary, the governor told aides that whenever possible they should refrain from making costly long-distance phone calls, and he then told them the story of how, as a poor boy growing up in San Francisco, he learned to turn out the lights when leaving a room.[27]

But there were more important initiatives to come. Major social and demographic changes were sweeping the state, and they demanded a bold and progressive response from the political leadership in Sacramento. Since the early 1940s, thousands of mostly middle-class white migrants had been thronging into the state. Lured by high-paying factory jobs in defense, aerospace, and other military-related industries, the migrants helped transform California into a national economic power and a booming center of construction. In the late 1950s, statisticians were projecting that sometime early in the next decade California would surpass New York as the most populous state in the nation. From his first days in office Brown realized that the vast human influx then underway was both his most daunting challenge and his greatest opportunity.[28]

Convinced that the needs of the migrants would be great, the new governor decided that he would have to improve the state's infrastructure, increase public works programs, and strengthen the social safety net. In his first legislative session in 1959, Brown enacted a slew of programs and policy reforms that marked one of the most far-reaching legislative successes for any governor in the history of California. In rapid succession, Brown won passage of a Fair Employment Practices Act (FEPA) that outlawed discriminatory practices in the workplace and created a commission to guard against such practices taking place;

created a new consumer protection agency to protect consumers from large corporations that might engage in unfair business practices or try to swindle customers; established an economic development agency to lure new businesses to the state and ensure the state's continued economic growth; enacted a plan to reorganize and make more efficient state government; won increases in Social Security and welfare benefits; secured new funding for mental health facilities, medical hospitals, drug treatment plans; and secured funds for the construction of new freeways, bridges, tunnels, highways, byways, rail systems, waterways, and schools. All told, he won passage of 43 of 44 of his major reform initiatives.[29]

Brown and his aides took great pride in the achievements of the first year. They considered themselves to be tough, strong-minded, politically astute liberals who understood the nature of the demographic changes and created a series of solutions to meet those changes. Aide Fred Dutton captured the burgeoning consensus among Democrats in Sacramento that Brown now had an opportunity to build a political coalition that would be as powerful as the one constructed by Franklin Roosevelt during the New Deal. "You have really made a major historical contribution in stabilizing the Party and reducing the internal frictions," Dutton gushed to Brown in 1960. "If the alliance of the Democrats with labor, the minorities, etc., can just be strengthened, you will have wrought a completely changed political foundation for the State lasting a decade or two after you leave office. . . . Once a coalition of that nature is put together its aftereffects go on for many years." Brown's ultimate responsibility, Dutton argued further, was to cultivate a corps of "vigorous younger men . . . who will carry on the fight for progressive government and the Democratic philosophy in the State long after this Administration."[30]

In 1960, eager to pass more programs and bold public works projects, Brown brushed off advisors who warned him that he was trying to do too much too fast. When, for example, Dutton told the governor that spending almost $2 billion on a water program and millions of dollars on state education was not feasible, Brown assured his aide that both projects were vital to California's future and that both programs would be enacted. "We'll build the water project, and we'll build new universities and new state colleges and new community colleges and elementary schools too," Brown told Dutton. "We've got plenty of money and we have to do it." Brown was true to his word, winning passage that year of a landmark bond measure that raised billions of dollars for a long-delayed but badly needed new water system for the state. He also shepherded through the legislature his Master Plan of Higher Education, another piece of landmark legislation that allocated funds for the construction of three new campuses in the University of California system, creating one of the largest and most successful systems of public higher education in the world.[31]

But Brown's second year in office was marked by two major political and personal setbacks. Flouting the advice of friends and aides, in February Brown agreed to a stay of execution for Caryl Chessman, a convicted rapist who had been languishing on San Quentin's Death Row for over a decade. Chessman had become a lightning rod of controversy in the state. In the 1950s he had penned several autobiographical tracts that detailed his plight on death row and whipped up considerable support for his cause. Brown had no personal sympathy for Chessman, whom he considered a conniving criminal. But he believed as a Catholic that he had a duty to preserve and protect the lives of all human beings, and since Chessman was not a murderer but a rapist, the governor decided to spare him.

Politically, Brown's decision was a disaster. Sixty days after awarding the stay, the California Supreme Court refused to overturn Chessman's sentencing and Brown had no legal choice but to let Chessman die. Activists on both sides of the issue were furious: Supporters of the death penalty attacked Brown for being weak, a vacillator afraid to mete out justice; foes called him a craven capitulator who in the face of political pressure abandoned moral principles and allowed a man to be executed. Brown's aides were also upset at their boss; they believed he had wasted precious political capital on the vicious "Red Light Bandit." In August 1960, Brown's fortunes plummeted further. Delegates, angry at his waffling on the Chessman matter, hissed and booed Brown during the Democratic National Convention in Los Angeles. Then, as if to add insult to injury, the governor proceeded to lose control over his own delegation. Kennedy's supporters had been counting on Brown to bring California into the Kennedy camp, and they were furious at Brown when the delegation initially split three ways—though eventually everyone unified behind Kennedy. Brown's growing number of critics now began assailing Brown as a waffling "Tower of Jell-O." The gibes hit Brown like a punch to the solar plexus: wounded, he fell into a deep despair. He even contemplated resigning.[32]

Yet again the governor proved resilient. Beginning in early 1961, on the advice of friends and aides, Brown made several changes in his personal appearance and tried to fine-tune a political style that was slightly awkward in the age of mass media and television. The governor started playing vigorous games of golf, trimmed fifteen pounds off his roly-poly frame (aide Hale Champion had proposed a bet to see who could lose more weight), and attended a spiritual retreat in which he did not utter a single word for three days. Aides now began instructing him in the finer points of television, teaching him how to wave his arms during debates, suggesting ways for him to perfect his sound bites and polish up his speech. Press aide Jack Burby suggested that Brown remove his glasses while on television and "wear lighter shade suits. This is primarily because of Los Angeles. Primarily to give the impression that you identify with strong sunshine more than with cool, foggy weather." But the road to political recovery entailed more than simply wearing better suits and removing his glasses during photo-ops. Brown also would need to remind voters of why they had elected him in the first place. He would need to recapture the ebullient, vigorous, straight-ahead political style that had won over Californians in 1958. With that goal in mind, the governor embarked in 1961 on a series of statewide speaking tours to rally Democratic activists and talk to the electorate about his accomplishments and future plans. He also delivered a series of speeches on the East Coast, impressing journalists and constituents alike as a vibrant and resilient leader with a substantial record of political accomplishments.[33]

Perhaps most important, Brown and his supporters began laying the groundwork for an all-out attack on their Republican opponents. In early 1961 administration aides started talking about bringing into the burgeoning Brown campaign a bare-knuckles Democratic political operative who could "knock every potential Republican candidate in sight." Dutton told Brown that if Democrats hoped to stay in power in California, they needed to engage in what he described as "razzle-dazzle aggressiveness initiated by a spokesman completely divorced from the Governor. Its purpose," Dutton explained, "should be to cut down George Christopher, Bob Finch . . . and anyone else who even begins to emerge. The attack should be in the form of substantively sound stories disseminated through local Democratic sources. . . . The overall attack program should be conceived and waged by someone specifically assigned to it. . . . It requires imagination, personal aggressiveness, literary style, and a little bit of downright nastiness."[34]

Democrats believed fervently in the efficacy of attack. They saw the Republican party in California as divided between moderates committed to Earl Warren–type reform initiatives and right-wing radicals who liked to rail against the communist menace. As it became clear that Richard Nixon would be their opponent, they knew they had to tar him as an extremist. Just a year earlier, Nixon had come within 113,000 votes of winning the White House. He had defeated John Kennedy in California, and although Brown considered him a controversial personality and a lightning rod for ridicule, Nixon was also one of the most powerful men in public life. An experienced and bare-knuckled campaigner who would stop at nothing to defeat his opponents, Nixon was a former congressman, United States senator, and two-term vice president. Nixon had traveled the world as an emissary for American ideals. He had established a reputation as a staunch anticommunist by pursuing Alger Hiss, braved rock-throwing crowds in Venezuela, debated Soviet Premier Nikita Khrushchev in Moscow, survived a surfeit of personal scandals, and enjoyed strong support from Republican fund-raisers and officeholders in California. Nixon, Senator Clair Engle predicted to Brown in early 1962, was certain "to be throwing these dead cats over the fence at you"; it was imperative that the governor "pick [the dead cats] up and throw them right back."[35]

Democrats began to do just that, launching private investigations into Nixon's financial history, feeding reporters negative stories about their likely opponent, planting hard-to-handle questions during Nixon press conferences (Was Nixon running for president? Was he in bed with the radical Right?). They accused Nixon of being someone who simply wanted to use the statehouse to put himself in a position to run for president. Early polls had shown Nixon with a sizable advantage over Brown, but the picture of Nixon as a carpetbagger who had his sights set on the Oval Office seemed to resonate as it had against Knowland.[36]

The anticommunist issue—which had earlier done so much to propel Nixon—now did the greatest damage to Nixon's candidacy. By 1962 the American consensus had changed. Domestic communism no longer seemed as troubling as it had in the late '40s and early '50s. Internationally, it began to seem that communism was here to stay. Champions of liberty during the early postwar years were now more likely to be viewed as zealots.

Brown viewed Nixon as a right-wing smear doctor and staunch anticommunist who would stop at nothing to win election. And Brown believed that Nixon could be made to pay a political price for his close ties to conservatives and for his incendiary, seemingly unstable ways. One internal memo from the Brown campaign portrayed Nixon as an alcoholic and a man prone to vitriolic outbursts and someone who suffered from bouts of paranoia. In February 1962, Thomas Page, one of Brown's aides, wrote the governor that Clint Mosher, a long-time Nixon supporter, had confided to Page that Nixon was a man on the verge of a nervous breakdown. The former vice president, Page wrote Brown, was

> embittered and bewildered by his defeat for the Presidency to the point where it affected him personally and may have

> affected his judgment and timing. Mosher feels that Nixon is a man who is "being led to the guillotine and knows it." Given a few drinks, Nixon's problems become intensified. For example, at a Republican dinner in Los Angeles, at which a prominent lady guest . . . asked Nixon about how to handle the Russians. The answer to the assembled group was, "Listen, screw them first before they screw us." The lady departed thereafter and for all practical purposes that was the end of the dinner party.

Page concluded his memo on an optimistic note. Nixon, he wrote, was "roaring and lashing out . . . [and] showing signs of what could be fatal weakness."[37]

In early 1962, Brown and his Democratic supporters began to attack Nixon as a right-wing radical unfit for the statehouse. The governor described Nixon as a man who had "surrendered" to the conservative wing of the Republican party and who shared a great deal in common with the state's crackpots who saw communists under every rock.

Just as Knowland had in 1958, Nixon provided Brown and his supporters with ample evidence of his right-wing, extremist credentials. Nixon, to be sure, had many factors working against him in 1962. He had not lived in California since 1953. According to Democrats, he failed to demonstrate more than a passing interest in key state issues, such as higher education, transportation, and water. By and large, the candidate failed to articulate a compelling vision of why he wanted to be governor and some larger vision of what he would do once he achieved that office. But Nixon's ties to the right-wing anticommunists did the most to sink his campaign. Nixon of course was not a conservative ideologue; many conservatives in California did not consider him a very strong political ally and they refused to campaign on his behalf in 1962. Yet to many voters, Nixon came across as an angry right-winger obsessed with the issue of communism. As the campaign progressed, a handful of Nixon's supporters tried to portray Brown as soft on the Left. Editors at *Human Events*, a leading conservative magazine, argued that "the man who served as district attorney of San Francisco, as attorney general for the state, and finally as governor of California, [was] . . . oblivious to . . . evidences of Communist activity. . . . Nearly all our elected representatives are aware of the Communist problem in our midst—but not Pat Brown." Nixon supporters in California derided Brown as a "willing puppet of the left-wing" and a man closely allied to the so-called California Dynasty of Communism (the CDC, a

Democratic interest group). Some of the most shrill Nixon backers even went so far as to doctor a photograph of Brown: Instead of greeting a Thai girl visiting California, the governor was shown bowing to Nikita Khrushchev, the leader of the Soviet Union.[38]

Some Nixon supporters had pasted bumper stickers on their cars that asked, "Is Brown Pink?" The charge backfired, deepening the impression that Nixon was an angry figure obsessed with fighting the communist menace. And Brown, by contrast, effectively reminded voters during the campaign that as governor he had enacted popular and mainstream reforms while ushering in an era of long-lasting economic prosperity. On the stump, Brown boasted about his accomplishments in the field of "human rights," hailed California's welfare program as a national model, and generally styled himself as a moderate reformer who in a second term would create a quarter million new jobs, crack down on dangerous drugs, eliminate slums, move people from welfare to work, provide Medicare for the elderly, increase funding for mental health clinics, "enact new protections against discrimination," work to improve "the strongest public school system in America," and build everything from rapid transit systems and freeways to parks and beaches.[39]

As his race against Nixon drew to a close, word came from Washington that the Soviet Union had placed in Cuba nuclear missiles within striking distance of the United States. Voter attention was diverted away from the campaign. Unable to communicate his message to voters, prevented from mounting a last-minute comeback, Nixon lost to Brown by more than 300,000 votes. Brown's victory was nothing like the million-vote trouncing he had administered to Bill Knowland four years earlier, but it was a historic triumph against an even more formidable opponent. Nixon reacted angrily, telling the press that "You won't have Nixon to kick around anymore." Brown meanwhile reveled in his new nickname, the "giant killer."

Brown underscored his dim view of Nixon and Nixon's anticommunist allies during a remarkable phone conversation with John Kennedy a few days after the election. Brown had just finished breakfasting with his son Jerry when Kennedy's call came through. Kennedy congratulated Brown for having won election to a second term and for "reduc[ing Nixon] to the nuthouse. That last farewell speech of his . . . it shows that he belongs on the couch." Brown agreed. "This is a very peculiar man," Brown told Kennedy. "I really think that he is psycho. He's an able man, but he's nuts! [Just] . . . like a lot of these paranoids." In their second term, Brown and his aides would not spend a great deal of time thinking about the radicals of the Right. The 1962 election results, they concluded, sounded the death knell of political extremism, and there was simply not a whole lot to say about the Nixonites and other anticommunists in the state. Conservatives were a shrill and impotent political force. They predicted confidently that in the new era the radicals of the Right would be bit players, horse-and-buggy naysayers flailing their arms against the inexorable, forward march of progress.[40]

They couldn't have been more wrong.

TWO

# THE ANTICOMMUNIST

> Governor [Brown] said there were no issues. That was the trouble with this campaign. There were no issues. . . . Well, there is an issue and it's an issue that is world-wide today—the issue of our times—totalitarianism versus freedom.
>
> —Ronald Reagan, 1962

In late 1962, the conservative movement in California and the nation was an object of derision to many. Governor Brown and President Kennedy were far from the only liberals belittling conservative activists in these years. Journalists, academics, and politicians routinely described conservatives as irrational men and women who were angry at the twentieth century and ignorant about the reality of contemporary American life. Right-wing radicals, liberals repeatedly charged, promoted a panoply of deeply unpopular political programs that seemed better suited to an earlier era in national history. In 1962, a writer in *The Nation* argued that conservatives were more interested in thinking up "frivolous and simple-minded" slogans than in developing intelligent proposals to national problems. A *Washington Post* reporter described members of one conservative group as "people who liked to complain about the twentieth century." And even a sympathetic commentator in *Commonweal* wondered whether a right-wing student group was a new political voice or "merely a new political organization out to repeal the twentieth century?"[1]

Of course, this was a caricature. The men and women who comprised the rank-and-file of the conservative movement in California tended to be intelligent, well-educated people thoroughly steeped in modern life. Conservatives worked as doctors, dentists, lawyers, businessmen, and pharmacists, resided in tract housing in typical Southern California suburban communities, earned good salaries from their jobs, used state-of-the-art household appliances, and did all of the other things that American families did in the early 1960s. But if conservatives were not irrational paranoids clinging to an earlier era in American life, neither were they dominant players in politics. California was a center of conservative activity in these years, but by and large right-wing Republican politicians and their gaggle of supporters had failed to establish themselves as a significant force. Conservative activists operated a number of right-wing bookstores in Southern California in which they sold buttons and bumper stickers that called on Americans to impeach Supreme Court Chief Justice Earl Warren, for example. Conservative intellectuals wrote incendiary books and tracts full of hyperbolic warnings about the communist tide that was supposedly lapping at American shores. Movement activists organized large and boisterous political rallies at which right-wing luminaries railed against the communist menace. A libertarian patriot by the name of Raymond Hoiles published *The Orange County Register*, a popular but shrill newspaper in which editors inveighed against sky-high tax rates and Washington plutocrats. The millionaire entrepreneur Walter Knott had opened the family amusement park Knott's Berry Farm, where he provided people with thrill rides and fed park-goers a steady diet of patriotic political symbols.[2]

On the whole, the conservative movement in California stood for a variety of political ideas and positions, but most conservatives agreed that the Soviet Union was a direct and immediate threat to the forces of democratic capitalism the world over. Rejecting the containment strategies that had guided U.S. foreign policy since the late 1940s, leaders and activists urged American policy makers to launch an aggressive military assault on Soviet satellites in Eastern Europe. On domestic matters, conservatives also generally concurred that communism was a sinister force that had made significant inroads into national life. Communists had penetrated the Washington bureaucracy, worked as top editors and reporters at the nation's leading periodicals, and also worked as professors and administrators on the nation's college campuses, tainting young minds and forging a base for worldwide revolution. Conservatives tended to blame American liberals for this sorry state of national affairs. Liberal planners had created invidious social programs, liberal politicians had raised income taxes to exorbitant and socialistic levels, and liberal academics and journalists continually ignored—much to the national peril—the evil and ubiquitous nature of the communist threat.[3]

In 1962 a handful of conservative politicians ran for high office in California, and almost without exception they suffered resounding rebukes at the ballot box. Spouting radical opinions and engaging in rhetorical excesses, right-wing candidates lost their campaigns in droves: Joseph Shell, a conservative former minority leader of the State Assembly, lost to Richard Nixon in that year's Republican party gubernatorial primary; Loyd Wright faltered badly in his bid to unseat moderate incumbent senator Thomas Kuchel; and Congressman John Rousselot lost his reelection campaign. Throughout the election year, conservatives could count on any number of right-wing political spokesmen to campaign for candidates and stump for votes. While there were many such prominent speakers in California in 1962, few were as shrill and radical in their political beliefs as Ronald Wilson Reagan. A well-known Hollywood movie actor who in recent years had become increasingly active in right-wing politics, Reagan was a principled anticommunist second to no one. In his speeches and public statements that year and in years prior, Reagan repeatedly depicted the Soviet Union as an evil and repugnant force bent on destroying the American way of life. Painting the conflict between East and West in Manichean and apocalyptic hues, Reagan argued that totalitarian hordes, with dreams of annihilating America in their heads, hovered just off American shores and could strike at any moment. "Today," Reagan told an audience in January 1962, "we are engaged in a great war to determine whether the world can exist half-slave and half-free. There are those who challenge the statement that war is now at hand. True, we do not hear the rattle of musketry or smell the burning cordite—that is, unless the wind is too strong from Budapest, Tibet or Havana. Whether we admit it or not, we are in a war. This war was declared a century ago by Karl Marx and re-affirmed by Lenin when he said that Communism and Capitalism cannot exist side-by-side."[4]

Reagan did not subscribe to the most outlandish conspiracy theories that were being propagated by some right-wing anticommunist activists in the country, but he believed that the greater danger to the American nation came from within. Communists, Reagan charged, were trying to overrun American institutions and topple the government, and naive liberals had failed to staunch the flow of subversives into domestic life. Liberals had failed to prevent communists from occupying positions of power in American government and they had further failed to see the national welfare bureaucracy for what it truly was—a one-way ticket to socialist Hell. In 1962, Reagan was a fifty-one-year-old man who had arrived at such political beliefs over the course of many years. Earlier in his life, Reagan had learned several important lessons about politics and culture, teachings that would inform his moral values and undergird many of his later political convictions. Though he was raised a Democrat, his attachment to conservative causes had early origins in his childhood home in Dixon, Illinois. These roots began to find their full expression during the anticommunist crusades of the late 1940s. During those first days of the cold war, Reagan concluded that government's primary function was to protect individual freedom, maintain the American economic order, thwart communist aggression abroad, and extirpate socialist forces at home. If Pat Brown's love for the New Deal came suddenly in 1934, Reagan's affection for cold war politics surfaced in 1947.

REAGAN'S FATHER JACK was a first-generation Irish Catholic who dreamed big, worked hard, and knew mostly failure. His chronic lack of success would serve as one of Reagan's first lessons—prosperity came only to those who avoided temptations. Ed Brown's vice was gambling; Jack Reagan's was worse: alcohol. Jack for years toiled as a general clerk in nondescript department stores across Illinois, dragging his wife and two sons from one dreary Midwestern town to another in a never-ending quest for business success. His big break came in 1920 when he became the manager and co-owner of the Fashion Boot Shop, a shoestore in Dixon. Despite Jack's qualifications—the local paper touted him as "an experienced shoe man and also a graduate practipedist"—the store flopped and Jack resumed his wandering ways. A flamboyant raconteur with a taste for the dramatic, Jack signed his name with a scrawling flourish and in hotel guest books listed his home address as "Dublin, Ireland" or "Molasses Junction." But he was neither a steady breadwinner nor a reliable father, and for Reagan he served mainly as a harsh reminder of the vagaries of life.[5]

Reagan's mother Nelle, by contrast, was a source of inspiration and security for her son, and it was she who inculcated him with the bedrock social beliefs that would form the basis of many of Reagan's later political convictions. Right around the time that Pat Brown's mother was taking him to a Wobblies meeting, Nelle Reagan, a teetotaler, was baptized into a popular religious sect called the Disciples of Christ. Reagan's mother did everything for the church, organizing sing-alongs, penning morality plays, and becoming a leader of the local Women's Christian Temperance Union.[6]

Reagan embraced the moral teachings of the church and participated actively in many of its social events. As a child he cleaned the church chapel, performed in his mother's plays, and at one point even dated the pastor's daughter. A serious and ambitious youth, Reagan evinced in these years little interest in politics, preferring instead to spend his time playing football and working as a lifeguard at the local swimming hole in Dixon. During his six summers on the job, Reagan saved scores of swimmers from the raging currents and quickly became a kind of legend to town locals. Reagan performed his duties with a seriousness bordering on obsession, and local newspapers depicting Reagan as a boy wonder who, "during his six years of service at the beach, . . . has never had an assistant and has watched a thousand bathers in the water at one time."[7]

Reagan decided to attend college at Eureka, a tiny Disciple-run school in upstate Illinois one hundred miles south of Dixon. And while he helped organize a student strike during his freshman year and won election as class president in his senior one, Reagan spent most of his undergraduate years immersed in nonpolitical extracurricular activities. He joined a fraternity and played on the football team (spending every minute of his first year on the bench), acted in school plays and worked on the yearbook.[8]

In 1932, immediately after graduating from college, Reagan set out for Chicago, the radio mecca of the Midwest, to look for a job in broadcasting. As the Great Depression rolled over the land, Reagan showed little interest in the larger political issues and social questions that were then roiling the country. To be sure, he was an ardent Democrat who admired President Franklin D. Roosevelt's fireside radio chats and had been impressed by Roosevelt's sunny disposition in the face of grave economic problems. But Reagan's devotion to the New Deal had as much to do with family ties as with any heartfelt set of liberal political beliefs. His father and brother were also staunch Roosevelt men, and in the early 1930s both Jack and Neil found jobs working for the Federal Emergency Relief Administration, one of the first New Deal relief organizations to hire people who suddenly found themselves unemployed and destitute. Jack would later hold jobs with the WPA and PWA, Harry Hopkins' relief agencies that built airplane hangars and employed idle artists to paint murals, and Reagan would later credit FDR with helping his family through tough times. But Reagan in these years mostly just wanted to find a job in radio, and he showed a steely resolve in pursuit of that goal. In Chicago, Reagan made the rounds at the major stations but received chilly receptions wherever he went. Told that there was nothing for a college graduate with no training or experience, Reagan returned home more determined than ever. Borrowing his father's Oldsmobile, he set out for Davenport, Iowa, where he met a crotchety old Scottish manager at the "World of Chiropractic" radio station. The manager told Reagan that WHO, as the station was called, had just hired a sports announcer, at which point Reagan turned away from the manager and grumbled, "How does anyone get a chance as a sports announcer if you can't even get a job in a radio station?" The manager pursued Reagan down the hall and rapped the strapping youth on the shin with his cane. "Not so fast, ye big bastard," the manager said, "didn't ye hear me callin' ye? Do ye perhaps know football?"[9]

Reagan's career as an entertainer was launched. His voice would soon become a staple of Midwestern play-by-play. Proving himself a major broadcast talent who possessed a deep and engaging voice and a flair for the melodramatic, Reagan became a master of invention in his craft, enlivening games that he neither saw nor heard with elaborate descriptions of ball parks and fans. Holed up in his booth in Des Moines, his assistant Curly nearby feeding him notes from the telegraph machine clacking in the background, Reagan broadcast games taking place in Chicago, more than three hundred miles away. One day Curly handed Reagan a note from the telegraph that read: "The wire has gone dead." In his autobiography Reagan describes what happened next: "I had a ball on the way to the plate and no way to call it back. At the same time, I was convinced that a ball game tied up in the ninth inning was no time to tell my audience we had lost contact with the game and they would have to listen to recorded music. I knew of only one thing that wouldn't get in the score column and betray me—a foul ball." Buying time, Reagan continued having the batter foul back pitch after pitch, inventing a red-headed youth who scrambled to retrieve balls that had landed in the stands. "My voice was rising in pitch and threatening to crack—and then, bless him, Curly started typing. I clutched at the slip. It said: 'Galan popped out on the first ball pitched.' Not in my game he didn't—he popped out after practically making a career of foul balls."[10]

Acting, however, had always been a part of Reagan's world, and after establishing himself as a regional radio personality Reagan decided to try something bigger and better: Hollywood. Aware that other radio celebrities had made the jump, Reagan took advantage of a trip to the Chicago Cubs spring training camp on Catalina Island in California to see Bill Meiklejohn, a Hollywood agent. Meiklejohn agreed to set up a screen test for Reagan at Warner Brothers studio, and Reagan began to think "that sports might not be the only course my life would follow." Twenty-six years old in 1937, Reagan stood at an imposing six feet one inch tall—an exceedingly handsome youth with chiseled features and a winning smile. Warner executives thought highly of the young talent and promptly offered him a six-month contract. Reagan's rise in Hollywood would be as rapid as his ascent in radio. In his first year as a movie actor, Reagan acted in eight films, gaining a reputation among directors as a solid performer well suited for lead roles in B movies.[11]

Most critics at the time considered Reagan's films mediocre products, but by 1940 Reagan had established himself as a bonafide Hollywood movie star. He starred in a string of successful blockbusters, winning considerable attention from film directors impressed with his good looks and from a public smitten with his Midwestern screen persona. In 1940 Reagan played the football star George Gipp in the movie *Knute Rockne; King's Row*, released two years later, marked Reagan's greatest triumph to date. In that film Reagan played Drake, a small-town Casanova injured in an accident in the railroad yards. Drake awakens from his coma to discover that a sadistic doctor, eager to punish the patient for dating his daughter, had amputated his legs. "It presented me," Reagan later wrote of the scene, "with the most challenging acting problem in my career." Reagan rehearsed for days, practicing his lines in bathrooms, before going to sleep, and while driving to work, and when it finally came time to shoot the scene Reagan recalled a sort of *über*-force seeing him through it: "I wandered over to the set to see what it looked like. . . . I stared at it for a minute. Then, obeying an overpowering impulse, I climbed into the rig. I spent almost that whole hour in stiff confinement, contemplating my torso and the smooth undisturbed flat of the covers where my legs should have been. Gradually the affair began to terrify me. In some weird way, I felt something horrible had happened to my body. . . . There were cries of 'Lights!' and 'Quiet, please!'" Reagan lay back, closed his eyes, and slowly "let my gaze travel downward. I can't describe even now my feeling as I tried to reach for where my legs should be. 'Randy!' I screamed. . . . 'Where's the rest of me?'"[12]

Reagan had talent as an actor and considerable presence on stage, and by 1942 he seemed destined for even greater movie successes. But World War II altered drastically his career plans. Reagan was a passionate critic of Nazi Germany and an eager participant in the fight against fascism. Believing that through hard work, perseverance, athletics, and his mother's homespun morality he had won a coveted spot in the cloistered world of Hollywood film stars, Reagan felt a patriotic duty to give something back to the nation. John Wayne could have fought but did not; Reagan had poor eyesight that kept him from combat. Instead he joined the Army Signal Corps and became an impassioned defender of God and country, making a series of propaganda films with appropriately martial titles (*Rear Gunner, For God and Country*). He became a regular at bond drives and troop send-offs, and also made Army training films with the "Culver City Commandoes" (the Air Force's film unit), in which he specialized in what one biographer called "uplifting, even devotional, tales about young martyrs serving a perfect cause."[13]

Reagan had high hopes for his acting career after the war, but they were quickly dashed on the shoals of a fickle moviegoing public and the vagaries of life in Hollywood. Several younger film stars had established themselves as up-and-coming talents, and although he was only thirty-four years old in 1945, Reagan struck movie executives as an actor who had passed his prime. John Wayne, who had made studio films throughout the war, emerged as a stronger older leading man for starring roles in Westerns and postwar war flicks. Reagan found himself struggling to land decent roles. His political interest piqued by the great struggle against Nazi fascism, and with his acting career on the wane, in the late 1940s Reagan began cutting radio spots and making speaking appearances on behalf of major Democratic political candidates and causes.[14]

In 1948 he actually appeared in radio advertisements sponsored by the International Ladies Garment Workers Union, in which he told the story of how "the Republican 80th Congress and the National Association of Manufacturers . . . [brought] on inflation and set back the cause of liberal government in the United States." Blending Hollywood humility ("You know me as a motion picture actor but tonight I'm just a citizen pretty concerned about the national election next month.") with assorted broadsides against Republican programs, which he held responsible for soaring inflation, draconian antilabor laws, and vicious reductions in Social Security benefits, Reagan proved himself a reliable Democratic spokesman and able celebrity-cum-politician. "President Truman knows the value of a man like Hubert Humphrey," Reagan said in another political advertisement that he cut in 1948, as Truman ran for the presidency and Humphrey for the Senate. "While Ball [Humphrey's Republican opponent] is the banner carrier for Wall Street, Mayor Humphrey is fighting for all the principles advocated by President Truman: for adequate low-cost housing; for civil rights; for prices people can afford to pay; and for a labor movement free of the Taft-Hartley Law."[15]

But despite his support for Democratic stalwarts like Truman and Humphrey, Reagan was slowly turning away from the liberal shibboleths of the Truman years and embracing positions that dovetailed better with his feelings of patriotism. Since 1938 Reagan had been a member of the Screen Actors Guild (SAG), a leading Hollywood union for high-salaried stars and screenwriters. During the war, Reagan worked his way up the ranks of SAG, becoming a member of the union's board of directors and later serving as SAG president. SAG was a relatively conservative union, and Reagan quickly established himself as a leading critic of the more liberal unions in Hollywood. He attacked as unpatriotic the movie technicians and other skilled workers who had occupied labor picket lines and participated in disruptive work stoppages during the war, and he began giving strong support to movie executives and strikebreakers who had lined up in opposition to the strikers. During one American Federation of Labor strike, in the early 1940s, Reagan skewered those walking the picket line as perfidious agitators. In the postwar years, Reagan generally sided with Hollywood executives and often went so far as to encourage employers to use scabs in their fights against striking workers. In July 1946, as waves of postwar labor strikes throttled the country, Reagan and SAG dismissed as merely "jurisdictional" the grievances of workers on strike. He urged actors to ignore the strike and cross picket lines, and later traveled to Chicago where during labor negotiations he adopted a position that aligned him with the producers and strikebreakers.[16]

In his 1965 autobiography, *Where's the Rest of Me?*, Reagan wrote that "the story of my disillusionment with big government is linked fundamentally with the ideals that suddenly sprouted and put forth in the war years." But in truth, it was postwar domestic anticommunism that did it. For in these years, for the first time in his life, Reagan began thinking hard about the burning political questions of the day, and when he did so he came down on the side of the hard-core anticommunists then on the march in America. Reagan had been a member of several liberal, antifascist organizations in Hollywood, including Hollywood Independent Citizens Committee of the Arts, Sciences, and Professions (HICCASP) and the Veterans Affairs Committee. Reagan's brother Neil and some of his acquaintances had occasionally warned him that communists were trying to infiltrate the motion picture business and overrun America, but Reagan had dismissed such warnings as the hyperbolic exaggerations of the militant few. As he wrote in his autobiography, he thought "the nearest communists were fighting in Stalingrad," and he did not in the early 1940s take seriously the rantings of those who said otherwise but failed to produce evidence to back up their claims.[17]

In the immediate postwar period, with the cold war gathering momentum, Reagan experienced what he would later consider his first direct brush with the communist menace. The experience would leave him scarred, and would alter the course of his life and career. Reagan was a member of the board of directors of HICCASP, and in 1947 one of his colleagues on the board, a woman whom Reagan did not know very well, started winning seats on the board for her friends and allies. Suspicious of the woman, Reagan retrieved a copy of the board's meeting minutes and realized what had happened: She had achieved majority control of the board of directors by internal maneuvering. She wasn't doing it just for friends, either. Distressed, Reagan called his brother late one night and, rousing Neil from a deep slumber, asked him to meet at the Nutburger stand in Hollywood, where Reagan was having a cup of coffee. "You wouldn't believe it," Reagan told his brother that night. "It just came to me tonight. We have a rule that if a board member misses two meetings without being excused, you're automatically off the board. There's a gal at [one studio]; I've been a little suspicious of her. All of a sudden, we had one of these cases come up tonight . . . and now we've got to find somebody else. It suddenly dawned on me that over the last several months, every time one of these cases came up, she had just the individual that would be excellent as a replacement. I managed to filch the minute books before I left. I can show you the page where her board members became a majority of the board, with her replacements."[18]

Reagan became suspicious that this was an organized communist plot. He tried to convince the board to pass a resolution condemning communism as a political force—this at a time when organizations across the country were doing so, including the AFL—but board members voted down the measure and Reagan, along with Jimmy Roosevelt (the president's son) and a handful of other moderates resigned in a huff. Whether Reagan had a genuine epiphany as to the evil nature of the communist threat remains unclear, but what is clear is that sometime around 1947 Reagan became a staunch foe of all things socialistic, plunging headlong into the struggle against the Soviet Union and dedicating himself to expunging from the American movie industry left-wing radicals who, he concluded, were trying to turn Hollywood into a worldwide propaganda base. Reagan's commitment to the cause of anticommunism came at a time of mounting antipathy toward left-wing movements. State and federal agencies began requiring that people in their employ sign loyalty oaths in which they pledged not to subvert the will of the American government. The Truman administration implemented new internal security policies designed to weed out radicals who had found their way into the State Department and other key federal bureaucracies, and even there, some felt the president was soft on the issue. The House Committee on Un-American Activities (HUAC) began holding public hearings into the size, nature, and scope of the communist threat in the country, paying special attention to Hollywood, where, it was believed, communists were on the rise.[19]

In the late 1940s, certain that he was witnessing firsthand communist attempts to overrun the film industry, Reagan decided that he had no choice but to take up arms against the radicals in his midst. He did so by gathering information for the FBI and by inquiring about communists in SAG union ranks. He traveled to Washington to testify before HUAC, and as a friendly witness to the committee he told committee members about communist efforts to "take over the motion picture business." He gave committee members names of left-wing producers, directors, and screenwriters whom he considered part of the conspiracy, and in so doing severed what few remaining ties he had to American liberalism. By 1947 he was established as a reliable warrior in the fight against communist evil, though he was not yet convinced that the Democrats were weak on the issue—after all, Truman helped to launch the cold war with the "Truman Plan," supporting anticommunists in Greece and Turkey, and visibly assuming the imperial responsibilities once shouldered by Great Britain. Why couldn't the Democrats oppose communism at home, like the AFL did? "The Reds know that if we can make America a decent living place for all of our people, their cause is lost here," Reagan told one reporter in May 1947. "So they seek to infiltrate liberal organizations just to smear and discredit them. I've already pulled out of one organization that I joined in completely good faith. One day I woke up, looked about and found it was Commie-dominated."[20]

Reagan's newfound passion, however, did not suddenly replace his lifelong dream of acting in movies. He continued seeking out lead roles in major Hollywood films. Such roles rarely materialized, however, and Reagan began more than ever to feel frustrated and disappointed with his career. In the early 1950s he appeared in several less-than-successful feature films: *Storm Warning*, about the Ku Klux Klan; *The Last Outpost*, a horse-riding Western; and *Louisa*, in which he played the aging father of an eighteen-year-old teenager. While such parts may have served as a springboard for an up-and-coming actor trying to establish himself in Hollywood, for a one-time star like Reagan they mainly indicated a career in decline. Reagan would continue acting in the early 1950s, but the well of good looks, talent, contacts, and talk-of-the-town buzz that had briefly made him a high-salaried star in the prewar years had run dry.[21]

One other part of his Hollywood-star biography fell away around the same time: his first marriage. As Reagan's career prospects began to look increasingly bleak, his wife Jane Wyman's picked up. Reagan put on a brave face when Wyman took a costar, instead of Reagan, to one of her premieres, but the marriage was on the rocks and by March of 1952 he had split with Wyman and married Nancy Davis, the daughter of an outspoken, conservative Chicago obstetrician. Otherwise, his life seemed a dead end. At one point Reagan even stooped so low as to accept, at his agent's behest, a gig emceeing variety shows in Las Vegas nightclubs. As Nancy later explained it, the Reagans were "not nightclub people," and they lasted in Nevada all of two weeks.[22]

Returning to Los Angeles, Reagan began giving speeches on behalf of SAG in which he defended the movie industry from critics and urged politicians to cut taxes for actors. A good public speaker, a popular drawing card, and president of a major Hollywood actors' union, Reagan had numerous opportunities to address audiences of all kinds, and he began accepting more and more speaking invitations. Eager to deliver his messianic message about the evils of communism, Reagan's speeches now more than ever began focusing on the dangers of the Soviet menace to the United States. In June 1952, Reagan delivered a commencement address before a group of Missouri students that included a bruising attack on socialism and an eloquent rumination on the genius of American society. America, Reagan told the graduates, was a great land, less a "place than an idea . . . that has been deep in the souls of man ever since man started his long trail from the swamps."

> It is nothing but the inherent love of freedom in each one of us, and the great ideological struggle that we find ourselves engaged in today. . . . It's the same old battle. We met it under the name of Hitlerism; we met it under the name of Kaiserism; and we have met it back through the ages in the name of every conqueror that has ever set upon a course of establishing his rule over mankind. It is simply the idea, the basis of this country and of our religion, the idea of the dignity of man, the idea that deep within the heart of each one of us is something so God-like and precious that no individual or group has a right to impose his or its will upon the people, that no group can decide for the people what is good for the people so well as they can decide for themselves.[23]

Reagan did not mention Stalin or the atomic bomb or the specter of communist hordes sweeping the world, but his message was clear enough. Reagan had spoken of a titanic struggle with evil—a war to the death—and he urged the young men and women in his audience to immerse themselves in that struggle: "You have an opportunity to decide now whether you will strike a match and whether you will help push back the darkness over the stadium of humanity. . . . If you embark on the right course and do this, you may bring closer the day when your sons and their sons will not have to prove their worth by bleeding all that they are and all that they ever hope to be into the sands of some far-flung beachhead."[24]

Making his way across the country, delivering similarly stirring speeches, Reagan caught the attention of Earl Dunckel, an advertising executive for General Electric in charge of audience promotion for the company's new television show. The company was searching for a celebrity who could host the program, hawk General Electric wares, and boost worker morale with plant visits. Dunckel thought Reagan perfect for the post: he was a moral and upright person with impressive skills as a public speaker and widespread name recognition. Reagan too found the job highly appealing. It offered him a chance to remain in the public eye, a good salary, and an opportunity to deliver his message. Hungry for new venues and careers, Reagan accepted Dunckel's job offer and quickly proved himself a wise choice for the slot.[25]

A charming celebrity and compelling public orator, Reagan was a natural on the stump. Tall, trim, dashing, he had the added advantage of being a movie star without acting like one, and to General Electric employees he came across as a down-to-earth celebrity. In his previous incarnations as radio broadcaster and movie actor, Reagan had displayed a knack for the public stage, and his time away from those jobs had not dulled his abilities one bit. Enduring a schedule so crammed with speeches and plant visits "it was almost beyond the limits of human endurance," Reagan, so long as he had his afternoon naps, proved an affable campaigner who could walk plant floors with ease, chat for hours with employees, and butter up company executives. He possessed a keen sense of timing, a facility for names, places, quips, and statistics, and an ability to give rousing paeans to free enterprise that inspired audiences, impressed plant managers, and wowed Dunckel. When Reagan appeared at plants, women workers would rush up to him asking for autographs with their hands outstretched. The men, by Dunckel's account, would stand to the side making derogatory comments about the Hollywood sissy ("I bet he's a fag," Dunckel remembers some workers sneering), but Reagan sensed the tension swirling around him and before too long he would leave the women and walk over to the men, engage them in conversation, and "when he left them ten minutes later, they were all slappin' him on the back saying, 'That's the way, Ron.'"[26]

Reagan did not always deliver the same speech verbatim, but he did strike over and over the same patriotic political chords, touting the merits of free enterprise and General Electric products, regaling audiences with stories from his heyday in Hollywood, and assailing large, suffocating government programs that, he said, smacked of socialism and damaged the business climate. For his efforts Reagan received $125,000 a year from General Electric, a spot in the public eye, and invaluable experience on what Reagan affectionately termed "the mashed potato circuit." On tour he also had an opportunity to refine his political beliefs, and in the late 1950s one thing about his leanings became abundantly clear: Reagan was no longer a Democrat. In talks and appearances, Reagan not only chastised liberals for spending taxpayer money with reckless abandon on ineffective social programs, but he also urged listeners, friends, and followers to dedicate themselves to rolling back the Socialist tide. Moving deeper into the world of right-wing politics, Reagan's speeches around this time began to strike increasingly strident, even apocalyptic chords about the great international struggle between East and West. Reagan's earlier defense of Hollywood and jabs at big government had now given way to scorching broadsides against liberal planners and collectivist cohorts. Reagan began to rail against communists and left-wing activists of all kinds, and he spoke in dark and ominous terms about the red menace hovering just off American shores. Arguing that the nation was engaged in a great war for freedom, Reagan argued that it was incumbent on every citizen and every patriot in every corner of the country to get active in the struggle against communism.[27]

In 1960 Reagan was still registered as a Democrat, but began to give strong support to Republican candidates who were running for high office that year. Reagan campaigned vociferously for GOP presidential candidate Richard Nixon, and in a letter that he penned to Nixon that year he revealed his almost visceral loathing of the liberal political program for which John F. Kennedy stood. Reagan urged Nixon to expose Kennedy for the socialist dupe he was: "Shouldn't someone tag Mr. Kennedy's 'bold new imaginative' program with its proper age?" Reagan wondered. "Under the tousled boyish haircut it is still old Karl Marx—first launched a century ago. There is nothing new in the idea of a government being Big Brother to us all. Hitler called his 'State Socialism,' and way before him it was 'benevolent monarchy.'"[28]

Reagan was developing a ravenous appetite for politics, and in the aftermath of Nixon's defeat he began to forge ties to the radical anticommunist movement in America, which at that time amounted to a smattering of grassroots political organizations and a growing number of activists and Republican party officials. Reagan began appearing at anticommunist political rallies where he shared a stage with the bombastic leader of the Christian Anti-Communist Crusade, Frederick Schwarz, and other fierce anticommunist luminaries. In 1961, Reagan delivered the keynote address at a $50-a-plate fund-raising dinner for Congressman John Rousselot, a controversial conservative and member of the John Birch Society whom Reagan hailed as a "warm personal friend." He appeared before patriotic business groups; endorsed Project Prayer, an organization dedicated to overturning a Supreme Court decision banning prayer in school; participated in the planning sessions of Project Alert, whose members included a retired Marine colonel clamoring for the hanging death of Chief Justice Earl Warren; and served as the keynote speaker at a Town Meeting for the Freedom,

Inc., awards ceremony. He recorded "Ronald Reagan Speaks Out Against Socialized Medicine," an album sponsored by the American Medical Association and designed to whip up opposition to health care reform legislation then pending in Congress. The AMA distributed Reagan's album to doctors' wives, and on it Reagan could be heard warning listeners that "one of the traditional methods of imposing statism or Socialism on a people has been by way of medicine." Reagan even went so far as to predict that if socialized medicine became law, "you and I are going to spend our sunset years telling our children and our children's children what it once was like in America when men were free."[29]

By 1962, Reagan had taken up a firm position on the margins of American politics. A member of a number of controversial right-wing groups, Reagan endorsed right-wing politicians running for office and he appeared on stage with some of the most reactionary men in American politics. Governors Orville Faubus of Alabama and Ross Barnett of Mississippi, segregationists both, gave Reagan awards for his steadfast devotion to public service, and Charlton Lyons, another Jim Crow southerner, enjoyed support from Reagan while running for governor of Louisiana. Reagan did not embrace the bigoted opinions and platforms of his southern friends, but the actor was more than willing to associate himself with racists and conspiracy theorists, demagogues and anticommunists. Reagan served as honorary campaign chairman for Loyd Wright, who was running in the GOP primary against moderate senator Thomas Kuchel, in a quixotic effort in which the candidate issued belligerent warnings to the Soviet Union, that "if we have to blow up Moscow, that's too bad" and voiced support for notorious right-wing political action groups. Reagan incorporated into his speeches material sent to him by the Liberty Amendment Lobby, an organization which called for (among other things) repeal of the income tax. He began publishing articles in *Human Events*, a leading right-wing opinion journal; joined the national board of Young Americans for Freedom (YAF), the first nationwide conservative student movement dedicated to political action; and taped advertisements for the Church League of America, a Chicago-based organization that had in its offices some 850,000 reference cards listing the names and identities of Americans suspected of being subversives.[30]

Increasingly well known as a speechmaker, Reagan began attracting attention from a host of liberal politicians, journalists, and political action groups. In the early 1960s COPE, the political action committee of the AFL-CIO, tarred Reagan as a right-wing zealot and included him in its list of dangerous anticommunists. Teachers at one Minnesota high school canceled an upcoming appearance by Reagan, noting in their resolution that Reagan had become too "controversial" for their taste. And Drew Pearson, the liberal Washington political columnist, began accusing Reagan of taking fees from General Electric and the AMA to lobby against the health care reform bill then making its way through Congress.[31]

Reagan felt wounded by the cacophony of critical voices, but he generally was restrained and even-keeled in his response. Refraining from the kinds of vitriolic outbursts and shouting tirades that had hurt Nixon in his race against Brown in 1962, avoiding enemies lists and plans for revenge, Reagan worked on fine-tuning his rhetoric and polishing his public speaking skills. Reagan's jeremiads against big government and communist aggression contained little that could not also be found in the speeches and writings of William Buckley, Barry Goldwater, Bill Knowland, Frederick Schwarz, John Rousselot, and a raft of other anticommunist leaders. Reagan called for more aggressive anticommunist measures abroad and a major reduction in the size of government at home, and he warned that communism was a sinister and ubiquitous force that was sweeping the globe. Yet he rejected most of the outlandish conspiracy theories about communism propagated by right-wing activists in the early sixties.

Reagan genuinely believed that communism was a serious threat to domestic tranquility. While campaigning for Nixon in 1962, he issued some standard warnings about Pat Brown, calling him a tax-and-spend liberal who had presided over huge increases in both the size and cost of state government. "Under the Brown administration, spending has gone up 47% and we've increased the number of state employees by 30%," he said at one point. "We have the highest per capita tax in the history of California, the highest per capita tax of all of the fifty states." Reagan also warned voters that they needed to be concerned about more than simply the size of the governor's tax plan. He didn't go so far as to suggest the governor was pink, but did describe him as oblivious to the communist threat. To Reagan, it all boiled down to totalitarianism versus freedom.[32]

ELECTION YEAR 1962 marked an important turning point for Reagan. In the spring of that year executives at General Electric, thinking him too controversial, fired him from his job as corporate spokesman. Reagan had been a model spokesman for the company, and after eight years of delivering speeches, staying in run-down motel rooms, and visiting General Electric plants, he now found himself with more free time on his hands, free time that he spent at Yearling Row, the family ranch in the Malibu Hills, riding horses (his favorite was a dapple gray named Nancy D.), hiking trails, donning dungarees, and entertaining friends with cookouts. Reagan enjoyed his life of leisure, but he also enjoyed the public acclaim and attention that went hand-in-hand with radio broadcasting, acting, and political campaigning, and it seemed unlikely that he would live out his days hosting barbecues and tending to horses in Santa Barbara.[33]

In 1962, he finally changed his registration from Democrat to Republican. It was his public appearances that had done the most to seal his reputation as a stalwart in the struggle against communism. Increasingly popular among conservative activists and fund-raisers in California, Reagan began to entertain requests from conservative leaders that he run for political office. He declined these offers at first, but he also was clearly a highly popular political figure for whom a campaign was no longer totally out of the question. And Reagan felt a strong obligation to the ideas and programs of the anticommunist right. Reagan had watched from close range while his friends and allies suffered a string of election defeats and sundry other political setbacks, and while he did not suddenly decide that he needed to run for office to save the conservative movement from oblivion, many of his friends, acquaintances, and ideological soul mates—Joe Shell, Loyd Wright, John Rousselot—had suffered defeat and left the movement in the state largely bereft of political leadership.[34]

It was by no means clear that taking a leadership role would produce any results. If politically aware Californians had been pushed in late 1962 to give their opinion of Ronald Reagan, they would have identified him as an extremist. A pleasant one, perhaps, but nonetheless a man on the edge of the spectrum. What they might not have realized, however, was that a series of little-noticed but ultimately turbulent social upheavals were beginning to roil California politics. Reagan had no way of knowing this either, but in the aftermath of Richard Nixon's failed gubernatorial campaign, the larger social forces that four years later would propel Reagan into the governor's chair were already congealing around him. The liberals were about to crack up, and the social order was about to disintegrate spectacularly.

THREE

# "ARE YOU NOW, OR HAVE YOU EVER BEEN, A *LIBERAL*?"

To the liberals in Sacramento, the last days of 1962 were a time of frenzied expectations and powerful possibilities, a moment of great promise born of the demoralizing lows and soaring highs of the last two years in office. Brown especially felt liberated from political restraints. Nixon had been defeated, economic prosperity seemed a permanent fixture of the landscape, and with his reelection victory, Brown had joined his role models Hiram Johnson and Earl Warren as one of three two-term California governors of the century. President Kennedy and Democrats nationwide were now celebrating him as a political titan. Brown had another four years in office in which to carry out bold reform experiments. He had a liberal legislature under Democratic control with which to work. His hyperactive first term had been ratified by voters. His aim could be set even higher.

But where? In late 1962, Brown and his men did not know exactly which programs and reform measures they would embrace, nor did they have a clear picture of what they wanted to accomplish in the second term. But they agreed that as the liberal arbiters of power in California, they had both a moral duty and a political obligation to employ the power at their disposal. Brown and his men believed that only visionary programs and public works would allow the state to meet the challenges of the coming decades. In late 1962, this crusading liberal mood was unmistakable, if inchoate and ill defined. It featured a free-floating enthusiasm about the ability of government to solve many of the major social problems of the day. Looking back from a post–Reagan revolution vantage point, the mood seems all the more remarkable.

It found expression in a variety of public pronouncements and internal administration memos. In the last weeks of the election, Brown asked advisors for a list of priorities for the next four years. Multipage, single-spaced documents brimming with bold plans and new programs were the response. Aides urged Brown to embark on a far-reaching reform agenda: improving the state's infrastructure, stamping out debilitating social wrongs, and creating a host of new social services to meet the growing needs of society's have-nots, the unemployed, the elderly, the indigent. They implored Brown to lure new industries to the state, strengthen the Economic Development Agency, and bolster the state economy; they suggested that he strengthen the FEPC, outlaw housing discrimination, pour more money into elementary and high schools and universities, and "assault . . . the problems of the big cities." It was hard to choose among these ideas—so much to do; so many social problems in need of redress, but they concurred that there was only one way to meet the needs of new migrants and the downtrodden, only one way to prepare California for the future—by manipulating the levers of power in Sacramento.[1]

Brown's second inaugural address was a ringing oration reminiscent of his first, and it gave voice to the reform spirit sweeping the state. Before lawmakers, family, friends, and aides, he articulated a far-reaching vision for his state. He began with the announcement that California was "in the midst of profound and historic changes," noting that "the western rim of a continent, which a century ago was as much legend as land to a handful of pioneers, now assumes the role of leader on that continent." Brown admitted that he longed for the much simpler era of boyhood days in San Francisco, "when the only cars on the silver hills of my native San Francisco were cable cars," but he said that those days were long gone and that it was just as well that they were, for Californians were forward-looking people who had never dwelled on the past and were not about to start doing so now. "We have always been pioneers and sons of pioneers, a vigorous, dynamic people who respect tradition, but scorn the status quo," declared Brown. "Through the turmoil of change, and sometimes chaos, Californians have pressed on toward the good society—not for the few, not for the many, but for all. . . . In the spirit of California's history then, we are here today to bear a lantern for the future, not carry a torch for the past."[2]

Moving on to discuss his specific legislative program, Brown promised constituents that he would balance the budget, improve education at all levels, achieve full employment, and solve the problems of the cities ("It is here or nowhere, now or never, that men will stand up to the challenge of the city"). Brown conceded that there was no great political or ideological consensus about what needed to be done in the coming years, but he went on to state that consensus or no consensus the governor intended to provide "bold, controversial leadership" on the key issues of the day.[3]

The soaring liberal hopes found expression in other ways as well in the days following Brown's victory over Nixon. Brown and aides believed that in the second term they would have a chance not only to do good but also to bolster their political standing, possibly even welding together a liberal Democratic political coalition that would rival the coalition put together by President Franklin Roosevelt during the New Deal. A few weeks after the election, Richard Kline, the executive secretary, captured the high hopes and sense of euphoria that held sway over liberals in Sacramento when, in a memo, he told Brown:

> [Your] opportunities are golden. You are the only Democratic governor of a major state in the Union, and it is the nation's first state. You have a friendly legislature to work with, and your margin of victory was large enough to constitute a mandate from the people, despite what the opposition press might say. The Republican party is, at the moment, without leadership or direction. Its chances of reemerging as a major force in California life depend largely on how well you succeed or fail in the next four years. It is only fitting that a Californian should make a successful bid for the Presidency in the next decade or so. Who that individual will be no one can say, but it is important that a political climate be created so that he can be developed and nourished. If that individual is to embody your own philosophy of government, it is your task to exercise leadership of the highest sort. In other words, your role as political leader did not end with the past campaign; it has only begun.[4]

OF THE MANY PATHS that beckoned, Brown seemed least apt to lead the struggle for racial justice in California. To be sure, he harbored a long-standing sympathy for the dispossessed and loathed racist practices of all kinds. He had been born to racially tolerant parents, raised in an ethnically mixed neighborhood in a cosmopolitan city, and as a young man he became a devout Catholic who considered racism a sin against God for which racists would be punished in the afterlife. Shunning white supremacists, in his younger years Brown had a general sense that racism was a sinister scourge that inflicted great harm on minorities and sullied the otherwise enlightened and heterogeneous social climate of California. And on occasion, while working as an attorney in private practice in San Francisco, Brown acted on his racial feelings and fought for integrated housing complexes in the city and also for the desegregation of local labor unions, going so far as to warn clients that if they did not integrate their union he would see to it that they were thrown in jail.[5]

But as the crime-fighting district attorney of San Francisco and the anticorruption attorney general of the state of California, Brown had demonstrated little interest in race reform. His constituents had not elected him to champion civil rights so much as to maintain social order. In keeping with the traditions of his offices and the political constraints of the time, Brown mostly avoided race questions and instead used the powers of his office to shut down illegal brothels and gambling parlors, prosecute murder suspects and mafia dons, and root out official corruption in Sacramento.

In 1959, for the first time in his political career, Brown embraced wholeheartedly the cause of civil rights. He appointed several black and Hispanic staffers, and more important, signed into law three civil rights measures: the Fair Employment Practices Act, to combat discrimination in the workplace; the Unruh Civil Rights Act outlawing discrimination in public accommodations and businesses; and the Hawkins bill banning discrimination in publicly funded housing. But in the remainder of his first term, Brown gave only sporadic attention to racial discrimination. In 1960 he appeared before a civil rights commission and denounced California realtors whom he accused of "hid[ing] behind the reactionary and discredited folk tale that segregation and discrimination are natural and tolerable because minorities prefer to be restricted to the ghetto." But otherwise, Brown made little effort on behalf of new measures in the field of antidiscrimination law. Worried about his political standing in the state, Brown avoided a contentious legislative battle on behalf of fair housing. In December 1960, Richard Kline captured the prevailing wisdom in Sacramento about housing and civil rights when he wrote the governor: "It would be unsound to initiate any major specific housing legislation at this time. We are simply not prepared for it. . . . Housing is such an explosive social subject. . . . The question is not what has to be done in this field, but what can be done from a politically realistic standpoint."[6]

In early 1963, what had recently seemed like an explosive social subject now seemed the perfect moral issue for the administration to tackle. By that time, of course, the national struggle for black equality was in full bloom. Massive civil rights marches gripped the cities of the American South, rocking the white political establishment in Dixie and provoking a violent racial backlash from governors, police chiefs, and city council members committed to defending Jim Crow laws in their states. In their effort to squash the protest marches and restaurant sit-ins, southern whites unleashed the full police powers at their command. The story is a familiar one—local authorities allowed angry white crowds to attack peaceful civil rights protesters. Black and white demonstrators trying to draw attention to segregated eateries, transportation systems, and hotels faced truncheon-wielding police officers with snarling attack dogs in Birmingham. Elsewhere, law enforcement officials routinely clubbed, beat, and jailed those working to abolish Jim Crow.

Treated to a steady diet of television images and news articles about the violent racial clashes roiling the South, Brown was one of many white liberals who was outraged. He began voicing strong support for the southern civil rights movement. He applauded Martin Luther King, Jr., for leading the struggle for black equality and began encouraging the young students in his state to travel to the South where they could join Dr. King and other liberals in the quest for racial justice. He made an important symbolic gesture on behalf of civil rights when he appointed William Becker to run a new state agency for human rights in California. Becker was a white, pipe-smoking veteran of the civil rights movement and he had amassed a record on the issue second to none. In his younger years Becker had helped unionize Mexican-American farmworkers in the Central Valley, served as chairman of the Committee for Fair Employment Practices, and won an NAACP freedom award for his devotion to the cause of civil rights. His appointment to the post of civil rights chief sent the signal to civil rights activists in the state that the administration was serious about enacting race reforms.[7]

In early 1963, for the first time, there was substantial political pressure put on Brown to take on the long-standing problem of housing discrimination. In early 1963, Mississippi, Alabama, and Georgia were not the only states to be rocked by massive civil rights activism. Protesters in California launched a series of demonstrations against business establishments and government agencies accused of discriminatory hiring practices. Led by the NAACP, CORE, SNCC, and a handful of other lobbies, waves of angry black and white picketers paraded in front of Sheraton hotels, Bank of America branches, federal buildings, city halls, and courthouses, holding aloft signs that asked onlookers whether they possessed the courage to stand up to racism in California, signs that asked, "Are you now, or have you ever been, a *liberal*?" Designed to appeal to the conscience of white liberals then in power in Sacramento, the demonstrations resonated with a liberal, sympathetic governor eager to strike out in bold policy directions. Still, Brown feared that the protests might spin out of control and turn violent and bloody. As he said at least once in 1963, Brown did not want California turning into the Mississippi of the West.[8]

Eager to temper passions and quell the demonstrations, Brown believed that the time had arrived for the housing issue. Brown considered racism a blight on his state. He saw the men and women on the front lines of the civil rights struggle as a kind of progressive vanguard for the liberal reform movement, and he abhorred the racist sentiments and discriminatory practices that he believed had a profound and deleterious effect on the social order: African-Americans tended to hold the worst jobs, attend the most dilapidated schools, and live in the most crime-ridden neighborhoods. Brown had passed bills outlawing hiring discrimination, launched an enormous expansion of the university system, and outlawed discrimination in public housing. But what about private housing?

Denied their constitutional right to live wherever they wished, most blacks had been relegated to the geographical margins of California society, a serious affront to Brown and to all liberals in the state. Basking in the glow of his reelection victory, with television images from the South generating widespread public sympathy for the cause of race reform, on February 14, 1963, Valentine's Day, Brown announced that he would embrace the cause of fair housing. In a major speech before a special session of the California state legislature, Brown called on lawmakers to pass a new and far-reaching civil rights measure to abolish race discrimination in California's housing industry. Depicting racism as a terrible scourge on the state that "aggravated . . . tensions" and undermined "American principles of equality," Brown encouraged Californians everywhere to rise up in opposition to the "serious injustice" of the status quo.[9]

Fair housing legislation appealed to Brown on several levels. In the late 1950s and early 1960s, a handful of prominent civil rights commissions and blue-ribbon panels, some appointed by the governor, others by the federal government, had documented a widespread pattern of race discrimination in the state's housing industry. Reports described how realtors used a welter of restrictive covenants and codes to keep African-Americans from buying homes in predominantly white suburban communities. In 1956, the Berkeley chapters of CORE and the NAACP conducted an experiment in which black and white prospective homebuyers tried to purchase homes in predominantly white neighborhoods. Realtors rejected black applicants but not their white counterparts. Other studies revealed that black students at the

University of California could not find decent housing in the area around campus, and in the late 1950s and early '60s, the U.S. Commission on Race and Housing and the U.S. Commission on Civil Rights echoed the problems on a broader scale, including in government agencies such as the FHA and VA. Advertisements for apartments often had "whites only" clauses to ward off black renters; realty boards tended to be lily white; and the Veterans Administration sometimes refused to sell repossessed homes to blacks. The result was unnatural and unfair. African-Americans had no choice but to live in dilapidated ghettos marred by overcrowding and poor public services.[10]

Brown refused to shrink from what he and his aides now considered one of the great moral challenges of the day. He had a lot of support. Liberals in Sacramento agreed with him and, in the heady spirit of 1963, believed that efforts to abolish housing discrimination would win broad backing from the public. Brown and his aides believed that with a new fair housing law they could allow blacks to live where they pleased, help destroy the ghettos, and thereby provide African-Americans with basic human rights and help stamp out the scourge of bigotry. They thought they had a winning issue that would improve Brown's political standing while rewarding civil rights lobbies for having supported Brown in his reelection campaign.

In the early spring of 1963 Brown mounted an energetic drive to win legislative passage of a fair housing bill. The Rumford Fair Housing Act extended the ban on discrimination in the sale or rental of all private dwellings except those with four units or less and with the owner in residence when sold by the owner. Brokers, however, were barred from discrimination in all transactions. That spring, the liberal state assembly easily approved the measure, as expected, but the real fight would be in the senate. That more conservative body was controlled by maverick rural Democrats with a long-standing antipathy toward civil rights reforms. The mavericks succeeded in sending Rumford to their Committee on Governmental Efficiency (GE), the so-called graveyard for liberal legislation where Luther Gibson and Hugh Burns, powerful conservative Democrats, held sway. Gibson and Burns had little interest in fair housing reform and employed a host of delaying tactics to keep the bill in committee, where it would presumably die a slow and little-noticed death.[11]

The bill would be anything but little noticed. Brown and fellow liberals now considered themselves in a war for the future of their state. Mounting a major assault on the recalcitrants, Brown began hailing Rumford as one of his "major objectives" for 1963 and promptly embarked on the most passionate fight since his 1960 campaign for a state water plan. Brown dangled before senate moderates and fence-sitters promises of judgeships and other plums. To conservatives he threatened retaliation—either release Rumford from the GE committee, or "You're not going to get your legislation through. Forget about it."[12]

The governor was far from the only politician and activist working on behalf of Rumford, but he did more than anyone to rally the troops. While aides pressured committee members and other senators, the governor encouraged grassroots groups, civil rights organizations, priests, rabbis, union leaders, and other leading liberals to come to Sacramento. Liberals responded in droves. The NAACP held a conference in Sacramento devoted to fair housing, and priests, rabbis, blacks, union organizers, the Jewish Community Relations Council, and the Jewish Labor Committee all descended on the capitol. As Brown aide William Becker recalled, the administration "had, for weeks on end, every day, one delegation from some place in the state of people who visited in the halls of the legislature. Between them and what I was able to do on the phone, we kind of kept this going."[13]

Brown had some big guns on his side. At a presidential rally at the Hollywood Palladium, Jesse Unruh, the powerful speaker of the state assembly, urged the White House to call Luther Gibson and threaten to close down the naval yard in Gibson's district if Rumford failed to find its way out of the senator's committee. Vice President Lyndon Johnson promptly called Gibson and warned him, "Senator, that fair housing bill that we think's in the public interest, that ought to come out. If it doesn't, there won't be any more contracts for the Mare Island Navy Shipyard. There won't be much work over there."[14]

In May, with only a few weeks remaining in that year's legislative session, the key Democratic committee members finally agreed to release Rumford from the GE committee. It was a ploy. Gibson and Burns were old legislative hands. They knew that the senate, with several hundred bills still pending on its docket, seemed unlikely to reach the fair housing bill before its session expired. June 21, 1963, the last day of the legislative session, was a study in chaos: files listing various bills circulated through senate chambers; bills from the state assembly continued to arrive; and mimeographed files cluttered senators' desks. Earlier that day Clark Bradley, a Republican, had passed a parliamentary motion requiring that every senate bill under consideration be read aloud three times before being voted on. The Bradley motion, one senator recalled, "made it utterly impossible to reach the Rumford fair housing bill before midnight. This was the strategy."[15]

Senators Edwin Regan and Joseph Rattigan, both moderate supporters of fair housing, decided to counter the Bradley strategy with a ruse of their own. In a last-ditch attempt to bring Rumford up for a vote, at eleven o'clock that night, with just one hour remaining in the legislative session, Regan and Rattigan called for a special order of business to move Rumford to the top of the legislative docket and put it up for an immediate vote. By 11 P.M. Regan, Rattigan, and other fair housing supporters had rounded up enough votes to pass their special motion, and the move caught Burns and other senate conservatives by surprise. Furious at the attempt to outmaneuver him, Burns, the senate majority leader, rose from his seat, approached Regan, gesticulated wildly at his colleague, and railed, "You know that we're not supposed to do this! It's a violation of all tradition." Regan simply shrugged his shoulders and laughed. Rattigan, meanwhile, was on the senate floor saying a few words about the merits of fair housing and signaling allies that the time to vote was at hand.[16]

Roll call commenced. Twenty-two senators voted in favor, twenty against. The measure had passed by the slimmest of margins. Around midnight, Brown signed the controversial bill into law. As news of the Democratic triumph spread through the capitol, Speaker Unruh and Senator Gibson warned administration aides that the new fair housing was not all that it was cracked up to be. They, at least, realized it was controversial and predicted that it would generate political heat for its sponsors. Unruh told Kline that Rumford "might reverberate against us" and Gibson predicted that Democrats who had supported fair housing would "go down like flies" in the next election. Gibson even warned a Brown staffer soon after the bill's passage: "You're going to regret this as long as you live."[17]

Brown and his liberal allies dismissed such warnings as the hyperbolic reactions of the unenlightened few. Richard Kline called "almost heresy" the Gibson-Unruh suggestion that Californians would turn on the Democrats who had supported fair housing. In the late-night hours just after Rumford's passage, liberals reveled in their major step forward in the struggle for racial equality. Roy Ringer, one of the governor's press assistants, believed that fair housing marked a major civil rights achievement for the administration. Arriving home that night, Jack Burby, Brown's press secretary, told his wife that the administration had just struck a historic blow for freedom. "By God," he gasped, "our kids might grow up never having to worry about racial tensions." CORE protesters had been occupying the state capitol for three weeks to protest the senate's refusal to pass fair housing, and when word of Rumford's passage reached them they celebrated by singing "We Shall Overcome." Senator Rattigan spotted the bill's sponsor, Byron Rumford, in the back of the Senate chamber. He embraced Rumford and as tears welled in his eyes he blurted, "Byron, I have just atoned for a Jim Crow boyhood."[18]

Brown did not have a Jim Crow boyhood for which he felt the need to atone, but he too considered the fair housing law a legislative landmark; it would help seal his legacy as a liberal titan, help eradicate urban slums, and bring California one large step closer to living out the ideals of equal opportunity spelled out in the Constitution. Brown was not quite so naive as to think that a single piece of legislation would suddenly wipe out all racial tensions in the state, but he did believe that the days of racism were numbered. The Fair Employment Practices Committee had visibly helped with employment discrimination, and Rumford seemed likely to do for the field of housing what the FEPC had done for the workplace. As Brown recalled, "this legislation was not just some symbolic legislation or something for the purpose of rubbing the landlord's face in the dirt. This was absolutely necessary to improve the lot of the Negroes . . . one of the great victories of my career [and] the beginning of our struggle to attack the problem of the ghettos."[19] The new law also seemed to confirm what he had believed since his victory over Nixon in November 1962. The forward force of responsible liberalism dominated the political landscape like few political forces of the century.

A LOOSE CONGLOMERATION of homeowners and realtors united by a mutual desire to protect property owners from government harassment, the California Real Estate Association (CREA), decided soon after passage of the Fair Housing Act to mount a far-reaching campaign to overturn it. L. H. "Spike" Wilson, president of the CREA, announced in November 1963 that he was forming a committee, "Americans to Outlaw Forced Housing," to circulate petitions and gather enough signatures to place a repeal proposition on the 1964 election ballot. The realtors had spent years lobbying against government regulations of California's housing industry, and they saw the new Rumford law as a fundamental threat to the housing market in California—not to mention an invidious infringement on the rights of property owners to dispose of their homes however they saw fit. "The whole country is watching," Wilson wrote colleagues that year. "And when they see that the people in the leading state in the nation had the courage to stand up and stop the erosion of individual freedoms threatening this great country of ours . . . we are going to be proud."[20]

In late 1963 aides informed Brown of the realtors' repeal campaign. Brown dismissed it as the noisy rumblings of the embittered business class. The governor did not believe that realtors had a legitimate chance of overturning Rumford, though he was somewhat concerned about the effects of a petition drive on the racial climate in the state. At worst, he feared a repeal effort might spark a bloody conflagration. In late 1963, Brown decided to do what he could to prevent such a scenario from taking place. He began urging realtors to lay down their clipboards and abandon their repeal drive. Operating on the assumption that fair housing threatened neither the real estate industry nor individual property owners in California, the governor reassured "realtors, builders, financial institutions and all Californians" that Rumford "in no way threatens property values or individual rights." He promised realtors that the FEPC, the agency responsible for enforcing the new law, would err on the side of caution when investigating complaints of discrimination.[21]

Brown also appealed to the conscience of people in the real estate industry and ordinary citizens in the state. Brown spoke passionately about the recent "terrible killings in Birmingham," which he called "a solemn reminder of our duty as citizens to uphold the law and to achieve what we know is right in our hearts—decent, fair treatment of all citizens." And he warned realtors that theirs was an "irresponsible approach" that would only "increase political bitterness and hate [in the state] rather than understanding and cooperation." Brown scolded CREA leader Wilson that his proposed ballot "initiative attacks the basic principles of America as they are spelled out in the United States Constitution. I do not believe we should submit sections of that document to plebiscite every time we are annoyed by them. I emphasize that your initiative attacks inalienable rights which the Constitution preserves for all free men." He predicted that a repeal campaign would "divide the people of California" and "leave a lasting scar on our communities," warned realtors about a possible loss of federal housing subsidies to the state, and argued that the real estate industry would suffer a crippling financial blow as a result of their actions.[22]

Aides called the CREA ballot initiative a "great tragedy . . . that . . . has evoked so much criticism . . . from constitutional officers, legislators, public officials and . . . the clergy and religious leaders of our great State."[23] Members of the Fair Employment Practice Committee offered to appear before local real estate boards and discuss the new fair housing law with realtors concerned about the impact of the measure on the housing market. Brown's aides sent legislators speeches in support of Rumford, and they also began urging civil rights organizations to get active in the struggle to preserve fair housing for California. Becker sent liberal allies pamphlets and informational packets that touted the merits of Rumford, and began urging unions and religious institutions to endorse the new fair housing measure. "As you know," Becker wrote one union organizer in Sacramento, "our hard-won Fair Housing Act is being subjected to the threat of an initiative and the CREA seems set on making California go through the terrible struggle of arguing this sensitive issue with slogans and emotion, instead of facts and reason."[24]

By November 1963, it became clear that all the arguments and cajoling had made almost no dent in realtors' support for a repeal initiative. Brown and his staff realized that they would likely face a repeal proposition on the next year's state ballot. "Unless we can reach more Realtors to take up the issue inside the CREA and the local boards," Becker wrote the governor that November, "they will certainly keep going." Brown, Becker, and others in the administration agreed that if the realtors did "keep going," if they succeeded in qualifying for the ballot, then liberals everywhere would have no choice but to wage "a full-scale campaign to win the popular vote."[25]

Jesse Unruh and other legislators knew better, but Brown and his aides were operating in a vacuum of their own making. They had little doubt that they would prevail in a ballot campaign and prove to the forces of reaction that hatred and bigotry were things of the past in California. They believed that fair housing was a prudent reform measure that had resulted in only a small number of citizen complaints against realtors. And the men behind the repeal campaign seemed a musty, antiquated group who were bent on halting the flow of progress. Senators Gibson and Burns were members of the "old Praetorian guard" in Sacramento, parochial Democrats from rural counties who had not yet stepped into the modern era. And others who had voiced opposition to Rumford looked like a list of *Fortune* and *National Review* subscribers—self-interested businessmen, libertarians, some boisterous bigots, narrow bands of wealthy property owners, and groups like the Citizens League for Individual Freedom, the State Chamber of Commerce, and the California Real Estate Association.[26]

Most telling to Brown and his backers were the arguments floated against Rumford. Some opponents claimed that "widespread discrimination did not exist" in California's housing industry; others had simply blasted the bill as a dangerous infringement on individual property rights, making the argument that an act outlawing racial discrimination was an assault on the very values—liberty and freedom—that made America the great bulwark of democracy around the world. Brown dismissed realtors as having little regard for the larger social consequences of the question. He continued to believe that they had almost no chance of igniting a grassroots revolt against the civil rights movement. Arthur Alarcon, Brown's executive secretary, summed up the administration's view of fair housing and those who opposed it: Rumford, he said, was a "mom and apple pie" issue "that no one could possibly be against," and those who were against it seemed like "totally foolish" people "not worthy" of being taken seriously.[27]

BUT IT WAS ONE THING to restrict employers and public-housing owners and quite another to restrict individual homeowners on the disposition of their castles. Polls taken in early 1964 showed Proposition 14 with strong support from California voters. Brown and aides believed that such numbers suggested only that the public was confused about the real issues involved. Realtors, they thought, had succeeded in distorting the scope and impact of the new Rumford law, fanning public fears about a government poised to roll back the rights of property owners. Brown believed that the arguments in favor of fair housing were still effective and potent, and that he and other liberals simply would have to put those arguments before the voters of the state. They remained confident that an all-out campaign to educate the public would quickly turn the tide. In early 1964, Brown and his supporters went public. They argued that Rumford was simply a way to give blacks a fair shot in life. They declared that under Rumford minorities had filed only a handful of complaints, and they portrayed fair housing as a modest reform measure that embodied the best in the civil rights and liberal political tradition. Blanketing the state with billboards emblazoned with the pictures of Abraham Lincoln and John F. Kennedy, American heroes martyred in the fight for freedom, Brown and others in the "No on 14" campaign argued that overturning fair housing would interrupt the march of progress. Indeed, in the wake of Kennedy's assassination, LBJ was whipping up support in Congress for major national civil rights bills like the Civil Rights Act, passed in 1964.[28]

Brown dispatched to Los Angeles several key aides, Richard Kline, Roy Ringer, and Lu Haas, to coordinate the "No on 14" election effort. Liberals secured endorsements from virtually every major moral, religious, and liberal leader in the state, from priests to rabbis to union leaders to civil rights organizers and even Hollywood stars. "Certainly, the reason we are in as strong a position [as] we are in is because of the church support which has been so spontaneous, so all-out," Becker explained to one ally in January 1964. Other liberals waxed equally confident about their ability to educate the electorate, with one summing up the mood by noting that he was "most encouraged by the broad support we are attracting." With virtually "all the good people in the state" firmly in the liberal camp, Brown and supporters believed that the realtors faced a daunting uphill battle that year. Becker, for one, had rarely seen so many people fighting for social justice, people from all walks of life pouring out of their homes and "campaigning in local communities, and writing letters to the newspaper, and putting out literature, and getting on radio and tv, and carrying ads."[29]

But the "No on 14" campaign was far from a harmonious coming together of progressive forces in California. It was a fractious affair marred by personal turf wars, low morale, and poor volunteer coordination. Bereft of funds, a single statewide coordinator, and a trenchant theme, Brown and his supporters had difficulty welding together the motley church groups, civil rights activists, and "random collection of citizens with good intentions." Aides and Democratic party leaders sent one another memos detailing myriad organizational woes: "Problems have developed in Los Angeles," Becker groaned to an aide in the attorney general's office at one point during the campaign. He was referring to staffing and fund-raising, among other things. In March, Democratic party activist Robert Coate echoed these complaints, telling Becker, "I shudder to contemplate the problem on a statewide basis." By June the campaign still did not have a finance chairman in the south, and campaign leaders were growing increasingly worried that they would not have enough money to mount an effective electoral effort. Kline told colleagues at one point that the need for cash was "critical and immediate," and other aides urged Brown to step up his fund-raising efforts.[30]

The biggest problem, however, was not internal campaign frictions or logistical snags but rather political strategy. Brown continued to believe that the electorate would see things their way and was deluded if it didn't. They sought to head off any such delusions with an all-out attack on opponents. Yet polls continued to show a public inclined to vote for Proposition 14. To Brown, realtors seemed to have confused people by calling their own repeal measure the "real fair housing initiative in California." Liberals now concluded that they had no choice but to launch a major attack on the enemy camp and depict opponents as dangerous demagogues who spouted vicious racist doctrines more appropriate to nineteenth-century America.

Liberal confidence continued to run high. Brown's allies believed that the great flow of American history stood on their side. They were the inheritors of Lincoln and Kennedy, while the realtors descended from Jefferson Davis and southern segregationists. Brown especially believed in a hard-hitting attack, and in mid-1964 he began wielding it with great aplomb, flaying foes as an unsavory combination of big business, seedy real estate brokers, and reactionary racists clinging to a discriminatory status quo. Brown vilified the Right and warned voters that Nazis, racists, and sundry other demagogues had glommed onto the initiative campaign in the hopes of touching off a racial firestorm. Before a gathering of real estate executives, Brown chastised the group for their "racist" ballot measure. When realtors responded coolly, the governor basked in the chilly reception, thinking it evidence of the bigoted nature of the opposition. At a statewide Democratic convention in Long Beach, Brown praised Democrats as "the champions of all that is progressive and dynamic in the political life of our state and nation," and he argued that the forces of reaction were on the march in California and had to be stopped. "Nowhere—nowhere," Brown thundered, "do we face the greater threat to California's liberal tradition than in the current initiative to repeal the Rumford Fair Housing Act. We did our best to keep it off the ballot and it's a tragedy we didn't succeed. And now, obviously, we must expend every effort to defeat the initiative. . . . We must learn from the mood of the civil rights demonstration in Washington last year that a reasonable cause demands a reasonable course of action." Brown railed further: realtors were not quite racists themselves but "they have not been able to keep the bigots out. Only last month, swastika-wearing members of the American Nazi Party paraded in San Diego with picket signs calling the Rumford Act a Communist plot. . . . California is not going to buy the extremist's wares . . . we are an intelligent people who respond to intelligent argument."[31]

At other highly charged rallies, Brown sounded similar refrains about the right-wing, antidemocratic threat gripping the state. In May, he told a Conference on Religion and Race, "Here in California a crest of extremist feeling riding these waves of unrest and doubt challenges the tradition of moderation in our state. In recent years we in government have worked hard to secure programs that would ensure equality of opportunity. . . . We have made consistent progress," culminating in the passage of the fair housing act eight months earlier. "But now powerful forces are . . . attempting to destroy the progress we have made . . . they are asking that Californians literally write a covenant of bigotry in California's constitution." The initiative, the governor concluded, offered voters a stark choice—peace and progress versus violence, bigotry, and a return to a much darker time in the history of American race relations. "Defeat the real estate lobby's initiative this fall, and you start the destruction of the ghetto. Destroy the ghetto and you start to wipe out de facto segregation in our schools. . . . And so I say there is no better target for you than the real estate initiative. And no greater victory for social justice and peace in the community than its defeat." In late August, at the Democratic National Convention,

Brown again blamed the repeal movement on vicious racists and reactionaries "for whom the burdens of a growing and powerful nation have been too heavy, [men] who seek the simple answer, the automatic thoughtless response."[32]

Aides waged the campaign with a similar sense of purpose and disdain for the opposition. Thinking it only a matter of time before voters realized just how radical and un-American Proposition 14 was, aides and supporters echoed Brown's remarks about a radical opposition composed of racist reactionaries out to squelch the spirit of equality then sweeping the land. During the campaign aides ridiculed opponents as "crackpots for housing." They dubbed Proposition 14 "the segregation amendment"; traced the web of extremist groups who supported the repeal initiative; and received reports from Anti-Defamation League activists who had infiltrated right-wing meetings and listened to racist diatribes against the Rumford Act ("[Wesley Swift] charged that forced integration is mongrelization, that Negroes were first imported as slaves by Jewish merchants," one such report read. "He said that Governor Brown is stalling the initiative from June to November in order to give pressure groups time to work and he said that every intelligent Christian should fight for this initiative.") Liberals also characterized Proposition 14 as an antiprogressive ballot initiative that sought to amend the state constitution, jeopardized federal housing subsidies to California, and amounted to a slap in the face to minorities everywhere. "Proposition 14 has one primary purpose," one anti-14 radio advertisement charged. "That is to give a few people the right to discriminate and segregate in housing."[33]

Nonetheless, by the fall of 1964, internal administration surveys and California state polls revealed that California voters continued to support Proposition 14 by overwhelming margins. In October a new Field Poll showed that 55 percent of likely voters said they intended to vote Yes on 14, 26 percent said they intended to vote No, and 19 percent were undecided. Polling techniques were not terribly sophisticated in 1964, so some of Brown's aides continued to argue that it was still possible to snatch victory from the jaws of defeat. Yet finally most of his aides seemed to realize that their cause was headed for a resounding defeat. It was as if they had woken up from a long sleep to the stunning preelection polling data. It left Brown confused and shaken; he had mustered his liberal troops, raised funds for the election, won endorsements from religious, civil rights, and union leaders, and stumped tirelessly throughout the state. All had been for naught.

In a last-ditch attempt to revive the campaign, volunteers and top advisors urged Brown to tone down his heated attacks on the opposition and work, as he had in 1963, to reassure voters that Rumford was a limited, modest reform measure that had only a limited, modest impact on the state. In August a volunteer for the "No on 14" campaign, Mrs. Stephen Brieger, warned Brown that his vitriolic rhetoric had undermined the election effort. "I've gradually developed the impression that there are far more people fearful of the implications in change than there are people who are outright bigots," she wrote the governor that month. "If we are to unify all people of good will . . . we must try to dissipate the public's false fears about the loss in property values, the incidence of crime and rioting in ghettoes, etc. There are reasoned and logical arguments covering these and all the other points that worry John Q. Citizen." Brown read Brieger's letter along with memos from Becker and Jack Burby that also urged him to cut down on the negative barbs and embrace a more positive approach to the campaign. Brown agreed that there was at least some merit to the charge that he had become overly shrill, and in the margins of one of the memos he scribbled to Burby: "Jack, I want to become more temperate." But Brown was a true believer that bigots and demagogues were behind the repeal campaign, and he couldn't bring himself to abandon his well-honed line of attack. Instead he continued lashing out at the conservative opposition. In October when Otis Chandler, the publisher of the *Los Angeles Times* accused Brown of provoking racial violence with his inflammatory attacks on the opposition, Brown scolded the *Times*' publisher, arguing that the real racists and radicals in the campaign were men like William K. Shearer, a publicist for Proposition 14 and "a writer of racist dogma. . . . It is not the Governor who is inflammatory. It is Proposition 14. And I submit that it is not the opponents of Proposition 14 who encourage the racists and bigots in this state, but those who support Proposition 14." Then Brown asked Chandler what he considered the key question of the campaign: "Will we solve our ancient problems of segregation and discrimination through legal processes? Or shall they be settled in the streets, with blood and violence?"[34]

Brown's fears about a bloody racial conflagration in the state were genuine, and his biting attacks on the opposition had some basis in fact. A number of white supremacists and radicals had indeed attached themselves to the repeal campaign, and such extremists spouted vicious canards about the black underclass and made incendiary statements about the havoc blacks would wreak on placid suburban communities in Southern California. During the campaign Robert Gaston, a well-known conservative leader, argued that "negroes are not accepted [into white neighborhoods] because they haven't made themselves acceptable." The state chairman of the National States' Rights party urged "white men" to unite behind the repeal drive, other activists lampooned fair housing as "the Rumford Mongrelization Act," and still others depicted Rumford as part of a vast left-wing plot to advance the "CommUNist course through racial agitation." That May the *New York Times* reported that the "radical right wing appears to have wide influence in the campaign to repeal California's fair housing law."[35]

Brown, however, had overestimated the role of true racists in the repeal effort, and painted a distorted picture of the men and women who sided with Proposition 14. While precise figures remain elusive, most leaders of the Proposition 14 campaign were steeped not in the dark world of right-wing racism but in the more murky realm of California real estate. They worked as brokers and developers and served on local and state real estate boards and had experience lobbying state legislators on issues of importance to the industry. They were not all rabid racists who simply did not like blacks. Most of all, Brown's repeated charges about the bigoted nature of the opposition failed to resonate with voters who were unsure about the fair housing issue and sensitive to any infringement, real or imaginary, on their property rights.

The liberals' misjudgment of the electorate was even more devastating than their characterization of the activists. Brown and his allies believed that fair housing was a clear and compelling moral issue that only the most narrow-minded people in the state would stand against. For years realtors had discriminated against blacks in California, prevented minorities from purchasing decent homes in good neighborhoods, and violated their fundamental right to liberty and the pursuit of happiness; and thus for years had sown the seeds of social enmity and racial discord. Such discriminatory practices were blatant and had to be stopped, and there was little question that Rumford would do the stopping. Brown believed that the new law promised to correct a longstanding moral injustice and would do so without adversely affecting the real estate industry, infringing on individual property rights, and turning suburban neighborhoods into seething cauldrons of ethnic tensions. Such an unswerving devotion made it difficult for Brown and other liberals to grasp a basic fact about fair housing and the 1964 repeal campaign: Voters were less worried about guaranteeing access to decent housing for inner-city blacks than they were about preserving and protecting their much-cherished right to sell and dispose of their property however they saw fit.

The realtors conducted a shrewd campaign aimed squarely at exploiting this visceral attachment to their homes. Sidestepping explicitly racist rhetoric and statements, proposition proponents instead hammered away at the sacrosanct issue of individual property rights and the every-man's-home-is-his-castle adage. They succeeded in tapping into latent fears that Rumford would bring about a drastic change in the nature of home ownership, telling people that Brown's fair housing law gave government bureaucrats the power to tell property owners what to do with their homes. They mounted a sophisticated, well-financed campaign that employed an array of powerful patriotic symbols—the flag, the Constitution, the Declaration of Independence—that effectively linked the ballot initiative to the cause of American freedom. At stake in the election was not civil rights for blacks, they said, but freedom for all Americans. Leaflets showed smiling American families standing proudly outside their suburban homes, and fliers that delivered to voters a simple and potent message: "Governor Brown opposes Freedom of Choice!"[36]

On November 3, 1964, the people in California made clear just how badly Brown had misjudged things: 4,526,460 cast their ballots in favor of Proposition 14; 2,395,747 Californians voted No. The margin of defeat was nothing short of astonishing. Only one county, Modoc, a tiny entity snuggled in the northeast corner of the state, rejected the initiative and even there it was a near thing. As liberals had expected African-Americans voted overwhelmingly against the measure, but whites from virtually every economic bracket and educational background supported it by a 58 to 22 margin. The tally was one of the largest and most unexpected political defeats of Brown's political career.[37]

True-believing liberals did not immediately know how to explain the election results. Hale Champion argued that it was white bigotry and hatred for the civil rights movement. Unwilling to tolerate even modest race reforms, whites had voted in overwhelming numbers. Becker believed that voters had supported Proposition 14 because they feared that Rumford would result in lower property values and more crime in their suburban neighborhoods. Arthur Alarcon had the most useful reaction; he blamed the liberal defeat on himself and other liberals who, he recalled, had become so swept up by the reigning progressive rhetoric of the times that they had lost touch with the concerns of the voting public. Richard Kline echoed this analysis. Liberals, he argued, had naively assumed that "people in the goodness of their hearts would vote no on 14. . . . I say the great miscalculation was that we felt if we could educate the people they'd vote our way. Well, the point was that we did educate them and they voted against us two to one."[38]

Lu Haas, one of Brown's press assistants, perhaps best captured the sense of depression that enveloped administration liberals following the election. During the campaign, Haas believed that fair housing was a clear moral issue and he was certain that most people shared his view. The passage of Proposition 14 was so unexpected, so shocking in its breadth, that it left Haas "shattered," as he put it years later. Haas failed to understand how a measure opposed by virtually every decent institution and every moral leader in California could achieve such a sweeping victory at the ballot box, and he argued that the vote on Proposition 14 "probably, ultimately did [Brown] in. Because . . . by the time Pat Brown was being kicked out of office, the state had washed its hands, politically, of liberalism. It was dead. . . . Liberalism died in '64, if you want to pick a date."[39]

The vote marked a major setback for liberals in California, but it did not irrevocably shatter the liberal coalition in the state or the consensus that undergirded it. True, voters had not only overturned Brown's fair housing law but had also elected a right-wing former song-and-dance man named George Murphy to the United States Senate. Murphy had defeated Pierre Salinger, a former Kennedy press secretary, criticized for carpetbagging (he had moved from New York to California just prior to the campaign) and for his strong support for Brown's fair housing law. Yet Brown remained the most powerful political figure in his state, Democrats still controlled the legislature, and Brown had over two years remaining on his term, a virtual eternity in politics. And the governor's reform agenda remained, by most lights, a popular agenda that appealed to the bulk of California voters. Just because voters had repudiated race reform in housing did not mean that they would do so in other areas. On the same day that voters overturned Rumford they also voted in overwhelming numbers for President Lyndon Johnson, putting a stamp of approval on the Great Society and the larger liberal reform program that Brown had championed, and repudiating a Republican party presidential candidate, Barry Goldwater, who was also widely seen as the unabashed leader of the conservative movement in the country. Brown had campaigned hard against Goldwater. With Goldwater's electoral collapse, most of the country agreed with Brown that as a political force conservatism remained marginal.

In short, fair housing was a turning point that liberals failed to notice. They still thought that their only opponents were the anticommunist crackpots. They still believed that the future was theirs for the taking, even if the populace was trailing behind the march of progress just a bit.

FOUR

# "RUN RONNIE RUN"

EQUALLY, ON THE OTHER SIDE, there were more reasons for despair than glee in 1964. For conservatives in California and in much of the nation, the 1964 presidential campaign began with a powerful political high with the nomination of Barry Goldwater, only to end with a dispiriting, overwhelming defeat. Though Proposition 14 was a victory for activists, it was not the main order of business. They had devoted most of their energies to Goldwater's campaign. In early 1964 the Right in the state achieved a stunning political coup, ousting Republican moderates from their positions of power within the grassroots organizations that dominated California party politics. Relying on a dense network of activists, immersing themselves in arcane bylaws and sundry parliamentary procedures, conservatives descended in droves on political conventions and succeeded in electing conservative stalwarts to leadership posts in the California Young Republicans (YRs), the California Republican Assembly (CRA), and the Republican party state Central Committee. The right-wing insurgency caught GOP moderates off guard and marked a stunning political triumph for a movement that had long been a minority faction.

In June 1964 conservatives notched an even greater political triumph with Barry Goldwater's victory in that month's California Republican party presidential primary. Conservative activists played a pivotal role in the victory, working long hours for weeks on end, distributing campaign pamphlets and registering new voters, sponsoring boisterous campaign rallies and raising money, walking precincts, and manning phone banks, crucial political activity that helped the candidate eke out a narrow three percentage point victory over the progressive Republican governor from New York, Nelson Rockefeller. California's eighty-six delegates were enough to secure for Goldwater the GOP presidential nomination, making him the first free-market, antistatist politician to win that exalted post since Calvin Coolidge in 1924.

But following these twin successes, Goldwater was swept away by the American mainstream. The results of that encounter were not pretty. The Johnson campaign blistered Goldwater as the poster boy for political extremism, deriding him as strident and dour—a crusading cowboy who wore as a badge of honor the extremist label that critics had affixed to him. Johnson strategists also aired the famous daisy advertisement, a scathing political spot that showed a little girl picking daisies in a sunny meadow as a nuclear warhead exploded in the distance, evaporating the child and leaving an ominous mushroom cloud in her wake while President Johnson intoned, "These are the stakes. . . . We must either love each other, or we must die." The spot only aired once, but it became so hotly discussed that its effects were magnified.

At that year's Republican national convention in July, Goldwater delivered his famous fiery acceptance speech in which he declared that "extremism in defense of liberty is no vice" and "moderation in the defense of freedom no virtue." The speech served as a rallying cry for the faithful but inflicted yet more damage on his already listless presidential campaign. In the fall, Goldwater also spoke nonchalantly about scotching Social Security and lobbing nuclear weapons into the men's room of the Kremlin. Goldwater advisors in California produced biting attack ads such as the twenty-eight minute docudrama *Choice*, an explosive film that offered up a nightmarish vision of America: bare-breasted women hung lustily out of windows in San Francisco, scantily clad dancers performed the twist, young black men razed inner cities, teenage gangs rampaged, and the president of the United States was shown tossing beer cans out the window of his large black limousine. Goldwater eventually nixed the spot, but the basic dynamic of the campaign had already been established. Liberals succeeded in depicting the senator as a right-wing firebrand too strident to occupy the Oval Office, a crusader who as president would try to return the country to an earlier era in American life, a man with a visceral, irrational hankering for a government shorn of vital social programs and a nation peopled with cowboys.[1]

Normally, anyone associated with such a resounding defeat would only be hurt by it. But the story of Ronald Reagan as the campaign's one bright spot is by now legendary. At the start of the campaign, he was still very much a marginal figure, acting in *Death Valley Days*, enjoying his leisure time, and giving occasional speeches. Goldwater, on the other hand, was the uncontested leader of American conservatism, a status he had held since 1960, the year he published *The Conscience of a Conservative*, a powerful political tract that articulated the key tenets of the conservative political program—more aggressive military measures and a drastic reduction in the size of government at home. The manifesto quickly became the bible of American conservatives, and Goldwater only solidified his reputation as a conservative hero when he urged activists at the 1960 Republican National Convention to go to work and take back the party from the Rockefeller moderates. As a political personality Goldwater was a powerhouse: rugged, gritty, and not known for mincing his words, the Arizonan was an impetuous daredevil who displayed little of the characteristic Reagan caution. He had ferried planes across the North Atlantic during the Second World War, and when the war ended began piloting his own Air Force jets. A hardy entrepreneur and two-term senator in 1964, Goldwater grew to love the desert and developed a keen interest in the Navajo Indians of his native Arizona.

Reagan, by contrast, craved control. Fastidious and fretful, he refused to fly in an airplane, let alone pilot one. Reagan too enjoyed the outdoors, but usually at his Santa Barbara ranch, where he could wile away the days riding horses or chopping wood. More solitary than Goldwater, and distant around friends and family, Reagan was both a Hollywood celebrity and a loner.

In early 1964, Reagan enthusiastically joined up with the Goldwater campaign. Like many conservative activists who made showy displays toward their hero, Reagan plastered the family station wagon and Nancy's Lincoln Continental with Goldwater for President bumper stickers and became perhaps best-known for glib gimmicks that he used to promote Goldwater's candidacy. In late March, he promoted a $100-a-plate Goldwater "Kickoff Dinner" at the Los Angeles Sports Arena by promising Goldwater enthusiasts a rousing display of patriotism such as they had never heard before, writing in a campaign newsletter, "you've never heard the Star Spangled Banner 'til you hear it Thursday [at the dinner]." On May 31 he led John Wayne, Rock Hudson, Raymond Massey, and a rally of Goldwater backers in the pledge of allegiance. And in July he attended the Republican National Convention as an alternate delegate who spent his time with his wife Nancy holding aloft placards that read "A Choice Not an Echo."[2]

At Goldwater's request, Reagan also began giving speeches for the candidate. But his talks amounted mostly to canned diatribes about the excesses of liberal government and the dangers of communism. His speeches rarely broke new ideological ground or veered from his standard spiel about a war between the forces of American light and Soviet dark. To be sure, they were popular, but to moderates and liberals, Reagan mainly deepened the impression that conservatives were anticommunist paranoids who saw subversives under every rock. Employing strongly worded denunciations of liberal enemies, Reagan came across as just one of many angry Goldwaterites on a quixotic crusade.

In the last days of the GOP presidential primary, Reagan excoriated Rockefeller Republicans when he opened a breakfast rally of 700 campaign workers with a searing parody of the enemy camp: "Good morning to all you irresponsible Republicans," Reagan greeted his listeners. He then accused Rockefeller supporters of conducting the "most vicious and venomous campaign against a candidate in our party we have ever seen," and he mocked moderates when he asked the audience if he should introduce Goldwater as the true voice of Republicanism or "as a Neanderthal man, a bigot, a warmonger, looking out at us from the 19th century?" Not long thereafter, at a Goldwater event at the Biltmore Hotel in Los Angeles, Reagan told dinner guests that "there [is] a conspiracy in the Eastern liberal press . . . we know what *they* are up to," the actor thundered ominously. "*They* are trying to discredit a great American by creating a false image and running against that. But *they* aren't going to get away with it."[3]

In their political reporting that year, journalists rarely mentioned Reagan, but when they did so they dismissed him as a huffy simpleton with strong ties to the Republican right. The *New York Times* described Reagan as "the youthful looking former Hollywood actor who has moved to the right of the political stage." The *Times* also noted that in one speech Reagan had issued a string of "attacks on the opposition" so "biting" that they seemed likely to sharpen the picture of Goldwater as a right-wing ideologue. Former Assemblyman Joseph Shell, Senate hopeful George Murphy, and a handful of other top conservatives even went so far as to snub their fellow-traveling Reagan as a latecomer to the conservative movement and an ex-liberal who was not to be entrusted with a leadership position within the campaign. A few of Goldwater's top aides considered Reagan something of a loose cannon, of little help to a candidate already dogged by charges of political extremism. And even some activists took a dim view of the actor, saying he was nothing more than a Hollywood has-been who spouted simplistic platitudes, "just an actor not of great substance," as James Hall, one of Reagan's future aides, recalled.[4]

But for all the knocks against Reagan in early 1964, a few wealthy entrepreneurs and millionaire businessmen in California viewed him in a decidedly different light. These Goldwater fund-raisers had heard Reagan speak and liked what they heard; Reagan was a crowd-pleasing and inspirational orator and a talented fund-raiser. He could be eloquent, witty, and self-effacing. In certain respects, key Goldwater supporters found Reagan even more appealing than the candidate himself. As a presidential contender Goldwater had been a large disappointment. Gloomy, dour, and prone to off-the-cuff remarks, the Arizonan seemed a conservative stalwart but not the politician to carry the conservative message to the American masses. By contrast, Reagan was a polished public performer who grinned frequently and told witty anecdotes about his time in Hollywood. He seemed sunny and sanguine and able to articulate conservative political positions without all the sturm-und-drang. Goldwater made flip comments; Reagan talked about the wonders of patriotism and the American free enterprise system.[5]

Reagan demonstrated the powers of his oratory on a number of occasions during the fall campaign. In August, during a heated meeting of the California Citizens for Goldwater-Miller, an organization of Goldwater volunteers, Reagan won election as co-chairman of the group with an impromptu speech on his own behalf. Southern California businessman Phil Davis was attacking Reagan at the meeting when Clif White, a national Goldwater organizer, rose in Reagan's defense. Reagan was sitting next to White and he reached over and grasped White by the arm and said quietly, "No Clif. This is my fight. Let me handle it." Reagan then conceded that he was a political neophyte and told his critics, "Folks, I'm the new boy on the block. I haven't been involved in a campaign like this in the past. But I can see that there's trouble here and there ought not to be trouble here." Reagan asked everyone in the room to get behind the Goldwater effort and his performance was so impressive that he and Davis were made co-chairmen on the spot. Two months later, in October, at an after-dinner party thrown by one of White's friends, Reagan again demonstrated his oratorical prowess by holding court in the living room and regaling party-goers with tales from the campaign trail. Everyone laughed at Reagan's stories and White for one came away impressed: Reagan had captured the spirit of the Goldwater crusade and had recounted "good stories about real people, amusing stories pertinent to our campaign, revealing vignettes of the hard-working men and women waging a tough, so often disappointing battle against . . . Lyndon Johnson."[6]

In the final weeks of the campaign, Henry Salvatori and Holmes Tuttle, top Goldwater fund-raisers in California, asked Reagan to speak at a $1,000-a-plate Goldwater dinner. Reagan was happy to comply with his friends' request. He delivered one of his patented stump speeches about the evils of socialism. Yet this time it really clicked. Reagan told horror stories about federal job training programs that cost "taxpayers about 70 percent more for each trainee than it would have cost to send them to Harvard." His multilayered lament about the liberal order thrilled conservatives in the room that night. After Reagan finished, dinner guests approached Tuttle and gushed about Reagan's performance. They said he had articulated the issues they cared about and they urged Tuttle to put Reagan on television for Goldwater. Tuttle liked the idea of getting Reagan before a larger audience and as dinner guests filed out of the nightclub he pulled Reagan aside and asked him if he would be willing to tape his speech for television. "Sure," Reagan replied congenially, "if you think it would do any good."[7]

Top Goldwater strategists later read a script of the Reagan talk and, thinking Reagan too "emotional and unscholarly," decided to nix the address. Their decision incensed Tuttle, Salvatori, Walter Knott, and other prominent California conservatives. They urged Goldwater's aides to let the broadcast go forward. Knott threatened to cut off advertising funds to the campaign while Tuttle, Salvatori, and others worked back channels to pressure Goldwater into airing the speech. Reagan himself had several conversations with the candidate about the spot, and he urged Goldwater to watch the speech and then decide for himself whether to air it. Goldwater finally did watch the speech. Afterward, he turned to an aide and asked gruffly, "What the hell is wrong with that?"[8]

On October 27, a week before election day, the speech ran on national television. Tan, handsome, comfortable before the camera, eschewing the bitter McCarthyite attacks on subversives in pin-stripes, employing rousing blasts against the federal bureaucracy, Reagan defended with strong words and ringing rhetoric the conservative program that was then under nationwide attack. He spoke in strong phrases about the wonders of the American capitalist system, defended a program of vigilant anticommunism at home and abroad, and blasted liberal elites for ignoring the communist menace in their midst. Liberals, he said, did not realize that the time for choosing had arrived, the time when Americans had to choose between the patriotic values of their Founding Fathers or the insipid amorality promoted by totalitarian regimes the world over.[9]

> This idea that government is beholden to the people, that it has no other source of power except the sovereign people, is still the newest and most unique idea in all the long history of man's relation to man. This is the issue of this election: whether we believe in the capacity for self-government or whether we abandon the American Revolution and confess that a little intellectual elite in a far-distant capital can plan our lives for us better than we can plan them ourselves. You and I are told increasingly that we have to choose between a left or right. There is only an up or down: up to man's age-old dream—the ultimate in individual freedom consistent

> with law and order—or down to the ant heap of totalitarianism. . . . You and I have a rendezvous with destiny. We will preserve for our children this, the last best hope of man on earth, or we will sentence them to take the last step into a thousand years of darkness.[10]

A few hours after the telecast Reagan received a phone call from Goldwater campaign headquarters. He had gone to sleep that night worried about how Americans would respond to his performance. The late-night phone call laid those anxieties to rest—the speech was a smashing success. A Goldwater aide informed Reagan that the switchboard at campaign headquarters was aglow with calls from around the country. Phone callers hailed Reagan's performance as a powerful call to arms, asked how they could obtain copies of Reagan's speech, and also asked how they could help Goldwater in the final days before the election. The outpouring did not slacken in the days following the broadcast. Thousands of conservatives wrote Reagan letters telling him he had articulated the issues they cared about: soaring tax rates, voracious federal bureaucracies, the struggle between East and West. Conservatives sent over $500,000 to Goldwater headquarters in the last days of the race, another half a million dollars poured in after Goldwater's defeat, and observers later estimated that overall Reagan's broadcast generated $8 million, a huge sum that astonished even grizzled political veterans.[11]

Journalists took note, and began arguing that Reagan's national television debut marked a pivotal moment for the celebrity actor. Reporters described Reagan's speech as a dramatic departure from previous conservative utterances and predicted that his performance had transformed him almost overnight from a minor political figure into a national political sensation. Shortly after the telecast reporter David Broder called Reagan's talk "the most successful national political debut since William Jennings Bryan electrified the 1896 Democratic convention with the 'Cross of Gold' speech." *Time* magazine hailed the speech as the "one bright spot in a dismal campaign." And one *Washington Post* reporter later described the address as a powerful rallying cry that had seared itself into the minds of many like-minded Americans: "If you were then an American inclined in your heart and mind to think of yourself as a conservative, and you saw [the speech], it stayed with you—not the precise words, but the feeling and the message. They were impossible to forget."[12]

What became known as The Speech indeed generated tremendous media publicity for Reagan. It impressed conservative fundraisers as a potent piece of oratory and convinced many activists that

Reagan was a rising star in his own right. But Reagan's speech was less a break with the conservative past than a reaffirmation of long-standing ideas and aspirations. Virtually the same speech Reagan had been giving for years, the "Time for Choosing" address amounted to a stinging rebuke of the welfare state. Reagan touted in fighting terms the virtues of a free-market system, excoriated liberal planners, and generally made a whole host of arguments familiar to any conservative politician or activist of the day. Full of threadbare refrains and blistering attacks on communists, the speech neither articulated a new conservative political vision nor catapulted Reagan into the American mainstream. Being a conservative star was one thing; a mainstream contender for office something else. These things would come to pass but they would have more to do with the larger right-wing insurgency on the rise in California than with Reagan's remarkable thirty-minute nationwide television address.

ON NOVEMBER 3, 1964, Lyndon Johnson trounced Goldwater by approximately 16 million votes, sweeping 44 of the 50 states and losing to Goldwater only in his native state of Arizona and in five states in the deep south—Mississippi, Alabama, South Carolina, Georgia, and Louisiana—where the race issue played in Goldwater's favor. In California, Johnson bested Goldwater by almost a million votes, a stunning margin that provoked a flurry of postelection commentary about the demise of the radical right in America. Commentators declared that the election sounded the death knell of the conservative movement. Goldwater's defeat was so thorough, so crushing, that he and the larger ideas for which he stood had virtually no chance of making a comeback. Reporters, politicians, and academics were in agreement on this issue, and within hours of the election journalists on the East Coast captured this fast-forming national consensus in their election postmortems. *New York Times* columnist James Reston spoke for many when he wrote that Goldwater "not only lost the presidential election yesterday but the conservative cause as well." *Time* opined that "the conservative cause whose championship Goldwater assumed suffered a crippling setback. . . . The humiliation of their defeat was so complete that they will not have another shot at party domination for some time to come." NBC broadcaster Chet Huntley described Goldwater supporters as a small band of right-wing crackpots—"segregationists, Johnson-phobes, desperate conservatives, and radical nuts . . . the coalition of discontent"—who now had virtually no chance of gaining a popular following in the country.[13]

Seldom has the punditocracy missed the mark so widely. In late

1964, conservative activists in California began talking about Ronald Reagan running for governor in 1966. Liberals, of course, dismissed the talk about a Reagan campaign as idle fantasies. Pollsters in California noted that Reagan enjoyed widespread name recognition, but they attributed his fame to his long acting career and Hollywood celebrity background and reported that only 12 percent of those surveyed said that he would make an excellent candidate for governor, while 39 percent said he would make a poor one. Leading Republican moderates cast aspersions on Reagan by telling journalists that Reagan was not a loyal party man but a fringe figure with little support from the reasonable men and women active in the Republican party. Some reporters continued to refer to Reagan only as a right-wing actor with close ties to Goldwater. Gladwin Hill of the *New York Times* seemed to speak for many in the press when he described the standard Reagan stump speech as a simplistic mish-mash of antigovernment rants. Hill further pointed out that Reagan had strong ties to the Christian Anti-Communist Crusade. The reporter poked fun at Reagan for being an actor who had introduced a recent episode of *Death Valley Days* this way: "By the way—I play the Senator"; there was, Hill noted, "a certain real-life aptness" to Reagan's statement.[14]

In the weeks following the November election, the critics seemed to have it right. In a series of public appearances and statements to the press, Reagan evinced little interest in binding party wounds and instead seemed keen on continuing to wage ideological war on GOP moderates. Reagan joined eagerly in the orgy of recriminations and regrets then dominating party politics. He blistered moderates for not supporting Goldwater in the '64 campaign and promised a group of Young Republicans that conservatives would not under any circumstances "turn the Republican party over to the traitors in the battle just ended. The conservative philosophy was not repudiated," Reagan roared. "We will have no more of those candidates who are pledged to the same Socialist goals of our opposition and who seek our support. If after the California Presidential primary our opponents had then joined Barry Goldwater at the national convention and pledged their support, we could very well be celebrating a complete victory tonight." In news interviews Reagan waxed equally caustic, boasting to reporters that the conservative philosophy had defeated the moderate one in the battle for control over the GOP. He told one newspaper that Goldwater was a fine presidential candidate and admitted to being a proud member of the "27-million-people-can't-be-wrong" school of Goldwater voters. Reagan also defended right-wing anticommunist groups as loyal organizations that bolstered the cause of freedom. He bragged that "assail[ing] the welfare state" was a legitimate endeavor as long as one had his "facts right."[15]

Still, Reagan, and California conservatives generally, had grown tired of losing elections to big-government liberals. The conservative movement in the state revolved around no single leader or party boss, and needed one. In the waning days of 1964 conservatives from all walks of California life cohered around a Reagan for governor campaign. They decided that Goldwater, for all his greatness, was simply the wrong man to carry the torch. The senator brought the movement closer than ever before to the promised land of American politics, but he came across poorly on television, displayed an uncanny flair for sticking his foot in his mouth, and had allowed a cabal of Arizonans close to him to dictate campaign strategy.

Pro-Reagan rumblings in fact began just hours after Goldwater's defeat. That night at a campaign party at the Ambassador Hotel in Los Angeles Reagan delivered a brief pep talk in which he urged Goldwater supporters to keep the conservative faith despite Goldwater's defeat. The talk had a tonic-like effect on the crowd, boosting morale and convincing many that Reagan would be their party's next standard-bearer. The next day in Ossowo, Michigan, several conservatives formed a Reagan for President club. A month later "Run Ronnie Run" and "Reagan for Governor" bumper stickers began popping up in right-wing bookstores in Southern California. Reagan also enjoyed strong early support from Goldwater and many of his California supporters. Goldwater described Reagan as a rising conservative star and a likely heir to his mantle, telling one reporter shortly after the election that he had "always looked on Ronald Reagan as one of the leaders of the conservative movement in this country. If he continues in his successful political career, I don't think you could deny that he would be the leader." In early December California conservatives assembled at the International Hotel near the Los Angeles airport for a Goldwater campaign postmortem. Activists agreed they had "a pretty good movement going" and urged one another to get active in the upcoming 1966 campaigns. When the day-long meeting ended John Gromala, a former president of the Young Republicans, and Vern Cristina, Goldwater's campaign chairman in San Francisco, stood in the hotel parking lot chatting when Reagan walked by them on the way to his car. The men spotted the actor and shot each other knowing glances: Reagan should run for governor; he was a wonderful speaker and "goddamned electable" candidate who would not "panic in front of a bunch of media people." They called Reagan over and urged him into the race.[16]

Among the first to recognize Reagan's potential were a handful of fund-raisers, the same men who had raised the money for Reagan's Goldwater address. In late 1964, Henry Salvatori, Holmes Tuttle, Ed Mills, Cy Rubel, and a handful of other prominent businessmen became the first conservatives to urge Reagan into a campaign. These men had seen each other frequently, sometimes several times a week, during the Goldwater campaign, and in the days following that election they continued to gather at dinners, barbecues, and cocktail parties where they talked about work and Republican party politics. They often gathered English-style after dinner, the men in one room, the women in another, where they enumerated the woes of the California GOP, told disheartening tales about the Goldwater campaign, and discussed what for them was the next big election in the country, the 1966 California governor's race. Angry at the sad state of affairs in Sacramento, the men agreed that Pat Brown was a tax-and-spend liberal and "do-nothing" governor who had to be ousted. They wanted Reagan to do the ousting.[17]

The men liked and greatly admired Reagan. Most had known Reagan on a personal level for over a decade. They viewed him as a man of deep political acumen and had been deeply impressed by the speeches he had given for Goldwater. Time and again Reagan had articulated conservative principles in a reasonable-sounding manner. He was charismatic, handsome, and cool under fire. He possessed incredible name recognition, and as Tuttle put it years later, Reagan had a warm and good-natured personality that would surely shine through on a campaign trail. Reagan "seemed steadier, less inclined to fly off the handle than Goldwater. He had more self-control, he could say the same things but in a more gentle way."[18]

Tuttle, Salvatori, Rubel, Mills, and others began urging Reagan to run. They did so in gatherings large and small, in private phone conversations and at right-wing social events. At one such gathering shortly after the election the men were discussing "Barry's troubles" when someone mentioned Reagan's terrific national television speech for Goldwater. Virtually everyone agreed that Reagan had performed brilliantly on that occasion and that Reagan had a future in politics. Then someone turned to Reagan, who was in the room at the time, and blurted, "God, Ron, you ought to get real active and get into this. We need people like you." Tuttle and colleagues visited Reagan at home, phoned him repeatedly, and offered to help him raise money for a campaign, including hiring professional political consultants to work with him on the issues, arranging his schedule of speaking appearances, and putting his financial house in order. In meetings that sometimes started at 8 o'clock at night and lasted until 3 or 4 o'clock in the morning they told Reagan that he had an obligation to conservatives and the country: Reagan was the only person in California who could save the GOP from the dustbin and rescue the nation from liberal ruin.[19]

Tuttle, Salvatori, Mills, and Rubel shared much. All had grown up poor, started their own businesses, and through hard work and ceaseless endeavor had joined the ranks of the super-rich. The men also embraced a similar view of American politics and the world order. Reagan's wealthy backers despised the New Deal and abhorred political philosophies—communism, socialism, fascism—that promoted strong centralized government as the solution to the problems of mankind. Though these men had made anticommunism a touchstone of their political ideology, above all they believed in the virtues of big business and the American free enterprise system. The quartet represented an older more traditional brand of pure laissez-faire conservatism that by the mid-1960s, even to most people on the right, seemed somewhat stale, and certainly no basis for a California gubernatorial campaign. Reagan would never formally break with his early backers, but in time he would move beyond their rather narrow political beliefs, casting aside the anticommunist laissez-faire rhetoric of the hard right and embracing a more nuanced set of positions. When Reagan made this leap, he took a crucial step toward a more popular form of conservatism, transforming a largely fringe movement prone to extremism into a more appealing, broad-based movement that could appeal to a vast swath of working- and middle-class whites in Southern California.

ED MILLS was a first-generation Dutch immigrant who followed his father into the bakery business, starting out as a stock boy in the packing department of Van de Kamp's bakery and moving slowly up the corporate ladder there until he became an assistant to Theodore Van de Kamp, one of the company's founders. Eventually Mills would be elevated to the job of company chairman, but long before that Mills was a staunch supporter of big business and of the Republican Depression-era president, Herbert Hoover. Mills' first real taste of politics came in 1935 when he campaigned for a California ballot measure to repeal the state's new tax on chain stores. In the early 1940s, Mills began organizing fund-raisers and other events for the Los Angeles Republican finance committee and also volunteered for a number of charitable and patriotic organizations, including Community Chest, United Way, and the Boy Scouts. By the 1950s Mills had become a fixture at Republican fund-raisers. He solicited donations for Dwight Eisenhower in 1956; supported Proposition 16, the controversial (and widely unpopular) right-to-work California ballot measure in 1958; and befriended a handful of moneyed conservatives who in 1966 would form the backbone of Reagan's gubernatorial campaign.[20] "The New Deal," Mills bitterly recalled, "was a welfare approach, and there were great problems in the country. Many people feel that Roosevelt saved us from revolution, but I think we would have solved our problems in another way. I don't think we would have had all the welfare we have today."[21]

Henry Salvatori shared Mills' reverence for the free enterprise system, but he was most animated by a hatred of communism. The most rugged and passionate of Reagan's early backers, Salvatori was a sun-tanned, wrinkly-faced, self-made millionaire and crack conservative fund-raiser who by the mid-sixties had become an institution in the city of Los Angeles. Born in Italy in 1901, Salvatori arrived in Philadelphia four years later, where his parents opened a family grocery store, later purchasing a farm in New Jersey. Educated in a one-room schoolhouse near the farm, he eventually attended the University of Pennsylvania, took a job with Bell Laboratories, and enrolled in a part-time master's program in physics at Columbia University. On the last day of classes Salvatori stumbled across a flier posted on a campus bulletin board outside the physics building. "Men wanted with graduate work in physics to do research work in Oklahoma," the notice read. "If interested, see Professor Wills." Salvatori was happy with his job and had little interest in looking for work elsewhere, yet the ad intrigued him and he soon found himself accepting a job with Geophysical Research Corporation, a pioneer in the oil industry. With the firm Salvatori developed new methods for locating oil fields, and in 1932 at the age of thirty-one, after a brief stint with Texas Instruments, he formed Western Geophysical, an oil company that became one of the largest in the world after discovering vast oil fields in remote parts of California.[22]

Like Reagan's other early backers, Salvatori believed that through endurance, innovation, and an up-by-the-bootstraps work ethic he had risen from poverty to wealth. But as odious as the welfare state was to this kind of self-made success story, Salvatori considered communism an even more invidious force for evil. Deeply concerned about the communist hordes that had overrun Eastern Europe and threatened other parts of the globe, angry at the United Nations, which he saw as a force for appeasement, Salvatori believed it his duty to serve his country. In 1949 he became chairman of the Republican Los Angeles County finance committee, two years later he assumed the chairmanship of the party's state finance committee, and soon he found himself fully engaged in the struggle. In the 1950s, Salvatori helped found the Anti-Communism Voters League, a nonpartisan group that rated candidates for political office based on their "awareness of the communist threat." Salvatori became a principal sponsor of Fred Schwarz's Christian Anti-Communist Crusade, donated $300,000 to an anticommunist research institute at the University of Southern California, and contributed another $1 million to a program for the study of individual liberty at Whittier College. Salvatori also began raising money for anticommunist candidates running for high office. He saw liberal Democrats as naive politicians "totally unaware of . . . the threat of communist Russia"—liberals appeased Soviet aggression and refused to allocate funds sufficient to maintain a strong system of national defense.[23]

Holmes Tuttle was also a lifelong Republican, a self-made millionaire, and a free-market maven. Part Chickasaw Indian, Tuttle was born the seventh of ten children on Indian Territory in Oklahoma in 1905, shortly before it became a state. He grew up poor on a family ranch and in the early 1920s made his way to Oklahoma City, where he took a job at a Ford factory. The work was not for him, however, and in 1926 he moved to California because he had heard from acquaintances that in the golden state employment opportunities abounded. Tuttle took a job selling cars at a friend's Ford dealership in Los Angeles, scraped by during the Depression, and emerged from the 1930s the lone remaining car dealer on the Los Angeles Westside. When World War II arrived he started a heavy-duty equipment business in which he manufactured big dump trucks for the American military, but as soon as the war ended he returned to the auto business and again established the only Ford dealership on the rapidly expanding Westside. Capitalizing on California's postwar prosperity, Tuttle became a fixture of the local business community and an exceedingly wealthy magnate who began dabbling in Republican party politics. In 1956 he helped his friend Justin Dart, the head of Rexall Drugs, raise funds for Dwight Eisenhower's presidential campaign, and while at first Tuttle was a reluctant participant in the political process he soon cottoned to the challenge of raising money for Republican political candidates. Tuttle believed in fact that businessmen had an obligation to themselves, their companies, and their country to become active in politics; disdainful of apathetic entrepreneurs and fiercely devoted to the capitalist system, Tuttle supported candidates who promised to protect big business from regulation-hungry liberals. He too worried about a nation drifting away from its free enterprise moorings and toward a more bureaucratic, top-heavy welfare state. "We were creating all these agencies," Tuttle complained about the New Deal years. "And, unfortunately, when you create one of those during an emergency, they are never dissolved."[24]

As a Goldwater delegate to the Republican National Convention, during the 1964 campaign Tuttle witnessed firsthand the unraveling of his party. Tuttle considered Goldwater a visionary ahead of his time yet he also believed the senator was too strident. He believed Goldwater should have selected as his running mate Governor William Scranton of Pennsylvania, a moderate who might have helped unite Republicans. Instead Goldwater had presided over a "fiasco" of a convention that only deepened party rifts. Tuttle took away from the debacle an important lesson—the GOP had to unite. Tuttle had been friends with Reagan since the late 1940s and he liked the actor immensely. In late 1964 he believed that Reagan was the one man who could unite California Republicans.[25]

Reagan was flattered by all this attention. At first, however, he harbored mixed feelings about a race. Fending off his friends and supporters with a variety of pat responses, Reagan said he was afraid to fly in an airplane and could not possibly traverse a state as big as California by bus or train. He insisted that he had no real experience in government and volunteered that surely there were others in the movement more qualified than he. He told friends that he still enjoyed acting and had no intention of giving up his movie and television careers for a gubernatorial campaign that by all accounting was a long shot. Reagan also had a family to take care of and he explained to supporters that Nancy would not allow him to quit his current job so he could embark on a quixotic crusade. But he was clearly tempted. When one friend urged Reagan into the race, the actor simply grinned and asked aloud, "It's a wild notion, isn't it?"[26]

Reagan enjoyed being in the public eye and at the center of so much attention. He enjoyed the cloying encomiums coming his way and he began reading his fan mail with a zeal that bordered on the frightening. Reagan marveled at this tremendous outpouring on his behalf and, susceptible to the pressure now being placed upon him, Reagan in February 1965 told Tuttle and Salvatori that if they raised enough money for the endeavor he would travel around California and appear before Republican groups, give some speeches, and test the political waters. "If by August or September we feel there's overwhelming support from the Republican Party to win an election, not just a primary, I'll do it," Reagan told his friends. In his autobiography Reagan described the statewide speaking tour as merely a way for him to fend off his supporters until he could identify an alternate candidate to run in his stead. But from the start of it, Reagan seemed genuinely interested in running for office. Conservatives plunged excitedly into the burgeoning Reagan election effort, turning out in droves to hear him speak, pleading with him to run for office, washing away his niggling doubts. The raucous reception that greeted Reagan on his statewide jaunt reached a fever pitch by the middle of 1965, convincing Reagan that he could win not only his party's nomination but also the governorship. He was propelled into one of the more unlikely crusades in California history.[27]

IN THE SPRING OF 1965, through his speeches and appearances, Reagan routinely won over listeners. Supporters rose in applause at the end of his talks, spoke in hushed terms about Reagan's political prowess, and urged him to declare himself a candidate for office. After an encounter with Reagan in December of the previous year, Vern Cristina, a Northern California Goldwater supporter, returned home and almost immediately called former assemblyman Joe Shell and urged Shell not to run for governor. "Joe," Cristina told the former minority leader, "I love you like a brother, but like a brother I have to talk to you, talk some sense into your head. You don't have the ingredients to win. Nobody's going to argue with me or anybody else about your ability and your knowledge, but that don't win elections." In early 1965 grassroots conservatives began contributing money to Reagan's still unannounced campaign, telling Reagan that he had the talents to deliver the conservative message to the California public and encouraging friends and acquaintances to join up with the Reagan juggernaut.[28]

The pro-Reagan feeling was infectious and it took expression in any number of ways. State Senator Vern Sturgeon watched Reagan address a state Republican Convention in Los Angeles and after Reagan finished turned to his colleague Jack McCarthy and blurted, "Jack, there is our candidate for governor." Victor Veysey, a state senator from Imperial County, and George Dukmejian, then a young assemblyman from San Diego, had a similar reaction after hearing Reagan speak for the first time, concurring that Reagan was the most impressive public orator they had ever heard. Reagan picked up support almost everywhere he traveled. When he and Nancy appeared at a big hotel in San Francisco a crush of people formed a line that snaked through the hotel lobby, out the door, and around the block, waiting for a chance to meet the conservative icon. The reception was so massive that Nancy, unnerved by all the attention, awoke the next morning stiff and unable to move her neck. In the spring, when Reagan appeared before 1,500 Republican women in San Diego and gave his usual pitch for free enterprise, the women in the audience spent the rest of the afternoon meeting with Reagan and peppering him with questions about the likelihood of his running for governor. Elizabeth Storrs, one conservative leader in the audience, asked Reagan excitedly, "When did you get into this? . . . We realized that you had the capabilities, you knew the state well, you had been an organizer, you had headed up your Guild . . . and kept peace in there . . . and we just felt that there was no question that you were the best qualified. When did you make up your mind that you had to do it, that it was an obligation and something that was necessary for this state?"[29]

The Reagan for governor boomlet also swept through the established conservative political action groups in the state. In March 1965 the Orange County chapter of the California Republican Assembly urged the larger, statewide CRA organization to endorse Reagan for governor. In Buena Park the local chapter of the United Republicans of California (UROC) started calling itself the Ronald Reagan chapter, and at UROC's state convention delegates passed a resolution urging Reagan to run for high office. In early April, Cy Rubel invited twenty of the top Southern California financiers, attorneys, and entrepreneurs to meet Reagan at the California Club in Los Angeles. Many in the group had supported Goldwater and they came away from the meeting impressed with the actor and with "the conservative ring of his statements." It became routine for Reagan supporters to approach the actor after a speech and urge him to challenge Brown in 1966. They told him he was terrific on the stump and the one conservative who could carry the Goldwater message to the American electorate. In April one poll revealed that "Movie actor Ronald Reagan" was beating out six potential rivals in a Republican party gubernatorial primary.[30]

Increasingly enthusiastic about running for office, Reagan invited Goldwater field workers and precinct coordinators to his home to discuss the upcoming governor's race. Reagan made no promises about a campaign, but he encouraged activists to go to work on his behalf. Goldwaterites found Reagan an impressive figure and in a now-familiar scene they encouraged him to take the plunge. "I am a citizen who now feels strongly enough about the need for political change that I am willing to expend personal time and energies to help see that the right kind of changes occur," one former Goldwater supporter wrote Reagan shortly after the meeting. "After an hour's discussion with you, I am strongly impressed with your views . . . I believe that you are easily marketable to the people . . . because of your obvious intelligence, wit, dedication, scope, and maturity—and most significantly, because of your unusual abilities in verbal communications." Reagan appealed to the activists because of his charismatic personality and his "unusual abilities in verbal communications" but above all because he articulated the principles conservatives considered fundamental to the country's future.[31]

Though he continued to nurse several serious reservations about running, by mid-1965 Reagan found himself on the brink of a campaign. He believed strongly in the conservative cause, felt a moral obligation to the activists who had fought in the trenches for Goldwater, and continued to believe that a creeping tide of socialism threatened to overwhelm California and its forty-nine counterparts. He also concluded that speaking on behalf of other candidates was not necessarily the best way for him to serve the anticommunist cause. "I believed in what I had been saying," Reagan later said of his decision to run for office. "I really wanted to prove that we could bring government back under the people's control." What Reagan had only a few months earlier considered a "wild notion" was becoming less and less so all the time.

COMPLAINING EARNESTLY about Democrats in America leading "us to ruin with too much power concentrated in Washington," increasingly accustomed to the klieg lights and media attention, basking in the glow of public acclaim, Reagan found himself caught up in something larger than himself, a crusading political movement buffeted by the sense that its time had arrived. Historians have often described the Goldwater crusade of 1964 as the Woodstock of American conservatism, the time when activists everywhere poured their hearts and souls into a movement about which they felt deeply passionate. But in California the Reagan for governor boom was at least as exciting as the Goldwater campaign had been, and the infectious energy that pervaded the conservative movement struck a strong chord in Reagan. Reagan began fighting with Nancy over who opened Reagan's fan mail and Kathy Davis, Reagan's personal secretary, recalled that Reagan was so "delighted" and obsessed with his "fan mail" that he seemed to have little time for anything else: Someone needed to sit down and "have a little talk with [him] about this *bad* habit. But he was loathe to give it up." Reagan tried but often failed to hide his excitement about running. He told the *New York Times* that he found the talk about a campaign "electrifying" and admitted that he was "honored by all the interest. Politics is nothing I'd ever thought of as a career. But it's something I'm going to give deep consideration and thought." He carefully stowed his fan mail in boxes and during one meeting with advisors proudly unveiled several large boxes full to the brim.[32]

By spring, he had clearly decided to go ahead. Yet a Reagan campaign by no means guaranteed the Right its long-awaited triumph. For all his raw political talent Reagan was not a Lone Ranger who would ride to the rescue of a movement that had spent years relegated to and roaming the political wilderness. Conservatives remained a minority political force in California and the politicians who championed conservative causes had still not demonstrated that the 1960s was a hospitable time for them or the larger ideas to which they clung. Derided in the press and by liberals as crackpots, kooks, and Goldwater fanatics, conservatives needed not just a candidate but also new issues, fresh strategies—and some luck. They would soon have it.

FIVE

# "YOU'VE GOT TO GET THOSE KIDS OUT OF THERE"

PAT BROWN SHOULD HAVE KNOWN he was in trouble when Joan Baez sang Bob Dylan's "The Times They Are A-Changin'." In the first days of December, Brown found himself swept up in a series of social protests that rocked the campus of the University of California at Berkeley. The Berkeley controversy had actually begun some three months earlier, in September, when university officials at the flagship state school, finding themselves under growing pressure from the *Oakland Tribune*, university regents, and local tourist companies, decided to impose a ban on political activity on campus. Consulting only a handful of relevant university officials, Berkeley administrators slipped the new rule into the university rule books in early September, under the cover of summer recess and before the start of fall classes.

The measure struck many undergraduates as arbitrary and authoritarian; it could not have come at a worse time. The ban not only trampled on a long-standing tradition of political protest at Berkeley but also came when Berkeley undergraduates had become increasingly active in the struggle for racial justice. Scores of Berkeley students had spent their summers braving snarling attack dogs and hateful police officers in Mississippi. The work associated with Freedom Summer 1964 was dangerous and exhilarating for the young men and women who did it, and as the student activists returned to Berkeley in September they had high hopes for what the fall would bring. They planned to keep up the fight for civil rights. They would set up political recruiting stations on campus, pass out civil rights literature, organize protest rallies and marches, and hurl themselves into the heated struggle over fair housing in California.

Word that administrators had banned such activities hit them like a conk on the back of the head. Students immediately denounced the new rules as part of an insidious attempt by conservative officials and local politicians to squelch the growing clamor for civil rights in the Bay Area. Determined not to allow a group of flaccid university administrators to foil them—after all, not even hardened Mississippi segregationists had beaten them—in September the student activists simply went ahead and set up civil rights recruiting tables on campus. Manning makeshift CORE and SNCC tables on Sproul Plaza, a modest strip of concrete in the heart of the campus, the students began passing out pamphlets and encouraging their peers to take part in the movement.

Administrators quickly tired of the repeated violations of university policy. On the first day of October they decided to put a stop to it. From their windows in Sproul Hall, several members of the Berkeley administration spotted a former student by the name of Jack Weinberg manning a civil rights table on Sproul Plaza. They approached Weinberg and asked him to fold up his table and leave the premises. Weinberg refused to do so. Flustered, administrators then called the Berkeley police and requested that they remove Weinberg from the Plaza. Officers arriving on the scene radioed a squad car onto campus to cart the trespasser to jail. By this time many students had gathered on the Plaza to watch the drama unfold as the black and white cruiser rolled onto campus. Angry at both the police and the administrators, the students in the crowd surrounded the police car. With Weinberg now handcuffed and inside it, someone in the crowd hollered: "Sit Down!" Under ordinary circumstances such an injunction would have likely been met by wayward glances and curious stares, but the circumstances at Berkeley that day were anything but normal. The youth assembled on the Plaza were well versed in the tactics of civil disobedience, and they responded immediately. Forming a human circle around the offending police cruiser, the students sat down and trapped the arresting officers on the Plaza.

University administrators moved quickly to quell the rebellion. University President Clark Kerr met with an ad hoc group of student protesters and reached an accord with the undergraduates that essentially ceded to students most of what they wanted. In exchange for freeing the police car from the Plaza and leaving the scene quietly, the administration promised not to punish those participating in the demonstration and to appoint a committee to review the ban on political activity. But the October accord quickly crumbled under an avalanche of internal in-fighting, bureaucratic bickering, and student ire toward administrators. After weeks of skirmishing between Berkeley students and university officials, Clark Kerr announced on November 28, a Saturday, with students away for the Thanksgiving holiday, that he had decided to suspend eight of the ringleaders of the October 1 police car sit-in. Activists were furious.

Leaders of what was now called the Free Speech Movement (FSM) decided to conduct a sit-in demonstration more massive and confrontational than anything they had tried before. On Wednesday, December 2, at a large noontime rally, thousands of Berkeley students jammed into Sproul Plaza as one speaker after another appeared on the makeshift platform and harangued Kerr and the Berkeley bureaucracy. The atmosphere was thick with defiance: Joan Baez performed her Dylan rendition; students joined in singing "We Shall Overcome," the anthem of civil rights marchers; and Mario Savio, an angry and articulate philosophy major, a veteran of Mississippi's Freedom Summer, and a leader of the student protest movement, articulated the student mood in the most fiery and memorable speech delivered that day.

Savio had established himself as a leader of the protest movement during the police car sit-in, when he climbed atop the roof of the black and white cruiser and delivered a series of rousing impromptu talks about the importance of free speech for the students on campus. In the weeks following this first confrontation, Savio had proven himself to be a potent orator: six feet, one inch tall and 195 pounds, the lanky twenty-one-year-old junior embodied the anger of the younger generation. He had long, sandy red hair, wore a defiant scowl, and his East Coast exuberance and fiery rhetoric captivated student protesters. Now, with another seething mass before him, Savio again captured the student fury with a speech laced with biting attacks on university administrators. Savio accused the institution of being corrupt and rotten. In words soon to become a signature speech of the student movement of the 1960s, Savio told rally-goers that "there is a time when the operation of the machine becomes so odious, makes you so sick at heart, that you can't take part. You can't even passively take part, and you've got to put your bodies upon the gears and upon the wheels, upon the levers, upon all the apparatus, and you've got to make it stop. And you've got to indicate to the people who run it, to the people that own it, that unless you're free, the machines will be prevented from working at all." Upon finishing, the junior led nearly a thousand of his peers into Sproul Hall. As the protesting mass occupied corridors and sat down in offices they succeeded in bringing the "odious . . . machine" to a grinding, screeching halt.[1]

Pat Brown had not paid a great deal of attention to the student strife on campus before then, but with over a thousand students occupying Sproul Hall a posture of aloofness was a luxury the governor could no longer afford. The upheavals on campus had already generated considerable media attention in the past two months and the takeover of Sproul Hall was sure to generate even more. As chairman of the board of regents and governor of the state, and with hundreds of students preventing the university from carrying out its functions as an institution of higher learning, Brown would have no choice now but to act.

Kerr, meanwhile, had spent days thinking about how he would deal with just the kind of massive protest demonstration that was currently underway at Berkeley. A Quaker and a longtime pacifist, Kerr may have struck many in the university bureaucracy as an imperious university president, but he was no fan of cracking down on student protesters and shuddered at the thought of calling in the police to make arrests. As a youth Kerr had spent three summers as a peace caravaner for the American Friends Service Committee during World War I and had worked as a labor negotiator in the Pacific Northwest during World War II. A witness to countless strikes, street demonstrations, and violent labor clashes, Kerr considered police action a blunt and radicalizing instrument that only made tense situations more uneasy. Worried about transforming the Berkeley campus into a battleground, Kerr believed that even in the face of provocation he should do what he could to negotiate a peaceful resolution. Confident in his abilities, yet eager to avoid confrontation, the UC president believed that the students should be allowed to remain in Sproul Hall so long as they did so peacefully. The first night of the demonstrations, Kerr updated three regents on the status of the occupation over dinner. He suggested to them that the administration seal off the building to prevent more students from entering Sproul, that they leave on the water and the lights, and allow anyone who wanted to leave the building to do so with impunity. He argued that as long as the student protesters did not damage property they should not be arrested. The three regents agreed with Kerr that a peaceful resolution to the crisis was the most welcome option. With the regents backing him Kerr called Governor Brown, who at the time was attending a banquet at the Beverly Hilton Hotel in Los Angeles, and urged him to fly to Northern California and come with him to Sproul Hall the next morning and reason with the demonstrators.

The governor agreed and promised that he would come. But Brown had grown impatient with Kerr and with the agitators. He had only a slight grasp of the issues involved in the controversy, and he could not understand why privileged elite attending the most prestigious collegiate institution in the state would launch a massive assault on the university that had given them such wonderful learning and life opportunities. He was not unalterably opposed to the tactics of civil disobedience, but Brown did not understand why the Berkeley undergraduates needed to engage in such militant and radicalizing tactics when negotiations, reason, and measured discussions would help them achieve their ends much better. In the hours after his conversation with Kerr, the governor decided to remove the students by force.[2]

His decision to order in the police came as the result of a series of conversations with students, administrators, aides, and law enforcement agents, though it owed something to Brown's long-standing commitment to upholding the rule of law. The governor did try to reason with the demonstrators, but his attempt at levelheaded negotiations got him nowhere. Jerry Brown, the governor's son and himself a future governor, was friends with someone who was friendly with Mario Savio. Jerry arranged for his father to speak with Savio. Five months earlier, from Mississippi, Savio had actually written a letter to the governor in which he pleaded with Brown to support the seating of the Mississippi Freedom Democratic Party at that summer's Democratic National Convention. Savio explained that he was spending the summer in Mississippi with over "800 compassionate human beings—mostly . . . students of both the Negro and white races"—who were working to "help bring freedom" to the state. Savio praised Brown for all his good work on behalf of civil rights, and especially for his pro–civil rights stands in the fields of housing and employment discrimination. You, Savio wrote the governor, are "a good friend of the work we are trying to advance in Mississippi." Savio then asked for political help, writing, "Governor, I have personally met with the violence of Mississippi whites, and the encouragement of such violence by local police. You have the power to help seat the Freedom Democratic Party. . . . Please help free Mississippi."[3]

In his phone conversation with Brown during the first day of the Sproul Hall demonstration, however, Savio adopted a much different tone toward the liberal governor. Making not even a passing attempt at negotiations, in clipped speech and fighting words Savio told Brown that day that by banning political activity liberals in the university bureaucracy had retarded the cause of civil rights in California, violated the civil liberties of students, and engaged in a form of authoritarianism that reminded Savio of the actions of the Johnson administration in Southeast Asia. Explaining that administrators had left students little choice but to resort to the politics of direct action protest, Savio was full of bluster and showed little of the respect and deference that

Brown believed was his due. Taken aback, Brown concluded that the students at Berkeley were out of control and unserious about negotiations. The conversation ended with the two sides being further apart than when they began. Jerry Brown summed up aptly how it had gone: "I don't think they communicated very well," Jerry told friends.[4]

Brown also had begun to lose faith in his longtime liberal ally Clark Kerr. The governor believed the university president had acquitted himself well during the police car sit-in, but Brown could not understand how the president had failed to quell student ire in the weeks since. Kerr struck Brown as both imperious and dithering. The governor believed that if he did as Kerr asked, and went traipsing into Sproul Hall the next morning to negotiate with the trespassers, he would have to do so with a bulletproof vest on his body. He would wade into a sea of disgruntled students who were trespassing illegally on state property and he would have to beg them to leave the premises. Certain that his chances of success were slim, Brown reconsidered his pledge to Kerr that he would seek a negotiated settlement to the crisis.[5]

As Brown contemplated his options, he also started to receive reports that the protesters had become disorderly and even dangerous. Around 10 P.M., Brown received a call from UC administrators who were in police headquarters in the basement of Sproul Hall monitoring events. Brown was told that the sit-in was not a spontaneous uprising but a well-planned demonstration that had been in the works for weeks: Students had brought into Sproul beds, mattresses, stockpiles of food, even menorahs which they were now lighting on the chancellor's office floor to celebrate the Chanukah holiday. Officials said further that UC and Oakland police could not handle the situation by themselves; they told Brown that they would need the help of the California Highway Patrol.

By this time Governor Brown had become, by virtue of his status as governor and chairman of the board of regents, the sole authority who would decide how to handle the sit-in. Taking command as best he could, the governor asked to speak with a representative from the district attorney's office. Told that Edwin Meese III, the assistant prosecutor for Alameda County, was nearby, the governor replied quickly: "Let me talk to Ed Meese." Brown had known Meese since the early 1960s, when Meese had served as legislative representative in Sacramento for the district attorneys and police chiefs of California. An expert in riot control who had taught classes on the subject to police officers, Meese had been called to campus to help monitor the situation, and in his conversation with the governor he argued that the students were unruly vandals who were wreaking havoc on the building and who "refused to leave" the premises. Meese told the governor that a UC police officer had peered into the office of Robert Gordon Sproul, the president emeritus, and that the officer had reported seeing papers strewn across the floor and other signs of vandalism. Meese warned Brown that if the governor waffled he would only make an already dangerous situation even worse. As Meese put it: "They're busting up the place. We have to go in."[6]

Meese was not the only official on the scene to report that the students had become violent. Alex Sheriffs, the vice-chancellor for student affairs and a conservative foe of the student agitators, called the governor's office to say that a freelance photographer by the name of Peter Whitney had complained that protesters who had seized Sproul Hall had physically assaulted him. Sheriffs, years later, recalled telling State Education Secretary Ronald Moskowitz: "A photographer-reporter called and said that he has been roughed up and he demands protection in some way, and who's going to do something for him? I don't know whether he was roughed up or whether his pride was hurt. There was no police in there with him because you guys and Kerr had an agreement on how to handle all this and that's the way it is. You want to know if anybody was hurt and I'm just telling you this." Moskowitz promised Sheriffs that he would inform the governor about the scuffle and that the administration would "take care of it."[7]

With the reports of chaos filtering in, Brown spotted UCLA Chancellor Franklin Murphy at the banquet and pulled him into the hallway to ask his opinion. Murphy had a dim view of the agitators, whom he considered spoiled brats who deserved to be arrested on the spot and expelled from the university. Murphy's opinion of Clark Kerr was not much higher, and the chancellor put little faith in the ability of Kerr to reach a negotiated settlement with the students. Murphy now urged the governor to crack down on the students, telling Brown simply, "There's only one thing you can do. You've got to get those kids out of there. That's all there is to it. It's a definite defiance of the law and it cannot be permitted."[8]

Brown agreed with Murphy's assessment of the situation, but he was a reluctant tough. He felt angry at the students for flouting the rule of law in California and considered their protest much too radical, misguided, and incendiary. But at heart he also liked the students and shared their passion for civil liberties and civil rights. He, like them, considered the university a sanctuary for dissenting opinions of all kinds, and he shuddered at the thought of bringing the police on the flagship campus of the University of California system and setting in motion one of the largest mass arrests in the history of the state. In the end, however, Brown felt he had no other choice but to remove the students by force; they were breaking the law, fomenting anarchy on campus, and trying to bring a state school to its knees. Brown called back Meese and instructed him to "take them out of there. Give them every chance to leave and tell them if they don't get out, they'll be arrested."[9]

At 3:30 A.M., after many students had bedded down for the night, Chancellor Edward Strong of the Berkeley campus entered Sproul Hall and announced over a bullhorn that anyone who did not leave the building would be removed by force. Student leaders had been expecting such a moment. They told followers to dispose of all sharp objects, to remove their rings and watches, to stay close to one another, to make no statements but give out only their names and addresses to the police, to ask for a lawyer, and above all to go limp when police tried to arrest them. Over the next twelve hours, 367 police made the largest single arrest in California history, dragging down flights of stairs and onto awaiting police vans 773 limp students and other protesters. The arrests took twelve hours to complete and lasted until well into the next school day. As police continued to remove the protesters from Sproul, hundreds of Berkeley students gathered to watch the drama unfold. Meanwhile a local alternative radio station, KPFA, replayed excerpts from a Brown commencement address delivered four years earlier, in which the governor had praised politically minded students who were willing to put their bodies on the line for civil rights and other such liberal causes.[10]

FOUR YEARS EARLIER, in the heady days of 1960, long before anyone had ever heard of Mario Savio or Jack Weinberg or Ed Meese, President Clark Kerr of the University of California had told Pat Brown that the public university system in the state had arrived at a critical juncture in its history. In the 1960s, Kerr predicted, "a tidal wave of students" would pour onto the college campuses in the state. These students would overwhelm current facilities, place great strains on faculty and administrators, and jeopardize the health of higher education in the state. Kerr noted that if the state failed to find a solution to the demographic bulge, the entire society would suffer the consequences. "The universities would not be able to handle the increased enrollments," Kerr explained, "construction would be delayed, the new campuses would take much longer to build, there would be a shortage of doctors, and the state's industrial growth would be retarded." But Kerr was optimistic about the future of the state and university system. He said that working together, he, Brown, and other such liberals could cope with the human influx and ward off the impending disaster. Kerr's plan was simple—infuse the schools with money. Increased funding, Kerr argued, would allow the state to construct more campuses, erect new buildings on existing campus sites, expand the capacity of classrooms, and hire more professors who could in turn teach more courses.[11]

Pat Brown did not need to be persuaded about either the problems related to the population boom or about the efficacy of state power to solve them. He considered education an integral part of California's future, and he was determined to build the biggest and best system of public education in the country. Beginning in 1959, Brown had embarked on the most far-reaching expansion of the university system in the history of the state. In 1960 he won passage of the Master Plan for Higher Education, which led to the construction of three new universities and established a new administrative arrangement for both the University of California and the California State systems. Brown expanded UC budgets so much that in some legislative sessions he won for the university more money than even Kerr had requested. Brown constructed classrooms, expanded the campuses, guaranteed free college education for every California resident with a high school diploma, and helped transform the public system of higher education into one of the best in the world.[12]

The governor had not attended college and always felt a twinge of jealousy toward those who had. But Brown had no doubts that as governor his mission was clear. He would provide the young people of his state with the opportunities that by dint of circumstances had been denied to him as a youth. Brown considered higher education one of the great engines of a progressive society, a force for economic growth and a waystation that could be used to equip young minds with the tools, knowledge, and critical thinking needed for future careers in business, public service, the arts, and the law. With an educated workforce the state would thrive economically, but it would also be able to meet the challenge of achieving a just and equal social order.

Brown considered Berkeley, the crown jewel in the University of California system, the embodiment of everything good and righteous in the liberal experiment. Brown touted the UC system whenever he had the opportunity. The iconoclastic Bay Area campus was, by 1960, teeming with the top undergraduate, graduate, and professorial minds in the state and in many cases, the world. Berkeley was home to a slew of Nobel laureates and boasted scores of other professors who were distinguished in their fields. Affirmation of the long-held liberal tenet that state power could be harnessed in the service of the social good, Berkeley also boasted tuition that was, remarkably, free.

For all the wonderful education that occurred on campus, the governor believed that Berkeley and institutions like it also had an obligation to teach their charges social responsibility and inculcate them with a commitment to public service. The university had a major role to play in the larger world of politics and society, he believed; in speeches and other public utterances Brown rejected the argument put forward by conservatives in California in the 1950s who spoke incessantly about the danger of permitting communist and other left-wing speakers on campus.[13]

In 1960, a handful of Berkeley radicals traveled to San Francisco to protest a meeting of the House Committee on Un-American Activities (HUAC); California conservatives responded to the demonstration by producing a film, *Operation Abolition*, portraying the protesters as a dangerous cabal out to topple the government. When in May 1959, a Subject A English exam asked incoming Berkeley freshmen to explain "the dangers to a democracy of a national police organization, like the FBI, which operates secretly and is unresponsive to public criticism," conservatives called the test subversive and FBI Director J. Edgar Hoover wrote a letter to the board of regents expressing "shock" that the university would permit such a perfidious question to be put before the young. The American Legion denounced "communist infiltration" on UC campuses, writing, for example, in one 1960 newsletter that there were "sub rosa espionage operations by Soviet intelligence agents at Berkeley." And on occasion, angry Californians complained to Brown about communists who had been allowed to speak on campus. "Stop the march of communism now in our Golden State," one woman urged Brown. "Stop communists from speaking on our publicly supported campuses."[14] Brown never paid any attention to these critics. He believed that activism among students was a good and even necessary thing.

In 1964, as students began taking part in civil rights demonstrations, right-wing politicians urged the governor to crack down on campus radicals. Oakland Assemblyman Don Mulford wrote Brown that he and other citizens of the state were tired of UC students who engaged in civil disobedience while attending college at taxpayer expense. They were not students but criminals, Mulford told the governor in April 1964, fomenting "anarchy by willfully, defiantly and cynically violating and conspiring to violate, the civil and penal laws enacted to protect all of the people of the State irrespective of race."[15]

* * *

UNTIL THE STUDENTS' Free Speech Movement, these arguments had gotten nowhere. In response, Brown had always posited an alternative vision of the role and purpose of the system of higher education. As attorney general and later as governor, Brown argued that in California, college students had the right to be exposed to a whole range of political thought and social causes. He argued that no matter how noxious or left-wing or subversive such ideas were, they would not penetrate the minds of the young wits and sharp students on campus. Radicals would win few converts to their cause, Brown theorized, because student bodies were too intelligent, too moderate, too forward-looking to buy the extremist wares.

Brown also said on many occasions that the university was a place where open inquiry and free speech could be pushed to the limits. Kerr liked to say that it was the job of administrations and college officials to make the universities places where students learn how to discern among ideas and discriminate in their political choices. The ideas floated on campus did not need to be made "safe" for students; the students would be able to sift through them on their own. Brown had spoken approvingly of students learning about the big issues of the day—the cold war, communism, poverty, civil rights, democratic governance—and thus awoken, becoming engaged by and excited about them.[16]

In 1961, Brown touted the merits of civil rights as a pressing moral matter worthy of student attention. In perhaps his best-known speech on the subject, the famed commencement address at Santa Clara University, Brown announced himself a leading proponent of John Kennedy's maxim that the young should ask of themselves not what the country could do for them but what they could do for the country. The time had come, Brown said on that spring day, "to put an end to the misguided *weltschmerz* for cultural unity—high time to have other goals than the material ones shown on billboards, television, and other forms of the great American daydream. . . . This creeping uniformity is deadly to the power of decision and self-rule. Against it, our colleges must throw their entire weight—and students must join the battle. Far from discouraging your students' social and public interests," he urged campus administrators, "I propose that you positively exploit them."[17]

> Here is an honorable source of college spirit; here is a worthy unifying and organizing principle for your whole campus

> life. I say: Thank God for the spectacle of students picketing—even when they are picketing me at Sacramento and I think they are wrong—for students protesting and freedom-riding, for students listening to society's dissidents, for students going out into the fields with our migratory workers, and for marching off to jail with our segregated Negroes. At last we're getting somewhere. The colleges have become boot camps for citizenship—and citizen-leaders are marching out of them. For a while, it will be hard on us administrators. Some students are going to be wrong and some people will deny them the right to make mistakes. Administrators will have to wade through the angry letters and colleges will lose some donations. We Governors will have to face indignant caravans and elected officials bent on dictating to state college faculties.
>
> But let us stand up for our students and be proud of them. If America is still on the way up, it will welcome this new impatient, critical crop of young gadflies. It will be fearful only of the complacent and passive.[18]

The speech proved to be wildly successful. It generated an outpouring of congratulatory letters and phone calls to the governor's office in Sacramento, with professors and students alike hailing a powerful rallying cry that summed up the best in the liberal tradition. One Santa Clara professor gushed that the talk "stirred up plenty of the right kind of thinking on this campus." Carey McWilliams, the famed California writer, told Brown that even at Oberlin College in Ohio, where McWilliams was teaching, students were abuzz about the ideas Brown had discussed in his speech.[19]

Brown realized, as did many Democrats in the early 1960s, that young people tended to be more liberal in their politics than their elders. And the governor believed that a politically active and engaged student body would redound to the benefit of his party and bolster many of the liberal causes for which he worked—students would supply the Democratic party with shock troops and campaign workers. They represented a key component in the political coalition that he had assembled in California. While the governor did not explicitly tell the students which causes they should support; while he did not lay out a point-by-point political agenda for them, he assumed that the students would be liberal stalwarts and fighting for issues about which he cared deeply. Brown's support for the students was partly political in basis; but mostly, it reflected a deeply felt commitment to liberal causes. As Ronald Moskowitz explained, Brown "was really proud that [the students] were active in the democracy they lived in, and all of us on the staff felt that way."[20]

Certainly Brown did not anticipate a wholesale revolt against the liberal and seemingly enlightened administrators on campus. His attention elsewhere for the most part, the governor had little inkling that in 1964 a protest movement at Berkeley would turn militant and highly inflammatory, rocking the university administration like nothing before it, sending his own administration into crisis, and provoking a stand-off between himself and the students that would touch off a chain of events that would contribute mightily to his electoral defeat by Ronald Reagan in 1966.

In the end there is probably precious little that Pat Brown could have done to blunt the impact of the Berkeley issue on the coming campaign. Brown was the governor at the time of the protests, and it was on his watch that things at Berkeley seemed to fall apart. Given all his pro-student speeches, however, he was in a worse position than he might have been. And in the days following his decision to arrest the students, the governor mainly succeeded in providing fodder to his critics and turning Berkeley into a political issue more explosive than it already was.

In the aftermath of the Sproul sit-in, Brown veered between feelings of confusion and outrage. He was, above all, miffed by the militance of the protesters and by the talk of Berkeley being an odious machine that stifled individuality and tried to mold students into mindless corporate worker bees. Brown and Kerr and other leading liberals in the state had devoted a great deal of time, energy, and public resources to strengthening the university system in the state, and they had worked especially hard to transform Berkeley in particular into a major center for higher education. The governor had trouble understanding how students, on whose behalf he had done so much, could be so unruly and so bent on destruction and so angry toward the liberals in the state. Two weeks after the arrests, Brown wrote a friend that the students "told a great university that they would bring its machinery to a halt, just at a very critical time in the life of a university." The young had undertaken this action without first consulting or expressing their grievances to Brown. He described to his friend his confusion about Berkeley: "If you had a revolution in your union tomorrow, with a sit-down strike in your office of 600 members, you would be as surprised as I was at the incident taking place at the university. Even our own revolutionary war was accompanied by some negotiations and only as a last resort did it result in the Boston Tea Party."[21]

But his confusion was accompanied by a deep outrage. Brown explained in the same letter that the student militants had hurt everyone in their path:

> I assure you that the young people did nothing but embarrass the university and my administration. If we had had meetings I am sure we could have made substantial progress. Clark Kerr is considered one of the best presidents of a university and he has fought against terrific odds for free speech on the campus. Now they are saying he made a mistake and to a majority of the people it will look like he has. As a matter of fact, his whole usefulness to the university has been impaired. The students are probably right on the free speech issue, but when they declared a strike they hurt an awful lot of good people.[22]

Brown also was offended by students who at the drop of a hat seemed willing to flout the rule of law. The former district attorney and state attorney general had strong feelings about the law and order, and those feelings had not changed substantially over the course of his career. The massive protests on campus, and the takeover of Sproul Hall especially, had rekindled a smoldering ember in Brown's heart.

In the first days after ordering the arrests, he began lashing the student protesters in public. He labeled them rebels and brigands, and argued that in their rush to demonstration they had abandoned the virtues of a society based on order and instead embraced a platform of political anarchy. He called their takeover of Sproul Hall an incendiary flouting of the law, and he promised constituents in the state that such acts of insipid radicalism would not go unpunished. On December 4, one day after ordering the arrests, Brown held a news conference in which he pilloried protesters for their hasty and radical actions. He warned that future uprisings on campus would "not be tolerated," and he declared that his paramount concern in dealing with the demonstrators was that "law and order on our campuses" would prevail. In private, the governor was equally adamant about maintaining the rule of law in the state. He reassured at least one UC regent that whatever the future held, he would make sure that students obeyed all of California's laws, no matter what cause they were protesting. There is "no question to what degree [the law will] be enforced," Brown wrote Regent Charles Canady; "No one has any alternative but to obey the law. This must be done."[23]

The law-and-order position was a popular one among the general public, as Brown knew. In the days following the arrests, the governor made a point of reading many of the letters, most written by constituents, that began pouring into his office in the wake of the confrontation in Sproul Hall. Brown told colleagues in Sacramento that he was eager to reexamine his own position on the Berkeley matter, and in his perusal of some five thousand letters that rolled in he paid special attention to the most critical missives in the batch. But the letters only deepened his conviction that the Free Speech protesters had employed militant, unacceptable tactics that were destructive to the university, the university administration, and to the state of California. And Brown concluded that his decision to arrest the trespassers was the correct one. In a letter to one constituent, he described the "young people today" as "complete idealists" who had accepted the terrible burden of "changing things overnight"; and he argued that the students were fomenting anarchy on campus and that they had to be stopped from inflicting further damage on the university: "At a very critical time to revolt against law and order and to demand, in such a blatant way, an unconditional surrender within twenty-four hours, is something I have never experienced in any strike or any other situation in my life."[24]

With a single decision, and by toeing a tough line, Brown believed he had reestablished himself as a law and order tough. District attorneys, police chiefs, newspapers, and average citizens seemed to be lining up behind him. People from around the state were condemning the student agitators, applauding Brown for his swift action. Brown had polls showing that the public was furious with the student demonstrators, but he did not need polling data to tell him what he had already gathered from the letters and confidential administration reports that were crossing his desk that December. Brown was confident that he had acted in a manner that suited the public mood; only hours after the arrests Judge Leonard Dieden, a deputy district attorney, informed Brown that "the universal reaction to the Governor's action was excellent. All reports indicate that the Governor did the right thing." A few days later, on December 8, aide John McInerny told the governor that at a meeting of peace officers and district attorneys in Los Angeles, police and prosecutors alike endorsed with great enthusiasm Brown's decision to arrest the lawbreaking students. McInerny explained to Brown in a memo that the crackdown at Berkeley did much to "restore public confidence in law and order in the state. The whole concept of 'the Rule of Law' in California has received a real shot in the arm by what you did, in their opinion." McInerny added that the chiefs of police had called Brown's decision the most important law and order decision of his six years in office.[25]

In mid-December, the governor's aides had read and analyzed the 4,510 telegrams, letters, and cards regarding the Berkeley matter that had been sent to Brown in recent weeks; and as aides reported to the governor, almost all of the correspondents were in favor of the governor's crackdown. A week later, on December 23, aides reported that the number of letters regarding the protests at Berkeley had skyrocketed, from less than five thousand to nearly eight thousand in number; and approximately three quarters of these letters, according to one administration tally, praised Brown and his decision to crack down on the students, and urged on the governor a posture of "continued firmness."[26]

But while the law enforcement community had rallied around Brown, a vocal group of students, professors, and civil rights activists in the state stewed. They felt that their ally had betrayed them. To their way of thinking, in the face of great political pressure, Brown, in a move that recalled for some the governor's waffling on the Caryl Chessman case, had capitulated to the forces of conservatism.

In the days following Brown's fateful decision, the political left in California expressed their outrage to the governor in letters, phone calls, and in raucous political rallies on the Berkeley campus. One day after the arrests, a massive student strike rocked Berkeley. Thousands of students descended on Sproul Plaza to hear speakers rail against the police and administrators and liberals whom they held responsible. Rally organizers blasted Brown as simply one of many liberal turncoats who had turned his back on his allies and his friends. Paul Jacobs, a visiting professor, told the throng that "this [was] the saddest day on the campus. Kerr and Brown are my friends. . . . [But] we have profound disagreement about what happened in Sproul Hall." As Jacobs spoke several policemen appeared in the window of Sproul, prompting hisses and catcalls from rally-goers below. Jacobs implored the crowd to stay calm, and in doing so he revealed a deep crack in the liberal political coalition in the state: "Do not be provoked by the police!" Jacobs urged listeners. "The police were introduced to the campus last night in a way not becoming to the university or to the Governor of this state."[27]

In the days after the arrests, several hundred UC Berkeley professors wired Brown a formal communique in which they criticized him for ordering the police onto campus. "[We] strongly condemn the presence of the State Highway Patrol on the Berkeley campus," read the faculty broadside. "Punitive action taken against hundreds of students cannot help to solve our current problems, and will aggravate the already serious situation." Forty students and professors from UC picketed Brown in Sacramento and called on the governor to grant amnesty to the arrested students. A Young Democrats student club at Berkeley passed a resolution that condemned Brown for his handling of the protests and cautioned Democrats against supporting Brown for a third term. Civil rights leaders also chastised the governor, reminding him that those arrested in Sproul were loyal Democratic voters and campaign workers, and that the student and civil rights left could not be ignored. On December 10, John Leggett, a Berkeley sociologist, warned Brown that if he did not take swift action to help the students arrested in the Sproul sit-in, James Farmer, the national director of CORE, would be forced to denounce Brown in public. "Issue a more favorable press release regarding the students," Leggett instructed the governor. He did not "want to have to see those students go through court trials without some kind of support from the Governor." Leggett told Brown that if he refused to meet with Farmer, the civil rights leader would have no choice but to attack the governor at an upcoming rally. Leggett also promised that Farmer would denounce the governor "at a press conference" after the rally.[28]

As a political matter, the prospect of a wholesale defection from within his Democratic camp concerned Brown. Men like James Farmer and Mario Savio and Paul Jacobs represented crucial parts of the Democratic political coalition in California, and for a governor accustomed to having in his camp blacks, students, and intellectuals, the outpouring of liberal anger left him dazed and concerned. But to his credit, Brown was most concerned not about the political impact of his actions but about their moral implications. The governor did not have many second thoughts about ordering the arrests; nor did he decide, at any point in the aftermath of the December 2 rally, that the students were justified in taking over a campus building and trespassing on public property.

Eager to prevent further upheavals on the Berkeley campus, however, and both confident that he had satisfied the law enforcement community and those sympathetic to the free speech issues, Brown started to extend to protesters a series of olive branches. He would not do as Farmer asked and pardon the students arrested during the protest, explaining to at least one acquaintance that a pardon was "something I would not consider under any circumstances." Still, in appearances before the media, in his letters to angry constituents and students, and in a variety of other public settings and statements, Brown tried to distance himself from his earlier attacks on students and fiery denunciations of anarchists on campus. He stopped mentioning the supposedly lawless hoodlums who had transformed the campus into a center of social chaos, and instead began describing the FSM activists as "misguided young men" who in the pursuit of a worthy cause had gotten carried away. Brown began telling student leaders that they had "an open door" to the governor's office. He encouraged them to work with Kerr and other administrators on achieving a peace accord for the campus that would be both just and lasting. And repeatedly, Brown made clear that he agreed with the FSM goal of achieving a campus community that permitted free speech and peaceful political activity. The governor even promised students that he would urge Berkeley officials to revise university regulations and reinstate the tradition of political activity on campus, telling protesters and other liberals that the free speech controversy was "the most unnecessary quarrel I've ever seen in my life." Brown spoke with Savio by phone, admitted to reporters that he had had a conversation with the militant student leader, and also acknowledged that he had personally promised Savio that if negotiations with the Regents collapsed, he would agree to meet with the Berkeley junior. When reporters asked Brown which side in the Berkeley dispute was in the right, students or administrators, the governor brushed aside the question as unimportant to the crucial period ahead and stated plainly that, "as to who's right in the last analysis I can't say. . . . Emotions rise in situations like this and each side thinks they are absolutely right. But one side can't unilaterally set themselves up as sole custodians of what's right and wrong."[29]

Brown worked behind closed doors as much as he could. The governor and his aides agreed that the most important thing for the governor to do was, in the words of Jack Burby, Brown's press secretary, to "blur the question of who won or lost long enough" to allow "the authorities and the students" to find a solution to the free speech controversy. Regents and administrators needed to show students that they were sincere in their desire to open the campus to political activity; students needed to demonstrate that they could keep their radical leanings in check and meet administrators halfway. Burby wrote the governor that "the next step is for the Regents committee to buckle down to work at once to demonstrate to the youngsters that they mean what they said about honoring the First and Fourteenth Amendments and I am given to understand that they intend to do just that. I think the Regents' action was so acceptable, as a matter of fact, that any attempts to stir up new demonstrations on the basis of it will fall flat."[30]

Ronald Moskowitz; Winslow Christian, the executive secretary; and Burby revealed the administration thinking about Berkeley in a joint memo that they wrote to the governor. The document, dated December 16, captured the emerging consensus within the administration that negotiation and compromise was the only solution to the campus wars. Brown, aides wrote the governor, needed to restore to undergraduates the right to engage in political activity on campus and reach out as well to a university administration reeling from the recent tumult on campus. Aides believed that Brown was in a strong position to accomplish both tasks: he would offer students a credible voice on the free speech matter because he had "built a marvelous reputation" as "a noted civil libertarian" (his Santa Clara speech had "put [him] on the road" in this regard, aides explained, and in the years since Brown had "lived up to" his "record" as a strong advocate for civil liberties). And Brown also enjoyed long-standing ties to law enforcement, strong backing from the California public, and many allies in the university administration.[31]

Aides believed, and the governor seems to have concluded as well, that two issues were involved in the free speech controversy, "maintaining the rule of law while allowing as much freedom of political advocacy and activity as possible for students." Everyone also concurred that Brown, in his handling of the protest movement, had acted in accord with both principles and now had within his grasp a chance to ward off all future such demonstrations. The trio of advisors argued that Brown, in the weeks ahead, should allow for a "cooling off period" in which passions on all sides of the Berkeley divide could be tempered, angry feelings blunted. Then, aides believed, the two sides would be able to return to the negotiating table in a frame of mind that would allow them to engage in serious negotiations. And it was at this point that the governor would put the Berkeley controversy to rest once and for all: Stress that the main cause of "all of this commotion seems to be a breakdown in communications between the students and the faculty and on up the line to the administration and Regents"; urge the Regents to adopt new rules allowing for "complete freedom of political activity and advocacy on campus"; and let it be known to the students that he and the Regents were committed to reaching an accord and putting an end to the strife.[32]

Brown and aides were confident that they could achieve just such a peace deal. In one memo Moskowitz told colleagues that the uprising at Berkeley was not such a disaster and could be handled without great fanfare. "The controversy and debate that has raged at times on the campus is what has made it a great university," Moskowitz wrote optimistically. And in mid-December Brown indeed began reaching out to all factions involved in the campus crisis, even meeting personally for ninety minutes on December 17 with Kerr, leaders of the Academic Senate, and seven regents. Afterward he told a waiting press corps that he was "optimistic" about the chances for compromise at UC and he described the meeting of university higher-ups as a "frank and friendly" exchange that had brought the warring sides closer to a settlement. Dismissing the free speech imbroglio as nothing so much as "a misunderstanding" between students and administrators that now "needed clarification more than anything else," Brown now had good things to say about virtually everyone involved in the controversy. He offered encouraging words to the protesters and defended as able men the university administrators. Clark Kerr, Brown reminded reporters, had helped make Berkeley "a preeminent" institution "in the world"; and as for Edward Strong, the chancellor of Berkeley and an enemy of Kerr's, well, Strong was "a good man, too. I can't say whether he's made mistakes. I'm certainly not going to add to the cross that he's carrying. I have confidence in him, too."[33]

In late January Brown agreed to meet with student-leaders at UC Riverside. The Riverside meeting, Moskowitz told Brown that month, represented a "marvelous opportunity for [you] to explain the two issues involved in the Berkeley situation to the students . . . to explain to [students] how it is possible for a man to believe in the goals of an organization without condoning or approving the methods they use to accomplish those goals." In his memo Moskowitz assured Brown that there would not be any "FSM spearheaders" in the student group and he proposed a number of tactics for blunting student ire. If students began complaining to Brown that the university administration had cut off all channels of communication and that civil disobedience was their only option, Moskowitz urged the governor to counter with the following: "Stress the positive aspects of all this trouble. If the demonstrations have done nothing else, they have made the Regents aware of the need for better communications between the students and faculty; between the faculty and administration; and between all of those and the Regents."[34]

By February 1965 Brown seemed largely content with the way he had handled the Berkeley demonstrations. He and his aides concluded that they had fashioned a coherent and effective response to the student uprising, striking a careful balance between law and order and civil liberties, police officers and the newly militant student left. With the Berkeley campus relatively quiet, Brown harbored high hopes that the period of turmoil was over and that life at school would soon return to normal. The governor could not have been more mistaken.

On March 3, less than two months after his meeting with UC undergraduates at Riverside, a New Yorker named John Thomson sat down in front of the Student Union on the Berkeley campus and held up a piece of paper that had the word *Fuck* written on it. Police arrested Thomson. In protest, one hundred and fifty student-activists held a noontime rally on the steps of the student store. Though not a large show of student strength, it was as incendiary as anything that had happened at Berkeley in the fall. At the rally protesters carried signs that read "Fuck Communism," chanted F-U-C-K repeatedly, read passages from lurid novels, recited angry poems about the alienation of the younger generation, and jump-started the short-lived Filthy Speech Movement on the Berkeley campus. The public read sensational news accounts of the licentious demonstrations and quickly reached the conclusion that once again Berkeley had spun out of control. The lewd rallies infuriated Brown as well. Recoiling in disgust, the governor urged administrators to quash the protests and restore a modicum of dignity to the campus.[35]

Clark Kerr was already coming under fire for failing to put a stop to the seemingly anarchic state of campus life and Brown soon ran into political trouble as well. He was in the difficult position of having to defend Kerr, and his inconsistent public statements now gave off the impression of a governor who had not acted tough enough. If not for the Filthy Speech Movement—all 150 members of it—Brown might not have been as badly hurt by Berkeley. It would not be the last time that a small group at the fringe of the Left caused serious damage to liberalism. When the opposite fringe, in the form of the John Birch Society, denounced Dwight Eisenhower as a communist, conservatism (at least, Barry Goldwater's presidential campaign) similarly suffered. When 150 students chanted "Fuck," the student movement took a big hit, as did its ally and friend Pat Brown.

Still, in the spring of 1965, it remained unclear just how big a role Berkeley would play in the coming gubernatorial campaign. Brown's record on education seemed strong enough to withstand whatever barbs might be aimed in his direction. He also believed that the California public would not want Berkeley bandied about in the sturm-und-drang of political debate, and that any attempt by conservatives to exploit the Berkeley issue might backfire. The Right had railed repeatedly against communist speakers on campus and encouraged the imposition of loyalty oaths on faculty members, but since the 1950s conservatives had done precious little to advance the cause of higher education in the state. Even if Brown was forced to pay a political price for Berkeley, what that price would be remained unclear. His right-wing critics did not immediately realize how to capitalize on the campus disorders and had little idea of how to link Brown and other liberals to the upheavals at Berkeley. Only later would Reagan score points with his attacks on moral decline and on "so-called free-speech advocates . . . [whose] ringleaders should have been taken by the scruff of the neck and thrown out of the university once and for all."[36]

SIX

# "A BUNCH OF KOOKS"

In March 1965, Reagan traveled to the California Republican Assembly (CRA) state convention at the El Cortez Hotel in San Diego to deliver a speech about the evils of big government. For three decades the CRA had been a staunchly moderate organization led by Earl Warren progressives, but now conservatives dominated the leadership posts. Convention atmospherics left little doubt where the CRA stood on the political spectrum. Racks of incendiary literature lined the hotel's lobby, with pamphlets attacking the usual icons and Governor Pat Brown; CRA delegates passed resolutions supporting the repeal of the federal income tax and an investigation of the United Nations; and Reagan was one of a number of speakers who took to the podium that weekend to rail against the liberal order. Government, Reagan complained to his admiring audience, was like a newborn baby—it had "an alimentary canal at one end and no sense of responsibility at the other."[1]

When his speech ended, a reporter from the *Los Angeles Times* caught up with the candidate to ask, What did he think of the John Birch Society? It was still eighteen months before the general election, and Reagan had not thought a great deal about how he would handle the issue of right-wing extremism. He gave a halting and muddled response, pointing out that a group of Sacramento Democrats had "found [the Society] not subversive" and that that was good enough for him. "I don't think those fellows in Sacramento would issue a false report."[2]

Reagan's critics were already beginning to describe him as a right-wing radical, a Birch ally well outside the political mainstream, and it was becoming increasingly apparent that whatever the candidate did in the months ahead, he would have to find a way to surmount the Birch issue. Much of his campaign—and conservative prospects generally—hinged on forging an effective answer to the Birch conundrum.

* * *

THE JOHN BIRCH SOCIETY—and the larger issue of right-wing radicalism—had long been the Achilles' heel of the California conservative movement. One of the largest and best-known political action organizations in the country, the society boasted thousands of activists committed to combating communism. Members spouted conspiracy theories about left-wing plots to overthrow the government, clamored for the impeachment of Supreme Court Chief Justice Earl Warren, published pamphlets detailing the nefarious ties between civil rights activists and communists, and painted former president Dwight Eisenhower as "a dedicated, conscious agent of the communist conspiracy."

Robert Welch, the society's leader, was especially controversial. Welch shared neither Douglas MacArthur's penchant for martial bluster nor Joseph McCarthy's reputation for violent outbursts; yet he was an anticommunist zealot all the same. A one-time candy manufacturer from Cambridge, Massachusetts, Welch seemed more a corporate accountant than a fierce anticommunist. Six feet tall and slight of frame, Welch was nevertheless a preacher of the anticommunist gospel. He had formed the Birch Society in 1958 and named it after an American captain who had been slaughtered by Chinese communists in the last days of World War II—"the first casualty" of a new war, explained Welch. Convinced that communist spies had penetrated the highest reaches of American government, Welch saw communist conspiracies everywhere, in the press corps, in private corporations, even in his audiences. Once, while delivering a speech, Welch noticed someone pacing the aisles asking if there was a doctor in the house. Welch stopped his speech and asked the man why he was "walking around like that." Without waiting for a reply, Welch then denounced the man's ruse as a "dirty Communist trick."[3]

The society bloomed quickly. Although its membership rolls were kept secret, historians have estimated that by 1962 Birchers boasted sixty thousand members and $1.5 million in annual income. By 1965 California alone—the Birchers' "banner state"—contained over ten thousand activists organized into a thousand chapters. Forty-one full-time workers staffed its Belmont, Massachusetts, headquarters, and 35 traveling coordinators roamed the country seeking new recruits. Welch repeatedly referred to his organization as nonpolitical, but it was in the larger world of American politics where the society made its presence felt most. Providing conservative candidates with a trained cadre of political organizers, envelope stuffers, and precinct walkers, in the early 1960s Birchers helped elect like-minded candidates to a spate of offices and capture leadership posts in venerable GOP organizations like the Young Republicans and CRA.[4]

The society also exerted significant influence at the local level, running candidates for school boards, city councils, and sundry other district offices, and infiltrating PTAs and other community groups in the hopes of spreading its anticommunist message to the masses. Grassroots activists did not always subscribe to their leader's more radical conspiracy theories, but they did see communism as a sinister force that pervaded American life. In the early 1960s, Birchers waged war on communists, liberals, and other left-wing sympathizers. They sent community leaders letters depicting Supreme Court Justice Earl Warren as a communist dupe supportive of civil rights and other subversive movements; attacked the federal income tax as a socialist tool, and argued that the fluoridation of public drinking water was part of a communist plot to poison American citizens. Birchers peddled their own textbooks to schoolchildren; pasted anticommunist bumper stickers on their cars; and sold sundry right-wing tracts, pamphlets, and movies at bookstores across Southern California. Soon, the society had become more visible than the anti–New Deal Liberty Lobby as a symbol of the excesses of right-wing Republicanism.

An April 1961 Gallup Poll revealed a public deeply suspicious of the society. Thirty-nine million Americans, according to the survey, had either read something about or heard of the Birchers, with 44 percent saying they had an unfavorable impression of the group and 9 percent, a favorable one. Even within the Republican party, the society became a flash point for controversy, a divisive wedge between moderates and conservatives vying for their party's nomination. GOP candidates of all stripes had difficulty escaping the issue. The Right defended Birchers as upstanding patriots, the centrists denounced the activists as disturbed and prone to paranoia. In 1958 William Knowland's support for Proposition 16, a deeply unpopular right-to-work measure, and reputation as an outspoken anticommunist, angered Republican moderates—and Pat Brown beat him easily. In 1962 Richard Nixon's attacks on Welch earned him the enmity of right-wing activists, seriously damaging his prospects in that year's general election—and again Brown won.[5]

In early 1965 Reagan faced a Knowland-like dilemma. The society was still an explosive issue in California, and after several years of experience with the Birch issue, liberal Democrats had become adroit at exploiting it. Reagan would be as vulnerable as Knowland to attacks on his pro-Birch position, and he didn't have anything close to Knowland's experience to make up for it.

Reagan's statewide speaking tour that spring had lent his candidacy a certain cachet and legitimacy. On television he did not appear strident. But the skills for which he would later become so well known were not yet tested in early 1965. Reagan had given only one major speech, and while it had been wildly successful, there was no guarantee that he would fare as well under the klieg lights and scrutiny of an eighteen-month campaign.

More troubling, right-wing activists engaged in fiery displays of support for their hero. At a Young Americans for Freedom (YAF) convention in Washington, D.C., in the summer of 1965, activists brandished incendiary bumper stickers and buttons that urged the bombing of Hanoi and the impeachment of Earl Warren, and combined the usual "Drop It (the big bomb)" with simply: "I am a Right-Wing Extremist." *National Review*'s William Rusher attacked the student left and bearded beatniks ("those roving slums"). Many activists sported buttons touting Reagan's candidacy. They cheered loudly for Reagan, and talked up his campaign to reporters, reminding some in the press of the Goldwater crusade. One CRA leader wrote Reagan that he would "support [him] all the way" and that "some former special agents . . . in the Bureau tell me there is a great grass root type support for you throughout the State." On July 1, Reagan received a letter from a right-wing organization called Citizens for Constitutional Government (CCG). The group had sent a questionnaire to the nearly 4,000 people on its mailing list, asking a variety of pointed questions probing the depth of conservative sentiment in California: "Do you feel that the police department should be allowed to stop you from protecting your home?" "Do you believe the split between Russia and Red China is genuine?" The organization then informed Reagan that of the 383 respondents, 275 had identified him as their top choice for governor.[6]

Reporters began depicting the actor as a darling of the radical right. In articles and biographical sketches, reporters routinely identified Reagan as a fringe figure with close ties to the activists. In July, a *New York Times Magazine* article reported that Reagan had the staunch support of conservative activists, and then described "the movement" as "almost a religion governing the lives of its adherents. It includes gun-toting psychopaths who think the John Birch Society is a club for sissies, Birchites and other white-collar radicals, tax-hating non-joiners, and regular Republicans who are simply more conservative than [Senator] William Scranton." Other newspapers and magazines devoted considerable attention to the right-wing extremists rallying around Reagan that spring. The *Los Angeles Times*, for instance, reported that the president of the Long Beach Young Republicans had been a member of the California Rangers, a right-wing militia, and had been convicted of trying to sell machine guns; the Rangers' secretary attended Nazi Party gatherings, wore storm troopers' uniforms, and marched in Nazi parades. The *New York Times* captured Reagan's dilemma when it editorialized that in 1966 the Republican party would either "represent a fairly broad spectrum of opinion or . . . be an organization committed to the reactionary radicalism of its extreme right-wing. The stakes are high." In typical *Times* fashion, the editorial took a centrist line: "If the liberals, moderates, and traditional conservatives unite and resume control, they could rebuild the Republican party in California and elsewhere as a viable alternative to the Democrats. If the far right . . . is able to consolidate and extend its power, it could irreparably ruin the national prospects of the G.O.P. The 1964 election returns for practically every office from assemblyman to President proved that the overwhelming majority of voters across the nation will not accept a party that is seriously tainted by reactionary extremism."[7]

Reagan seemed oblivious to the extremist question. In his initial forays that spring, he did little to dispel doubts. Reagan paid lip service to the importance of party unity, but mostly he spoke in strident tones about the enemies within and urged conservative activists to steel themselves for a fight with party moderates. His speeches amounted to lengthy attacks on encroaching government power, and bore scant resemblance to the polished, knowledgeable disquisitions on state issues considered a prerequisite for any serious gubernatorial candidate. In late April, Reagan appeared before 1,200 cheering Young Republicans in Santa Ana and urged his followers to "rise from defeat" and fight with everything they had to "defend the Republic." He complained bitterly of "an intellectual elite" and the entire "misguided Democratic leadership." His performances were compelling, right-wing tours de force, and aimed mainly at firing up the faithful.[8]

Reagan was no great admirer of Robert Welch. He disagreed with Welch's radical conspiracy theories, voicing outrage at the accusations that Eisenhower was a communist agent. But Reagan seemed reluctant to distance himself from the Birch Society. Reagan had long believed communist conspiracies existed, and often complained about "Communist plot[s]" in "the motion picture industry" and socialists who ruined the careers of promising Hollywood actors, writers, and directors.[9]

Such beliefs dovetailed nicely with the society's, and for the most part Reagan applauded the men and women who peopled its ranks. They were, he implied on more than one occasion, patriotic Americans who deserved recognition for their steadfast devotion to the Republic. As a candidate, he had only a dim grasp of the pitfalls of the Birch issue. Reagan understood that moderates did not like the

Birchers, and that he had to somehow dispel the image of him as a keeper of the radical flame. Yet he was loath to denounce the society; such a move would go against his deeply felt anticommunist convictions and make him seem like the politically expedient moderates he had so long opposed. Reagan, as one United Press article noted, seemed keen on winning Birch backing, arguing that while he did "not agree with everything about the Society," he did believe that the group "has never been found to be subversive or desirous of infringing on individual rights." Reagan told other reporters that he had "no basis for the blanket indicting of people, or of applying loyalty oaths," and that he would not renounce an entire organization just because it contained a few unsavory characters. The Ku Klux Klan was much worse than the Birch Society, he argued further, because "the Klan would deny some people their constitutional rights and it is in the area of organizations officially declared subversive."[10]

The most vocal attacks on Reagan came from GOP moderates. Alphonzo Bell, a Los Angeles area congressman, phoned his friends in the business community and urged them not to support Reagan—a Goldwaterite sure to drive away moderates and wreak havoc on the Republican party. Other moderates lashed Reagan as a "shallow" and dangerous candidate bereft, in the words of one disenchanted Republican, of "new proposal[s] or program[s]. There was [sic] no new ideas presented on the old issues," the critic huffed to Reagan's aides, adding that the candidate had only an elementary grasp of "certain basic issues." Another moderate worried that Reagan was a divisive figure who would only exacerbate party rifts. "His candidacy," he warned Reagan backer Cy Rubel, "would develop another throat-cutting operation. . . . [The party] simply cannot stand another fiasco such as we have had repeatedly since 1960."[11]

Moderates began scrambling for a candidate to oppose Reagan. Former governor Goodwin Knight began talking about coming out of retirement to rescue his party from political extremism, and United States Senator Thomas Kuchel also began making noises about a primary run. Kuchel, California's leading GOP moderate, seemed the perfect man to halt to the Reagan juggernaut. He would have both enough money to run a campaign and top political advisors; he had recently won a libel suit against four right-wing activists who had falsely accused him of being a homosexual, and he enjoyed passionate backing from party moderates. When he confessed to reporters that he "wake[s] up in the middle of the night wondering about" a primary campaign, he only fueled speculation that Reagan would have difficulty surviving the bitter and bruising primary battle to come.[12]

Reagan was in no position to preempt an assault from the moderates simply by renouncing the Birchers. In the summer of 1965, a handful of conservative activists had already begun complaining that Reagan was intent on denouncing the Birch Society and abandoning conservatives in favor of party moderates. During a CRA meeting on July 12, a Saturday, Cyril Stevenson, Jr., the CRA president, placed in members' seats copies of a *Newsweek* interview with Reagan's new professional consultants—a certain duo named Spencer and Roberts. Stevenson argued that they were convictionless spin doctors trying to wrest the campaign away from the conservative activists. The president wanted his organization either to dump Reagan as its candidate of choice or pressure the campaign into dumping the consultants.

In a batch of confidential memos to CRA members and Reagan, Stevenson warned that the new advisors would try to transform the candidate into a moderate and demanded that the candidate renounce his ties to the anti-Birch wing of the party. "How do we know we will even know the candidate when the P.R. men finish with him?" Stevenson complained to his activist friends. The president reminded members that "both the candidate and the P.R. firm know what we want, but they won't give in unless they have to" and urged activists to demand more of a role in Reagan's campaign. Until the candidate agreed to such terms, Stevenson suggested the activists withhold their support.[13]

Stevenson also threatened Reagan directly, warning the candidate that to win conservative backing, he first had to prove himself worthy of right-wing support. He could not be the "standard bearer for a cause" unless he promised activists a large say over campaign decisions. "Will you consult UROC, YR's and CRA on all campaign chairmen, vice-chairmen and coordinator appointments?" Stevenson demanded to know. "Mr. Reagan, since your entire excuse and strength for running comes from the grassroots conservative movement, why is it you refuse to accept them as 'General Partners' in your campaign? Are you ashamed of the Volunteers? . . . Do you feel the Volunteers are a liability?"[14]

It was the moderates, however, who posed the greater immediate threat to Reagan's candidacy. Excited by the prospects of a Kuchel run, and eager to discredit Reagan, the moderates believed the Birch issue offered the best chance of torpedoing Reagan's campaign. In late July they found themselves in a position to attack.

That summer, Republican leaders had searched in vain for ways to minimize the impact of the extremist issue on next year's campaign. Members of the Republican state central committee had suppressed a resolution condemning Birchers, thus averting a full-blown ideological battle within the committee. Yet Welch had promised to make the society a presence in the 1966 campaign, and the Birch issue continued to appear in most discussions and analyses of the Republican party. The Reagan campaign had not yet decided how to handle the issue, and the candidate himself seemed not to recognize the dangers it posed to his candidacy. An aide had informed Reagan that John Rousselot, the society's public relations director and a longtime friend of Reagan's, had offered his services to the campaign, telling managers that the society was at Reagan's service; if Reagan wanted a Birch endorsement, Rousselot would deliver it; if he wanted the society to attack him, Rousselot promised to arrange that, too.[15]

Neither Reagan nor his aides took the offer seriously. They wanted little to do with Rousselot, and agreed that whatever tack they took, they would not strike secret deals with the Birch high command. On July 21, at a CRA meeting at the St. Francis Hotel in San Francisco, however, Reagan told the dozen or so Republicans in the room about Rousselot's offer. "Johnny Rousselot is a terrific fellow," the candidate said. "[He] offered all his help in the campaign. In fact, he said he would do anything from calling me names in public to endorsement—whatever we want."[16] Reagan was joking. Hoping to deflect what he knew to be a contentious issue, Reagan reached for a touch of humor. He only succeeded in touching off the first firestorm of his political career.

Jane Alexander was a CRA director-at-large and a moderate opposed to Reagan, and she saw in Reagan's remarks a golden opportunity to derail his campaign. Angry that Reagan would make such a deal and then brag about it, Alexander decided to leak Reagan's statement to the press. She told reporters that Reagan had admitted that he had the full support of the John Birch Society. Mike Young, a Young Republican also at the meeting, confirmed Alexander's charge. "What she says is true," Young assured the media. Reagan "sounded like he was enamored of Mr. Rousselot. Reagan's more of a shallow image—if elected, we'd have to go along with whoever pulls the strings on him; he'd have to be led around by the nose."[17]

The charges resonated with what reporters knew about Reagan's ties to the far right, and newspapers ran lengthy stories on Reagan's Birch ties. Reagan found himself on the defensive. He issued a series of half-hearted denials and convoluted answers, initially telling reporters that he had never discussed his campaign with Rousselot or any other Birch official, and that he had never made such a deal with the society. "No such . . . arrangement exists or has ever been considered by me," he stated flat-out. A few days later the candidate reversed course, recanting his earlier statements and admitting that he may have said something at the CRA meeting about an offer from Rousselot, but that he had done so only in jest. He then went on the attack, complaining bitterly about Alexander, griping that he couldn't "go rushing into print answering every irresponsible woman who starts swinging a hatchet in my direction." Privately, the campaign was in turmoil. Reagan called at least one aide and asked him to spread "the message" that Rousselot had never offered him a deal and that his comments were meant as a joke; at another point, Reagan instructed aides simply to ignore the "whole thing."[18]

Reagan's response to the charges did not bode well and served mainly to embolden his growing number of critics. Reporters now began poking fun at Reagan and his Birch allies, and political pundits predicted that the controversy had placed his front-runner status in jeopardy. Journalists continued to dismiss the candidate as "Hollywood actor Ronald Reagan, darling of the Goldwaterites and choice of the John Birch Society"; in *The Beverly Hills Courier*, a local Los Angeles newspaper, editors denounced the Reagan-Rousselot deal as a "shocking and disgraceful" pact between extremists.[19]

By early August, the issue confronting Reagan was clear: The campaign, as Henry Salvatori recalled, "had to convince [people] that we weren't a bunch of kooks." The odds of doing so seemed long. Knowland, Shell (the former California Assembly minority leader), and Nixon—seasoned professionals all—had failed to navigate the shoals, and there was little to suggest that Reagan could do what these veterans could not.[20]

SINCE AT LEAST THE 1950s, Pat Brown had viewed the conservative movement generally as an antiquated force going against the basic grain of American life, and its candidates seemed hopelessly mired in the American past. Adherents championed long-discredited notions about the efficacy of individual initiative, attacked venerable government social programs as dangerous threats to the social fabric, and peddled fantastic tales about communist hordes infiltrating American shores. This last seemed especially ludicrous.

Like most liberals, Brown abhorred communism and supported the containment foreign policies popular in midcentury America. Yet in his view communism posed little threat to American institutions. Run by enlightened men eager to wield power for socially beneficial ends, federal bureaucracies, large corporations, and universities big and small seemed forces for progressive social change and immune from communist coups. "There was no communist conspiracy," Brown argued in these years. "There were liberals, and there were people that maybe wanted a socialistic form of government. But . . . there were also a group of psychopaths that saw a communist under every rock." As attorney general, Brown opposed the loyalty oaths conservatives wanted to impose on public employees, and looked askance at F.B.I. reports detailing the left-wing affiliations of judicial nominees—"junk stuff," Brown recalled, that sought to smear fine people based on their youthful associations with communist groups from the 1930s and '40s.[21]

Beginning in 1961, the governor helped launch a crusade against the John Birch Society and other radical anticommunists. Like many of his fellow liberals, Brown took his cue from Thomas Storke, the feisty elderly publisher of the *Santa Barbara News-Press*. Liberal scholars had for years been warning Americans about the growth of the radical Right, yet it was Storke's groundbreaking expose of the Birch Society that catapulted the extremist issue to the political fore.

A throwback to the muckraking journalism of the Progressive Era, Storke took an instant dislike to the Birch Society. He received scurrilous letters bad-mouthing his friend Earl Warren and heard rumors that a tiny handful of radical anticommunists were organizing in Santa Barbara. Storke instructed Hans Engh, one of his reporters, to investigate the group. Engh discovered that the society had infiltrated a student organization at UC Santa Barbara and was wreaking havoc on the beach community as a whole. The patriotic Storke felt duty bound to speak out against the group, and on January 22, 1961, he did just that, publishing the first in a series of articles detailing Birch activity in Santa Barbara.

Storke ran several such stories, and began painting the society as a fascistic group engaged in "a reactionary rebellion against the twentieth century." On February 26 Storke published a front-page editorial excoriating the society for its smear tactics and wild conspiracy theories. Referring to himself in the third person, Storke captured the growing liberal antipathy toward the hidebound authoritarians: "He lived when conditions were rugged," Storke wrote of himself in typically dramatic fashion. "When West was West and men were men. He lived during periods when if a man or a group of men . . . called our President . . . and others at the head of government, traitors, they were made to answer. He lived when men were considered cowards when they hid behind their women's skirts and clothed their identity through anonymity." Storke condemned "the dictatorial, undemocratic structure of the society" and dared Welch to "come up from underground" and fight like a man. The next day Storke boasted to a friend that he had "expose[d] these fakers" and that his was "the first paper in the West to take them on . . . these rats."[22]

Storke's series sparked a nationwide outcry against the society, transforming Birchism into a major political issue almost overnight. The *New York Times* and *Time* followed Storke's series with similar exposes, liberals pressured Congress to launch an investigation into society practices, journalists began painting right-wing activists as part of a mentally disturbed clique, and Storke received credit for having struck a powerful blow for American democracy. Fifteen thousand requests for copies of his editorial poured in, and Americans across the country hailed the octogenarian as a champion of freedom. Newscasters cited Storke's work, journalists awarded him the Pulitzer among other top prizes, and the publisher's friends applauded his stance as a courageous defense of the liberal order. *Los Angeles Times* publisher Otis Chandler said he was "fed up on all these attacks on Chief Justice Earl Warren" and praised Storke for his timely expose. Warren himself expressed appreciation for Storke's attack, telling his friend, "I am more amazed how some people can in the name of freedom advocate totalitarian measures to accomplish their purpose. . . . As far as I can see there isn't much that can be done except to smoke them out a little as you are doing and as others following your lead are doing. . . . I do appreciate the manner in which you have taken up the cudgels for us." Robert Allen, a nationally syndicated columnist, thanked Storke for being "the spearhead in what is increasingly becoming a nationwide hue and cry against this pack of vicious and sordid social desperadoes. You and your paper fired the opening guns against this would-be insidious totalitarian conspiracy."[23]

No one took up Storke's cudgel with greater glee and zeal than the governor of California. Sensing a potent political issue in the making, Brown believed that as the liberal leader of the state it was also his obligation to speak out against such dangerous antiprogressives. He praised Storke's expose, hailing the editor as a state treasure who had exerted a profound influence on the political landscape. "Up here in Sacramento," Brown wrote Storke, "some of the peanut politicians are following the John Birch line, and we are running into the extremism of the radical right. . . ." Later, he told him: "Yours was the first paper in the country to recognize the danger of these ultra-right groups. . . . I know of no one who has approached the problems of our country more objectively, more moderately, or more courageously than you. . . . I rate you with the giants of California."[24]

Brown saw the Birchers as somehow both a national joke and a genuine threat to political democracy, and he moved swiftly to announce his opposition to them, opening, with martial-like bluster, a multipronged effort to relegate Birchism to the margins of California politics. Brown asked state Attorney General Stanley Mosk to launch a probe into the society. Concerned about conducting a McCarthy-like witch-hunt, Mosk rejected Brown's request and instead wrote the governor a fifteen-page letter detailing what he and others already knew about the society. Dated July 7, 1961, the report became the leading liberal statement on the Birchers. The society, Mosk wrote in the report's most famous passage, was made up "primarily of wealthy businessmen, retired military officers and little old ladies in tennis shoes. [Birchers] are bound together by an obsessive fear of 'communism,' a word which they define to include any ideas differing from their own. . . . In response to this fear they are willing to give up a large measure of the freedoms guaranteed them by the United States Constitution in favor of accepting the dictates of their 'Founder.' They seek, by fair means or foul, to force the rest of us to follow their example. They are pathetic."[25]

Mosk argued that activists inhabited a Manichean world characterized by an irrational fear and hatred of an implacable communist foe. He portrayed them as mentally unstable, disturbed men and women who would not survive national media scrutiny. Mosk quoted journalists who lampooned the society as "ridiculous" and cartoonists who did sketches entitled "Malice in Wonderland," and he suggested that Birchers would prove rich targets for liberals' barbs. As for Robert Welch, Mosk dubbed him an "embittered candy maker"—a paranoiac who rarely granted interviews and prattled incessantly about impending communist coups.[26]

The report fed the anti-Birch momentum then gripping the country. The *New York Times Magazine* reprinted it, and oddly enough the phrase "little old ladies in tennis shoes," a symbol of the "pathetic" nature of the opposition, quickly became the rallying cry for Birch foes everywhere. California Democrats urged the Brown administration to do something about this new scourge. One activist warned the governor that Birchers were "playing upon the emotions of the voters" and had to be stopped. Chairman of the State Democratic Party Roger Kent told Fred Dutton that Republicans had begun showing two Birch films—*Operation Abolition* and a "much worse one" called *Communism on the Map*—at military installations, defense plants, and police stations around the nation. "It appears that some Republicans have decided that their only chance to win is the old communist issue," Kent griped, noting that the problem was especially acute in California and "one that . . . needs attention right now."[27]

Brown agreed. He believed the issue to be a winner: Forced to

Governor-elect Edmund "Pat" Brown arrives at election headquarters on election night, November 4, 1958, with wife Bernice (left), and daughters Cynthia and Kathy (far right) after winning a stunning, million-vote victory over nationally known William Knowland, the "Senator from Formosa."

Pat Brown displays the front page of a newspaper announcing his second electoral victory as governor, over former vice president Richard Nixon. The 1962 election seemed to sound the death knell of the Right in California and raised Brown into a pantheon of greats, earning him the nickname "Giant Killer."

TWO PHOTOS: BETTMANN-CORBIS

AP/WIDE WORLD PHOTOS

BETTMANN-CORBIS

Nixon lost California to Brown by 300,000 votes. Two years earlier he had lost the presidency to John F. Kennedy by just over 100,000, and he thought his political career might be over. During this infamous November 7 press conference he told the newsmen angrily, "You won't have Nixon to kick around anymore."

Two years after Nixon's loss in California, film star and former General Electric spokesperson Ronald Reagan appeared as an alternate delegate at the 1964 GOP convention in San Francisco. Reagan's "Time for Choosing" speech would be one of the few highlights of Barry Goldwater's divisive, dismal campaign. When Goldwater was routed by Lyndon Johnson, many observers believed the conservative movement to be permanently discredited.

AP/WIDE WORLD PHOTOS

Mario Savio, a philosophy student from New York, led the University of California, Berkeley's Free Speech Movement. Here he indicates victory after having won university backing in the students' battle against restrictions on political demonstrations. Brown sympathized with the students, but proved unable to appease them.

March 13, 1965: UC president Clark Kerr (right) holds a press conference with Brown and Berkeley chancellor Martin Myerson (left) on the unrest at the school. Brown supported Kerr, who was perceived as increasingly ineffectual as the turmoil dragged on.

PETER WHITNEY ARCHIVE PHOTOS

A drunk-driving arrest of a black motorist was the spark that ignited the Watts riots in August 1965. Brown was on vacation with his wife in Greece. His deputies, feuding with Los Angeles Police Chief William Parker and firebrand Mayor Sam Yorty, were slow to call out the National Guard despite Parker's pleas.

The riots left 36 dead and 879 wounded. Police arrested more than 3,500 people, and the damage done to Brown's political standing was immense. The black community attacked him for not having done enough to fight poverty; conservatives, for having done too much.

TWO PHOTOS: ARCHIVE PHOTOS

TWO PHOTOS: BETTMANN-CORBIS

ABOVE: The riots in Watts came as "no surprise to me," said L.A. Police Chief Parker. Brown said Parker's post-riot remarks about "racial war" were "very unfortunate," but whites in L.A. applauded the straight-talking chief, and journalists portrayed him as the only one to emerge from Watts "with the image of a hero."

ABOVE RIGHT: L.A. Mayor Sam Yorty was a Democrat, but could not have been more unlike Brown. Yorty's immensely popular "get tough" rhetoric allied him with Parker. Here Yorty holds up an "inflammatory" handbill distributed to the citizens of Watts. Communists, Yorty claimed, were trying to incite the blacks of Los Angeles to riot. Later he would challenge Brown in the Democratic gubernatorial primary.

AP/ WIDE WORLD PHOTOS

RIGHT: Democratic Assembly Speaker Jesse Unruh calls the house to order for the 1965 session in Sacramento. Unruh, physically imposing and politically outspoken, was the emotional antithesis of the reserved, nonconfrontational Brown. He wielded massive power within the state, however, and considered challenging Brown in 1966, one sign that the liberal Democratic coalition was falling apart.

Reagan on the campaign trail during the 1966 gubernatorial race. A political neophyte, Reagan showed incredible savvy in the race against Brown, putting a smile on Yorty's law-and-order policies while downplaying the anticommunism of his own earlier speeches. Here he leads a Mexican Independence Day parade.

On the stump Reagan quickly overcame his naivete and ignorance of California politics, using massive binders that contained cards with data on every possible local issue to bone up before each speech. He proved a dynamic speaker, quickly convincing voters that he was a good guy in real life, as he had been on film. In this case, however, several women in the front row have found something else equally compelling.

TWO PHOTOS: AP/WIDE WORLD PHOTOS

AP/WIDE WORLD PHOTOS

Robert Welch, the founder of the anticommunist John Birch Society, was political poison for many conservative candidates. He had called Dwight Eisenhower a communist and was just the sort of extremist that Reagan would have to avoid to capture the middle ground in 1966.

Stuart Spencer, half of Spencer-Roberts, the famous team of political advisors, was the man on whom Reagan relied to coordinate local committees and set up events, like Reagan's popular Q & A sessions, that showcased their candidate's wit and flair. Spencer and Roberts helped to brief Reagan on every possible political issue.

BETTMANN-CORBIS

Sam Yorty lost to Pat Brown in the Democratic primary, but in so doing the conservative mayor gathered over a million votes and badly damaged Brown's chances for a third term. After the primary, still burned from party infighting, Yorty refused to endorse Brown, and much of his support swung to Reagan. Here Yorty appears at Reagan's November 9 celebration party to congratulate the governor-elect.

Brown and Reagan meet for the first time since the election as Brown welcomes Reagan into his office in the Capitol following the Republican's landslide victory.

TWO PHOTOS: AP/WIDE WORLD PHOTOS

choose between right-wing extremism and Democratic liberalism, voters would choose the latter every time. During a statewide speaking tour that May, Brown spoke in ringing terms about the Birch threat, warning repeatedly that extremists of all stripes wanted to destroy the tough, rational, and proven program of progressive liberalism, and replace it with an authoritarian state not unlike Nazi Germany or Communist Russia. In letters to constituents, the governor charged Birchers with trying "to convince people that there is a vast Communist conspiracy motivating the campaign in many of our cities for the fluoridation of water," which he considered a scurrilous "campaign against democracy." Birch "smears . . . undermin[e] the confidence of our people in our government," Brown argued further. "I have great faith that free speech and democratic discussion will expose the extremists . . . and that good sense will prevail when the people are exposed to the facts."[28]

Brown indeed saw his popularity soar the more he railed against the radical right. Storke told Brown that he had helped "save us when the hoodlums were exposed by me and others." "There is great fear among many people of my acquaintance," another admirer wrote the governor, "and a great need to hear men in your position declare openly against those who try to bring the McCarthy era back." One professor said he supported Brown's plan for a "statement of liberal principles which might be set against Senator Goldwater's *Conscience of a Conservative*," and the attorney and informal advisor Warren Christopher told Brown that his recent statewide tour was "uniformly excellent. . . . I think this is an important turning point." Brown, basking in the public adulation, declared that "the tide [was] turning" in the liberal direction.[29]

Swept up in the spirit of the day, Brown pressed his campaign with a passion that bordered on the evangelical. He instructed citizens in the art of attacking Birchers, rhapsodizing that "the best tool" for discrediting radicals "is informed and incisive criticism. We should exercise this right . . . at every available opportunity and then trust in the good sense of the majority of Californians who believe that anyone who can follow a philosophy which says democracy is a fraud is, himself, a fool." In early 1962, in the midst of his reelection campaign against Nixon, Brown dispatched Frank Mesple, a legislative aide, to gather information about anticommunist rallies in Los Angeles. Mesple's subsequent findings revealed the hardening liberal view that American conservatism was no longer a legitimate political force.[30]

The rally, Mesple wrote the governor, was sponsored by the rabid anticommunist General Edwin Walker and took place at the Los Angeles Sports Arena before a near-capacity crowd of angry whites. In the parking lot outside the arena, Mesple counted fifty idle buses and an array of incendiary bumper stickers which he described for the governor as follows: 24 Goldwater strips, 16 Joe Shell for Governor stickers, one "Impeach Earl Warren" sign, eight "The only 'ism' for Me is Americanism" stickers, and "for whatever political implication is involved, 'Buy Girl Scout Cookies' stickers. I knew Welch made candy bars," Mesple joked, "but I didn't realize he was behind the Girl Scout Cookie movement also."[31]

Mesple depicted rally-goers as a shrill lot composed of inept activists unschooled in the art of American politics. Walker was a poor and lumbering public speaker, lacking spontaneity and reading his talk with difficulty. "If Walker had any ability to manipulate this crowd, it could have been a fearful spectacle," explained the aide. "He spoke for one and a half hours; largely a recitation of the abuses that had been heaped upon him. . . . His pomposity and arrogance are appalling. He went out of his way . . . to antagonize the Press. . . . I don't think he will make a good demagogue." Mesple dismissed other speakers as dangerous naysayers, disillusioned men harboring an array of grievances against American leaders, heaping invective on "their favorite whipping boys. . . . The 'Alger Hiss Gang' was blamed for the deportation of 2 and a half million anti-Communists into the Soviet Union. . . . Dean Acheson got his lumps . . . Ike bore the major brunt of the attack . . . [And] Harvard and Columbia Universities were singled-out as, 'Leading the subversion of our educational system.'" Mesple noted that "any mention of the John Birch Society" drew "wild applause," and that Birchers "were the real organizers and supporters of this program." Mesple promised to investigate the groups sponsoring the event, concluding that the Birchers were "a nasty outfit" but not a serious threat to the governor's power.[32]

Content to dismiss the radical right, and focused on his second term, the governor and aides adopted an increasingly derisive tone toward the Birchers, poking fun at activists and urging radio stations to play songs spoofing the group.

*We're the John Birch Society . . .*
*Here to save our country*
*From a Communist plot*
*Join the John Birch Society*
*Help us fill the ranks*
*To get this movement started*
*We need lots of tools and cranks.*[33]

The issue didn't die, however. The 1964 Goldwater contest reignited administration fears about a right-wing resurgence. He and aides again felt "an obligation," as Roger Kent noted in late September of that year, "to create a catastrophe for Goldwater and the right-wing nuts around him." The governor eagerly reverted to his anti-Birch mode, lashing conservatives as Nazi fascists who represented a dangerous departure from the moderate consensus. "Throughout the recent history of our great country," Brown said shortly after the Republican National Convention, "leadership of the two major parties has been maintained by moderates—thoughtful Americans who realize there are no easy answers to the complicated problems which grip this nation today."[34] Goldwater, however, was a dangerous throwback to a darker era.

> By asserting that extremism is not a vice, he ruthlessly encouraged the racist, the bigot, the Ku Klux Klan, and even the Communist to assault the constitutional rights of those who oppose him. You may define extremism as an act of Nathan Hale, but we no longer live in a nation whose problems are as simple as those of the era in which Hale lived. Today the extremists are the organized haters who burn churches in Mississippi or wreck private property in Harlem—all in the name of "liberty." History shows that other nations which tried to solve their complex problems by giving leadership to a man with simple answers have all fallen in bitter defeat. They were defeated by nations of moderate leadership. Must history repeat itself?[35]

Once again, it was a winning issue. When the two philosophies were pitted against one another, Birchers—and their Goldwater-style candidates—were no match for Brown's program of responsible liberalism.

In 1966, Brown would try the same approach. In early 1965, the governor did not overly concern himself with a Reagan candidacy. Yet he and aides were quietly preparing an all-out assault on the radical right. On January 6, William Becker urged Mesple to encourage state Senator Hugh Burns to conduct a second investigation of the Birch Society, on the grounds that the administration would benefit from "a more critical analysis of the Birch Society." Other aides began monitoring right-wing activity in the state, reporting to the governor that the society was still a shrill and hostile organization trying to topple the administration, and that it was a salient issue that could be exploited for political gain.[36]

One aide informed Brown that at a "Giant [Birch] Rally," members of the Constitution Defense Committee circulated a Recall Brown petition and Karl Prussian, an anticommunist leader, accused Brown of taking part in the communist conspiracy to muzzle Prussian. The aide described Prussian as a hate-monger who gripped the edges of the podium during his harangue, his face growing red with rage as the blood drained from his knuckles. Prussian assailed Brown, Mosk, and State Controller Alan Cranston as "the epitome of the Communist plan . . . to make California the first Soviet state in the U.S. . . . They have been accommodating, appeasing, and capitulating to the Communists in their drive to make California into a Communist dictatorship."[37]

On April 6 Becker captured the growing enthusiasm for taking on the Birchers yet again. He told colleagues Jack Burby and Winslow Christian that "an anti-Nazi rally is scheduled for May 7th in Glendale. Ronald Reagan is the featured speaker." The event, Becker wrote, was "obviously an attempt by these right-wingers to clean up their image." Becker gave the "right-wingers" little chance of success, pointing out that Reverend A. E. Peterson of Burbank—a radical anticommunist spearheading the Recall Brown drive—was behind the rally, and that Reagan and others would have a difficult time distancing themselves from their radical brethren. "Perhaps, at the appropriate time," Becker suggested hopefully, "[Reagan and Peterson] should be asked to be consistent and repudiate the more dangerous forms of totalitarianism in California, such as the Birch Society."[38]

IN LATE JULY, Reagan and allies were working hard to distance the candidate from the GOP fringe. First, however, they had to make sure that his right-wing support was solid. Despite the earlier threats of revolt, they were soon reassured on this point. Conservative rank-and-file had grown wary of the Birch issue; reluctant to make the society a litmus test for Republican candidates, the grassroots revealed in July the depth of its support for Reagan. In response to Cyril Stevenson's charge that at heart Reagan was a political moderate, CRA activists and leaders mounted a vigorous defense of the candidate's credentials, defending Reagan as a dedicated conservative who would not abandon the movement faithful.

Other allies came to Reagan's defense as well. Reverend W. S. McBirnie, a right-wing radio evangelist and friend of Reagan's, delivered a speech before the CRA entitled "Cannibalism in the Republican party." In it he beseeched the rank-and-file to cast aside their long-standing enmity toward fellow Republicans and concentrate on their real enemies, the Democrats. Activists responded enthusiastically to McBirnie's plea, and quickly made clear that they wanted no part of Stevenson's attempt "to force concessions from Ronald Reagan." A. L. Bane, a CRA board member, assured Reagan's staffers that McBirnie's speech was well received, noting that the candidate's campaign managers could not have performed any better than the Reverend had. Bane also estimated that only about 25 to 30 percent of the activists supported the Stevenson position, while the remaining 70 to 75 percent were "thoroughly disgusted with his tactics."[39] According to one Reagan ally, Charlie Lavis, a CRA leader, said he regretted bringing Stevenson into politics and nominating him for CRA president, and his colleague Frank Adams voiced his disgust with "Steve and those whom he chooses to do his dirty work."[40]

With the right flank assured, the campaign moved to the center. CRA members—and conservative activists generally—defended Reagan from Jane Alexander's charge that the candidate had aligned himself with the Birch Society. They worked with Reagan and his campaign staff to isolate Alexander and other moderate critics. "Kay" was a Reagan ally, a CRA leader, and Reagan's point person on the Alexander controversy. She told Reagan that conservatives were working with Reagan's aides in Northern California to shore up support for his candidacy and meeting "on the q.t." to discuss ways to discredit Reagan's critics. CRA officers, Kay assured Reagan, were even considering resigning to protest Stevenson's failure to repudiate Alexander. CRA leaders held a press conference denouncing Alexander as an embittered troublemaker; Reagan's Birch remark, they added, was nothing more than a facetious aside made behind closed doors; it was not to be taken seriously.[41]

CRA activists also looked to conservatives outside their organization to repudiate Alexander. Kay, for example, told Reagan she had friends who "might have good contacts in the Young Republicans, and ward off potential YR's confirming Alexander's charge." One of her contacts even went so far as to call Alexander directly, perhaps to reason with her, but Alexander hung up on him. The same contact, Kay added, "also called the YR, whom he suspects of being [Alexander's] liaison, told him to stay away from the press but the guy denies having anything to do with Alexander." Kay, meanwhile, was urging other movement friends not to speak with reporters and to do "their 'housecleaning' quietly and without public notice. They all pledged their willingness to do this. . . . Frankly I'm not sure they can do it quietly . . . maybe [Stevenson] will resign. Ha!" On September 1 Kay told Reagan's aides during a meeting in San Francisco that as far as she could tell, the California right was still firmly behind Reagan; she noted that her neighbor was also unhappy with "this Alexander woman" for spreading nasty rumors about Reagan.[42]

The conservative response to the Alexander-Stevenson controversies confirmed for aides what they long suspected: Reagan had strong activist support. This allowed them to focus on the more pressing need to convince the rest of the state that Reagan was not a Birch ally. In the last weeks of summer, the extremism issue still hovered ominously over the campaign, threatening to engulf it at any moment. Fred Haffner, a top Reagan aide in the North, complained that Alexander was still "feeding stuff to the press," that the *Los Angeles Times* had run a series of articles about the controversy, and that the Birch issue was still a powerful one capable of damaging Reagan's candidacy.[43]

Immediate responsibility for the problem fell on Stu Spencer and Bill Roberts, the top GOP political consultants who had agreed to run Reagan's campaign. The two men were determined to avoid the Birch pit into which Goldwater had stumbled, and by temperament and experience were particularly well suited for such a task. They had cut their political teeth in the California Young Republican movement of the 1950s, at a time when Warren moderates dominated the organization, and had grown into shrewd political operatives sensitive to the extremist issue that had so long plagued the Republican party. Spencer and Roberts were, by their own admission, ardent moderates. But their allegiance owed less to ideology than to political calculation. They believed in the efficacy of free enterprise and less government intervention in the marketplace; yet above all they wanted to win elections. Convinced that politics was less about ideas and policies than about winning, Spencer and Roberts had concluded by 1965 that conservatives made poor political candidates.

They were hard-nosed operatives cut from the same mold as Murray Chotiner and Robert Finch, two of Nixon's top aides. Attracted by politics, the men had decided in the late 1950s to quit their jobs—Spencer was working as director of parks and recreation for the city of Alhambra, Roberts as a television salesman—and devote themselves full-time to their new love. In June 1960, after a stint with the Los Angeles County Republican Central Committee, the men put up $500 apiece, took out a month-to-month lease on a dingy office in the back of a travel agency, and formed "Spencer-Roberts." They flipped a coin for the best office and started with three clients, little capital, few resources, and no secretary. At the time only two such consulting firms existed, Whitaker-Baxter and Baus and Ross, yet these firms impressed Spencer and Roberts as a wave of the future and a way to achieve stability in an inherently unstable, ever-changing profession. Such a business, they reasoned, would bring in good money, not have to depend on a single patron or politician (an arrangement conducive to a long career), and provide Republicans with the organizational skills sorely lacking from current campaigns.

The men made a formidable team, and quickly established themselves as the leading Republican political consultants in the state. Spencer worked well behind the scenes, poring over campaign polls, mapping strategy, and directing operations. Roberts preferred the higher-profile positions and became adept at firing up activists and cajoling candidates. Spencer liked to manage dark horses; Roberts favored front-runners. Tough, energetic, and stocky, Spencer took chances; easygoing, patient, and soft-spoken, Roberts oozed caution. Often sitting across from one another, the men engaged in free-wheeling dialogues about their campaigns, keeping one another abreast of developments and strategies. It was, Spencer explained, "just like a marriage—you've got to get along and we did."[44]

In 1961, they won their first two races. Soon thereafter they helped elect several candidates to the Los Angeles City Council. In 1963, they steered two unheralded Republicans to victory in special congressional elections, prompting an avalanche of publicity and enhancing their reputation as can-do wunderkinds. Working almost exclusively for moderates, Spencer-Roberts quickly developed an aversion to right-wing ideologues. In 1964, they ran Nelson Rockefeller's California primary campaign against Barry Goldwater; although Rockefeller lost that race, Spencer-Roberts came away from the contest convinced that extremists had little chance of winning general elections.

The consultants' strategy against Goldwater was simple. They hammered relentlessly on Goldwater's ties to the Birch Society. They played up his off-the-cuff gaffes and sent out campaign mailers that asked: "Whom do you want in the room with the H-bomb?" The strategy almost worked. Early polls showed Rockefeller behind by thirty percentage points; the New York governor ended up losing by only three.[45]

The fact that these two moderates came to work for Reagan should have been a warning sign to Pat Brown. In April 1965, Spencer and Roberts entertained the notion of working for Reagan. They met the would-be candidate at the Cave de Roy in Los Angeles, Reagan's favorite lunch haunt, and came to several quick conclusions about the actor. They found him "nice and pleasant," charismatic, affable, "very retentive," and a man with more depth than Goldwater; Reagan, the pros reflected, might have a future in politics.[46] Yet they harbored serious doubts about Reagan's electability. His inexperience worried the consultants, but most of all they were wary of his reputation as a right-wing radical. Could he break with his radical allies and defuse the Birch issue?

They had heard Reagan "was a real right-winger," a "martinet," and "difficult to get along with . . . that he was just tough and not easy to work with." "At first I didn't know if he was for real, politically," Bill Roberts recalled in an interview years later. "He was a charming fellow, and he was an ideologue. In those days the John Birch Society was quite prominent, and a right-wing movement emerged in the Republican Party, vis-à-vis the Goldwater candidacy of 1964. In the context of all that, we didn't know where Reagan was coming from."[47] In their initial meeting, the pros warned Reagan that they would not take part in another "Goldwater-type campaign." Roberts was especially blunt about their concerns. He reminded Reagan that "politics isn't like Hollywood," and that Spencer-Roberts was a professional operation and would not work for "dogmatists or prima donnas. A candidate cannot be a star and treat his staff like dirt."[48]

Reagan responded amiably to such admonishments, and after a series of discussions the consultants became convinced that with the proper training and strategy, Reagan could indeed distance himself from the Birch taint. For all his anticommunism, Reagan nevertheless remembered well the Goldwater-Rockefeller wars and had let it be known that he wanted no repeat of that fiasco. He understood the public's antipathy toward the Birchers, recognized the dangers of being identified with Robert Welch, and expressed a willingness to compromise on the issue. One night, Reagan asked the consultants to his home for dinner. When the men arrived they found Reagan sitting on a couch, his legs crossed, a pair of brightly colored red socks visible to everyone in the room. It was a nice touch of humor. When the meeting broke up that night, the men looked at each other, smiled, and said they were prepared to "go all the way if things went right."[49]

California's Republican moderates, many of them old allies, greeted Spencer-Roberts' decision with a chorus of criticism. They sent nasty mail, drubbed them as turncoats, and voiced disbelief that they would agree to work for a right-wing radical like Reagan. San Francisco reporter Jack McDowell had followed many Spencer-Roberts campaigns and considered himself well acquainted with the firm's talents; he considered them "bonkers" for choosing a long-shot like Reagan. "You guys," he told them bluntly, "are absolutely crazy."[50]

Spencer and Roberts did not know for certain that they could distance Reagan from the extremist issue, but they recognized early that Reagan bore little resemblance to the party's firebrands. The men saw Reagan as a fresh political face, a skilled communicator, a terrific storyteller, and a generally genial candidate. He was by no means a perfectly polished politician, but he seemed well suited to television and a man of moderate disposition.

The men began to work on the Birch problem almost immediately. Aware that moderates would try to build "a fence around our operation," the consultants moved swiftly to convince voters that Reagan was not an incendiary radical. Yet it was not a simple task. Roberts, for one, had little interest in repudiating the Birch Society as a whole. He remembered well Nixon's ordeal, and feared that if Reagan started attacking the activists, he would come across as a politically expedient hack who had abandoned his longtime allies. "Everyone would have seen through that," Roberts reasoned, "and Ron would have lost credibility. If he had become 'Mr. Expedient,' he would have lost the activists but he would not have gained anywhere else. The Democrats would still have hit him with the Birch issue by planting the idea that he was accepting back-door support from them." If Nixon's experience in 1962 was a lesson in how not to handle the Birch issue, Goldwater's campaign two years later offered a full-blown course; whatever they did, Spencer-Roberts had to assure the public that Reagan was no Goldwater acolyte.[51]

Reagan, Spencer-Roberts decided, would have to repudiate the more extremist elements in the society without antagonizing the bulk of the Birch membership. In a June 1965 interview with *Newsweek*—the same interview Cyril Stevenson found so repugnant—the advisors made few pretenses about their stratagem. *Newsweek* reporter Karl Fleming asked the men how they planned to turn their client into a viable gubernatorial candidate—how, as *Newsweek* put it, these "remarkably successful promoters [would] win one for the Gipper in 1966."[52] Spencer-Roberts responded candidly. They admitted Reagan had "supplanted Goldwater in people's minds. But we are going to try to shift that image. In fact, we've got to if we're going to win." To do so, the men said they might go so far as to ask the CRA, UROC, and YRs, right-wing groups all, not to endorse Reagan; they also vowed to seek the support of Rockefeller Republicans and predicted that people would be "surprised when they see the list of liberals and moderates who come out for Reagan." The candidate, they further noted, had to become less hyperbolic and more moderate-sounding—someone "who is not the darling of the extremists, a sensible, reasonable guy who leans to the right but who doesn't spout all this nonsense about the Liberty Amendment and fluoridation. Our toughest job is going to be proving that he isn't a right-winger."[53]

Fleming pointed out that only a year earlier, while running Rockefeller's campaign, the consultants had compiled a list of Goldwater's fringe backers and that Reagan had come in at number 22 on the list; next to Reagan's name was the following description: "Another Liberty Amendment stalwart." In the interview Reagan dismissed "the same old business of pinning a label on somebody" and promised that such labels wouldn't "stick if people will listen to what I've got to say." Fleming noted that Reagan then abruptly ended the interview, because he was due at a dinner in Burbank to accept an award from the Town Meeting for Freedom, an "arch-conservative" organization honoring Reagan's patriotic devotion to right-wing causes.[54]

Spencer-Roberts had no desire to alter Reagan's basic convictions about communists or Birchers, and Reagan had little interest in such changes. When some aides suggested that he denounce the society, the candidate replied testily, complaining that Birchers were not simply a "Republican problem. I see no reason to indict or repudiate an organization of which I am not a member and have no intention of joining."[55] In mid-September, Reagan made it clear that he was not about to abandon his Birch allies, writing John Rousselot a letter thanking him for his support during the recent Alexander imbroglio: 'I assure you I'll keep my words in line with yours, and I want you to know how sorry I am if my attempt to get a laugh caused you any embarrassment. I solemnly pledge that from now on I'll only tell dirty stories suitable for male company, and thus there will be no chance of Jane Alexander having anything to quote."[56]

But Reagan agreed with Spencer-Roberts that they would have to repudiate Welch, the society's founder, and that they should issue a statement spelling out Reagan's position on the society. Debates broke out among aides about the wording of such a statement. An early draft called on Reagan to urge Birchers themselves to repudiate Welch. But this approach, one aide warned, "might come back on him over the next year—say about Labor Day 1966—with the following question: 'It's been nearly a year now since you said that Birch Society members have a moral responsibility to disavow statements of Robert Weisch [sic] and that you would not indict the society until it was evident that they had failed this responsibility—don't you think they've had enough time to put their house in order?'" Other aides agreed, and one scribbled to Spencer in the margins of one early draft that the paragraph was "not needed—extraneous—might be used later?"[57]

On September 24, Reagan issued his first and only formal statement about the Birch Society. It proved a deft political juggling act. He began by noting that in recent months many articles and discussions had linked him to the organization, but denied that he had ever been a Bircher and said he had no intention of becoming one. Reagan then "reaffirmed" his criticism of Welch, calling "utterly reprehensible" the candyman's Eisenhower smears and his other outlandish conspiracy theories, and urging members to repudiate their leader's more far-fetched ideas. The statement also tried to assure activists that he welcomed support from anyone who supported his political philosophy. "In all fairness to the members," Reagan continued, both the FBI and Burns' subcommittee had cleared the society of subversive activity. Reagan quoted from a recent report about the group, and then came to the crux of his argument, stating that he had decided not to solicit support from "any blocs or groups," but would seek support from individuals "by persuading them to accept my philosophy, not by my accepting theirs." The statement totaled one page.[58]

Overall, the statement was a big success. Of course, a handful of Birchers felt betrayed by Reagan's attacks on Welch, and they excoriated the candidate for abandoning them in the heat of battle, renewing fears of a Nixon campaign redux. "I did not see or hear that you had denounced the communists or any of [their] many insidious activities," one Bircher complained angrily to Reagan. "This statement, charging a very fine group of people of being lunatic, is exactly what the communists want you to say . . . if what the news media says is true, Mr. Reagan, you can not count on any more support from me and I am sure the other Birch members feel the same way."[59] Frank Cullen Brophy, a national Birch leader, told the candidate's mother-in-law that by attacking the society, Reagan was unwittingly helping the communist cause. The society, Brophy opined, "is the only organization in America that has the Communists worried, and they will go any route to destroy it."[60] Another member argued that Reagan had "given Governor Brown a big boost towards another term," while one hate-filled letter-writer informed Reagan that the real enemy was the "Negroes . . . a vicious, thieving, murderous gang that takes the law in their own hands." As for the Birchers, "I will admit there is a rotten apple in every barrel and there are a few in the KKK but most are trying to preserve the white race. . . . Now you and the Republicans are trying to woo the Negroes but not the John Birchers. Will you please tell me ONE thing that the John Birchers have done that is not patriotic and that is vicious, thieving, murderous?"[61] Another angry supporter mused that the candidate "ought to go after left-wing conspirators. . . . I am not a John Bircher," the man rambled, "but I know many very dedicated, patriotic Americans who are. In war, one needs all kinds of troops." Reagan thanked this supporter for his "kind letter and good suggestions" and added that he was in "complete agreement."[62]

But the majority of conservatives remained firmly in Reagan's camp. John Rousselot issued a supportive statement that also managed to defend Welch—a terrific leader whose allegations about communists "have always been backed up by a careful accumulation of facts." Rousselot chose to indict journalists who distorted Reagan's words. John Schmitz, the lone Bircher in the California State Assembly, attacked reporters who tried to pit Reagan against the society and assured Reagan he would personally work to "recoup some of the losses in this area." Schmitz pointed out that Reagan did not have too much to worry about in any case, because "the John Birch Society members and friends are becoming thick-skinned."[63] In October, one of Schmitz's Birch colleagues echoed this optimistic appraisal, telling Reagan "that the Society was satisfied with [his] stand."

Reagan, in turn, reassured Birchers that he had no intention of abandoning them. He touted members as "fine upstanding citizens" whose support he welcomed, and confided to members that he liked most Birchers, was only criticizing the group's lunatic fringe—a segment that did not "represent the thinking or policy of the society"—and that an uncharitable few had misinterpreted his statement. Reagan also reminded Birchers that he had risked his life in the war against communism, "liv[ing] for the better part of a year with a police guard for my family as a result of communist threats against me. I will match my record for fighting, not talking about, Communism with anyone you care to name," Reagan added confidently.[64]

Reagan now seemed better prepared for questions about the society, and more adept at responding to his critics' concerns. When opponents tried to bait Reagan into defending Birchers, Reagan responded deftly, noting that he too found Welch's views distasteful and shared the moderates' concerns about the GOP fringe. At other times, he dismissed the Birch issue as a red herring that was not "pertinent" to the campaign, charging his critics were "reaching for an issue." On October 1, a group of journalists caught up with Reagan as he was boarding the Republican party "happy train" for the state convention in San Francisco. One reporter asked Reagan for his opinion on the society. "I think the charges made against Dwight Eisenhower were utterly reprehensible," Reagan replied strongly. It was enough to change the subject.[65]

Aides, too, worked to keep Birch members out of the campaign and away from the candidate. They ordered colleagues not to allow supporters "to organize as Goldwaterites for Reagan" and at campaign events, fearful of pictures in the next day's newspapers, aides obstructed the path of Birch leaders, including John Rousselot, trying to greet the candidate. Lyn Nofziger, Reagan's press secretary, felt badly about their treatment of Rousselot, "but damnit he should've known better that he was not gonna be a help." And when aides learned of a Reagan fund-raiser at a Bircher's home in Pasadena, they canceled it.[66]

Later in his career Reagan would become famous for his deft use of sound bites, such as "Government is not the solution, government is the problem." In 1965, in his major Birch statement, the line about "persuading them to accept my philosophy, not my accepting theirs" was just such a line. In the span of a few months, the campaign had made major strides on the Birch issue. Reagan was freed up to talk about the failings of the opposition and articulate his own positions on the pressing issues of the day. Events would provide Reagan with plenty of other issues to trumpet.

SEVEN

# "CHARCOAL ALLEYS"

By August 1965, Reagan had gone a long way toward blunting the John Birch issue and the larger matter of right-wing radicalism. Pat Brown had little idea that Reagan had accomplished anything of the kind. The Right, he continued to believe, remained marginal, and Democrats had a vague sense that they could tar Reagan with the brush of extremism. Brown's attention was elsewhere: nine months after the sit-in in Sproul Plaza, he still had to figure out how to heal the rifts left by the protests. In August Brown was on vacation in Greece, touting the merits of the California economy, and preparing for a peaceful sailing trip through the Aegean Sea with his wife, Bernice. If he was thinking of the campaign at all, he was probably thinking only about Berkeley.

Around 7 p.m. on Wednesday, August 11, 1965, a white California Highway patrolman named Lee Minkus received a tip from a motorist that a black youth was driving drunk through the streets of South Central Los Angeles. Minkus spotted the driver, Marquette Frye, and promptly placed him under arrest. It was a scorching summer evening, and residents who had been standing on porches and milling outside their homes flocked to the scene. Frye's brother Ronald, who had witnessed the arrest, ran home to tell his mother what had happened. Mrs. Frye arrived on the scene and scolded her son for drinking, when a seemingly routine arrest suddenly morphed into a major confrontation between blacks and police.

While she was haranguing him, Marquette pushed his mother away and moved toward the small crowd that had gathered around him, swearing and shouting that if the officers wanted to jail him they would have to kill him first. Soon the crowd numbered about 250, and more police came to the scene to keep the situation in hand. Their presence, however, accomplished the opposite. Residents resented the heavy police presence in their neighborhood, and when one woman spat on an officer trying to keep order, the officer waded into a sea of black faces, plucked the offender from the crowd, and placed her under arrest. Rumors now flew that police had abused a pregnant woman and that the Fryes had also been handled roughly. Riled up by rumors and by the police, residents began throwing rocks at police cruisers that were now leaving the area in an attempt to calm residents. With the police gone, rioters turned on random passers-by, stoned cars, and dragged white drivers from their cars and beat them.

At approximately 2 P.M. the next afternoon, the Los Angeles Human Relations Commission conducted a meeting at an auditorium in Athens Park, eleven blocks from the Fryes' home, to help defuse the racial tensions in the ghetto. Organizers hoped residents would talk, community leaders would listen, and everyone would agree to stay cool and not riot that night. The meeting went poorly. Reporters were out in force for the event, and as cameras rolled, angry residents launched heated complaints about Watts and other poor black ghettos. They spoke of living in run-down homes, bad public transportation, a lack of jobs in the area, and brutal police officers who stopped residents at random and abused them at will. With the crowd on fire, a youth ran to the microphone at the front of the meeting hall shouting that the time had come to go into the suburbs and attack the real enemy, the white man: "They not going to fight down here no more," the youth predicted. "You know where they going? They after the whites. . . . They going to do the white man in tonight."

Human Rights Commissioner John Buggs pleaded with local stations not to show the clips of the youth at the microphone. Producers ignored Buggs's pleas. Airwaves that night were thick with the inflammatory images, and their main effect was to ratchet up tensions in a city already rife with fear. One journalist reported that by Friday afternoon, August 13, "many normally sober-minded fathers and husbands" were flocking to sporting goods and hardware stores and buying guns, bows, arrows, knives, slingshots, and any other weapons they could find. Nightmarish visions of an all-out race war seemed a real possibility as whites hunkered down in homes and thousands of angry blacks took to the streets, smashing windows, looting groceries, overturning cars, directing sniper shots at firemen, and hurling Molotov cocktails in various directions.[1]

Several miles away, in downtown Los Angeles, William Parker, the city's chief of police, sat in his office and railed against the situation. Parker was a tough, no-nonsense officer, and he had made sure that his men were in street-fighting shape—well trained, highly disciplined, and just as militant as he about maintaining law and order in Los Angeles. But Parker had come to the realization earlier that day that the situation in the streets was not breaking his way, and the realization pained him. He knew that he had several thousand officers under his command, but that rioters now numbered in the thousands, too. He reluctantly concluded that he would have no choice but to put in a request for the National Guard.

Asking for troops, he thought, would be a simple matter. The chief would issue a formal request for the Guard and the politicians would grant his request immediately. So Parker phoned Sacramento, put in his request, and sat in his office and waited for a response from the state. Several hours passed. By afternoon, Parker was still waiting for a response, the troops were nowhere in sight, and so he concluded that the politicians, for reasons beyond his grasp, must have rejected his request. Agitated, Parker wondered how any person in a position of power could prefer to debate the pros and cons of troop deployments rather than launch a crackdown on rioters. The politicians had now left Parker in a quandary. His men were under siege, the riots continued to rage, citizens were petrified, firemen were the targets of sniper practice, stores were being looted, buildings burning, people dying, and Parker did not have many options. But as he contemplated those that did exist he also clung to a single angry thought about the men in Sacramento: They had let him down.[2]

ABOUT EIGHT HOURS EARLIER that day officials from Parker's police department had told Lieutenant Governor Glenn Anderson that the violence that had flared on Wednesday and continued into Thursday was now "rather well in hand." Anderson had arrived in Los Angeles on Thursday to survey the riots for himself. Convinced the violence had ended, he felt free to resume his duties. Under normal circumstances a lieutenant governor's comings and goings would not matter much, but circumstances on this day were anything but normal. The state's elected governor, Pat Brown, was vacationing in the Mediterranean.[3]

Lieutenant governor since 1959, Anderson had spent a total of almost a year as acting governor, filling in for Brown when the governor was away on official business. And in that time Anderson had learned how to deal with disasters of all kinds. He had inspected National Guard training sites, familiarized himself with Guard call-up procedures, and generally understood the different options open to him during floods and fires, labor strikes, and political riots. On Friday, August 13, Anderson was confident a disaster was in the making—but in Berkeley, not Watts. In recent months the UC campus had become a magnet for antiwar organizers and hotbed of student strife. Undergraduates had taken part in protest rallies, sponsored teach-ins, and marched in the streets shouting angry slogans about Lyndon Johnson and other prowar leaders. Anderson had solid sources telling him that major protests were scheduled for that Friday. Newspaper articles and administration reports warned that activists were planning to block a train that was slated to pass through Berkeley that morning, carrying men and materials on the first leg of a trip to Vietnam. A UC Regents meeting had been scheduled for that day, and Anderson wanted to attend it. Later he reflected how it made sense for him to travel to Berkeley and leave behind Watts. "I had been told at 7 o'clock [in the morning] that [the riots had been] contained, they weren't going to need the Guard," he told the commission that would later investigate the riots. "I could have stayed in Los Angeles and something could have broken out up [North] and they could have said, 'How come you weren't up in Berkeley where all this thing was going to happen and you were told so in all of the morning papers?' "[4]

Around 9:15 A.M., shortly after Anderson departed for Berkeley, new riots rocked Watts. That morning dozens of social workers and other Good Samaritans had gone into the streets and pleaded with black Angelenos to stay cool and not riot. Instead, in the sweltering early morning heat, angry mobs gathered on street corners and began cutting a path of destruction through the ghetto the likes of which Los Angeles had never known. By midday chaos engulfed the city. Gunfire was ringing out in routine and frightening intervals, and plumes of black smoke rose from several blocks.[5] By midafternoon the rioting in Watts had become so overwhelming and destructive that it had already earned a place in history as the largest domestic disturbance of the century; not since the New York City Draft riots of 1863 had such violence convulsed a United States city.

Around 11:00 that morning, with riots raging, Chief Parker had placed his fateful phone call to Pat Brown's executive secretary, Winslow Christian, and urged the administration to call out the National Guard. Christian responded tersely to Parker's request, telling the chief that Acting Governor Anderson was at a Regents' meeting in Berkeley but promising to inform the governor of Parker's request. Fifteen minutes later Christian called Anderson and explained what was happening. Anderson listened and quickly came up with several reasons not to grant Parker's request. Anderson considered himself a strong leader when it came to the issue of law and order and realized, in fact, that "the moment a sheriff or city official . . . asks for the Guard, it is my job to go in and back them up." But Anderson harbored serious doubts about the police in Los Angeles. Two hours earlier they had told him that riots were under control but now Parker was saying just the opposite. Christian argued that Brown's people had no independent information about the riots—only Parker's word that they were happening—and Anderson concluded that before deciding anything he should gather more information about events on the street. He gave Christian three executive orders: to get him on a plane to Los Angeles; to arrange for him to meet with National Guard General Roderick Hill and top advisors to Pat Brown, as well; and to arrange a meeting with Chief Parker, Mayor Sam Yorty, and black leaders in Los Angeles.[6]

These seemed three relatively straightforward, easy-to-achieve orders but aides had trouble fulfilling two of them. After hanging up Christian tried to locate and secure Pat Brown's normal plane, *The Grizzly*, only to learn the craft was being used for an errand in Northern California. Scrambling for alternate modes of transit, Christian called Richard Kline, a Brown staffer in Los Angeles, updated him on the situation, and asked that he call Parker and schedule a meeting between the chief and the acting governor.[7] At around noon, Kline called Parker. The chief took the call hoping Kline would have new information about the status of his troop request; instead Parker listened while Kline explained that Anderson was heading toward Los Angeles eager for more information about the riots. Kline asked if Parker would be willing to meet with the acting governor that afternoon.

Parker's response came fast: No. Parker deemed the notion of a meeting ludicrous—"a delaying tactic that would further jeopardize the security of the community and accomplish no useful purpose," and he was indignant.[8] He could not fathom why anyone would hold a meeting while riots were raging. No one, black or white, could negotiate with the mobs wreaking havoc in South Central Los Angeles. He told Kline as much, then snidely said that if Anderson wanted more information about the riots he should call the police command center and get a whiff of the violence that way.[9] Later Kline recalled that Parker "was obviously very agitated. We had a lack of communication and coordination on our part and the part of the Police Department of exactly what should be done. We found ourselves floundering a little bit in not being able to determine, frankly, whether we should take more of an initiative than we did or whether we should make the Police Department make the decisions."[10]

As Parker and Kline floundered, Christian tracked down a National Guard jet at McClellan Air Force base outside Sacramento. Anderson had to take a circuitous route to the airfield, but by early afternoon he was airborne, lumbering toward Los Angeles. Over the deafening roar of the jet's engines, Anderson held a hastily arranged meeting with Hill, the Guard commander, and several key Brown aides. The meeting was important, producing a snap consensus about the riots, Chief Parker, and the immediate status of the National

Guard. Aides argued that they had only a smattering of information about the riots and that Parker was a hot-blooded police chief with a penchant for hyperbole. They asserted that the rioting might not be as vicious as Parker described, warned Anderson about Parker's reputation as an intimidator, and said the massing of troops could be seen as a capitulation to Parker. Aide Sherrill Luke told Anderson not to do anything "precipitous . . . without knowing more about the situation," and Bill Becker urged Anderson to meet with black leaders before making decisions. In agreement about the loose cannon in police headquarters, Anderson instructed 2,000 troops—a fraction of the total Guard force—to assemble in armories and await further orders.[11]

Parker, meanwhile, was fuming. Infuriated by Anderson's dithering, unable to suppress the viciousness in the streets, Parker decided to take his feelings public. A clutch of news reporters had flitted in and out of his office that day, and now Parker sat in his office and went on record to denounce the riots in his city and the craven politicians in his state. Parker called streets in Watts "charcoal alleys," and complained that Anderson had failed to call the Guard. Around 4:15 he held a press conference, broadcast live on television, in which he escalated his rhetoric even more. He blamed politicians for not deploying the Guard, implied that all city residents were in danger, and warned viewers that he was thinking about asking the president of the United States to send in the Army.

In Los Angeles, Brown staffer John Billett spotted Parker on television and could not believe the words droning out of his set. Parker had just told the city that Anderson had failed to call up troops at a time of mass mayhem; he was dispensing false information and ratcheting up tensions mightily. Billett had it on good authority that the Guard had in fact been deployed—that troops would be on the streets soon. Alarmed at Parker's rant, the aide called Pat Brown's top advisor, Hale Champion, and told him that Parker was on television telling the city that Anderson had failed to deliver on Parker's troop request.

"Well, for God's sake," Champion replied, "straighten them out."[12] Billett rushed to police headquarters and in the middle of Parker's press conference announced that there had been a misunderstanding—Parker had his facts wrong about Anderson and the National Guard. The state had activated troops, Billett assured the press, and armed forces would be flooding streets in a matter of hours. Taken aback by Billett's announcements and taking umbrage at the interruption, Parker responded with a series of prickly questions aimed at Billett: "Why," Parker demanded to know, "weren't we told about this? How do you know this is so? How do I know that is true?" The exchange was rancorous, in Billett's recollection. "There was a general falling apart between him and I," Billett later told commissioners investigating the riots in Watts. "There was definitely disagreement as to what the facts were."[13]

Around this time Anderson touched down at Los Angeles International Airport. He was in the dark about the fraying of relations with Parker, did not know what exactly was happening with the riots, and still expected to meet with Parker, Yorty, and civil rights leaders. On the ground, Hale Champion was anxiously awaiting Anderson's arrival. Angry that the acting governor had subordinated his civic judgment to political advice about Parker, Champion finally spoke with Anderson by phone and told him what was happening. Riots were raging, he said, and Parker was in no mood for a meeting; Brown, he added, though still in Greece, wanted the troops deployed immediately—a course of action Champion himself supported. Trusting Champion's judgment, Anderson held an impromptu press conference at the airport and announced that he was activating the Guard.[14] With nightfall fast approaching, the riots' end still nowhere in sight, property damage rising, and many lives already lost, the state's acting governor went before the media and urged residents to remain calm, pledging the restoration of order in the near term and the triumph of the National Guard in the street fighting to come.

THOUSANDS OF MILES AWAY Pat Brown struggled to impose a measure of control on the situation, but that task proved impossible. On Thursday night Athens time Winslow Christian had called and told him that a tiny section in black Los Angeles had erupted in violence but that the rioting had been sporadic and was now contained. The next morning Brown read a brief article about the flare-up in the *Athens Daily Post*, and the article only confirmed what Christian had told him, that the riots were small and within the control of the LAPD. The next night, however, Brown received a phone call that dramatically altered his opinion. This time Hale Champion, acting as Brown's eyes and ears in Los Angeles, told the governor that the rioting had mushroomed into a horrible spasm of death and destruction. Thousands of angry blacks were in the streets, Parker's police were outmanned, and the chief had placed a formal request with the state of California for the National Guard. Champion added a few other sketchy details, explaining that Anderson was on his way to Los Angeles and Brown had better return on the first flight home.

In this initial cross-Atlantic conversation with his aide, Brown did not discuss the precise reasons for the rioting or the aims or intentions of those sowing such destruction. Instead he told Champion to take action. "You certainly call out the National Guard," Brown instructed. "I would put a curfew on, too." Brown felt he had no choice but to cut short his trip and head straight to the scene of destruction.[15]

After speaking with Champion a second time (the aide had little new to report), Brown boarded a plane for Rome. During the arduous twenty-four-hour journey home, Brown stopped in New York and Omaha, Nebraska, before finally touching down in Los Angeles. At each stop he deplaned to confer with aides via phone, discuss antiriot strategy with White House officials, and grant interviews to reporters. In his public and private utterings Brown offered a window onto his initial thinking about the riots in Los Angeles; and in those musings he made two basic points about the violence. First, he repeatedly said that the most important thing in the near term was to suppress the rioting. On this point he waxed tough; adamant, he implored aides to put as many troops on the streets as possible as soon as possible and also kept pressing them to impose a curfew on the riot zone. Second, Brown told reporters that based on the reports he was receiving, the largest city in his state had taken on the characteristics of "a war." The city was in a "state of insurrection," Brown said bluntly, adding that his top priority was to stop the rioting and make city streets safe again.[16] Shortly after arriving in Los Angeles, he bragged to a reporter, "It was my idea to call out the troops"; he then promised to restore "law and order" to the city and jail the "hoodlums" and thugs responsible for the disorders.

But for all his tough talk and bold pronouncements Brown struggled to explain the riots. He did not have a wealth of information about who had started the riots or why, but on his initial flight home he began to wonder about the forces that underlay the horrific uproar. Brown did not have a compelling answer to that question; he was baffled. As district attorney, attorney general, and governor he had spent decades in public life—and never had he experienced the kinds of disturbances and insurrections now taking place in Watts. He did not see how large chunks of the citizenry could rise up en masse and without warning revolt against the social order. He also failed to grasp why blacks were so angry. Brown of course knew that life in the ghetto was hard, but he also believed blacks in his state were much better off than those in southern citadels of segregation and the old, dilapidated cities of the American East. Blacks in Watts owned their own homes and moved about without legal constraints and generally reaped the benefits of having liberals in Sacramento who championed their plight and fought on their behalf. On his first stopover, in Rome, Brown disembarked and suggested the conundrum that would haunt him in the months to come: the riots, he told reporters, were not simply a horrible moment of mass violence but also an "unbelievable" event that was "beyond my comprehension."[17]

Brown had spent many years thinking about the problems of the cities, and believed prior to Watts that he had gone a long way toward resolving the most debilitating aspects of urban life. In March 1959, still flush with excitement over his November success, he established a state commission to investigate the nature of California's urban woes. He had written a letter to the commissioners announcing that California's population was growing at warp speed and predicting that the unprecedented influx would tax the strength of government and stretch local resources to their utmost. New migrants will "crowd our streets, overburden our transit lines, threaten a dangerous pollution of our air, create water shortages, and [lead] to new cost and complexity in local government. Numbers will lead to nightmares unless we plan our growth and meet its challenges."[18]

Six years later Brown believed he had helped stave off this apocalypse. Averting urban disaster was a major accomplishment—and a commentary, in Brown's view, on the benefits of having enlightened leaders in power in California. His administration had tackled urban woes in every possible way: by building things (miles of freeways, schools, community centers, recreational facilities, and public parks); with income transfers (welfare assistance to elderly illegal aliens, increased funding for unemployment insurance, expanded job training programs); and with treatment (drug rehabilitation centers, mental hospitals, groundbreaking programs in psychiatry).

Brown was not a sociologist-politician who spent a great deal of time poring over academic treatises about the roots and consequences of black poverty in America. Rather, armed with a gut sense of right and wrong, open to new ideas and advice, and inclined to go into cities and streets and glimpse firsthand the problems there, Brown simply had decided that he would make a point of eliminating injustice in all its forms.[19]

Brown considered nothing so unjust as the long, sordid history of racism in America. Sympathetic to African-Americans who fled the American South for the West, Brown saw his state as a place of opportunity for people of color: In its cities jobs abounded, racism was not so deeply etched in the social fabric, living conditions were a dramatic improvement over conditions elsewhere, and blacks could sit in the same restaurants, sleep in the same hotels, drink from the same water fountains as whites.

Beginning with the passage of the Rumford Act in May 1963, the administration launched a wide-ranging, aggressive antipoverty war of which it was exceedingly proud. Brown and his aides implemented affirmative action programs to bring more minorities into state government, promoted job training programs and a youth corps, and hailed California as a laboratory for social experiment and themselves as antipoverty trailblazers carving a progressive path for the rest of the nation. Hale Champion captured the fighting spirit of the antipoverty push when he bragged years later that Sacramento liberals "were famous. We were the sons of the New Frontier and the Great Society."[20] The Urban League agreed with this assessment, announcing in 1964 that it had just completed a major study of urban conditions and found that Los Angeles was far and away the best for blacks. Watts, the league and others noted, was a special forty-mile stretch shorn of the worst features of city life.

The passage of Proposition 14, in November 1964, deeply upset Democrats in Sacramento but did not alter their basic sense that race relations in Los Angeles were on the right track, poverty on the wane. That summer small riots had erupted in New York, Chicago, Birmingham, and four other big cities but Brown did not see the uprisings as danger signals for his own state. He did ask Chief Parker to travel East and talk to police officials about their handling of the riots, but Brown pointed out that riots occurred in the southern and eastern parts of the land where ill will between blacks and whites cut deep. He did not pay much attention to five straight days of protests at the Los Angeles Federal Building that March; to the rancorous exchanges between Mayor Yorty and local black activists over federal antipoverty grants; to the inflammatory CORE protests that rocked the mayor's office in June; let alone to the shortcomings of the War on Poverty and the hard, bitter feelings that ran heavy in Watts. Like many liberals, he was well meaning but out of touch.

During the 1950s more blacks migrated to California than to any other state in the union. The black population in New York more than doubled, and in Detroit it tripled, but in Los Angeles it increased by a factor of eight. When blacks had arrived en masse in the 1940s, they found well-paying jobs in aircraft plants and military shipyards, but once the fighting stopped and whites returned home, the good jobs ran dry, and unemployment in Watts skyrocketed. By 1965, in certain pockets of the ghetto, unemployment stood at a crushing 31 percent. Almost 90 percent of the homes in Watts had been built before 1949; slumlords ruled and rarely did repairs. The population density in Watts stood at 27.3 per acre as opposed to 7.4 per acre for the rest of the city, and virtually any resident with sufficient funds fled the ghetto for the much nicer middle-class suburbs in nearby Baldwin Hills and West Adams. In his 1968 book *Soul on Ice* the prison-inmate-turned-author Eldridge Cleaver captured the keen sense of despair for which Watts would soon become known: "To deride one as a 'lame' who did not know what was happening," Cleaver explained, "the 'in-crowd' of the time from L.A. would bring a cat down by saying that he had just left Watts."[21]

But perhaps Brown's greatest misjudgment about Watts before the riots was in police-black relations. Brown had mixed dealings with Parker and the Los Angeles police department, tussling with the chief and Sheriff Peter Pritchess in the early 1960s over the merits of crime prevention and drug rehabilitation. Mostly, Brown styled himself as a friend of law enforcement. In 1963 Brown refused to read a report by the United States Civil Rights Commission about California police-minority group relations. Throughout his tenure, in fact, he made frequent appearances at police conventions, touted his roots as a crime-busting district attorney, and rejected proposals to create civilian review boards to investigate charges of police brutality. Brown countered that district attorneys made better investigators, saying civilian boards would drain taxpayer dollars, create press controversies, and sour blacks on police and police on blacks.[22]

Aides echoed such arguments. After riots shook Harlem in 1964, Bill Becker, Brown's most liberal civil rights staffer, warned Brown that review boards would be "a serious proposal of the Negro community in the next period" but argued that the state would be better off creating a one-stop-serves-all complaint center, an ombudsman, than independent police review bodies. Brown and Becker did not think the Los Angeles police were taint-free but nor were they the bigots civil rights activists made them out to be. Becker, expressing Brown's view as well, wrote a constituent in 1964: "Unfortunately, many Negro people bring to the North and the West the bitter attitudes toward police which they so understandably developed when they were in the South."[23]

Nothing better reflected the administration's dismissive attitude toward the issue than the fate of a memo written in 1964 by Howard Jewel, assistant attorney general for civil rights. The year prior Jewel had read stories about noisy civil rights protests in San Francisco and decided to take stock of race relations in the state. Jewel perused black newspapers, interrogated civil rights and police officials, and laid out his findings in a remarkably prescient memo raising the specter of massive black rioting in Los Angeles. Jewel said black-white relations were mixed overall but had grown ugly and frayed in Los Angeles. The reason for the fraying? Chief Parker was one, civil rights leaders the other. "Soon the 'long, hot summer' will be upon us, the evidence from L.A. is ominous. . . . Chief Cahill of S.F. has met every effort to convince San Francisco and his own police department that the civil rights struggle is not between the demonstrators and the police, but that in fact the police department is a third and neutral force. Chief Parker, by contrast, has made it clear that the struggle is *between the police department and the demonstrators.*" Jewel assured Stanley Mosk, the state attorney general, that Parker's police force was strong enough to handle civil rights demonstrations but warned that "the true danger" lay not with protests but a massive civil uprising. "In Los Angeles, if demonstrators are joined by the Negro community at large, the policing will no longer be done by the L.A. police department but by the state militia. If violence erupts, millions in property damage may ensue, untold lives may be lost and California would have received an unsurpassed injury to her reputation."

This scenario, Jewel wrote, was not far-fetched. Parker and civil right leaders loathed one another—blacks saw in Parker a racist brute and Parker hated the blacks who attacked him in public. "One cannot contemplate the personalities and emotional makeup of the chief antagonists to the struggle without being struck by the similarities. Each is independent and strong-willed. Each regards himself as a champion of a beleaguered minority. . . . Each is determined to prevail no matter what the cost. . . . Each is currently embarked upon a course of conflict which is designed not to *avoid* violence, but to place the blame for violence upon the opposing parties. . . . Each has as his motto 'not one step backward.' "[24]

In 1964 Attorney General Stanley Mosk read this memo and forwarded it to Brown's office. Administration aides read the report as well but took "no action on it"—Brown later testified—because "it confirmed findings they already had. . . . My people didn't regard it of significant importance to pass it along to me. My staff took care of it and never showed it to me. . . . Perhaps they should have."[25]

A few days before the riots, Brown sat for an interview with the leading Greek-American paper in Greece, *Ethnos.* He told his interviewer that California was a wonderful state with a vibrant economy and model social structure. He made no mention of race relations or tensions in L.A.[26]

The riots were a political disaster for Brown. He was away for the bulk of the disorders, his Sacramento surrogate had failed to deploy the Guard in a timely fashion, and he had failed to see it coming. But in the aftermath surprisingly few foresaw the impact of the riots on Brown's political chances. No one thought the riots would help him, but Brown and others believed that they did not wreck all hopes for 1966. Watts was the first major race riot of the 1960s, and Democrats did not yet know how it would play in a campaign. Brown styled himself a clairvoyant who could glimpse future patterns and adjust himself accordingly. He believed the riots had presented him with a major opportunity: he could repair the social fabric and keep fighting poverty as a hero.

If this window of opportunity existed, Bill Parker slammed it shut quickly. Following the riots, Parker acted much more like a politician than a police chief. He focused, it seemed, on raising his public profile more than on crime sweeps and cadet classes. Appearing on television, granting frank interviews to reporters, appealing baldly to whites worried about black thugs, Parker catapulted himself into the national spotlight by taking very public positions on hot-button social issues. He spoke of disintegrating social order and spineless liberals who harbored too much sympathy for blacks and not enough for his men in blue; and he let it be known he would not sit by while civil rights leaders bad-mouthed his force and blamed him for the riots. Parker had transformed himself into an unofficial national spokesman for anyone concerned about urban looters and law and order in the cities.

Born in 1902 to a South Dakota mining family, Parker arrived in Los Angeles twenty-one years later and joined the police department four years after that. A diligent worker and devoted officer, Parker rose quickly, earning a law degree at night, passing police exams, surviving departmental purges, and becoming the chief policeman in his city in 1950. At the time of Parker's ascendance the LAPD had a well-earned reputation as a place of graft and corruption; police officers purchased promotions from station chiefs, higher-ups accepted bribes from defense attorneys. The department as a whole was much like the San Francisco district attorney's office of the 1930s—in need of new blood. At the outset of his reign Parker offered the much-needed infusion. Touting the merits of an efficient and disciplined officer corps, the chief began a far-reaching effort to combat corruption, instituting tough exams for new recruits, refusing to hire high school dropouts, encouraging men to attend college at night.[27]

But in the fifties Parker became best known for his zealous devotion to the rule of law in his city. Parker boasted a strange but simple philosophy about life in Los Angeles. He said human beings were "the most predatory of all the animal kingdom" and required "restraints" to keep them from doing bad things. Parker loved his men, was proud of his profession, and hailed both as important bulwarks against anarchy. He said officers were the people who maintained law and order in cities and protected citizens against the gusts of chaos that sometimes swirled over urban streets. He denounced social movements, fads, and ideologies for encouraging social rebellion and cultural upheaval, and adopted a Manichaean worldview that pitted police and law-abiding citizens on one side of the social divide against criminals, social workers, and political liberals cowering on the other.

In 1964 Howard Jewel had written in his memo about race riots that Parker did "not dislike Negroes because they are Negroes, but because they dislike the police department. This, in Parker's book, is the only unforgivable sin." Parker, however, did harbor a special animus toward blacks, singling them out for abuse, treating them with contempt. He dismissed civil rights protesters as purveyors of social disorder, called civil disobedience a "short step from . . . mob violence," said poor blacks were lazy, and welfare cheats were work-averse people who committed a disproportionate share of crime in America. In the fifties the LAPD as a whole held similar attitudes. Rumors had it that one Los Angeles police station hung a photograph of Eleanor Roosevelt with the words "nigger lover" scrawled across the bottom. Parker's police were known for calling their batons "nigger knockers," pulling over black motorists for no reason, and preparing themselves for inner-city patrols by invoking the mantra, "LSMFT—Let's shoot a motherfucker tonight."

Jewel was right about Parker's greatest ire being reserved for critics of the LAPD. Parker issued strident attacks on civil rights leaders, liberals, and others who dared to criticize him or his men, or to speak in glowing terms about the rights of criminal defendants. Parker dismissed criminologists, social workers, and any social program designed to transform criminals into law-abiding citizens. He called the "coddling" of criminals a waste of time, abolished police department programs aimed at keeping troubled youth off the streets, and told people who called him irresponsible that he was "a policeman, not a social worker." Parker railed against communists, too, because like criminals and civil rights activists they had made a point of undermining the social order. One time, Parker appeared at a state assembly committee hearing to testify in support of a bill that would clamp down on male prostitution on the Sunset Strip in Hollywood. Refusing to confine his testimony to the evils of the male sex trade, Parker spoke in dark terms about communists who had infiltrated the United States Supreme Court, the California Legislature, and other important civic institutions.[28] At one point his testimony grew so outlandish that Chairman of the Committee Gordon Winton rapped his gavel and scolded Parker for not sticking to the matter at hand: "Chief Parker, we are here to find out what the problem is and how this bill will solve it. And your ranting and raving about communists isn't going to help the solution."

Parker ignored Winton and launched another attack on communism. "One more outburst like that," Winton finally fumed, "and I'm going to have the sergeant-at-arms remove you from the hearing room."[29]

After the riots Parker was everywhere. He developed a scorecard on the riots divided into two basic categories, upstanding citizens and fomenters of social disorders. He called Brown and other state liberals misguided, said social programs were worse, dubbed rioters thugs, and defended policemen as God-fearing patriots who stood tall during the most vicious days of violence. Parker made many incendiary comments but his most egregious pertained to riotous masses and the black penchant for violence. He explained the riots by saying blacks had simply run amok in the same manner that animals run wild: "One person threw a rock and then, like monkeys in a zoo, others started throwing rocks." Parker pointed out that blacks made up only 16 percent of the city's population but committed approximately 60 percent of the violent crimes—a staggering figure that explained why he had so many men patrolling the ghettos. He predicted that by 1970 45 percent of Los Angeles would be black, adding, if Californians wanted to "live with that without law enforcement, God help you."[30]

Racist overtones cut thick through much of this rhetoric, but the chief's main message was that society should respect the police and maintain a strict social order. Millions of mostly white Americans agreed with this message, and in the frenetic postriot political mood Parker emerged a hero. Before 1965 was over 120,000 mostly white Americans had written the chief thanking him for his strong stand during the riots. Most public officials, one journalist reported, came away from the riots "something of a villain [but] at least one man came through with the image of a hero."

Had he lived longer Parker might have proved less likable, but in July 1966 the irascible chief suddenly dropped dead of a heart attack in the middle of a military function while Marines were standing and applauding him. Mayor Sam Yorty, a staunch Parker supporter who witnessed Parker's demise, told reporters that Parker's final act was fitting: It "was a wonderful way for Chief Parker . . . to die. He was a great chief, and he really made the L.A. Police Department into the best police department in the world." At Parker's funeral Yorty echoed his earlier praise: "God may not be dead, but his finest representative on earth has just passed away."[31]

* * *

On August 16 the *Los Angeles Times* aptly declared Watts "a holocaust of rubble and ruins not unlike the aftermath in London when the Nazis struck, or Berlin after Allied armies finished their demolition." The day before an anxious Pat Brown had swooped into the riot zone bearing little resemblance to Churchill after Berlin or Hitler after London. Instead Brown moved through the rubble like a man under siege; accompanied by fifteen cars of troops, passing signs in storefront windows that read "Blood Brother" and "Negro Blood," inside and outside the ghetto Brown suffered a series of rebukes and encountered a frightening hostility. Mayor Yorty, spotting Brown and aides at the LAPD's command center, sniffed that Brown had three "public relations men" in tow. Conservative editorialists called Brown's war on poverty a joke, left-wing columnists condemned it as too timid, and almost all commentators dwelled on the fact that Brown had been in Greece when the explosion hit. While Brown was touring the riot zone, Watts residents and National Guard troops also offered criticisms. One Guard member told a reporter that Brown was a good man but had no business being in Watts at that time. After Brown lunched with troops, Guard General Hill informed him that with gunfire erupting nearby and live electrical wires laying in the streets, Brown would have to leave the zone, the tour was too dangerous. During one particularly tense meeting in Watts, a black activist supposedly spit in the governor's face.[32]

The riots had left thirty-four dead and property damage in the millions; part of Los Angeles had been reduced to rubble; allies had suddenly become enemies, and friends, foes; and an area once thought a pillar of the administration's progressive program had become a symbol of good intentions gone bad. Brown was reeling.

At first, Brown talked tough about the evils of disorder and maintaining the rule of law in Los Angeles. He spoke of social and legislative efforts to curb riots and punish rioters, trumpeted his credentials as a former district attorney and attorney general, and paid little mind to nattering militants prattling about corrupt racist "establishments" and romanticizing rioters as revolutionaries blazing an admirable trail for blacks elsewhere. Brown found such arguments perverse. Instead he praised the LAPD and the Guard, vowed to keep troops in the streets "until they are safe," and railed against "hoodlum criminal elements" whom he fingered as responsible for the violence. Over the next several months he would also make several half-hearted attempts to ally himself with Chief Parker, stating at one point that he had "known the Chief for a long, long time" and had "always had a very high respect for his ability."[33]

If Brown had entertained the notion of siding with Parker and Parker's law-and-order supporters, he did not do so for long. Brown understood that embracing Parker meant repudiating civil rights and urban agendas—casting aside two ideological pillars on which his administration rested. Brown found Parker's talk about blacks distasteful, considered his attacks on civil rights ugly, and viewed him a huffy simpleton whose solution to urban woes was a night stick. On August 23, on national television, Brown blasted Parker, saying the chief "talked too much," made postriot statements that were "very unfortunate," and was a lightning rod who had undermined "the whole cause of race relations in Los Angeles."[34]

As a political matter, Brown did not think a break with Parker would prove costly. In 1964 a raft of commentators started interpreting the "white backlash"—a new political phenomenon that was supposed to sweep the country and wipe out liberalism in the process. That year Brown and aides looked at polling data, discussed the backlash issue, and concluded, or at least many did, that antiblack sentiments ran strong in the state but not strong enough to unseat liberal officeholders. In late July William Becker sent Brown a poll and wrote, "The attached . . . , which measures to some extent the white backlash, was done before the Harlem and Rochester riots which may, of course, change this. But it does indicate . . . that we should be careful in overestimating the backlash."[35]

In the wake of Watts, Brown remained confident. In late 1965 backlash talk blossomed into a full-blown, noisy national debate. Pundits and politicians argued loudly that whites, upset by riots, frightened by marauding dark masses, would flock to conservative law-and-order politicians preaching the virtues of police sweeps and criminal crackdowns. One Rowland Evans and Bob Novak column described well-to-do Jews in Beverly Hills and other Westside suburbs frantic with fear; black anti-Semitism had thrown whites "into such unreasoning panic that scores of families laid off Negro servants." Liberal politicians would be the next targets; Sam Yorty "has a new popularity among whites" and Ronald Reagan, another bumptious right-winger, "also rides the white backlash."

Brown dismissed the issue as media hype and described the backlash as a modest-sized beast ready to be tamed by men of good will. In late September the administration took stock of the public response to the riots; in just over a month Brown had received 5,920 letters, postcards, and telegrams about Watts. Some people praised the governor; most "correspondence was almost unanimous in deploring that the riots occurred." Many voiced "strong support" for Yorty and Parker and "law and order." Aides dismissed the writers as bigots. "A large number [of letter-writers] said they are more prejudiced since the trouble," aides told Brown, and many seemed to have mental problems. One white said he had sent $1 to the NAACP to make Brown an "Honorary Negro" member, another asked Brown for "an operating site on Mulholland Drive" to perform rain rituals, and a third attacked him for once offering Alabama Governor George Wallace advice on race issues.[36]

Brown headed into the fall of 1965 eager to tamp down the ugly racial feelings in the state and to launch a sweeping response to the ghetto violence. He saw extremists on both his left and right flanks, and believed the moment called for cool heads, rational analysis, and a modicum of calm. Brown thought himself well equipped to handle all these tasks.

At various points Brown blamed the riots on Parker's racist rhetoric, the blistering August heat, the legacy of slavery, and poor police work in the ghettos, but mostly he argued that a slew of social ills lay at the heart of what ailed Watts. Aides came away from meetings with residents chastened about conditions in the ghettos, and in memos to Brown they argued essentially that blacks were angry because conditions in their neighborhoods were rotten. "It is hard to convey the full flavor of these meetings in a summary report," Becker wrote Brown shortly after the riots. "They represent some 40 to 50 hours of listening by myself . . . and others. . . . These people reflected an almost universal *bitterness* toward the 'establishment,' both white and Negro." Residents complained of filthy stores, overpriced food, haughty shop service, a dearth of youth recreation halls, police brutality, and welfare centers located miles outside the riot area.[37]

Stamping out poverty, aides realized, would not be easy. They worried that Oakland, East Palo Alto, San Francisco's Mission District, and Hunters Point might also turn violent and that the bulk of the forty-nine federally funded government programs then in place did not provide aid to eighteen- to twenty-five-year-olds, the hard-core unemployed. "Many of these people have never worked and are not eligible for unemployment insurance payments," an aide wrote the governor a few weeks after the riots. "Most do not fit into any conventional category for welfare assistance. . . . Many of the unemployed are not employable. . . . Functional illiteracy runs high. Low skill levels are the rule. . . . [And] more than 50 per cent of the unemployed in Watts have police records."

Bringing jobs to the city was indeed a hurdle, but ultimately aides did not doubt their capacity for clearing it. They urged Brown to treat Watts "in the same manner as a natural disaster," said "a program of relief must be launched free of the usual political and administrative delays," clamored for "public service projects" offering "the most promising approach to the immediate employment problem," and warned that only "prompt intervention by government at this time could prevent [a] return to violence by frustrated minorities." Brown agreed with all points. Eager "to bring a sense of hope and relief" to the ghettos and with memories of the riots spurring him on, he launched a new round of social spending.[38]

In late 1965 administration Democrats increased welfare spending, worked to convert "gang energies to constructive purposes," helped rioters hire defense attorneys, provided residents with medical assistance, landed jobs for several hundred youth, and urged federal officials to spend more money on "areas of extreme need."[39] They viewed these projects as major steps in a broader war—one, it seemed, that was theirs for the winning. Waxing optimistic about fighting poverty, in early 1966 Winslow Christian remarked that the administration "expect[ed] to make excellent progress in such fields as protective services for children, preschool educational opportunities, very significant reductions in class size in the areas of hazard, some job development and several other areas of concern."[40] Years later, Hale Champion recalled the feelings of those days, marveling, "we were out in front. We were, in effect, telling [federal agencies] what we thought their standards ought to be. They generally trusted us to go ahead. . . . We were more liberal than the federal approach."

On December 6, the administration received what it considered a much-needed boost when the McCone Commission issued its long-awaited report on the riots. Brown had created the bipartisan commission on August 19 and had high hopes for it for many reasons. He realized the riots had national implications and that conditions in Los Angeles resembled those in other large cities; he hoped a commission run by well-respected men and competent staffers would blunt post-riot recriminations, calm public passions, and do for the riots what Earl Warren's Commission had done for Kennedy's assassination—discredit vicious rumors that communists were behind the violence.[41]

But Brown also had a powerful political agenda that he expected the commission to promote. Brown said he wanted commissioners with "the stature and integrity to remain above the political charges and counter-charges," and after naming his eight appointees he touted the body as a neutral coterie of civic-minded citizens. But the commission was his. He had appointed John McCone, a conservative former CIA director, as chairman but also tapped Warren Christopher, a close friend and advisor, to be vice chairman. Hale Champion recalled that Christopher was the administration's voice on the commission, the man who would ensure the production of a sensible report that meshed with Brown's own analysis of the riots.[42]

For two months the commission, with $250,000 in its operating budget and 16 secretaries and 26 consultants on staff, had interviewed witnesses, culled evidence, and held closed-door hearings. Drawing on testimony from Brown, Parker, Yorty, Anderson, and most of the other major players in the riots, the body published an 86-page report, "Violence in the City—An End or a Beginning?," that fit Brown's earlier instructions to the commission.[43] Brown was not happy with everything in the report (commissioners, for example, criticized the state's welfare benefits as too generous), but he got most of what he wanted. Written in a style of cool detachment from the horrors being described, the report chronicled the riots in precise detail, noting the exact time of day phone calls were made, orders issued, stores torched, blazing temperatures reached. Commissioners mildly criticized the rioters and chided Anderson for not calling up troops more quickly, but the report's silences were more conspicuous than its noises. It failed to fault liberals for raising black expectations with their utopian talk about an end to poverty (a criticism conservatives lodged against Brown) nor did it fault Parker or Yorty for antagonizing blacks with their snide remarks and fiery actions (an oft-heard criticism from the civil rights community). Commissioners argued that rioters represented a thin slice of a much larger black community, called the event itself a mindless insurrection, and embraced the analysis, popular among Brown supporters, that riots did not result from a racist, deeply flawed social order but from the same set of social ills that had caused so much consternation in the Brown camp.

The most hopeful aspect of the report as far as Brown was concerned lay in the commission's recommendations for how to heal Watts—massive social spending. Commissioners noted their shock at listening to rioters and residents describe the depth of despair in Watts, and argued that lifting that gloom would be a difficult, though not impossible, task. "The road to the improvement of the conditions of the disadvantaged Negro . . . is hard and long," commissioners wrote. But "there is no shorter route. . . . To travel the long and difficult road will require courageous leadership and determined participation by all parts of our community, but no task in our times is more important. Of what shall it avail our nation if we can place a man on the moon but cannot cure the sickness in our cities?"[44]

No sooner had the report appeared than Brown began brandishing it as a call to arms. He applauded its analysis of the riots and suggested the report supported his contention that poverty, not racism, was eating away at the ghettos and that something had to be done about that problem. "Some day," Brown predicted over the radio shortly after the report's release, "a scholar will read this report, in a generation or more, [and] he [will] say one of two things. He will say it was delivered in time and Los Angeles did something about it, or he will say we were warned and we didn't pay attention."[45] The report, Brown later gushed to John McCone, had provided society with a powerful "blueprint" for "the immediate future. . . . If we can accomplish 50% of the things you have recommended, there will be far less chance of another Watts riot. My goal is 100% and that is what I intend to achieve just as soon as possible."[46]

Yet if Brown hoped to use the report as a personal endorsement, its release did nothing of the sort. Instead it fanned the prevailing political winds, which in December 1965 were blowing down a growing ideological canyon between conservative law-and-order politicians and civil rights activists. The report drew criticisms from the likes of Parker, Yorty, and sundry other supporters of law and order. It was even more condemned by the Left. In past years black activists, liberal academics, and civil rights leaders would have been allies of Brown and likely supported whatever race initiative was on the administration's agenda. But not in late 1965. Many one-time liberal allies broke openly with the governor over the report, denouncing it and the commission as craven political products that failed to address the key issues in the rioting. Critics assailed the report as a much-too-timid document that glossed over underlying causes and accused Brown of giving the commission a meager 100 days to complete its work—a time frame, critics huffed, that precluded a "deep and probing" analysis. Critics said commissioners failed to grasp the nature of racism in America and the scope of police brutality in Los Angeles. Harvard political scientist Robert Fogelson dismissed commissioners as "California's establishment" and depicted riots not as irrational acts of violence but "articulate protests against genuine grievances in the Negro ghettos." The report's recommendations also drew fire. The U.S. Commission on Civil Rights criticized commissioners who "prescribe aspirin where surgery is required." Civil rights activist Bayard Rustin noted commission solutions "boil[ed] down to voluntary actions by business and labor, new public-relations campaigns for municipal agencies, and information-gathering. . . . Like the liberal consensus which it embodies and reflects, the commission's imagination and political intelligence appear paralyzed by the hard facts of Negro deprivation it has unearthed, and it lacks the political will to demand that the vast resources of contemporary America be used to build a genuinely great society."[47]

Brown believed that if anything he was going out on a political limb by giving such vocal support to social spending programs, and he downplayed left-wing broadsides about his timidity and pressed full speed ahead with his social spending agenda. In late 1965 he continued to argue that government—through job training programs, public work projects, and one-stop service centers—was the best solution to the problems in Watts. Indeed, new service centers offered classes teaching such skills as typing, upholstery, and television and auto repair, and social workers offered people services from welfare and legal advice to job referrals and tips on money handling. Brown urged the White House to adopt a crash program to give blacks jobs, writing to Senator Murphy, "We have identified some 50,000 potential jobs, socially useful jobs that could be filled immediately under such a program."[48]

But by early 1966 Brown's antipoverty efforts had failed to dramatically alter conditions in Watts. Brown was not single-handedly going to bring about a revolution in the ghettos, not, at least, the kind of revolution he envisioned—and certainly not in the span of a few months. In 1966 a prominent black lawyer in Los Angeles told White House aide Marvin Watson the obvious, that "the basic condition of the Negro in that part of Los Angeles . . . is fundamentally unchanged since the riots."[49]

On March 15, 1966, in an airplane over Grand Junction, Colorado, airline pilots informed Brown and his staff that they had reports of new rioting in Watts. Aides asked TWA to reroute Brown's flight, pilots did so, and Brown was soon on the ground relieved to learn that the rioting had been contained. These riots had had about 600 participants and produced two deaths, a distant number from the thirty-four killed during the earlier upheavals. Police had little trouble restoring order—they did so in a matter of hours—and Brown declared soon after touchdown that "everything is well under control."

But the *San Francisco Chronicle* suggested all was not well with Brown's political prospects. The paper reported that one white man had died "as he battered on doorways trying to get away from a Negro mob" and that "Negroes" were "rampaging through the streets . . . shooting, stabbing, and throwing bricks and bottles." Rioters had worn yellow T-shirts with pictures of the recently slain Malcolm X emblazoned on the front, and other shirts proclaimed, "Participant, first annual Los Angeles riot." Nationwide polls showed that the riots had replaced the war in Vietnam as the top political concern of voters. Years later Hale Champion recalled his concern that the riots had turned next year's election into a "whole new ball game."[50]

EIGHT

# THE GEORGE WALLACE OF CALIFORNIA

PAT BROWN very nearly decided not to seek a third term. The political situation in the state in early 1966, he confided to Vice President Hubert Humphrey, was a mess. Both parties were divided and he was under attack from both sides within the Democratic party. Republicans, he told Humphrey, were using social issues "more viciously than at any time in my career, and there are a whole slew of them who slug at me every hour on the hour."

Brown's wife, Bernice, begged him to retire from politics and spend more time with his family. Worried that Brown's heart might give out, Bernice told Brown's aides that the governor might even have trouble surviving a third term, saying, "You guys are really talking about shortening his life." Brown was certainly showing signs of fatigue and flagging interest in his job. When he first arrived in Sacramento, he routinely called aides at 5 A.M., waking them because he was preoccupied with a political matter. Aides would then rush over for breakfast at the mansion to discuss the legislative agenda or other pressing problems; before they were finished, the governor would have received a half dozen calls from people who knew the early morning was a good time to reach him.[1] Understandably, after eight years of this pace, Brown was worn down and had lost some of his earlier zest for the job.

But for all the reasons to step aside, there were others pushing Brown into the race. Brown was eager to match Earl Warren in both deeds and longevity, and Warren had the distinction of being the only governor in the century to serve more than two terms. It was not uncommon for aides to debate who was the greater governor, and Brown realized that he would forever stand in Warren's shadow without another four years in office. Aides also urged Brown to take the plunge, telling him that he was the only hope for November. And Brown, finally, was determined to hold his party together and fend off the newly vocal radical Left and the newly powerful Right. In early 1966, the California Democratic party was in crisis. It is difficult to convey the sense of the angry recriminations and bitter feelings that were sweeping the state. In December 1964, students at Berkeley had bolted the party, leading a mutiny on the Left; now, the signs of a larger upheaval had begun to appear. Many civil rights activists and a small but vocal number of intellectuals were beginning to attack Brown for failing to eliminate poverty, his stand on the riots, and distancing himself from their critique that the entire social order was racist. The final defection on his political left came when the California Democratic Council (CDC), the most veteran liberal ally of the governor and a great symbol of Democratic strength in California, broke with Brown over his handling of the burgeoning war in Southeast Asia. A dramatic blow to the governor, the CDC defection helped pave the way for what would prove to be a crippling primary challenge from a politician firmly to Pat Brown's right.

The CDC, established in 1953 to revitalize the Democratic party, had played a pivotal role in Brown's rise. It had endorsed him for governor in 1958 and 1962, and over the years thousands of members had campaigned for Democrats in precincts around the state, handing out literature, attending rallies, writing newspaper editorials. Though the group often staked out positions to the left of the governor on such issues as recognition of Red China and loyalty oaths, most CDC members were middle-class liberals who supported an activist government and considered Brown an ally and a leading progressive.

Brown saw the CDC in a similar light. He had worked with the group to pass fair housing and other liberal legislation, and together they had helped maintain a strong Democratic party in California. Brown was not reticent about showing his support for the liberal group: he attended CDC conventions and delivered rousing keynote speeches that praised the group as the vanguard of the progressive movement. In January 1960, aide Fred Dutton expressed his faith in the alliance, telling one of Brown's speechwriters that he should pen for the governor a CDC convention speech that was thick with the emotion of liberalism. "I have always felt this can best be accomplished with the CDC through mentioning a few magic words," Dutton told his colleague. "Just offhand, I would imagine that the primary magic words that come quick and hard in the speech are Stevenson; civil rights; Poplarville, Mississippi; Nixon; sacrifice; India; people in need in the world; dangers of atomic testing; loyalty oaths at the University, etc., etc."[2]

Yet by 1965, the CDC had lost many members since its heyday in the 1950s, and it found itself competing with a number of single-issue, left-wing social action groups, including the Congress of Racial Equality (CORE), the NAACP, the Free Speech Movement, the Vietnam

Day Committee (VDC) in Berkeley, and the United Farm Workers in the Central Valley. The CDC also stood as an object lesson in the problems of success. In the 1950s, the group attained the goals it had set for itself, breaking down barriers for Democratic candidates, installing Democrats in high office, infusing California with the fighting spirit of Adlai Stevenson liberalism; by 1960 it was unclear how the group was to stay strong in an age of Democratic dominance. In 1960, CDC President Tom Carvey captured the dilemma, writing colleagues that the CDC would have to place less emphasis on campaigns, elections, and preprimary endorsements and more on a select set of liberal social issues. The CDC had responded, to some extent, to Carvey's exhortation, setting up conferences to hash out positions on issues and taking up arms in the struggle for civil rights. But the campaign had produced mixed results, and in 1965, though it remained the state's great symbol of Democratic prowess, the CDC was in need of fresh faces and new liberal blood.[3]

In 1965, the governor supported Simon Casady, a liberal newspaper editor from San Diego, for CDC president. An outspoken advocate of civil rights, Casady seemed like a solid choice for the position, but turned out to be an embarrassingly fierce opponent of the Vietnam War. He saw in the conflict a dark, arrogant strain of American liberalism, considering it a reckless, immoral endeavor. Touring the state in his private plane, Casady spoke early and often against American intervention in Asia. He ridiculed President Johnson, encouraged young men to burn their draft cards, established ties to other burgeoning antiwar groups, and attacked Brown for refusing to break with American foreign policy in Asia. As governor, Brown had little influence on American foreign policy and absolutely nothing to do with the military action in Southeast Asia. Privately, he harbored doubts about the wisdom of the war. But Brown was the most important Democrat in California, a strong supporter of Lyndon Johnson, and a symbol of American liberalism; he saw no alternative but to support the war, and his position cost him.

One day Brown and Alan Cranston, a CDC founder, encountered the fifty-seven-year-old Casady at a fund-raiser at the Fairmont Hotel in San Francisco's Nob Hill. After dinner, Brown pulled Casady aside and said, "I understand you're doing a great job, Si, but I think you ought to soft-pedal that Vietnam business a little." Cranston appeared next to the two men and seconded Brown's opinion: "It might be a good idea if you stuck to state issues, Si—like smog. Or saving the redwoods."[4]

But Casady was an impassioned critic of the war, and he refused to be muzzled. Instead of toning down his attacks, he stepped them up, deriding LBJ as a "cowboy who shoots from the hip and not a very good cowboy at that." Again Brown tried to silence him, calling him from Sacramento and saying, "Si, I've been back in Washington and the President is very disturbed about what you're saying about Vietnam." The governor suggested that Casady go to Washington, where he could receive a briefing on the war effort. "If you come back and still have the same opinions, well, that's fine," Brown promised.[5]

Casady went to Washington and came away from his briefing more disillusioned than ever. Lyndon Johnson's cronies, the CDC president complained, had told him Johnson was in Vietnam because, in Casady's angry words, he didn't "want to see the white world which we've built up since the Reformation besieged by the rest of the world in the next ten or twenty years." More defiant than ever, Casady returned home and back to his antiwar tirades. At a function in Petaluma, someone told Casady his attacks on Brown had damaged the governor. "Governors come, and governors go," Casady replied.

The next day Casady received a call from the governor.

"How are you, Si?"

"Fine. How are you?"

"Fine. Did you get my letter?"

"No. What letter?"

"I asked you to resign as president of CDC."

"Oh. What's the problem?"

"Si, I just don't think you should be saying the things you're saying about Vietnam, criticizing the President and criticizing me, while you're still president of the CDC. You have a right to your own opinion. But you occupy an official position within the party, just like I do. We can't always say the things we feel like saying. And Si?"

"Yes, Governor."

"I hope this won't interfere with our friendship."[6]

As word spread, members of Berkeley's Vietnam Day Committee got in a car and drove to Sacramento to protest the governor's action; demonstrators held aloft placards that read *Upside Down with Brown* and *LBJ—Governor of California.* Over the next months, the battle between Brown and the antiwar forces grew increasingly rancorous. Once enthusiastic supporters, the CDC and other antiwar Democrats now dismissed the governor as a liberal lackey kowtowing to Washington's warmongers. Brown made several attempts to quell the uprising, but to no avail. Liberal-minded groups and factions that he normally relied on for political support abandoned him in droves. A furious Casaday refused to step down.

In February 1966, at the CDC convention in Bakersfield, Brown maneuvered to oust Casady from office and install a more sympathetic person in his place. Brown delivered an angry speech on LBJ's behalf, and left with Bernice beside him as members booed him and then nearly blocked the police car that whisked him to safety. The next day he spoke again, urging delegates to sack their organization's president. Speaking directly to Casady, the governor said, "When you treat the President with contempt, me with contempt, the congressmen with contempt, you have forfeited the right to lead a Democratic organization." Brown's pressure succeeded: The CDC voted 1,001 to 859 in favor of Gerald Hill, Brown's candidate. But the victory was pyrrhic. The controversy had crippled Brown's support from the one constituency on which he should have had a lock.

Ironically, little had changed. Hill, like his predecessor, toed the antiwar CDC line, and immediately declared that his election did not change the group's opposition to the war in Vietnam. A reporter mentioned to Brown that Hill seemed "more liberal than Casady."

"He may be more liberal," Brown said, "but I think he'll be more discreet."[7]

WHILE BROWN WORKED to contain his left-wing base, he faced an even bigger challenge from the right. It began with a very personal feud with the Speaker of the California Assembly, Jesse Unruh. "Big Daddy," as reporters called Unruh, liked whiskey, women, and power, and in Sacramento in the early 1960s he had all three. Three hundred fifty pounds with jowly cheeks that made him look more like a professional wrestler than a legislative titan, Unruh had transformed the state assembly into a locus of political power, building up a sizable slush fund, providing assemblymen with campaign funds in exchange for political support, and hiring a full-time staff that allowed members to research issues, cull information, and operate more freely of the governor. The son of a Texas sharecropper, Unruh grew up so poor he had slept in a chicken coop, and became well known in California for his slovenly appearance (throughout the 1950s he persisted in wearing sandals, his feet unwashed and grimy), his legislative brilliance, and his political prowess.[8]

Relations between Unruh and Brown had never been good. His eye always on the governor's office, Unruh moved quickly to solidify his power in the legislature, winning appointment in 1959 as chairman of the powerful Ways and Means Committee, the gateway for all appropriations bills. Unruh was not particularly ideological; he was interested mainly in power. Surrounding himself with a tight-knit clique of freshmen Democrats, a group that in time would come to be known as the Speaker's Praetorian Guard, Unruh shepherded most of the governor's program through the legislature with skill and rapidity. "Jesse made his reputation on my program," Brown said of that first legislative session, "and I made mine on the way he handled it. . . . I would never have achieved what I did, particularly in the 1959 session, had it not been for the tremendous ability and help of Jesse Unruh."

Brown considered Unruh "a rising young politician and a damned good legislator," appreciated his deft help on the budget, and rewarded him by convincing Speaker Ralph Brown to accept an appointment to the Court of Appeals and make way for Unruh. But he soon discovered he had made "an awful mistake."[9]

On a personal level, the nonconfrontational Brown clashed with the behemoth Speaker. Politically, Unruh was disappointed that the governor refused to reduce the size of the bloated civil service, and criticized the executive branch for buying too many children's schoolbooks and then building bonfires to burn the unused texts. Unruh usually took positions that were to the right of Brown, and resented Brown's close ties to the CDC, which Unruh considered a bunch of do-gooders eager to undermine his power.

Brown, for his part, disliked Unruh's expansion of the assembly staff—he thought it created a rival to the executive branch that would result in "a stalemate because you've got two groups of experts"—and thought the Speaker's casual, contemptuous attitude toward him outrageous.[10]

In 1962, Unruh supported Brown for governor under the mistaken assumption that he would have Brown's endorsement for the same in 1966. When it became apparent that he would not have it, relations between the two became so frayed that Brown thought Unruh "simply was out to destroy him."[11]

By 1964 the rivalry had spilled into the open. The Speaker began telling reporters that he'd "be lying if I told you I hadn't thought of being governor," and he began working behind the scenes to line up support for a gubernatorial run. "I want your support in 1966 for governor," he told Pierre Salinger that year.

"You mean, if Pat doesn't run?" Salinger asked.

"No, no, I want your support for governor."[12]

Determined to revive his chances for 1966, Unruh underwent a remarkable personal transformation, embarking on a crash diet and cutting out wine and women. It was necessary, he realized, if he wanted to become governor. "I think he decided," his top assistant, Larry Margolis, explained, "'I'm just goddamn fed up with being fat and ripping my clothes and having to grunt to get into the seat of my car.'" In four months he lost ninety pounds, limiting himself to one meal—"never . . . more than a steak and a salad or a hamburger and a salad or meat and a salad without dressing"—a day. Sometimes he ate only one meal every other day. He gave up cigars and decided to forgo his beloved scotches and martinis.[13]

The discipline was the forced product of a boundless love for power. One evening Assemblyman Gordon Winton and Unruh sat in Frank Fats, a local Chinese restaurant that was one of Unruh's favorite haunts, eating and drinking. "I think I'll run for governor, Jess," Winton needled his colleague. "What do you want to be when I'm governor?"

"President," Unruh responded.[14]

Margolis urged his boss to oppose Brown in the primary. The Democrats were splintering, and something dramatic needed to happen for the party to regain the initiative. You can beat him, Margolis said. The bureaucracy was out of control, with examples of waste or corruption everywhere, and Brown was to blame. Margolis had the unusual foresight to realize that Reagan was a strong candidate, difficult to beat; only Unruh could play the role of giant killer. "The other reason I wanted him to run, apart from the giant killer potential, was that Jesse had momentum at that time," Margolis recalled; he believed in momentum. Just after the 1964 elections, in December, Unruh's people gathered in Palm Springs to discuss his gubernatorial campaign. They all hoped Brown would step aside, thinking that if he ran he'd lose and that it was Unruh's turn to get a crack at the governorship.

It wasn't. Unruh's marriage was falling apart, and his children were having problems. Unruh felt like he'd failed them, and he worried that news of his philandering would seep out. He complained that his head was not "screwed on right" for the mission, and he knew the chances of defeating Brown were slim.[15]

Above all else, Jesse Unruh was not a man to embark on fanciful crusades. He was not afraid of dirtying his hands, should it come to that with Brown. But why bother, if someone else would do it for him? Don Bradley, Brown's campaign manager, told Roger Kent, the former California Democratic party chairman, that Unruh was behind a challenge by Los Angeles Mayor Sam Yorty. The governor complained that Unruh would stop at nothing to deprive him of a third term. Kent concluded that Unruh was hoping Yorty would "get in the race in the primary and break Brown's leg in a primary race." Afterward, perhaps Unruh would step into the void created by Brown's departure.[16]

EVEN MORE OMINOUS than Brown's rift with Unruh was the growing rift between Brown and the two most powerful men in Los Angeles: Yorty and William Parker. It was this rivalry, more than Vietnam, that would rip the Democratic party apart. The Democratic infighting of the sixties is often described as a split between liberals and leftists; but the divisions were both more complex and more damaging than that. Brown endured an equally potent, and in many ways more popular assault, from the Right. Men like Yorty and Parker—even Unruh—challenged Brown on the issue of law and order that would also be instrumental in Reagan's rise.

In the grand progressive tradition, Brown was a reformer, with a deep-seated and very genuine hatred of racism and a powerful desire to do whatever he could to improve the lives of blacks in his state. To Brown then, the us/them mentality that Yorty and Parker thrived on and the white backlash it engendered were not just grating but potentially dangerous. But both men were immensely popular—more so, even, than Brown and his staff would ever realize. Brown stepped into a brawl with battle-scarred bruisers. It was a scrap that, win or lose, would cost him.

In the wake of the Watts riots, the same day Brown first blasted Parker, Sam Yorty offered a heated defense of the LAPD, stepping quickly to the side of his increasingly popular friend. On August 28 Yorty wrote the L.A. district attorney that "the 'big lie' technique has long been used in the area to label all police 'brutes.' Communists, fellow-travelers, and demagogues have drummed the charge of 'police brutality' into the ears of the people of the area, deliberately fomenting antagonism to law enforcement officers, inciting the residents to resent and resist officers in the proper professional performance of their always difficult and often dangerous duty." It is not the blacks who have suffered innuendo and unfair treatment, the mayor argued, but the police. They have "had their rights, authority, and powers curtailed and made extremely complex by a series of very technical decisions of the courts expanding the rights and defenses of persons accused of crimes. In the meantime, the crime rate soars. . . . In the face of the foregoing it is not easy to sustain police morale; to give them the desire and the courage to continue to do their job—a job upon which the whole fabric of our society is dependent."

Yorty, like Parker, held a simplistic view of events in Watts. The California Highway Patrol, he believed, had botched the initial arrests. They had "fooled around . . . if they had taken the suspect and gotten out of the area . . . it wouldn't have happened. . . . There's no doubt there were conditions there, particularly the unemployment and all that sort of thing, and agitators, that were going on . . . but because you're out of a job doesn't mean you have to riot." The housing was not as bad as some would have blacks believe—"agitators" had been required to fan the flames at crucial moments, and African-Americans in L.A. had been watching too much news of late, especially all the nasty footage of black protests and police attacks on the protesters in the South. It "got the Negro people all upset and tense," Yorty told an interviewer. "Irresponsible" liberals were also to blame.

As Yorty saw it, Bobby Kennedy and Sargent Shriver, two of the leading exponents of the War on Poverty in Washington, had made promises to the black community that they had no intention of keeping. Brown had encouraged inflammatory sit-ins and marches. Yorty also faulted the governor for being on vacation in Europe during the worst of Watts, criticized him for attacks on Chief Parker, and chastised Lieutenant Governor Anderson for wanting "to confer with the black ministers before he called out the National Guard."[17]

Yorty, unlike many of his southern counterparts, was not an out-and-out racist. Though blacks had come to revile the mayor for his outspoken defense of Parker and unremitting hostility toward civil rights demonstrations, Yorty felt that he had often spearheaded the attack on segregation in California. As he explained it to the McCone Commission, when he entered office, the fire department was segregated, and Yorty had single-handedly integrated it with a "Look, Chief, time's up. Either everybody eats together or we abolish the mess." Yorty pointed to a series of (minor) accomplishments in the field of civil rights. "I put a Negro on the fire commission. I also gave control of the police commission to minorities. I left Mike Cohn on. I added an attorney. . . . I did this with quite a few commissions, including my staff," the mayor boasted. "And I was determined to make this a model city from the standpoint of race relations. . . . And I felt that it was successful. And I still think that Los Angeles basically has very good race relations." Yorty said he even tried to "correct the nomenclature" of the LAPD, implementing programs to teach officers not to say things that blacks might find offensive. Had he been successful? In his mind, he had bent over backwards, but had been rewarded only with abuse.[18]

Samuel Yorty's harsh words received a surprisingly positive response from the public. Emboldened, the maverick Democrat took his next big step in March 1966 and challenged the incumbent governor in the Democratic primary. Vitriolic and irascible, Yorty seemed an unlikely gubernatorial candidate. In many ways, he was the George Wallace of California politics, an acid-tongued conservative Democrat notorious for his scalding attacks on liberal elites. The most reviled Democrat in the state, the mayor, as one biographer admitted in 1966, "arouses strong feelings. Many love him. Some detest him. Few are neutral." Will Rogers used to say that he never met a man he didn't like, to which Senator Fred Harris of Oklahoma quipped, "I met my fellow Oklahoman Will Rogers, and I'm sure of one thing, that he never met Sam Yorty."[19]

To most Democrats, then, the mayor's campaign resembled nothing so much as a hoax, another in a long line of fanciful crusades against more powerful foes. Prone to overblown rhetoric and angry tirades, always running for one office or another, Yorty was a loser—an annoying nuisance but not a serious challenge to Pat Brown.

Yorty, more brawler than politician, got his start in politics in the spring of 1933, when he attended a banquet of the Municipal Light and Power Defense League in Los Angeles and made an impressive speech to local leaders on behalf of Chas Dempster, a mayoral candidate. "It still seems a fairytale dream," Yorty wrote his father a few days after the speech. "The room was all in orange and beautifully decorated." Yorty spoke last. Nervous, the twenty-four-year-old upstart was sure that if he performed poorly he was "done for." But he gave a rousing peroration that brought invitations from other candidates to speak on their behalf. "I'm going to be careful who I speak for," Yorty explained to his father, "because I am going to be running before many years and I don't want to make any mistakes. . . . I would rather give a speech than eat."[20]

His prediction came true. A native Nebraskan devoted to the famed Democratic orator William Jennings Bryan and President Woodrow Wilson and an outspoken champion of the working class and underdogs everywhere, Yorty won an assembly seat in the California legislature in 1936, where he quickly established himself as an avid New Dealer working on behalf of the working-class poor.

A mustachioed five feet, nine inches, 155 pounds, Yorty was from the start a scrapper. (Later commentators would note that he "seems to take pleasure in playing the underdog even when he knows that he is top dog.") Yorty thought he had been sent to Sacramento to fight for the little guy, the voiceless man on the street who wanted a fair shake in life. He aligned himself with the motley collection of socialists, left-wingers, and reformists in California at the time. As his first reelection campaign approached, Yorty had secured a reputation as a "wild-eyed," violently pro-union and antipoverty liberal. Shortly before his 1938 reelection, a front-page article in the *Los Angeles Times* linked Yorty and other top Democrats to the Communist party.

"I felt sick, disgusted, and angry," Yorty said after seeing the headline. Yorty believed that the accusations, which had been released by HUAC, were part of a plot against him that came from HUAC's Republicans, who in turn, he thought, must have been supplied with their information by the reds. After meeting with Democrats, however, the always-suspicious Yorty concluded that the real culprits were his colleagues: "All manner of lies were concocted and spewed out at Democratic party meetings. . . . People who had been friendly suddenly quit speaking. I could practically identify the Communists and their cohorts by the change in attitudes. The campaign against me was virulent and vicious. It was calculated to destroy me and drive me out of the Democratic Party."

By the start of World War II in 1939, Yorty had completely soured on the Left. He began accusing local fishermen of spying for the Japanese but refused to say where he got his information. "We must awaken to the threat," the assemblyman said. Though his views increasingly diverged from those of the Democratic mainstream, Yorty never seriously considered switching parties. A life-long Democrat, the maverick mayor believed all citizens had a duty to support the best candidates and not necessarily toe the party line. By offering a dissenting view, Yorty felt he was helping a party that stressed—but increasingly failed to achieve—unity over consistency.[21]

Yorty thought that he could most benefit the party by working from the outside to purge it of reds. Convinced that they were seizing control of the State Relief Administration, Yorty broke with his longtime liberal ally, Governor Culbert Olson, and shepherded a bill through the legislature establishing a committee to hold hearings on communist infiltration in California. Serving as committee chairman, Yorty exploded in rage and frustration at uncooperative witnesses. "Communists are rats!" he cried during a hearing, "a bunch of rats!" Spectators booed loudly, and the scene degenerated; eventually police had to clear the auditorium and restore order.[22]

In his committee report to the legislature, Yorty warned of an impending communist takeover of the state and displayed his penchant for bare-knuckles politics. "These traitors probably do not have the power to accomplish this objective without outside assistance," Yorty wrote. "But they are preparing to strike whenever we face a crisis of sufficient gravity to weaken our resistance. As part of our national defense we must stop them before they are able to attain sufficient strength." Yorty, as one California Democrat remembered, "kept a constant campaign plank almost geared to be on the alert against any kind of communist infiltration."[23]

By the 1960s, Yorty was firmly established on the right edge of his party. Never one for restraint, Yorty complained that the CDC was "wired, packed, rigged, and stacked" and published a scathing pamphlet, "I Cannot Take Kennedy," in which he accused the Kennedys of trying to buy the presidential election and wrecking the Democratic party. He concluded by admitting that he was a pariah within his own party, but that he would continue fighting for what was right. "In California today," Yorty wrote, "the position of a militant anti-Communist in the Democratic party is an uncomfortable one. Most of the leaders are anti-Communist but they are in many cases either naive or too cowardly to do anything more than merely talk about the evils of Communism while contending that the threat is greatly overrated—a theme the Communists foster and love to hear repeated."[24]

For all his incendiary statements Yorty was an adroit campaigner. He railed against large, wealthy, powerful institutions, often coming across as a heroic struggler ready to defend the people's interests from sinister outside forces. In 1961, Yorty ran for mayor of Los Angeles and won. Waging a crusade against the "downtown interests" and the *Los Angeles Times*, which he accused of using its financial and media clout to control the city, Yorty tapped into a latent dissatisfaction with urban life. He attacked everything from inefficient garbage collection to smog, traffic, and property taxes. Backed by George Putnam, an inflammatory local right-wing television commentator, and aided by intelligent managers who made him shave his mustache for TV, Yorty had broad appeal, putting together a powerful coalition of blacks and lower-middle-class whites in the San Fernando Valley and other suburbs, and defeating the two-term incumbent Norris Poulson.

As mayor, Yorty earned the everlasting enmity of Pat Brown. Resentful of the growing power of the administration in Sacramento, Yorty repeatedly refused to support the governor. In 1962, when Brown ran against Nixon, Yorty issued two demands in exchange for an endorsement. "Yorty has two basic projects on which will depend whether he endorses you for reelection, repudiates you, or maintains strict neutrality," an aide told the governor that January. Yorty wanted a senate reapportionment plan more favorable to Los Angeles and more money for L.A. rapid transit. Only full compliance, the aide wrote, would result in an endorsement.[25]

Brown's aides urged that he comply with Yorty's wishes, but there is no evidence that Brown did so. In the end the mayor remained neutral in the campaign. Brown aide Paul Ward complained to a colleague after the election, "Since you are in charge of metropolitan problems, and since Mayor Yorty is no longer my special campaign problem, perhaps you should keep this file for further reference. The material in this file is so deeply embedded in my poor mind that I shall never forget it anyway."[26]

Yorty's grievances against the governor were equally embedded in his own unforgiving mind. For instance, in 1954 Brown, in his attorney general race, had solicited support from the GOP and "ran out on the rest of us on the Democratic ticket." Yorty eyed Brown with contempt for switching parties during the New Deal. Yorty had served in the military and survived the jungles of Guam during World War II; Brown had stayed home and ran for district attorney. "I always resented the fact that he got his start in politics while the rest of us . . . went into military service," Yorty recalled.[27]

In turn, Brown thought Yorty's military service a mere publicity stunt, his tough talk about the Vietnam War ridiculous: Knock out Haiphong harbor, the veteran-mayor urged. Step up the bombing campaign. Lift the restrictions on the fighting. "No President," he told the president, "has [the] right" to send American boys with one hand tied behind their backs. "If you're sending them out there and you're asking them to risk their lives, we have an obligation to back them up. This country has got to back them up. But when people tell you don't escalate, what they're saying is 'Let the boys risk their lives, but let's don't do anything to risk ours.' I think that's cowardly. I think you should change it and take some of these restrictions off and win this war, wind it up." To Brown, LBJ, and like-minded Democrats, Yorty's opinion was as uninformed as it was unwelcome. "I went to Vietnam and I studied the situation," Yorty protested.[28]

Practical differences, however, outweighed the theoretical divide. In 1956 Brown had supported Yorty's primary opponent and later had refused to invite Yorty to the Democratic National Convention. Resentment built on resentment and enmity between the two political powers deepened. As Brown tersely remarked in late 1965, "I have not had a friendly relationship [with the Mayor]. I wouldn't say it was unfriendly, but there has never been that close relationship that exists between the Chief and myself."[29]

In 1964 Yorty continued to hammer on the governor, accusing him of running "a bad Tammany Hall type of political machine and . . . a sordid kind of power politics" and of wanting "to be Vice President."

"If I've tried to establish a political machine," Brown replied that year, "I've been very unsuccessful." When the *Los Angeles Times* reported that Brown had tried to make peace with Yorty, one of the governor's supporters captured the Democratic consensus on Yorty when he sniffed, "What has this noisy little man done to deserve such political recognition?" He then called Yorty a "shameless apostate" who "throughout his spotty political career . . . has been consistent in only one thing, the smearing of . . . others in political life, especially if they are Democrats."[30]

The mayor responded with a press conference in Sacramento in which he accused the governor of political cronyism and knuckling under to interest groups lobbying to keep Percodan, a dangerous painkiller, available over the counter. In 1965 Brown responded to Yorty's sniping by trying to end the mayor's political career once and for all. In Yorty's reelection campaign, Brown threw his support to James Roosevelt, a moderate liberal congressman, the eldest son of Franklin and Eleanor, and Yorty's toughest opponent.

It was then that Yorty first started making noises about a gubernatorial bid. In September he announced at a news conference that several Brown supporters had soured on the governor and had asked him to seek the Democratic nomination. "There is quite a defection, yes, within the Democratic party, from Brown, and many of his former supporters are trying to get me to run," the mayor said. Yorty predicted that Brown would be vulnerable in next year's election and attacked Reagan as a right-wing actor who read from a script. "I must say in all truthfulness," he said, "that I never feel sure whether he's acting out a part, or whether he really says these things himself. . . . I always wonder if he's got a script writer, and he's playing on the stage."[31]

Yorty's victory for mayor had put him in a position to challenge Brown for the nomination in 1966, and he decided once and for all in March of that year—a mere three months before the primary election—to seek the Democratic nomination for governor. Motivated only partly by personal animus and the years of bickering, Yorty also had serious political differences with the governor. Seeing Brown as soft on crime, riots, welfare cheats, and protesters, Yorty offered a vision of government markedly different from that of the incumbent.

By 1965, Yorty had abandoned his earlier liberalism in favor of a conservative, law-and-order approach to race, crime, and social upheaval. Resentful of federal social programs that threatened his power and empowered black activists, Yorty began wrangling with Sargent Shriver over the composition of Community Action Boards and the distribution of federal funds. Yorty also dismissed talk of rehabilitation, criticized judges for expanding the rights of criminals, and sided resolutely with the man he had once resolved to "school," Chief of Police William Parker. As Tom Bradley, the future mayor and a Yorty critic, recalled, "from that point on, anything that Parker wanted, he got."[32] When President Johnson failed to appoint Parker to the President's Commission on Crime, Yorty lashed out at the administration. "To me it is disgusting. If I am classified as a friend of the administration, it would be nice to have at least the courtesy of minor consultation about matters affecting my city, including confusing W.O.P. [War on Poverty] directives. These have not only caused me to be embroiled in unnecessary controversy, but have deliberately fostered racial problems which we have not previously experienced."[33]

Soon the mayor had become a frequent target of civil-rights protests and, in the eyes of many, a symbol of segregation. Yorty's handling of the riots only deepened the picture in the black community of a callous reactionary hostile to minority concerns. Opponents blasted him for traveling to San Francisco during the initial outbreak and accused him of depriving minorities of federal largesse, tolerating a racist police department that ran roughshod over the city's black residents, and making inflammatory comments about Martin Luther King and other civil rights leaders.

For all the criticism, the riots helped Yorty to solidify his reputation as a tough-on-crime mayor. Though he believed that some communists were behind the insurrection, a charge the McCone Commission later refuted, Yorty was careful not to appear too conspiratorial-minded. Instead, he adopted a more multifaceted—and much more popular—explanation for the violence. Yorty argued that civil rights protests had inflamed passions in the inner city, and he derided civil-rights leaders as intransigent, irresponsible radicals more interested in attacking the mayor and the police than in solving the problems of the ghettos.

At every opportunity, Yorty hailed Parker as a great law enforcement officer, and blamed the violence in Watts on a criminal cabal of hoodlums and black radicals. Yorty's alliance with Parker would do much to bolster the mayor's political standing. Sharing a penchant for pugnacious public displays, a withering disdain for liberals, and a commitment to law and order, the two men became fast friends.[34]

Together they also blamed Brown for contributing to the confusion during the riots by "setting up a corps of press agents in a hotel instead of using his own offices in the State Building across the street from mine in the City Hall where we could have conferred, and issuing misguided press releases." Yorty complained that when Brown was in Rome, on his way home, he had likened the riots to a war; but when the governor arrived, he had "caused untold trouble by insisting upon going into the riot zone at a time when desperately needed officers had to be diverted in an attempt to protect him, and he was finally compelled to turn back because of the very violence about which he had been warned."[35]

Yorty proved a powerful spokesman for the increasingly popular view that the solution to mass violence was better-equipped, more efficient policing, and quickly became a leader of the growing nationwide cry for law and order. Articles in the *New York Times* featured the mayor as an outspoken defender of the police and characterized his debates with Sargent Shriver and other liberals as part of a larger nationwide exchange over the problems of race and riots. Shriver called Yorty's charges "intemperate, unfounded, and untrue," and leading national politicians had to choose sides. Former President Dwight D. Eisenhower echoed Yorty when he announced at a news conference on Capitol Hill after a breakfast meeting with Republican leaders that the riots represented a trend toward lawlessness in America. California Senator George Murphy concurred, explaining that the riots in both Berkeley and Watts had nothing to do with "ghetto conditions. They're both a result of the growing disrespect for law and order."[36]

A fawning biography of the mayor published in the mid-1960s captured Yorty's growing appeal. "During the tense days of the rioting and looting," Ed Ainsworth, the biographer, wrote, "Mayor Yorty and blunt, courageous Police Chief William H. Parker emerged as the firm and unyielding advocates of law enforcement. They stood fast amid hysteria and criticism and provided, in the long run, the only bulwarks to whom Negroes as well as whites could turn in the confusion and inconsistencies of other officials, particularly on the state level."[37]

Emboldened by polls showing him with a better shot than Brown against likely Republican nominees, Yorty began accumulating a war chest for his campaign. In November 1965, shortly before leaving for a goodwill trip to the Far East, Yorty attended a $100-a-plate dinner in his honor at the Hollywood Palladium. The mayor pulled in more than $100,000 from the 1,800 guests. He promised the funds would go toward "voter education," but said they might also be used for funding his campaign.[38]

Yorty was never a stickler for playing by the campaign finance rules. Every eight months or so the mayor would host a $100-a-plate testimonial dinner for himself, according to Roger Kent, the head of the Democratic party. Kent had hated Yorty since the 1950s, when Kent was starting out as party chair. He recalled that the state's top Democrats had agreed to send out a joint mailer with their pictures on it, the cost to be shared by Brown, Yorty, Stanley Mosk, Claire Engle, and others. Yorty sent in his picture along with a blurb to go under it; Kent printed up around 1.5 million copies before realizing that Yorty had no intention of paying. "Just plain fraud," Kent had moaned.[39]

With a small but growing slush fund, and events breaking his way, Yorty confided to friends and aides that his political prospects looked good: "I don't know any Democrat who could possibly challenge [Brown] next June except myself." Experts estimated that the riots had cost Brown around 4 percent of the Democratic vote. As the *Los Angeles Times* reported, "[Brown's] firm position in support of civil rights and against the highly popular Proposition 14 at the 1964 general election became a hindrance to him as the white backlash began to develop on the opening days of the riot." Of course, noted the *Times*, "it is impossible to forget that Brown has the capacity to come from behind and has done so twice before. In 1961," the article said, "at approximately this time of the year, the governor trailed all Republican opponents in several public opinion surveys and then won re-election."[40]

As the two men jockeyed for position, Brown made token efforts to ward off a Yorty candidacy, but he had little influence on the mayor. Told by an aide that "Yorty is still toying with the idea of seeking the Democratic nomination. . . . However, the best available information is that . . . the first statewide office that he will seek will be U.S. Senator in 1968," the governor offered in late January to help Carmen Warschaw, a Yorty ally, in exchange for help "bring[ing] Mayor Yorty's support into our effort."[41]

The Brown campaign assigned aides to attend Yorty events and analyze the mayor's performance, but aides were not overly concerned about a Yorty campaign. In late January, Brown's top advisors learned from their man on the scene that Yorty was taking digs at Brown for being on vacation during the riots and that he would decide around the end of February if he was going to run. "All in all it was pretty routine, dry stuff," the aide opined, "and I felt Sam was off form for the day." Uninspired research and the occasional attempt to get newspapers to spin a Yorty event one way or another aside, the Brown campaign generally dismissed Yorty's effort as a fanciful undertaking not worthy of a response. If Yorty's challenge helped push Brown into the race, it must be said that Brown had unrealistically high hopes for the coming campaign. He thought the ideological divisions in the GOP more serious than those in his party, and he dismissed GOP criticisms as election-year bluster.[42]

By now the party had become such a jumble of personalities and factions, ideologies and turfs, that the only true kingmaker remained, at least in the eyes of Brown and his backers, Pat Brown. There was no one with his experience, political clout, and popular following. He thought no one else could win, and most friends agreed. Jesse Unruh was a "crook and a bungler," Yorty a renegade who had alienated Democrats by supporting Nixon over Kennedy in 1960. The Democratic party would unite around Brown because it had no choice—only Brown could win.[43]

In March Pat Brown held a press conference in which he mapped out his vision for a third term. Surrounded by a clutch of family members, Brown announced that he was embarking on a "great new adventure." He told reporters that his greatest satisfaction as governor had been "working on behalf of all the people of this state . . . [Government] is too important to the coming generations to turn over to either the radicals of the right or the radicals of the left." He then paused for questions.

"Do you anticipate anyone challenging you in the primary?" a reporter quickly asked.

"I anticipate that I haven't made every Democrat in the State of California happy, so maybe someone will run."

"What about Sam Yorty?" came the follow-up.

"I've understood that Sam might run and that's his privilege."

Another reporter asked him about Reagan.

"He is a Goldwater Republican," Brown said derisively, "and I don't think he'll deny it. He was the leader of that campaign. He's been an exponent of the far right for the last three or four years at least, and there isn't any question about it and I'll be very surprised if even he would deny that he is a conservative of the right-wing school."[44]

Brown had trouble grasping the Reagan and Yorty appeal: Reagan was an actor, Yorty a renegade, both were conservative on the social issues. Later that month, Yorty announced officially that he would challenge Brown in the Democratic primary. Like so many of the mayor's previous campaigns, this one was a last-minute undertaking. Brown responded by going on television and blasting the mayor as a hothead who had failed to solve his city's problems. The governor recognized that Yorty had strong support among Los Angeles suburban voters. Beyond that, he thought that Yorty couldn't do much. He was running with little money and less Democratic support against a two-time incumbent. One of Brown's campaign managers summed up the governor's confidence when he predicted that the governor would "murder Sam Yorty in the primary."

When Brown was not attacking Yorty, he was ignoring him. "I can best describe Sam by classing him as a SKUNK," Norris Poulson, the former mayor, wrote Brown in early March. "Therefore you do not want to fight him as 'only they can fight.' He tells the BIG LIE and keeps enlarging it," Poulson cautioned, adding that "[California senator] Tom Kuchel absolutely ignored him except for a few cutting remarks about the ridiculousness of his statements and he defeated him handily." Poulson also told Brown that a group hostile to the governor was behind the Yorty campaign. The anti-Brown forces, Poulson explained, knew Yorty had no shot, but "they think he can mess you up for the finals." Poulson praised Brown for agreeing to speak in San Diego, "Goldwater territory," and urged him to talk about his accomplishments. "Regardless of 1964, these people [in San Diego] think of their immediate needs, and Water Recreation and new University strikes their pocketbooks. 'Let the Governor Brown Team' finish the job," Poulson suggested, should be the governor's campaign slogan.[45]

Poulson's advice reflected a long-standing liberal consensus that Brown could stave off right-wing challenges by emphasizing his record of achievement while attacking opponents as embittered extremists outside the political mainstream. Before a radio interview, an aide suggested that the governor point out that the opposition had no concrete solutions to state problems, only hackneyed slogans and far-fetched ideas.

Brown's supporters also ridiculed the mayor as pathological—a man unfit to govern. "He was a cocky little guy and just the damnedest liar that I've ever had anything to do with," Roger Kent recalled. "He could lie more convincingly than anybody I ever had anything to do with, and he consistently did it."[46]

Such a strategy had worked effectively in years past, but in 1966 it backfired. The administration was so contemptuous of Yorty, and so accustomed to beating extremists, that it failed to grasp that to many voters, his issues—the issues that Reagan would soon take up with such effect—were not just lies, Yorty's complaints not just demagogic extremism. To Brown, Yorty was a liar prone to "paranoia"; to Yorty, Brown was hopelessly out of touch. "Whoever wrote the speech you read on TV," Yorty told Brown in March, "should take an elementary course in California government. He caused you to accuse me of your failures—I hope out of ignorance rather than conscious deception."[47]

The Brown administration, Yorty charged, had failed on two fronts: It had taken power out of the hands of local leaders, leaving mayors and other community activists helpless to address urban woes; and it had given little support to officials trying to crack down on crime. Brown, Yorty argued, had done so much damage to California's judicial system that it would "take decades to correct." The mayor mailed constituents booklets on the California crime rate designed to draw attention to the rising levels of violence in the city. The response was overwhelming. "I am among the many thousands of citizens who are becoming increasingly indignant and concerned over the wholesale release of convicted criminals through the technicalities of DORADO, ESCOBEDO AND CAHAN decisions," one person wrote the mayor, referring to liberal judicial opinions that expanded defendants' rights. "We are rapidly approaching a situation that affords the criminal greater protection than the law-abiding citizen."[48]

When Watts' aftershocks hit in March 1966, Yorty immediately requested stringent antiriot laws to help the police "to cope with present conditions." A fight between black and Mexican-American youth had spiraled into free-floating, mindless violence. Two were killed, and the images of sullen black youth and baton-wielding police flickered on television sets around the state, reigniting fears of a race war. Brown, thinking that these more minor disturbances did not occasion any major legal shifts, turned him down. He was soon proved correct; the police moved swiftly and with overwhelming force and the disturbance was quelled. But to voters, the mini-riot was a grim reminder of its predecessor. To Yorty, Brown's response was "a shocking but customary display of arrogance. . . . It seems inconceivable that any Governor could brush aside such a request from the largest city in the State under existing circumstances."[49]

The governor was soft on criminals, Yorty said, and he was soft on communists, too. At the end of April, the mayor challenged Brown to a debate on the issue, a discussion, as he put it, of communist infiltration of the Brown-backed CDC. "Is the CDC Communist-infiltrated?" Yorty asked, "and did Brown, knowing this, seek its support?"

Asked for evidence of communist infiltration in the CDC, Yorty cited the group's resolutions on Vietnam and Red China, and said that he had tried to identify communist members, but that he was unable to access party records. Yorty's assault seemed ludicrous to Brown—"This little man has flipped his lid"—but it reflected a growing unease with the antiwar movement in California. Linking Brown to the antiwar left, Yorty claimed that "Governor Brown has chosen to seek and accept the support of groups that advocate holding the war in Viet Nam on the Communists' own terms."[50]

Yorty's hard-hitting tactics were scoring points. In late April, friends warned Brown that he was in trouble in Southern California. "Certainly, your people are underestimating Yorty, who is taking advantages of all your weaknesses," one acquaintance wrote. "His daily T.V. and radio programs are unfair to you—but very effective in further dimming your image. . . . Either your strategists down here are ignorant of the terrain or they don't give a damn about building a tremendous plurality for you at the Primary. If Mayor Yorty gets the large vote he and many of us think he will get in the south, you will be in real trouble in November."[51]

Brown resolved that in both the primary and the general election, should he reach it, his pace would not slacken. He vowed to Hubert Humphrey, "we will work as hard as we can to see that [Yorty] is defeated."[52] The governor attacked the mayor as a loose cannon. A Brown campaign pamphlet, for example, drubbed Yorty as a Republican dupe and the author of a "vicious" anti-Catholic smear against the late President Kennedy. "Yorty has used the same right-wing nonsense in other pamphlets and mailing pieces," the leaflet read, "attack[ing] our courts under the lurid headlines of 'Narcotics, Murder, Mayhem.'" He was "an unprincipled demagogue who has turned a serious national crime problem into a political issue" and a fearmonger who posed a threat to "the tradition of responsible leadership in politics."[53]

Behind the scenes, aides maneuvered without success. The Brown campaign asked Yorty to leave Vietnam and other incendiary issues out of the fight. In February, Brown's Southern California campaign chairman, Charles Rickershauser had written, "It should be clear to you that your repeated attempts to make political capital out of the nation's involvement in the bitter South East Asian conflict constitute a distinct disservice to the American cause, cheapen the nation's sacrifices there, put new propaganda weapons into Communist hands and certainly contribute nothing toward public understanding of the problems in Los Angeles." Yorty ignored the plea and continued to hammer on Vietnam and other issues. The distance—ideological and emotional—between the two Democratic candidates was just too great.[54]

The June primary put an end to the mudslinging, at least momentarily. At first, as the early results trickled in, revealing a massive advantage for the governor, the mayor remained hopeful. Those votes, he remarked, were all from the Bay Area, a much more "provincial" part of the state. When the final results were in, Yorty had lost, though he had performed remarkably well, garnering almost one million votes, only 300,000 less than the number cast for Brown. Yorty's strong showing led analysts to describe the vote in general as "anti-Brown." The political editor of the *San Francisco Chronicle* noted that "despite the months of campaigning by the Governor and his lavish expenditure of campaign funds," the election showed that "the people want a change."[55]

Most politicians would have eased off; Yorty was defiant to the bitter end, arguing that he would have won if Republican moderates had been allowed to vote in the Democratic primary. "The election clearly demonstrated the fact that the discredited Brown machine has become an albatross around the neck of the Democratic Party.... Brown and his supporters appear determined to hang on until they drag the Democratic Party down to defeat." The mayor promised to work for electoral reform to give voters greater choice in the primaries. He added that he would not decide whether to endorse anyone in the coming campaign. "As Mayor," he concluded, "I am in a nonpartisan office and I like it."[56]

After the primary Brown tirelessly wooed his rival in an effort to bring him back into the party fold. He wrote the mayor letters promising fast action on antiriot legislation and other matters important to Los Angeles; and he invited Yorty to Sacramento for a four- or five-hour session and lunch at the Mansion, at the mayor's convenience.[57] Aides converged on Yorty's press conferences, carefully reporting the mayor's utterances, looking for signs of what he might do.

They did not have long to wait. Yorty's June 1966 press conference was a tour de force, even for Yorty. He unveiled examples of what he deemed inflammatory literature that subversives were passing out in his city. He displayed a poster that, he charged, Progressive Labor—"a Communist group"—was distributing; it was a picture of Chief Parker accompanied by the words "Wanted for Murder." He disagreed with Brown that current law-and-order legislation was sufficient. Most important of all to the Brown camp, he said he wouldn't discuss politics until Brown met with him later that afternoon and wouldn't decide who to endorse until October. Yorty did hold out some hope, however. He did not dispute Roger Kent's prediction that Brown would receive 75 percent of Yorty's vote in November, saying, "after all, these are Democratic votes and I think they will want to vote for the Democratic candidate." Yorty then announced that had it not been for the "black backlash," he might have beaten Brown.[58]

Yorty's half-hearted conciliation notwithstanding, the Democratic party in California was in trouble, disjointed, and fractured. November would tell how many voters shared Yorty's strange sense of party loyalty.

PRIOR TO THE PRIMARY, in his more than three-decade political career, Brown had come to despise only one man: Max Rafferty, a state superintendent of schools and vitriolic right-winger. Not even Jesse Unruh made the cut. "Other people—Reagan and Nixon and other people—I fought hard, but never really disliked them, and don't dislike them today," explained Brown. To Brown's list of one he added one more: Yorty, "a contemptible, under-the-table fighter with a capacity of meanness second to none . . . in my long political career they're the only two people that I actually disliked."

Brown and aides had good reason to loathe Sam Yorty. But the administration's disdain, however justified, undermined Brown's reelection bid. The campaign viewed the mayor as someone outside the political mainstream—someone who could be ignored. But Yorty's politics presaged Reagan's, and thus Brown's defeat. Yorty himself seemed to grasp this. Long after he had left office, an interviewer asked the mayor if he thought of himself as a man ahead of his times. "That's been my trouble, one of my troubles," Yorty responded. "It's a shame, really, but somebody has to start things off." Someone, Yorty could have added, needs to finish them, too.[59]

NINE

# THE SEARCH FOR ORDER

IN OCTOBER 1965, it was not at all clear that Ronald Reagan could pull it off. Could he unite his party? Could he capitalize on the social upheavals that had caused Brown so much trouble? In August, Reagan had succeeded in blunting the issue of the John Birch Society, yet he still needed to prove that he could handle the rough-and-tumble of a statewide political campaign. He had to learn how to handle tough questions from the media, deal with the hostile attacks on his personal character and political positions, and prove to voters he was not simply a know-nothing actor with extremist views. His campaign faced the daunting challenge of preventing the kind of internal GOP fratricide that had hurt Nixon in 1962 and Goldwater in 1964. Finally, Reagan and the Right had to shed their image as single-issue anticommunist fanatics, and forge popular positions on such matters as taxes, education, civil rights, black riots, and student protesters. These were major obstacles all.

IN OCTOBER 1965, after seeing internal campaign polls showing Reagan as the Republican front-runner, Holmes Tuttle and other backers told the candidate to cancel his television and movie contracts and devote himself full-time to the campaign. On October 17, key Reagan strategists and fund-raisers gathered at the candidate's home for a major strategy session. Though Reagan would not formally announce his candidacy until January, Bill Roberts left little doubt that the campaign was well underway. "In many areas," he told steering committee members and the Friends of Reagan, "the effort has gone way beyond the fondest hopes of all those concerned." Roberts wanted the group to discuss the budget, the candidate's schedule for the next two months, new polls, when to establish a more elaborate statewide campaign organization, and whether they should launch "a major attempt . . . to encourage elimination of possible primary opponents."[1] The key opponents they expected included George Christopher, former mayor of

San Francisco; Joe Shell, former Minority Leader of the assembly; Laughlin Waters; and, possibly, Senator Thomas Kuchel.

Reagan was enthusiastic about the campaign, telling confidants that he offered "the best chance of winning" and that he was going to run. Yet for all his bravura, he understood the daunting task ahead of him. He would have to quit his jobs, forfeit his income, and abandon the cushy ranch life to which he had grown accustomed. He would have to convince the media and the public that he knew the issues, could stay calm under pressure, and had enough experience to be a serious gubernatorial contender.[2]

Journalists and some scholars then and since have portrayed Reagan as an automaton who excelled mainly at foolish quips, television, and following directions. He made few decisions, critics have complained, held few campaign responsibilities, and employed a slew of handlers to train his mind, focus his thoughts, ghostwrite his talks, and find him time for much-needed midday naps. Indeed, Reagan had a showman's talent for winning over audiences and charming television viewers, but only a poor grasp of important matters of public policy. As Reagan himself admitted, he had devoted so much time to researching "the overall philosophy, national and international policy, that I did not know anything about the organization of state government, the problems and what would be the issues in state government. . . . I had just a citizen's resentment of certain things that had happened." As one Republican complained after meeting Reagan in late 1965, "He is far from well enough versed on specific issues. (Some of the people there were very sharp and quite well informed on particular issues. They were not happy.)"[3]

Everyone knew Reagan was a former actor and a relative newcomer to Republican Party politics. Critics quickly dismissed his candidacy as a joke. "Reagan for Governor?" movie mogul Jack Warner would quip. "No, Jimmy Stewart for Governor, Ronnie Reagan for best friend." Editorialists piled on. "The latest innovation in political life is the acceptance of actors as creditable political figures, even though they lack the background and experience in government which are prerequisites to success in public office," the *Sacramento Bee* editorialized in 1965. "Ronald Reagan is making the most of this innovation. . . . There is something scary about the idea of actors in politics. . . . What happens when an actor simulates a role so well he is called upon to perform it off stage in real life? Then you have Raymond Massey actually attempting an appendectomy or Ronald Reagan actually making crucial decisions of government. Frightening thoughts."[4]

Reagan was determined to prove his critics wrong. He boned up on California issues. He urged Spencer and Roberts to let him take more chances on the stump. "I've got a suggestion," Reagan ventured. "From now on, why don't I just say a few words to whatever group I'm with, no matter how big it is, and then just open it up to questions and answers? People might think somebody had written my opening remarks for me, but they'll know it would be impossible for somebody to feed me answers to questions I didn't know about in advance."

The advisors were leery. Reagan was adamant, however, insisting that he give the new format a try.[5] Spencer and Roberts finally gave him the go-ahead. "To get around the problem that Ron is just 'speaking a part he has memorized,'" Bill Roberts wrote a party activist in Santa Cruz, "we have asked for question-and-answer periods following most of his major engagements. These certainly are not prepared and people get an opportunity to test his intellectual capacity. He does not have all the answers; he is not a professional politician. . . . But, as time goes by, he learns more and more to add to the backlog of understanding which, we feel, he has."[6]

Reagan proved adept in the Q and As, blending humor and wit with articulate statements on state issues. Reporters, skeptical that Reagan could handle himself under duress, watched the sessions closely for signs of a meltdown; they came away disappointed. "It was apparent to those of us who really had spent time covering the guy on the campaign trail that he was not dumb," the California journalist Jack McDowell recalled. "Really the thing that drove that home was under Q and A. He would throw back sensible answers—not just at press conferences, but to audiences. He did very well in it, and so well that Stu Spencer was saying, 'We want Q and A every time we can.'" McDowell, after listening to one such session, changed his mind about Reagan. This guy isn't so stupid, McDowell told himself; "he's handling these pretty well. . . . So if there was a turning point in my evaluation of the guy, that was it."[7]

As Reagan impressed audiences, Spencer and Roberts came up with a novel idea for defusing the experience issue. The partners had long, rambling discussions about the coming campaign, and out of one of these sessions emerged the concept of the citizen-politician. The idea was fairly simple. Reagan, the consultants conceded, had little political experience and scant knowledge of state government. "He was green," Spencer acknowledged.[8] Aware that Reagan could not match Brown's or Christopher's knowledge of state issues, the advisors decided to turn one of Reagan's most glaring weaknesses—his lack of experience—into a plus. "We decided not to show brilliant knowledge, which he did not have," Roberts recalled shortly after the campaign ended. "We tried to operate on the level that he is not a professional politician, that he is a citizen politician, Joe Doakes running for office." It was, he explained, "one of the best ways he could compete with Brown on knowledge of the issues. It was a defense measure, but later on it turned into a real asset. At the end, Brown was defending himself against being a professional politician."[9]

Prior to 1965 most California politicians and reporters believed that all credible gubernatorial candidates had to be intelligent and have some experience in government and a basic knowledge of state issues. But in the 1966 race this axiom no longer held true. As the public grew more disillusioned with rising crime rates, student protests, the war in Vietnam, and ghetto riots, they also became more suspicious of traditional, liberal politicians who had spent their careers expanding government entitlements, building state infrastructure, and reaching out to minorities. It was the beginning of the run-as-an-outsider trend that would soon sweep presidential politics.

Spencer and Roberts approached all their campaigns the same; they first tried to identify large blocks of potential swing voters—Democrats who might be inclined to vote Republican—and then spent an inordinate amount of money, resources, and the candidate's time to woo these voters. As Bill Roberts once boasted: "We decide where our candidate goes and how he uses his time. We say when and how he should spend his dollars. We decide to whom mailings should be made. We put precinct workers in position to tell them what to say. We control the timing—when you move on different issues."[10]

Relying on computer programs that performed sophisticated demographic breakdowns for each district in California, Spencer and Roberts came to realize that many white working- and middle-class Democrats in Southern California were increasingly unhappy with the political climate. In time this discovery would help turn Reagan's attention toward a set of increasingly contentious social issues. But in late 1965, it mainly served to confirm Spencer and Roberts' belief that Reagan could style himself as a citizen-politician and still attract key voters.[11]

Was Reagan merely Spencer and Roberts's face man? In their rush to debunk Reagan, critics have overlooked the degree to which the Reagan campaign was a group effort that coalesced around a talented candidate. Obvious as it may sound to dispassionate observers today, to critics of the 1960s it was not at all clear that without Reagan, there was no Reagan campaign. Handlers, supporters, and the state party helped, but it was Reagan who recognized early the political conundrums plaguing conservatives, understood what needed to be done to address those problems, and worked hard to turn himself and his movement into a politically popular alternative to the dominant liberal approach.

If there was a rock on which the Reagan campaign was built—other than the man himself—it was the GOP machine. By the time of Reagan's candidacy, it was a jilted and determined dynamo and an engine for making money. Much of its work, however, was invisible to the public, and Reagan has long maintained that it was not until June 1966, after the primary election had ended, that he received support from state Republican officials. "Under the law in California," he explained to an interviewer in the 1970s, "dating back to Hiram Johnson, the political parties cannot preprimary endorse. So you have no contact or support or help or anything in that regard. All the party did was . . . try to unify the party and go forward when the election was held."[12] Reagan's argument is more myth than history. Under the deft leadership of Gaylord Parkinson, an obstetrician–turned–political operative from San Diego, the GOP did indeed do a lot for Reagan long before the primary votes were tallied.

Young, impeccably dressed, and conservative on most issues, Dr. Gaylord Parkinson seemed an unlikely pol. "Parky," as friends called him, was a Chicago native and a Presbyterian who had come to California in 1928. A self-described bookworm who at one time wanted to be an international lawyer, Parkinson instead attended medical school at Temple University in the early 1950s, where he studied to be a gynecologist. He also developed a second passion, politics. Captivated by the Alger Hiss spy case, Parkinson traveled to Washington to attend HUAC hearings. There, he met Richard Nixon, an up-and-coming California congressman who urged the doctor to get active in Republican party politics.

He did. Upon finishing his residency, he returned to California. Though busy with his bustling medical practice, Parkinson began reorganizing the Young Republicans in San Diego, worked on a Republican congressional campaign, and took a deep interest in the local political scene. One aspect of it rankled: The party, he discovered, was amateurish, poorly organized, and had in its ranks only a handful of businessmen and other professionals. Teaming up with several acquaintances, he founded Republican Associates, a group for young professionals that raised money, endorsed and trained candidates, sent out mass mailings, and provided campaigns with professional political consultants. Eager to make party politics more efficient and businesslike, Parkinson wanted to do for politicians in San Diego what Spencer and Roberts had done in Los Angeles. With the help of Robert Walker, a Spencer-Roberts protégé, Parkinson recruited 1,200 dues-paying members, helped local assembly candidates to victory, and as he immodestly recalled, "became rather prominent, rather quickly."[13]

Despite these efforts, the California Republican party remained a shambles of warring factions, ideological splinters, and clashing personalities. For this state of affairs the GOP could thank a series of party-gutting reforms passed by Governor Hiram Johnson in the 1910s. Determined to wrest control of the legislature from corrupt oil and railroad lobbies, Governor Johnson instituted a series of measures, including recall, referendum, and initiative, that placed more power in the hands of voters and left parties with few funds, scant coordination, and little say in primary elections. Unable to endorse candidates during the primaries, the parties ceded most of their power to grassroots volunteer groups who could raise and disburse money, make endorsements, and do all the other little things that made for a successful campaign. The party was paralyzed in other ways as well. Party conventions, which determined platforms and elected officers, took place between the primary and general election—a formula for discord in which one faction of the party would carry the candidates through the primary and another through the general election. Statewide party fund-raising was virtually nonexistent, and the GOP state central committee was almost always divided between Southern and Northern California. Moreover, the state party resembled more a Byzantine bureaucracy than a modern-day political operation, besotted by committees, subcommittees, and chairmanships that bore little or no relation to one another. County committees, for example, had almost no involvement with the state central committee, and top local activists had little say in state affairs. Candidates were left to fend for themselves for the most part.[14]

Parkinson explained the conundrum of Golden State GOP politics this way: "You have every candidate running on his own. He can run on his own as long as he can get in the primary; then he turns to the party and says: Okay, help me. Well, he looks around and there's no party. He's alienated half of them to begin with and then there isn't any party—no Republican finance—no nothing. . . . It's the most screwed-up system I ever saw in my whole life. I never saw a worse system. You couldn't perfect a worse system."[15]

In 1962, eager to win control of the state central committee and then reorganize and unite the party, Parkinson won election to its vice-chairmanship. During his campaign, worried about being identified with the party's liberal wing, Parkinson urged Caspar Weinberger, the party chairman, at that time seen as a moderate, to keep his distance. "At that time his coming out for me was a kiss of death," explained Parkinson. "We actually had threatened to go to court to get him not to run with me as a slate. He was passing petitions around. We had to stop that because I had the delegates down here without him and I did not need him to get elected. Consequently, when I became vice-chairman, he largely ignored me." So at first he could do little. It was that year that many right-wing Republicans, upset with Nixon's denunciation of the Birch Society, defected from Nixon's gubernatorial campaign.[16]

But in 1964, the year of the Goldwater debacle, Parkinson became state chairman. In the aftermath of the 1964 elections he embarked on a crusade. He began to reach out to both moderates and conservatives, arguing that to win statewide office, the two sides needed to put aside their differences and come together. He reminded party leaders that Republicans had lost in 1962 because Joe Shell and the conservatives "sat on their hands" and in 1964 because the liberals bolted. "This is not the time for recriminations," he admonished GOP elders. "We've got work to do. We're going to make this a party of consensus."

First, he turned the chairmanship into a full-time job. Second, Parkinson appointed a Fair Campaign Practices Committee, composed of prominent moderates and conservatives, to monitor candidates and quell nasty primary squabbles. Parkinson recalled the committee's success, saying, "I think it worked. They were a big enough group and an outspoken enough group that if some candidate said something in Fresno, he was called by one of them who said, 'Now what is this? What did you say? We saw what the press said. What did you say and what did you mean? Do you think that's wise, and are you going to go on doing that?' . . . That was their role, and I think it helped again moderate the primary."[17]

He also implemented, with the help of Spencer-Roberts, a new Republican political strategy. The Cal Plan, as it was called, was simple: Instead of distributing valuable funds and resources evenly across the state, the party would focus on target-districts that seemed the most promising for Republican candidates. Impressed with Reagan's conservative views and with his rapid ascent, Parkinson, who had been looking for a "succinct, poignant, sellable form of my philosophy," began in late 1965 working behind-the-scenes—though he later denied it—to squelch moderate attacks on Reagan's campaign and help the front-runner maintain his lead over George Christopher. Robert Walker also helped. Convinced that colleagues had grown "sick and tired of blood baths," Walker came up with the idea of an Eleventh Commandment, an edict that said, "Thou Shall Not Speak Ill of Any Republican." Eager to minimize attacks from moderates, Parkinson and Reagan's aides quickly cottoned to the concept.[18]

Reagan's conservative supporters helped, too. When, for example, the former assemblyman Joe Shell complained that Reagan was a back-stabbing usurper who had promised to support him for governor (Reagan denied the charge), right-wingers—among others—began pressuring Shell to stop his attacks.[19] Rus Walton, the president of UROC, flew to Phoenix in 1965 to meet with Goldwater, who pulled Walton aside and asked, "Hey, Rus, can you get Joe to step aside and not run against Reagan?"

Holmes Tuttle traveled to Shell's house to convince him that Reagan was an honorable man, a credible candidate, and a good Republican with solid conservative credentials. Though he did not tell Shell directly, his message to the forlorn former assemblyman was clear: Reagan represented conservatives' best chance for victory. "I was tired of losing," Tuttle recalled years later. "I had gone through the 1964 campaign, . . . and we were in bad repair throughout the country. I wanted to win. I tried to convince [Joe], but [he] never did quite forgive me." Cy Rubel and Tuttle then invited Shell to Reagan's headquarters, where they offered him a prominent role in the campaign, which he refused.[20]

Reagan, for his part, tried to stay focused not on his immediate opponents but on the problems of Pat Brown and the Democrats. It helped make him sound electable to many Republicans. He scoffed that Brown's only solution to problems was more government programs and executive edicts. "We've increased our expenditures in the state 10 times faster and greater than we've increased our population," he said.

> Twenty years ago 2 and a half percent of our population were receiving public welfare, and today in the midst of what we're told is unprecedented prosperity, that figure has risen to more than 15%. . . . We've had a great university built by the people of California, cheerfully and willingly, and I'm sure many of them built it with a dream that they were creating a great opportunity perhaps denied to them in their youth, but for their children. And now they see many of their own children denied admittance because of a lack of space while that same great university has been brought to its knees and humiliated by a neurotic, dissident minority. In crime, we're first place in the nation, and this year they just admitted that the increase for narcotics arrests of youngsters under the age of eighteen is up 40%. The spectacle of our chief executive officer going to Washington seeking the solution to unemployment by asking for $250 million to provide 50,000 jobs doing odd jobs and chores around the public buildings and schools—this isn't good enough for Californians. Why not

> turn to the business community and ask how can we remove the shackles, how can we improve the business climate in this state? . . . Let me say we can't do this if we don't win. This is the name of the game. We can't win if we continue to remember past bitterness, past divisions, and make them more important than the responsibility we have to the people of this state.[21]

Despite his attractive rhetoric, party moderates continued to bristle at the thought of a Reagan-Brown matchup. Senator Kuchel's supporters began calling businessmen and other politically connected Republicans, urging them to leave Reagan's campaign. His nomination, Kuchel men explained, would split the party along liberal-conservative lines and leave moderate Republicans little choice but to vote for Brown in the general election. They also began pressuring Kuchel to oppose the actor. Some of Kuchel's backers, like Los Angeles Congressman Alphonzo Bell, even began making noises about running and offering primary voters an alternative to the liberal senator and the right-wing actor. "I could decide to offer myself as an alternative for all Republican voters to self-destroying, exclusionary extremes that might reemerge in our Party," Bell wrote editors at *Time* magazine.[22]

In reality, Reagan's only serious primary challenger would be George Christopher, a Greek San Francisco businessman who had served two terms as mayor of his city from 1955 to 1963. The son of an immigrant who earned enough money to bring his wife and family to America by selling peanuts in Sacramento, Christopher started out working at a hamburger stand south of Market Street fourteen hours a day to help support his ill father and six siblings. He later moved into dairy consulting, hopping from plant to plant trying to straighten out their businesses. He began to get discouraged, feeling that six months after his visits, each dairy factory would be back to its old tricks. When one small dairy shop closed, Christopher told his wife that he was tired of his life and desired a change. He would take all he had, $3,000, and put it into the dairy store. He built it into a multimillion-dollar operation which he eventually sold to Berkeley Farms.

Christopher was originally a Democrat, but when he expressed interest in politics, wanting to run for supervisor, the head of the San Francisco Democratic party told Christopher that he had no hope because Greeks had no future in politics. Christopher hopped on a streetcar, stormed into city hall, and changed his registration to Republican. He would have been more comfortable as an independent. He won mayoral elections by what at that time were the biggest margins in the history of San Francisco and earned a reputation as a builder of Bay Area Rapid Transit and Candlestick Park. He was an ambitious politician who coveted statewide office. He quickly gained a reputation as a perennial loser, however: In 1958 in the Republican primary for U.S. Senate; in 1962 for lieutenant governor. Dour in demeanor, with jowly cheeks, Christopher was a less-than-scintillating personality and by 1966 an old face. But above all, he was a political moderate. That, more than anything else, proved to be his downfall.[23]

Christopher kicked off his announcement in the gubernatorial race on October 26, and plunged into a whirlwind tour of the state, holding press conferences up and down California in San Diego, Los Angeles, San Francisco, and Sacramento, and ending the evening with a cocktail party at the El Mirador Hotel Skyroom, overlooking the lighted dome of the Capitol. "The Republicans," the mayor said, "are going to be in a sad state unless we disavow extremism. I would advise Reagan or any other candidate to look at the polls and see who would win in the finals."[24]

Christopher had been the Northern California chairman of Governor Rockefeller's 1964 campaign and warned that a Reagan nomination would set the party back another ten to twenty years. "I ask no aid from the radical left," he told reporters. "I ask no aid from the extreme right. If I thought the difference between winning and losing required embracing any extremism, I'd prefer to lose. Anyone who requires three or four paragraphs to try to explain his position on extremism is not only deluding himself—he is trying to delude the people."

The California Field Poll showed that in a head-to-head matchup with the incumbent, Christopher beat Brown handily, outperforming even Reagan. His campaign stressed his experience in government, his success as a businessman, and his "constructive philosophy" that could save the Republican party from internecine warfare—though at the same time he took shots at Reagan, the front-runner. He thought he not only had more smarts than Reagan but also "knew more about government than" him. "Who has the qualifications, training and experience for the highest office in our state?" one Christopher campaign release asked in 1965.[25]

As early as February 1965, Christopher began blasting Reagan as an extremist unable to unite the GOP. Senator Kuchel had made it clear he would not run, leaving Christopher as the only serious moderate contender. Christopher chastised the right wing of the party for being intransigent and said that the Republican party would have to "disassociate itself" from the John Birch Society to win. He made strong appeals for civil rights, hoping to bring some minorities into the GOP fold. He boasted of his role in forming the California Republican League, a moderate bunch that opposed the growing right-wing presence in Republican political groups.[26]

The mayor knew his candidacy was doomed, however, when one night in Santa Barbara he found himself in a question and answer session with Reagan before several thousand people. Someone asked Reagan what he would do about the $5 billion budget that he'd inherit as governor. Eliminate 10 percent of all state employees, Reagan replied—a simple statement that drew great cheers. Christopher cut in that he had had great experience with such issues, but that "my experience in government tells me that you just can't do this automatically, cut ten percent. You have to work, number one, through the elimination of duplications but through the process of attrition." It would be very difficult, he said, to cut that much from the payroll. A chorus of boos erupted from the crowd. Moderation was just not a winning formula.[27]

Meanwhile Reagan's camp was trying to get Christopher to run for lieutenant governor, but Christopher was tired of playing second fiddle. People approached him and said, "Step out of the picture. You're from the north and Reagan's from the south. This will make a great team. You can't beat it."[28] But Christopher didn't want to be lieutenant governor, especially behind an extremist. As the election neared, he harked back to the problems of Goldwater. "When the Republican Party . . . let itself be splintered in 1964 and produced that riotous, roughshod Republican convention, it lost its wide-based support. The Presidential election of that year was a catastrophe for the Republican Party, regardless of where the fault lies."[29]

Later, on February 20, the *San Francisco Examiner* reported that a deal had been struck between Christopher and Reagan as early as the previous June. The terms were simple: Both candidates would campaign furiously until January, then the one who had the least chance of defeating Brown according to polls, would step aside and back the other. According to the story, Arch Monson, San Francisco businessman Prentiss Hale, and Christopher himself met with Reagan advisors Henry Salvatori and A. C. Rubel and other key supporters in an upstairs private dining room of the Broadway-Hale stores in Los Angeles. Christopher promised to withdraw if he were not the most likely candidate to defeat Brown; Salvatori said that Reagan would do the same. Christopher aides complained that Reagan had "double-crossed" them by reneging on his agreement. Reagan denied the story, protesting that he had "never made a deal in my life" and that "I am in this race to stay." Christopher, too, was emphatic—no deal had been made.[30]

It is unclear where the truth lies, but higher-ups knew that the candidates would need a firm hand to help them negotiate the straight and narrow. During the primary and the race itself, the search for unity would be directed by a higher power—Parkinson. When Christopher stepped up his assault on Reagan, the chairman ordered the mayor to save his ammunition for the Democrats. He also threatened to cut off funds to candidates who violated his commandment. When word reached Parkinson that a member of the GOP state central committee was planning to stage a play "to ridicule Reagan," he announced that the play would be a violation of the Eleventh Commandment, asked to see a copy of the script, and warned that jokes about actors and anti-Reagan spoofs were off-limits.[31]

Christopher supporters complained bitterly about Parkinson's actions, saying that he was stifling the mayor in favor of the Gipper. They accused the Friends of Reagan of giving Parkinson $33,000 to help defray the doctor's expenses, and Christopher himself flouted the commandment by attacking Reagan and poking fun at Parkinson's nostrum. During an appearance with Parkinson at a hotel in San Diego, a reporter asked Christopher what he thought about the Eleventh Commandment. The mayor responded, jokingly, that he wasn't going to abide by it because he already had enough trouble with the first ten.[32]

Parkinson's commandment significantly improved Reagan's political standing, yet by no means did it ensure a victory over George Christopher. As 1965 came to a close, Reagan still faced several obstacles: Christopher continued to snipe at him, and Reagan was growing frustrated with his inability to strike back. Reagan could not resist the occasional emotional outburst, an ever-present danger for a candidate trying to distance himself from extremists and avoid lashing out at opponents. "He couldn't understand why guys in his own party would go after him like that," explained Bill Roberts. "What the hell, he figured, we're all Republicans. We're the guys in the white hats, we ought to be saving our ammunition for the bad guys. Ron really got hot when they insinuated that he didn't keep his word."[33]

One day, Reagan returned to Los Angeles after a long road trip. He was scheduled to appear before a group of newly inducted American citizens and Lyn Nofziger, who had been on the road with Reagan, had little interest in attending the ceremony, complaining to Bill Roberts, "I'm tired, nothing's going to happen down there, I don't think I'll go." However, Roberts insisted that Nofziger accompany Reagan.

George Christopher was at the event, and in his speech administered a blistering assault on his opponent. Reagan, more prone to outbursts when tired, was now furious. According to Nofziger, Reagan was so mad he could have assaulted Christopher. "He wanted to go hit him. I was saying, 'But you can't do that.'"

"'Well, by God, you don't know how I feel!'" Reagan complained.

"'Well, you just can't do it.'"

"'Well, if I can't hit him, let me go find Arch Monson [Christopher's campaign manager], I'll hit *him*!'" The press secretary was still nervous when Reagan rose to speak, not knowing if the candidate would keep his cool. But Reagan acquitted himself well, making what Nofziger thought was "the most beautiful speech," telling the inductees that their native countries were not losing children, but that the United States was gaining them. Relieved, Nofziger left the building with Reagan. As the two men walked out, Reagan looked at his aide, chuckled, and said, "Oh ye of little faith."[34]

Reagan was far cooler about intraparty attacks than even his closest confidants could have predicted. When Laughlin Waters, a far less popular primary opponent, attacked Reagan, the front-runner didn't return the blow, but complained that the party once again looked "like a bunch of hopelessly quarreling children." Instead of making things worse, Reagan encouraged aides and friends to complain to Parkinson about opponents' unseemly conduct. The Eleventh Commandment, he knew, would lead him to the promised land.[35]

The Eleventh Commandment, however important, would never have worked if it was merely enforced; it had to be believed in. This wasn't possible unless Reagan and his advisors could find a piece of common, appealing ground. Spencer knew that for Reagan to win the primary and the election he had to (like most candidates during a major election) run toward the middle to capture the votes of white conservative Democrats and white liberal Republicans, many of whom were clearly angry over Berkeley, Watts, fair housing, and antiwar protests. But if it was Spencer who emphasized the importance of these groups, it was Reagan who defined the nature of the new appeal—law and order.

As THE CAMPAIGN PROGRESSED, Reagan adopted much of the rhetoric of Sam Yorty; he tried to win Yorty's endorsement; and he openly appealed to Yorty Democrats, at one point acknowledging that he had "met with Mayor Yorty because I believe that the people who voted for him represent a protest against Brown. I'm going after those votes."[36] Reagan stood alongside the mayor during a parade celebrating Los Angeles' 185th birthday; he lunched with him, touted the many Yorty leaders now active in his campaign, reminded reporters that he was the only candidate to defend Yorty from "attacks by two eastern liberal

Democratic Senators," and sought to widen the Brown-Yorty rift by calling attention to Brown's "paranoia" comment.[37]

Reagan realized, as had Yorty, that the morality theme—whether Vietnam and the excesses of the Left, the trouble at Berkeley, or riots in Watts—was a convenient catchall, an umbrella that allowed him to weave together an effective and articulate assault on everything bad that happened in the state during Brown's tenure. On Vietnam, Reagan wrapped himself in the cause of American patriotism, and assailed antiwar radicals at every opportunity. Reagan sensed early that citizens were frustrated with the stalemate in Southeast Asia and with the left-wing opponents of the war. On social disorder and crime, Reagan had an even better, almost empathic understanding of public sentiment and fears, and he played perfectly to the new mood of anger.

Unlike Brown, Reagan had the advantage of being close to the scene when violence first erupted in Watts, but distant enough from political power that he had little to do, except avoid the appearance of racism and give his opinion. On the day Watts went up in flames, Friday, August 13, Ronald Reagan was having lunch with Lyn Nofziger, then a Washington-based political reporter for the conservative *San Diego Union*. Reagan's advisors had decided that Nofziger would be a good press secretary for the campaign. Nofziger was a brash and bright up-and-comer in the conservative movement who had not been part of the 1964 fratricide. Short, stocky, and balding, he had the reporter's mien—wrinkled sports coat, tie hanging limply around his neck, one shirt button undone, and rumpled slacks—and he reveled in the role.

But he was skeptical of Reagan's offer. He had liked Reagan's famous speech for Goldwater, but he did not consider Reagan an especially formidable politician. Nofziger had first met Reagan at a cocktail party on a farm outside of Columbus, Ohio, on June 8, the reporter's forty-first birthday. Reagan had traveled to Ohio to attend a dinner for Ray Bliss, the Republican party's national chairman, but the cocktail reception was in Reagan's honor. Reagan arrived late, and only a few stragglers, in Nofziger's dim recollection, were "still partying."

Drunk, Nofziger approached Reagan and introduced himself as a friend of Reagan's brother, Neil. They chatted briefly, but Nofziger quickly got the sense that Reagan "was not greatly enamored of inebriated reporters." Intrigued by the talk about an impending Reagan candidacy, Nofziger had scribbled some notes that evening for a story he was considering. But too far gone to write legibly, Nofziger later couldn't decipher what he had written.

Two months afterward, Nofziger called up Neil Reagan and said, "Hey, I'm coming to California and I'd like to interview your brother because I'm convinced he's going to run for governor." Nofziger wanted to speak, sober, with the gubernatorial hopeful, thinking he might get a good story out of it, as well as a free lunch from Neil. The three men met at the Hollywood Brown Derby, one of the Reagan brothers' favorite hangouts. Reagan arrived fifteen minutes late.

"You may not remember, but we've met before," Nofziger said sheepishly. Reagan stared back at him and said simply, "Yes, I do."[38]

It was an inauspicious beginning to what would prove to be a highly successful political pairing. In the coming election, Nofziger agreed to handle the press for Reagan. More than that, he would consistently be there for his candidate with sound advice, humor tempered with loyalty, and the political connections to effect crucial behind-the-scenes changes. Nofziger would provide direction, too, though for Watts little was needed.

Reagan saw the explosion there as a way to blame Brown for the breakdown of order in the cities. Reagan said publicly (and disingenuously) that he didn't know what the political impact was of the riots, but added that anytime disturbances occurred it must mean that there was a problem with those in power. He said that it "has never been my intention . . . to attempt to capitalize on such a tragedy for political purposes." Reagan then argued that several factors caused the riots. New arrivals from the Deep South had expected to see streets "paved with gold," misled by the liberals who had promised they would eradicate poverty. When asked if Brown was to blame, Reagan replied, "Oh, I wouldn't like to specify an exact blame now as to who made promises. I would say that an entire philosophy of government is [at fault with] the Governor turning to these government programs as an answer to poverty."[39]

Christopher also joined in the attack on Brown. The administration, the San Francisco mayor and Republican gubernatorial hopeful complained, "fiddled while Los Angeles was burning." Reagan went even further, linking Brown to a pattern of general lawlessness that, he said, gripped the state. Reagan recollected that he had once said that the "skyrocketing crime rate began eight years ago," but "was corrected in the press by one of the Governor's henchmen, who pointed out that the rapid increase in crime began more than eight years ago. It began when the Governor was Attorney General and directly responsible for law enforcement in our state." He attacked Brown's "flagrant dereliction of duty. If the Governor took the warnings seriously enough to alert the National Guard, then he certainly should have taken them seriously enough to inform the Mayor of Los Angeles and the Chief of Police . . . the Governor's failure to keep the mayor informed is inexcusable." Reagan added that for the second time in the last year (meaning the riots in March 1966), Brown had been out of the state "on non-state matters" at riot's start.[40]

Pundits would later charge that Reagan played a race card with Watts. There is some truth to this accusation. At various times Reagan had opposed the 1964 Civil Rights Act, the 1965 Voting Rights Act, and fair housing reform, arguing that government did not have the power to trample on the rights of states and individuals, even if such power were harnessed to stamp out something as scurrilous as segregation. "There is a limit as to how far you can go through the law," he said on one occasion. "You cannot benefit one person by taking away the freedom of others. I believe that the right to dispose of and control one's own property is a basic human right, and as governor I will fight to uphold that right."[41]

But mostly Reagan shied away from the civil rights issue, distancing himself from segregationists and talking about riots and order instead. The strategy was a winner. Law and order was a concept that Reagan latched on to instantly, and he did so in a way that seemed reasonable, not extremist. Reagan modified L.A. Police Chief Parker's arguments, softened the rhetoric, and transformed law and order into a potent political weapon. The candidate worked hard to avoid statements that could be construed as racist, and came across as too good natured a person to be a demagogue. His statements were for the most part genuine and helped distinguish him from other, less adroit colleagues who refused to denounce segregation and other racist practices. Reagan also had a positive solution to the issue of racism and poverty, arguing that a combination of individual initiative, private enterprise, and creative energy could best solve the problems of the cities. These ideas struck many liberals as ludicrous, given the depth of problems in Watts. Yet, they served to blunt accusations that Reagan was simply another nay-saying conservative in the mold of Goldwater.

Reagan's ideas also appealed to whites disillusioned with costly liberal social programs. He cautioned that the problem of race was "most difficult" and that it would not be solved overnight. He asked aides to look at volunteer programs in inner cities around the country, and said that the answers lay with individuals, not with more programs and bills.

In October 1966, when Watts had been reduced to just another bad memory, Hunter's Point, a black neighborhood in San Francisco, exploded in violence after a police officer shot a sixteen-year-old boy who allegedly was trying to steal a car. Mayor John F. Shelley imposed an immediate curfew, Brown called out the National Guard, and both candidates made promises not to make the riots a political issue—a far-fetched pledge under the circumstances. Indeed, Reagan quickly abandoned his promise, pointing out that the riots revealed "how little leadership has been exerted in Sacramento to head off such violence," and urging Brown not to "reward" the looters. One reporter explained this tactic: "Ronald Reagan hedge-hopped across California yesterday and at every stop deplored Negro unrest but denied that the 'white backlash' is of any significance in his campaign for governor."[42]

The law-and-order issue was easy to exploit and easy for Republicans of all stripes (and even Democrats) to unite around. And Reagan was helped by rising rates of crime. From 1965 to 1966 murder in California rose 14.4 percent; robbery, 9 percent; and rape, 5 percent.[43]

Berkeley, too, was wonderful fodder for Reagan, who did not instinctively know how to capitalize on what he would later call the Berkeley Mess. A batch of aides and supporters supplied the campaign with memos on Berkeley. The issue started to show up in Spencer and Roberts's polling results. And people started asking Reagan at events what he planned to do about Mario Savio and other Berkeley radicals.

Conservatives for years had been trying to make hay of the Berkeley issue, railing against communist speakers on campus, making sporadic attempts to depict Berkeley as a haven for subversives and malcontents. In 1960, activists produced a harrowing film showing anti-HUAC Berkeley students in San Francisco as a left-wing cabal trying to topple the government, and circulated the movie, *Operation Abolition*, at Birch meetings and right-wing rallies. The American Legion often denounced "communist infiltration" on UC campuses, writing, for example, in one 1960 newsletter that there was "sub rosa espionage operations by Soviet intelligence agents at Berkeley." And angry citizens sometimes took pen to paper to complain about communist speakers on campus. "Stop the march of communism now in our Golden State," one woman urged Pat Brown in 1963, "stop communists from speaking on our publicly supported campuses."[44]

Such complaints had landed in the public arena with a dull thud. But in late 1964, with massive protests rocking the campus, student radicalism became one of the most talked about issues in the state. Conservative papers and television commentators charged that campus sit-ins were more about youth rebellion and drug-inspired anti-Americanism than serious political dissent. Reporters played up ties of students to outside agitators and communists, and trained a spotlight on liberal bumbling. *U.S. News & World Report* admonished "school authorities" not to "back down from masses of student rebels." *Life* did stories about Berkeley, and the anticommunist weekly *Tocsin* denounced Clark Kerr for his "liberal-extremist policies."[45]

In late 1965, as Reagan toured the state, people began complaining to him about dissidence on campus. "What are you going to do about those bastards at Berkeley?" audience members asked him. Others vented outrage through letters to Reagan headquarters and to newspaper editorial pages. Someone from the state of Oregon wrote Reagan that Berkeley students had raised $1,000 for the Viet Cong: "This is too much! . . . You are one of the very few men we have ever heard speak up courageously and realistically against communism." One letter to the editor urged Savio to join the Army and fight in Vietnam ("They make my boy toe the mark. So why shouldn't you serve for freedom?"); another read, "Go to Hell, all you Rotten Beatniks!" One citizen left a note on Savio's trash can in which he asked collectors to let the garbage accumulate to the point of overflow. "The fire department needs an excuse to close down this communist sponsored, pink-oriented, slack-jawed, rabble-rousing, unpatriotic, dribble-spouting . . . malodorous, mafia of overprivileged, underbrained, bleeding-hearted megalomaniacs."[46]

From the first Reagan displayed a quick wit and shrewd understanding of public anger. He began reading articles on Berkeley, gathering as much information as he could, and prepping himself for voters' questions. As early as October 1965, he blasted antiwar marches in Berkeley—and the failure of liberals to quash them—as "the fruit of appeasement. The time to have stopped it was when the students first blocked a police car on the campus. The administration should have taken the leaders by the scruff of their necks and kicked them out, and it should have put the rest of them back to work doing their homework." Reagan also grew adept at turning hecklers to his advantage. One aide recalled a group of "scraggly" protesters, long hair and sandals, at a Reagan appearance at Occidental College holding aloft placards that read, "Down with Reagan, Down with Nancy" and "Who Wants Boraxo [one of Reagan's former sponsors] in Sacramento?" Protesters stood in the balcony trying to shout down the candidate. When the hecklers finally grew quiet, Reagan turned to them and, referring to the Boraxo sign, said, "That may be only soap to you, but it was bread and butter to me."[47]

Nonetheless Reagan's aides and supporters considered Berkeley a dangerous issue, one that could brand the candidate an extremist if he did not play it right. Some Reagan supporters went so far as to produce a five-minute film about riots in Berkeley; the footage was so violent that Spencer and Roberts refused to show it, telling Holmes Tuttle, "Hey, that's not going on the air." Spencer liked the great footage from police libraries, but considered the overall film a "brutal show" that made Reagan seem like a right-wing radical.[48]

The campaign walked a fine line between an incendiary all-out attack on Berkeley and a more tempered stance. Some supporters wrote Reagan memos suggesting ways to capitalize on Berkeley without sounding shrill. Former assemblyman Caspar Weinberger, for example, worried that Reagan would turn the issue into a political football and antagonize alumni, telling the candidate to tone down his rhetoric. "A great many University alumni in influential positions throughout the state . . . are concerned about the thought of any public investigation of the University by a legislative witch hunting committee or others," Weinberger warned. Nixon aide H. R. Haldeman gave advisors pointers on how to frame the issue. Aides would ply Reagan with note cards on "the Berkeley problem," filled with details about student excesses, yet generally steering clear of the communist charge. Instead they suggested he cast the issue as a matter of public morality.[49]

By shifting the focus from the tired issue of communism to the more accessible concern over morality, Reagan's strategists found a way to tap into the fears of ordinary Californians. In notes to the candidate, aides pointed out that student protesters were radical anarchists who had imbibed the writings of Paul Goodman and Henry Thoreau (whose book *Walden* represented "a symbol of rejection of society") and had opened the door to chaos and Marxism. Aides also charted the sinister origins of the Vietnam Day Committee, and called Berkeley one of the first and most vocal centers of dissent. Berkeley, in short, was in the throes of a complete moral collapse. Homosexuality was said to be rampant on campus, taking over bathrooms and even seeping into fraternity houses.[50]

There was also the problem of "free sex." "A free love movement has followed the filthy speech movement," aides informed Reagan. "Students, former students, and nonstudents continue to test the limits of the permissible at Berkeley"; the past month had seen "six naked parties" at Berkeley; members of the UC Sexual Freedom Forum set up campus tables and sold buttons that read, "Take it off" and "I'm Willing if you are." "They distribute pamphlets on birth control, abortion and venereal disease" and have lectured on these subjects with university approval." The group's president, aides added, was a wild figure who went around arguing "that the only test of sexual conduct should be: 'Do I want to do it?'" Reagan heard that approximately 10,000 UC students had experimented with LSD, and that "no one can even guess how many more self-styled 'acid heads' there are among oddball cult groups." (The acid heads were described as "life's losers—dissatisfied, restless people, afflicted with problems they can't handle.")

The campaign had also amassed a number of inflammatory documents from the Berkeley uprising, including transcripts from a Filthy Speech Movement rally in which a featured speaker defended the right of citizens to say "Fuck" in public. "Love fuck," a document in the Reagan files quoted the dissident as saying, "Love-Fuck. Seriously, honestly. It means something to me. It means a great deal to me. . . . Why is it people are so afraid? . . . Why can't people come out and call a spade a spade—call a fuck a fuck?" Little escaped the campaign's attention; its files bulged thick with items such as poems, published in campus magazines, about the vacuity of middle-class life: "Grow old push on junior exec maybe have kids wife mistress mortgage grey hair ulcer split level no heat children . . . IM TWENTY TWO GODDAMN YEARS OLD YOU MOTHERFUCKER/unemployed bum free high all week free see the shrink once a week . . . free soul free mind free body free no job free free."[51]

The key for Reagan was not to characterize students as a "mob of rebels"; rather, he had to link Brown, as well as Kerr, to the disorders. Again, aides supplied suggestions. One argued that Kerr had knuckled under to student demands, paving the way for anarchy. Tuttle felt strongly about tying Brown to Berkeley, and in late March, another aide advised Reagan to come out in favor of academic freedom but against the most vicious anti-American activities on campus. The university, the aide reasoned, was not a place for students to attack U.S. foreign policy "or promote an alien ideology. Academic freedom also does not mean allowing a minority of students and 'non-students' to intimidate or interfere with the educational process of the majority of students." He suggested that Reagan promise to expel malcontents, establish "clear guidelines of acceptable conduct," and order professors to set a good example for students; this would distinguish him from liberals, help restore order, and "once again, all Californians would be proud of their university and state college system."[52]

In May, a state senate committee published an inflammatory report on Berkeley, that gave the campaign a golden opportunity. The committee was run by Hugh Burns, the crusty Democratic majority leader of the state senate, and it struck many liberals as a throwback to the days of McCarthyism. Burns and Richard Combs, a strident anticommunist who often did legwork for the committee ("I venture to guess Combs is a John Bircher," Tom Storke once told Clark Kerr), had a long-standing interest in communism on campus, and had several informants. In the late 1950s and early '60s, they eagerly passed

Kerr information about subversives in the system. Kerr, however, dismissed such documents and angered Burns. It is not surprising, then, that the May report laid the blame for the revolt at the feet of Kerr and other liberals. Berkeley, the report noted, had become a "haven for Communist influence and sexual misconduct under . . . Kerr," a campus "teeming with Communists, homosexuals, and other unsavory types."[53]

Reagan made dramatic use of the document. On May 12, he appeared at San Francisco's Cow Palace, the site of Goldwater's "Extremism is no vice" speech, and delivered a major address about the Berkeley matter. With "the biggest flag in the world" looming in the background, Chuck Connors, star of TV's *Branded*, walked up to the microphone and introduced Reagan as "a man in a state that needs a man." Buddy Ebsen, another television star, quipped, "better an actor than a clown in Sacramento." To rousing applause and hollers, Reagan then took the podium and gave his most forceful talk yet on Berkeley. He harped on "a small minority of beatniks, radicals and filthy speech advocates" who had "brought shame to a great University. . . . So much so, that applications for enrollment have dropped 21% and there's evidence that they'll continue to drop even more." Blaming small groups for polluting California's educational environment, Reagan seized on the Burns report and unleashed a blistering attack on student "misconduct." He admitted he had not yet read the Report—"I've never seen the report, I only know what I've read in the papers about it"—and then unveiled a different "report from a District Attorney of Alameda County," which "verified at least in part what the press has said about" the Burns Report. Opening the report to a description of the Vietnam Day Committee dance in Harmon gym, Reagan warned the audience that "the incidents are so bad, so contrary to our standards of decent human behavior, that I cannot recite them to you from this platform in detail." Then he read an excerpt:

> The total crowd was in excess of 3,000, including a number of less-than-college-age juveniles. Three rock-n-roll bands were in the center of the gymnasium playing simultaneously all during the dance, and all during the dance, movies were shown on two screens at the opposite ends of the gymnasium. These movies were the only lights in the gym proper. They consisted of color sequences that gave the appearance of different-colored liquid spreading across the screen, followed by shots of men and women, on occasion, shots were of the men's and women's nude torsos, and persons twisted and gyrated in provocative and sensual fashion. The young

> people were seen standing against the walls or lying on the floors and steps in a dazed condition with glazed eyes consistent with the condition of being under the influence of narcotics. Sexual misconduct was blatant. The smell of marijuana was prevalent all over the entire building.

Pointing up a "leadership gap in Sacramento," Reagan charged that Brown "had permitted the degradation of the once great University of California," called "for decisive action to restore the university to its once high standard," and announced that the issue could no longer "be dismissed or swept under the rug."[54]

Frank Coakley, the Alameda County district attorney, had never authored a report on Berkeley, and he figured that one of Reagan's speechwriters had gotten the information about the dance from an article in the *Oakland Tribune*, in which Coakley had been badly misquoted. The article, the DA later said, was "highly inaccurate. . . . The *Oakland Tribune* had received a report on the dance from another source and then hung the story on me." Coakley and new Berkeley Chancellor Roger Heyns did eventually investigate the dance at Harmon, and they found Reagan's claims to be grossly exaggerated. Only a few policemen and janitors had witnessed the evening's events, and they had described nothing like the display of sex, drugs, and rock and roll documented by Burns and Reagan. They turned up only a few minor acts of immorality. A Berkeley vice chancellor who had researched the dance admitted that it "got off to a bad start"—there were delays opening the doors and parking was difficult" but he said that no marijuana had been found. There was only a sweet-smelling odor wafting through part of the gym, only a few empty beer bottles had been discovered, and, despite rumors of a topless dancer, "no police officer saw quite that much," a university official wrote. "In sum, there appear to have been several instances of genuinely unseemly behavior, but certainly not warranting the political outcry which ensued. . . . The reader [of the Burns report] gains the impression that one outrage has succeeded another through the year in a monotonous uniformity. In fact, however, the year has been marked by constant progress in eliminating undesirable activities."[55]

Yet despite the exaggerations of the Burns report, Reagan easily won the battle over Berkeley. The issue was his to lose from the beginning. When the troubles began he was not governor, mayor, or the president of a university. He had not been the one who failed to exercise needed leadership and strength during a moral crisis. Here as later, Reagan's political innocence was a blessing, his articulation of the angry mood shrewd. Reagan, not Yorty or Brown or Christopher, would emerge from Berkeley, Watts, and San Francisco's mini-riot with a claim to the political middle.

By the fall of 1965, Reagan had a lead on Christopher, but, according to some polls, he was still trailing Pat Brown and the Democrats, and unlike his Republican foes, these opponents were not inclined to pull punches. In early January, on the eve of Reagan's official announcement of his candidacy, Pat Brown captured the prevailing wisdom among liberals when he told reporters, "The thought of Ronald Reagan sitting in the governor's chair moves me to great lengths." Democrats began printing bumper stickers that read, "Elizabeth Taylor for H.E.W.," and Democratic Party Chairman Robert Coate accused Reagan of hiding his right-wing bonafides and trying to fool voters into thinking he was a moderate.[56]

Reagan was already proving the naysayers wrong. On January 4, 1966, the candidate announced before a statewide television audience that he was now officially a candidate for governor. The announcement was greeted by those in Hollywood and Sacramento with the usual guffaws. What most critics failed to notice, however, was that Reagan had begun to pick up on themes that would take him to victory. He had written the bulk of the address himself, scribbling in his difficult-to-decipher scrawl a speech that addressed the major issues of the campaign and unveiled a more modern, appealing version of his conservative philosophy. In a clear departure from the gloomy defiance that had characterized Barry Goldwater's presidential campaign, and in a conscious attempt to distance himself from his earlier statements about communist hordes and totalitarian tyrannies, Reagan showed a sunny, sanguine disposition that emphasized the possibilities and glories of California life. "California's problems are our problems," he began. "It won't matter if the sky is bigger and bluer out there if you can't see it for smog, and all our elbowroom and open space won't mean much if the unsolved problems are higher than the hills. Our problems are many, but our capacity for solving them is limitless."

The heart of his address was a critique of the moral turpitude sweeping the state. Disorder, Reagan said, had descended on California like a plague. "Our city streets are jungle paths after dark, with more crimes of violence than New York, Pennsylvania, and Massachusetts combined. Will we meet [the students'] neurotic vulgarities with vacillation and weakness, or will we tell those entrusted with administering the university we expect them to enforce a code based on decency, common sense, and dedication to the high and noble purpose of the university? That they will have the full support of all of us as long as they do this, but we'll settle for nothing less."[57]

Reagan's rhetoric was appealing, but he still lacked specifics. Immediately after the speech, he embarked on a crash course on California politics. The candidate also benefited from a raft of memos and papers written by a pair of behavioral psychologists named Kenneth Holden and Stanley Plog, which gave Reagan ammunition on the law-and-order issue and more credibility as a candidate.

Their role has been the source of considerable controversy. Scholars and critics, including biographer Garry Wills, have argued that the two men turned Reagan into an effective candidate, scripting his speeches and spoon-feeding him information. This impression was created partly by Holden and Plog themselves, who later claimed that they whipped Reagan into shape, accompanying him everywhere, revising his speeches, offering him advice, prepping him for hostile questions, grooming him for office, and educating him on everything from the minutiae of state water policy to agricultural concerns. "We worked a lot with him on strategy, how he should handle himself in a campaign. It was not just providing information; we worked on the whole concept of the man," Plog explained. Holden inserted into Reagan's speeches impressive quotes from Edmund Burke, Alexander Hamilton, John Adams, Abraham Lincoln, and Benjamin Disraeli, and took credit for making Reagan look like an intellectual. "You should have seen those newspapermen jump when Ron first quoted Jefferson to them," he recalled proudly.[58] But if anything, their key contribution was in helping Reagan forge positions on the social issue.

Professors at UCLA and San Fernando Valley State, respectively, Holden and Plog ran the Behavior Science Corporation of Van Nuys (BASICO), a cutting-edge research firm that provided psychological testing services for school districts and consulting for corporations. Experts in behavioral psychology, the scholars adopted a distinct approach to problems of the workplace, one that stressed the primacy of psychology in office spats, business failures, and slumping sales.

They agreed to work for Reagan in January on two conditions: they wanted unfettered access to the candidate and a few days alone with Reagan so as to familiarize themselves with his political beliefs. The Kitchen Cabinet of Bill Roberts, Henry Salvatori, and Holmes Tuttle arranged for the men to spend three days together in a beach cottage in Malibu.

Holden and Plog liked what they saw. Reagan, Plog thought, had a well-developed ideology and a set of fundamental beliefs rooted in the Constitution. Shortly after their first meeting, Holden jotted down some notes on Reagan. He gave Reagan his seal of approval, writing, "Charismatic personality. Knows his position and the position of others. . . . He is not a map reader, he is not a reactor. Reagan knows who he is and what he stands for. His library is stacked with books on political philosophy. He can take information and he can assimilate it and use it appropriately in his own words."[59]

But the problems were obvious. The candidate, one of them recalled, "knew zero about California when we came in. I mean zero." "He didn't have a secretary," Holden said, "and he was assimilating stacks of material on state issues, clipping newspapers and magazines. It was a monumental task." Plog concurred, explaining, "[Reagan] knew practically nothing about California. . . . He was clipping articles from newspapers himself. . . . He was organizing all of his speeches. He had no background information of his own." At times, the candidate also seemed unserious, like the day he suddenly put down his reading material and announced, "Damn. Wouldn't it be fun to be running now for the presidency? Wouldn't that be great?"[60]

Holden and Plog divided campaign issues into seventeen major topics, including transportation, education, water, and the economy; put together a staff of 31 statisticians, sociologists, political scientists, and psychologists; wrote position papers; and assigned researchers to put together black binders stuffed with hundreds of five-by-eight-inch index cards containing facts, figures, and arguments for and against each issue. Carried by one of Reagan's bodyguards, the black binders were the candidate's constant companion, dispensing last-minute information at campaign stops and before appearances. Holden and Plog's system was thorough, well ordered, and well suited to Reagan's style.[61]

"We made certain that Reagan came across as a reasonable guy," Holden explained, "not as a fanatic who wanted to tear down all government." Holden urged Reagan to stop using "that terrible phrase, 'totalitarian ant heap'" ("It just sounded too harsh," he recalled) and embrace a fresh and positive approach to state problems. Holden later explained, "You had to be for things, and everything we worked on for him was focused on developing a positive program, with conservative underpinnings. . . . This was positive candidate speaking out positively on conservative issues, and that's not an easy thing."[62]

They also suggested ways to capitalize on the law-and-order front. Welfare, crime, Berkeley, and the immorality in Sacramento all bulked large in BASICO's black binders, with note cards containing statistics, quotes, and anything else on these issues that might prove damaging to Pat Brown.

Holden and Plog urged Reagan to hit hard on the issue of welfare, suggesting that he promise to trim bureaucratic fat, make welfare agencies more efficient, and reduce spending. They provided him with detailed accounts of the battles between Brown and Jack Wedeymeyer, his director of social welfare, over new welfare regulations. Wedeymeyer, the advisors noted, had called Brown's "current convictions . . . in substantial conflict" with views held by a board of welfare activists that Brown had helped create. "It should be emphasized that these principles [i.e., lavish welfare spending] were created and fostered by Brown until the public's contempt for the rising costs of welfare necessitated [Brown's] poor attempt to pass the buck to his appointee and, in turn, to make himself appear as a fiscal knight-in-shining-armor." Brown's about-face on welfare, his talk of budget cutting, seemed nothing more than a politically calculated attempt to obscure his true record on welfare.[63]

Initially, Reagan was reluctant to harp on welfare. "There was a time when I thought [welfare] might be a dangerous subject, something like Barry and Social Security," Reagan wrote an assemblyman in February 1966. But armed with Holden and Plog's statistics, Reagan slowly discovered the issue's worth; everywhere he went, audiences wanted to know how he planned to reduce it. "I am becoming more aware that the man on the street has decided he's supporting too many families not his own, and he wants something done," Reagan explained.[64]

On other, more controversial issues, such as abortion, Reagan showed restraint. Cardinal McIntyre suggested to Ron that before speaking out on the topic, he wait to see what the state legislature did with it, and Reagan took his advice. "Until we know what the legislature will do," Reagan explained to one supporter, "it is impossible to discuss this [abortion] measure because then with the specifics in mind, we can go for the necessary advice to men of science, men of medicine and men of God. I believe [McIntyre's] position is a sound one, and I'm going to try to hold to it."[65]

The Reagan camp was not nearly as reticent when it came to discussing crime, however. Holden and Plog adopted a typically strident approach to the issue, informing Reagan that FBI statistics showed that the total number of crimes committed in California had increased from over 250,000 in 1959 to over 438,000 in 1964, a 72.5 percent rise. The crime rate, aides argued, was soaring. "Anaheim, Garden Grove, and San Francisco reported increase[s] in all categories except rape. Glendale has increases in every category except murder, Riverside in all except robbery, and Pasadena in all except assault." Index cards gave Reagan a brief history of antiriot legislation, noted that the attorney general had called a conference to discuss ways to reduce drug use among students, and said that Brown had called hearings on whether to regulate LSD.

Brown's gaffes were part of Reagan's cheat sheet, too. Under a section entitled "Brownisms," Holden and Plog compiled a lengthy list of Brown blunders, including his (in their eyes ludicrous) statement that Roger Heyns, the new Berkeley Chancellor, had the campus under control. Another was his admission, "I think that the fact that I have been Governor for seven and a half years is the greatest difficulty I'll have in overcoming." Reagan was quick to portray the Brown administration as a redoubt of corruption and cronyism, attacking the governor for appointing incompetent friends and relatives to key posts.[66]

Racial issues also were an opportunity, albeit one that demanded careful handling. Reagan had never been terribly interested in winning over black voters, but by early 1966, he abandoned even the pretense of doing so, writing a Democratic supporter that although the campaign would "make an effort with regard to our negro friends . . . I must say, however, I doubt in the limited time of the campaign if we can make great inroads on their heavy Democratic leaning."[67] Instead, he adopted a shrewd approach to the race issue. He distanced himself from right-wing racists, denying that he was a bigot and denouncing racism. "I always surrounded and prefaced any such remark with my belief—well, my opposition to prejudice and bigotry," Reagan recalled. "I emphasized that I thought that anyone . . . should use their moral leadership to publicly disavow anyone who did anything of this kind, to try and create a climate in which it would be—well, you would almost morally outlaw people who discriminated." And in October 1965 he adopted, at least temporarily, a more moderate position on civil rights, telling the San Francisco Republican Assembly that he favored the Civil Rights Act and saying that "it must be enforced at gunpoint if necessary." When a black Republican politician asked Reagan if he would refrain from supporting black candidates, lest he alienate white supporters, Reagan responded angrily. "I told the entire assembled [audience]," he recalled, "'If I understand you, you're saying, would I not want to help you run for office for fear that someone would not vote for me because I was doing that? I will tell you now, I don't want the vote of anyone who would vote against me for that reason. I am going to do everything I can to help every one of you.'" Later in the campaign, Reagan even boasted to the mayor of Oakland that he was making significant progress on the racial front, writing, "We are turning the corner in changing our image."[68]

But it was not a smooth road. Reagan, despite his October statement, remained opposed to civil rights legislation and argued for a voluntary solution to the problem of racism. On March 5, 1966, Reagan appeared at a gathering of black Republicans in Santa Monica for a debate with George Christopher. To Reagan's advisors, the event was largely meaningless; realizing that their candidate had little chance at capturing the black vote, which represented only a minuscule portion of all GOP voters, Reagan's handlers would have preferred to ignore it. But they decided to send Reagan for a simple reason: "We knew Ron wasn't going to get anywhere with Negroes," Stu Spencer explained, "but he had to go anyway because it would look bad if he stayed away."

Reagan was tired. Accustomed to afternoon naps—"He mustn't be overtired, [he] must have his naps," one memo implored—he had spent the last three days traveling and trying to overcome a flu that had dogged him throughout the campaign. Though advisors had briefed Reagan about his appearance and warned him that he might be in for some rough treatment, Reagan did not heed their warning.[69]

The debate began poorly. Christopher, a staunch civil rights supporter, drubbed Reagan as a reactionary in bed with right-wing racists. Goldwater's opposition to the landmark 1964 Civil Rights Act, Christopher argued, had sullied the reputation of the Republican party. He urged right-wingers like Reagan to expunge from their circles vicious racist dogma, and reminded black audience members that as a moderate, he had a long history of fighting racism. Reagan tried to respond to Christopher's barrage, but his answers seemed rambling and vague, and it was clear that he was not in top form. He said that he opposed dividing Americans by race and ethnicity and implored, We're all one people, and we should be seen as such. Reagan announced that as governor, he would use "the prestige of the governor's office" to speak out against bigotry and turn to the private sector for solutions. When a reporter asked the candidates if they thought Proposition 14 was constitutional, Reagan deflected the query, saying only that it would be better not to comment since the issue was still pending before the state supreme court; then he added that racism was a moral problem "that must be solved by the people."

When Ben Peery, a Los Angeles businessman, rose from his seat and asked Reagan, "How are Negro Republicans going to encourage other Negroes to vote for you after your statement that you would not have voted for the civil rights bill?," the candidate again had trouble connecting with his pro–civil rights listeners. Reagan explained that he supported the principles behind the act but that the bill was a "bad piece of legislation"; he then defended Goldwater as a fine human being. "If I didn't know personally that Barry Goldwater was not the very opposite of a racist," Reagan said, "I could not have supported him."

Sensing an opportunity, Christopher rose from his seat and snarled, "Contrary to my opponent, I would have voted for the bill if I had been in Congress. . . . The position taken by Goldwater did more harm than any other thing to the Republican party, and we're still paying for that defeat. This situation still plagues the Republican party, and unless we cast out this image, we're going to suffer defeat."

Reagan had had enough. Indignant, he got up from his seat and, breaking with the debate format, demanded "a point of personal privilege. I have tried my utmost and as sincerely and honestly as I can to tell you what is in my heart and how I feel," he began. "In all my life it would be impossible for me to feel prejudice of any kind. . . . I would like to have the information by anyone here that there is anything in the nature of bigotry in my personality. I resent the implication that there is any bigotry in my nature. Don't anyone ever imply that I lack integrity! I will not stand silent and let anyone imply that—in this or any other group." He then slammed his fist into his hand, balled up a piece of paper, flung it into the audience, and stormed off the stage muttering expletives. "I'll get that S.O.B.," Reagan vowed.

Lyn Nofziger, who had been sitting in the audience, acted fast; he left his seat and caught up with the candidate, who was still swearing to himself as he stomped down the aisle. "Shut up, Ron, shut up," Nofziger whispered. In the parking lot, the two men, along with aide Kenneth Holden, huddled together to figure out the next move.

"Well, what do we do now?" Reagan asked.

"Well, I think you better go home, while I figure out what to do," responded Nofziger, wishing Spencer or Roberts were there.

Reagan climbed in his car and was whisked away by his driver. Jim Flournoy, a black Republican, emerged from the auditorium and asked Nofziger where Reagan had gone. "He's gone home," Nofziger explained.

"I think it would be a mistake for him not to come back," Flournoy responded. "People here think he walked out on them."

Nofziger drove to Reagan's house, where he found Reagan and Nancy furious and in deep discussion. Nofziger tried to coax Reagan into returning. "They're having a cocktail party and they're expecting you and if you don't show they'll think either that you don't like blacks or that you're afraid to face them." The pressure worked, and Reagan finally returned to the event.[70]

For the campaign, the episode was a near disaster. It seemed to confirm rumors that Reagan was a right-wing racist and a man of uneven temperament, provided foes with a tailor-made campaign issue, and raised serious doubts about the candidate in the minds of some supporters. Newspaper articles recounted the blow-up in detail, opponents urged reporters to listen to tapes of the incident, harped on Reagan's ties to right-wing crackpots, and suggested that the actor did not have the mental stability to be governor. "Mr. Reagan, of course, has been ill, and I extend my sympathy in this moment of emotional disturbance," George Christopher told reporters. He characterized Reagan as a "temperamental and emotionally upset candidate whose sole escape from problems is to dash hysterically to his dressing room," and then promised to donate $5,000 to charity if anyone could prove that he had accused Reagan of racism.[71]

One statewide poll taken a few days after the blowup revealed that Reagan's lead over Christopher had fallen to single digits, from 13 percent to 8 percent. Reagan's efforts at damage control seemed ineffective. "My wife says I'm very even-tempered," a grinning Reagan assured reporters at a press conference in Sacramento four days after his walkout. At other times, he adamantly denied shedding tears and maintained, implausibly, that he "only walked out because I thought the meeting was over."[72]

The chorus of criticism was so great, in fact, that many previously staunch supporters contemplated abandoning Reagan for a more seasoned politician. GOP leaders who had gathered to discuss the political repercussions wondered aloud how the candidate would hold up under even tougher barbs from Pat Brown and the Democrats. Newspapers reported rumors that at least one prominent Republican had urged colleagues to dump Reagan, and campaign advisors such as Stu Spencer were worried, fearing that another explosion could ruin Reagan's reputation and sink the campaign. Even more troubling, Henry Salvatori, one of Reagan's most prominent supporters, had decided to abandon Reagan for former Governor Goodwin Knight. For the most part, Salvatori and other members of the Kitchen Cabinet were restrained on campaign matters, deferring decisions to the political professionals Spencer-Roberts. But when Salvatori read newspaper accounts of Reagan's blowup, he decided to persuade Goody Knight to enter the race. He didn't get very far.

While with the candidate in Placerville, a small city near Sacramento, Nofziger received word that Robert Mardian, another Reagan advisor, wanted to speak with him urgently. Mardian was "frantic."

"You've got to get down here right away and talk to Henry Salvatori," Nofziger remembered Mardian urging him. "He wants to dump Reagan and run Goody Knight."

"You can't be serious," Nofziger scoffed.

"Get down here right away and talk him—Salvatori—out of it," Mardian said again.

Two days later, a Sunday, Nofziger, Mardian, and Salvatori met. The three men spent much of the afternoon debating Reagan's strengths and weaknesses. Salvatori finally relented, believing, after much cajoling from Nofziger, that there was little he could do at such a late hour anyway.

Salvatori's angry response, however, was the exception. Though most supporters were not happy with the blowup, they were not terribly troubled by it either. Aides decided to make sure that Reagan was well rested before appearances, Stu Spencer told reporters that the incident was nothing more than a normal reaction to Christopher's attempts at character assassination, and Reagan iterated that he would not stand mute while his character was being questioned. He denied swearing and explained the tantrum by saying, "Frankly, I got mad. There was no outright charge . . . I felt in the manner of answering, there were inferences that placed me over in that category. It was the sum total of the afternoon. I'm not a politician. There are just some things you can't take as a man."[73]

If anything, the incident had its greatest impact on the opposition. To many Republican moderates and Democratic liberals, the blowup confirmed that Reagan was a loose cannon and that he could be effectively attacked as an angry right-wing extremist and a man temperamentally unfit to govern. Confirmed in his belief that conservatives could not win statewide office, Pat Brown and aides made the mistake of thinking that Reagan would be easy prey in a general election. Oblivious to the growing appeal of conservatism, the governor decided to play dirty to help Reagan win the nomination. It would prove a crucial—and a classic—miscalculation.

In the early spring, not long after Reagan's infelicitous remarks, Brown and several of his top aides began discussing ways to affect the outcome of the GOP primary. Almost every aide agreed that Christopher would be much tougher to beat than Reagan; the question was, what could they do about it? The group came to a simple conclusion; as Joe Cerrell recalled, the consensus was that "We have to screw Christopher, because he's gonna be tough in November and we can roll through Ronald Reagan."[74]

Not all Democrats agreed with this consensus, but their arguments failed to sway the governor. Some warned Brown that Reagan might not be such a pushover. Manning J. Post, a fund-raiser for Unruh, told the governor,

> Pat, you don't really understand. You've got advisors around who tell you what you want to hear. Now stop and analyze it . . . Reagan has always been a good guy. . . . He's always

> been good to an animal. He's always been good to a kid. He's always played the hero role. He's been the Boy Scout troop leader, the choir guy in the church, the husband, the family man. . . . He's the guy with the white hat. He's the Shirley Temple of the male set. This sonofabitch is going to beat the shit out of you . . . because the first thing you've got to have in politics is recognition, that's what you pay all the money for. All this shit for recognition. You take an actor who had the image of a good guy; man, you can't overcome it. You just can't make him a bad guy any more.[75]

Occasionally the governor voiced concerns. "Everybody tells me that it's better to run against Reagan and it will be to our advantage if Christopher loses in the primary and we have Reagan as an opponent," the governor told Nancy Sloss in early 1965. "But I'm not sure, I'm not sure that's right. But everybody agrees. Everybody agrees."[76]

Not Joe Cerrell, a campaign consultant and Brown aide. He had recently watched Pierre Salinger lose a bruising Senate campaign to the right-wing actor George Murphy, and he reminded colleagues that trying to determine the outcome of the GOP primary was dangerous business. "Jesus Christ," Cerrell remembered saying, "I just lost to an actor, who is not as well known as Ronald Reagan. Why don't we just mind our own business?" In hindsight, Cerrell wished he had been even more forceful in his opposition, and told them that Reagan, not Christopher, was the best candidate. But he had lacked the courage to do so.[77]

Instead, Brown, with the near-unanimous consent of his staff, went on to make a massive mistake. In 1940, George Christopher, then still a dairyman, had been convicted of violating state laws regulating the milk industry. Arrested and charged with buying milk from Marin County farmers at rates above the legal limit, Christopher pled guilty to a misdemeanor and paid a modest fine. Fifteen years later, in 1955, Marin County District Attorney A. E. Bagshaw, who had handled Christopher's case, all but exonerated the dairyman of wrongdoing. "Any attempt to use that prosecution as a basis for creating the inference that Mr. Christopher has ever been charged with or convicted of serious crimes involving dishonesty, immorality or moral turpitude, would be a low form of political deceit, which should be exposed, if possible," Bagshaw wrote that year.[78]

But Christopher could not wipe the blot from his record. When Christopher had been arrested, police fingerprinted him and then took a mugshot of the future politician for their records. In the 1950s and early '60s, years when Christopher ran for office, opponents had dredged up the conviction and exploited it for political purposes. In 1962, when Christopher ran for lieutenant governor, Democrats put out a scathing expose that drubbed Christopher as "the only mayor of a major American city with a criminal record," a thug with a history "so atrocious" that he was a walking embarrassment even to then gubernatorial candidate Richard Nixon.[79]

Nor did Brown's aides like the mayor; they considered him corrupt and lazy and joked to one another about his scandal-ridden past. As Hale Champion later confessed, "We didn't have a very high regard for Christopher."[80] The idea of using the arrest to help Reagan seems to have originated with Richard Kline, who, according to at least one account, first suggested that they investigate Christopher's background and somehow publicize the mayor's criminal record. Harry Lerner, a long-time Democratic political consultant with a reputation for hard-knuckle campaigning, expressed support for Kline's idea, and the governor, over the objections of his campaign manager Don Bradley, told aides to go ahead with the project. Like Joe Cerrell, Bradley had little interest in rehashing the scandal. The story, Bradley reasoned, was old news, plus he did not see Christopher as any great threat. Christopher was obviously going to lose to Reagan, Bradley argued, and nothing the Democrats could do would change that.

Bradley was overruled. One Sunday that spring, with Bradley away from the offices, Hale Champion and Harry Lerner convinced Brown to put out the milk story. They decided to feed the story to Drew Pearson, a tendentious, nationally syndicated columnist with a record for carrying out political attacks. A staunch Brown backer, Pearson, the Republican assemblyman William Bagley recalled, had torpedoed Caspar Weinberger's campaign for attorney general in the late fifties by suggesting that Weinberger was Jewish, which he wasn't.[81]

Throughout the primary, Brown's men had given Pearson bits of information for his columns. Lu Haas, an assistant press secretary, pointed out to Pearson several items favorable to Brown, and suggested ways to attack Sam Yorty and other opponents on issues ranging from education to crime. *Time* magazine, Haas told Pearson, had called California's supreme court "'the nation's most aggressive and progressive state court.' This is the court which has come under attack from Democrat Yorty and right-wing Republicans as being soft on crime. Yorty, incidentally, recently has been blasted by two former State Bar presidents for his attacks on Governor Brown's appointments to the courts. . . . The bar presidents say appointments have been the best in state history. . . . It is impressive," Haas continued, "and any mention of our progress would be greatly appreciated."[82]

To feed him information on Christopher, the campaign recruited

Dick Hyer, a former reporter, and also, according to William Bagley, Fred Bagshaw, who was related to the Marin district attorney who had prosecuted Christopher and was a director of public works in the Brown administration. Bagshaw reportedly passed information on to Don Bradley.[83] Hyer also forwarded his information to campaign higher-ups, and Lerner too was busy combing Christopher's background.

Brown had hoped that by going through aides and underlings, he could avoid the taint of having smeared an opponent. Personally, the governor found such smears distasteful, and he tended to shy away from vitriolic, personal attacks on opponents. Harry Lerner, by contrast, had no such reservations about going negative. As Fred Dutton explained, Brown "never could bring himself to be a hatchet man or negative about his opponent too much. He'd do it . . . but he was not effective about it. [He usually had] a hatchet man on the side. . . . Lerner was sort of the ultimate one."[84]

While Lerner helped coordinate anti-Christopher activities, Don Bradley personally sent Drew Pearson the information about Christopher's background. In many respects, Pearson was the perfect man for the job. Though based in Washington, he considered himself something of an expert on California politics, which he had closely followed since the early 1950s. He admired Pat Brown and had even written a controversial column attacking Fred Howser, Brown's opponent in his race for attorney general. (Howser responded with a million-dollar, unsuccessful libel suit against Pearson.) Iconoclastic and full of braggadocio, Pearson styled himself as a crusading columnist who excelled at extirpating corruption and other political malfeasance. (Pearson once boasted to a friend that one of his anti-Nixon articles "turned out to be a hundred percent correct . . . and was eventually published all over the United States.") Plus, he didn't like Christopher.[85]

In early May Pearson wrote a column blistering Christopher as a criminal and a swindler. Learning of the impending attack, Christopher's campaign did everything it could to prevent the article's publication. Arch Monson, Christopher's campaign manager, was backstage at a campaign event at the Pasadena Auditorium when he received a call from Christopher headquarters. An aide told Monson that they had just gotten word that someone was distributing to newspapers a Drew Pearson column about Christopher's arrest and conviction for violating milk laws.[86]

The campaign was frantic. Christopher flew to San Francisco, met with his attorneys, and had one of his lawyers call editors and ask them not to run the column. Christopher's attorney told publishers that the milk scandal was an old, worthless story that had been used years before. The response was favorable. Many newspapers as a rule did not like to run articles containing revelations about California politics that had originated outside state lines. Some of the publishers decided not to run Pearson's piece simply because they did not like it. The article, in fact, was so scathing that two of California's most venerable dailies, the *Los Angeles Times* and the *San Francisco Chronicle*, refused to run it.

But the quest to suppress the article was fanciful from the first, and on May 9, 1966, a small newspaper in Vallejo, California, ran it. Pearson began the article by offering his readers a mea culpa, explaining that he had supported Christopher's campaigns in years past but that in doing so he had made a mistake. "I . . . was fooled," he wrote. "I have dug into Christopher's record," which, the columnist announced, "shows conclusively" that the mayor was dirty. He had, Pearson continued, received $10,000 in kickbacks from farmers eager to sell him milk, flouted health laws, ignored scores of warnings from city officials, and dodged the draft during World War II by claiming he was an agricultural worker. Pearson then quoted former governor Goodwin Knight, who in a 1962 letter to Thomas Storke called Christopher's record "the worst I have ever seen." To drive home his point, Pearson, chagrined that some newspapers had refused to run his column, took the unusual step of flying to California and holding a press conference. Before a gaggle of colleagues and cameras, Pearson brandished the unflattering mug shot photo of Christopher. As campaign manager Arch Monson recalled, "the game was up."[87]

The biggest beneficiary was not Brown but Reagan. As the story wended its way through the state, Reagan kept a low profile. For the most part, he was content to keep quiet and let the Christopher and Brown camps trade charges in public and crumble under an avalanche of recriminations and attacks. Privately, Reagan may have applauded the attack on his opponent and perhaps wanted the story spread, but in public Reagan made every effort to stay above the fray, lest he antagonize Christopher supporters. Reagan assured his opponent that he had nothing to do with the "scurrilous literature" and reiterated his commitment to the Eleventh Commandment. "It is my deep-seated belief that nothing must be done to split our party and thus make it impossible to vote out of office an opposition administration that would stoop to slander and mud-slinging of the type you mentioned," Reagan wrote.[88] When Christopher accused Reagan's supporters in San Diego of distributing the Pearson story, Reagan asked Parkinson to investigate the matter. Reagan then ordered everyone in the campaign to refrain from talking about the article "or in any way [taking] advantage of it." "I know of one occasion when four young men tried to make it appear that they were spreading the smear in my behalf. We immediately investigated and found that all four were members of the very left wing 'Students for a Democratic Society.' . . . Every one in our camp knew that I would disavow and walk away from anyone who took advantage of this smear attempt," he wrote.[89]

Word eventually leaked that Brown was behind the smear, and the news infuriated George Christopher and his moderate supporters. Earlier in the primary, Christopher had seen California Field Polls that showed him gaining ground on Reagan. But in the aftermath of the Pearson piece, his numbers sagged, leaving him a sure loser in June. The article damaged Christopher most in Southern California, where voters, unfamiliar with the San Francisco mayor's record, were hearing for the first time about Christopher's arrest. Moderate Republicans were furious at the governor, whom they considered an occasional ally.

Assemblyman Bill Bagley sent a note to Don Bradley accusing him of being "the architect of Pat Brown's political outhouse." Bagley then distributed the missive to reporters and issued a press release decrying the vicious attack on George Christopher. Bagley called Pearson's piece "putrid," explained that "Brown, of course, wants to . . . destroy George Christopher, and thus have Ronald Reagan nominated," and fingered Bradley as the "smear man."

"Mr. Christopher is a cry baby," Bradley retorted. "George Christopher's arrest record . . . [is a matter] of public record which Mr. Christopher has yet to explain adequately. Mr. Christopher has been ducking the truth for years." Brown's campaign manager then wrote Bagley a twelve-word memo on official campaign stationery adorned with the governor's seal. It read:

> *To: Bill Bagley*
> *From: Don Bradley*
> *Subject: New Smear*
> *Fuck you! You can quote me.*

Bagley, a cameraman in tow, promptly brought the memo to FBI agents, complaining that Pat Brown's campaign manager had sent obscenities through the mail. The bureau took no action.[90]

Pearson, for his part, denied Christopher's charges, defended his attack as a legitimate expose of a corrupt public official, and told reporters that a fawning biography of Christopher, given to him by the mayor, had drawn his attention to the scandal. He said he had hired a former San Francisco city hall employee to research records from the health department, called Christopher's allegations about him and Brown "absurd," and denied ever pressuring Christopher.[91]

It was Pat Brown, more than anyone else, whose reputation was tarnished, and moderate Republicans who were antagonized. A week before election day, with rumors sweeping the state, Brown admitted to reporters that his staff had given Pearson material on the milk scandal. The revelation provoked a new round of hostile editorials. "Apparently Brown was seeking votes from Christopher supporters in the November election," a columnist wrote of Brown's mea culpa, "but it is doubtful many of them will support Brown." Another reporter noted that the smear had undercut the governor's image as a decent and honorable chief executive. "Some people thought that Pat Brown was indecisive or bumbling but no one denied his sincerity or dedication," wrote Harry Farrell. "After the Christopher smear he was just another politician." Hale Champion later recalled the impact of the smear on Brown's campaign. Reagan, Champion explained, "played that very well . . . and Reagan's managers and Reagan's supporters played on the theme of Republican unity and this is the chance to win." Had it not been for the Pearson article, Champion went so far as to speculate, the Republican party "might not have reunited. It was touch and go right after the primary, I think, as to whether or not we could bring in major Republican support of the old Warren stripe back into play."[92]

Historians have only a poor understanding of why Pat Brown wanted to face Reagan in November. It was not primarily because Reagan was an actor, though that was a factor, nor because he was inexperienced and of modest intelligence, nor because he was a novice; it was because he was conservative. Hale Champion admitted later,

> I think that all of us, the governor included, made a wrong calculation: that George Christopher would be a tougher candidate than Reagan—or at least would be harder to handle. That was made in the traditional context of California politics which was that, as with Warren or Pat or others, somebody who could occupy the center would have liberal Republican support . . . and that fringe candidates or people who were viewed as fringe candidates, did not do as well; were usually the losers.
>
> Based on Reagan's history—involvement in the Goldwater campaign, basic support which really came from people who had always been very conservative and so on—the dangerous candidate was the guy who might try to take the middle away. That was especially true because of the Governor's

> activities in 1964 in support of the Rumford Act which, in our view, had cost Salinger the seat in the Senate to George Murphy and was probably, sub rosa, the single most important issue in California.[93]

THE WEEK BEFORE THE PRIMARY, confident of victory, the Reagan camp sent out a mass mailer to all the Christopher supporters they could find, as well as some Yorty faithful, announcing that if Christopher won Reagan promised to support him. But if Reagan won, he said in the mailer, he wanted their support. To Yorty supporters, the Reagan camp sent a personal message: You're interested in the same issues as we are, "so come aboard." "All those things hit on election day," Tom Reed explained, and it "wasn't accidental."[94]

On June 8, 1966, Reagan beat George Christopher handily, garnering 77 percent of the vote, improving on Goldwater's margin in the 1964 California presidential primary by 25 percent. He made huge inroads into the politically moderate sections of Los Angeles and surrounding suburbs. Lou Harris explained the trend, writing, "before this year, southern California was 40 percent conservative. The rest of the state was 18 percent conservative. Now southern California has increased to 50 percent and the rest to 30 percent conservative." It was a new "conservative belt" that cut a wide swath through the southern part of the state.[95]

Soon after the primary, at a meeting at Reagan's home, Robert Finch, Reagan, and others agreed that they would bring together other nominees in Sacramento and make a unity pitch. Finch implored them to bring Christopher aboard and unify the party. Reagan called on the Republican candidates for attorney general and other statewide offices, his top aides and fund-raisers, to meet with him in Los Angeles. They decided that as much as possible they'd run as a team. The party, Reagan and his men were determined, would be behind them.[96] Within a few days Reagan had forgotten about the moderates, but the job had already been done. Christopher was bitter and difficult to reach, but those below him were not, and Reagan's men were successful in recruiting them. The Eleventh Commandment, they thought, so successful a doctrine in the primary, would sweep Reagan into the governor's office and beyond.

The *New York Times* argued that "California voters of both parties very nearly brought off a double disaster in Tuesday's primaries. The Republicans, against all counsels of common sense and political prudence, insisted upon nominating actor Ronald Reagan for Governor. . . . The Democrats, however, managed to pull back from the rim of the abyss and mustered a majority for Governor Pat Brown. . . . Mr. Yorty has aggravated the explosive racial situation in Watts by his frivolous comments and his failure to push effective programs. . . . He deserved a much more resounding defeat."[97] As usual, the *Times* underestimated Reagan's appeal.

TEN

# PRAIRIE FIRE

By the late summer and fall, the Reagan campaign was firing on all cylinders, while Brown was imploding. In the first poll after the primary, Reagan was shown to be ahead of Brown by 15 percentage points. Reagan had the edge on major wedge issues, and his vulnerability as an extremist paled in comparison to the crackup of the Left. Other candidates would have struggled against the Democratic incumbent in a hugely Democratic state, so soon after Goldwater's embarrassing defeat; Reagan's success owed much to his own decision making, his campaign's superior organization, and his ability to take advantage of events well beyond the range of his—or Brown's—control.

A week before the primary election Barry Goldwater predicted that Reagan would win the nomination and that "this victory will bring me great personal joy." He then offered the campaign his services. "If you ever need me in your general campaign, feel free to call. In fact, I am speaking to the women in LaHabra on June the 25th and if Ronnie is the winner, I will extol his virtues, and I know a few, to the skies."[1]

Reagan responded to the senator with a warm reply, thanking his mentor for blazing the trail that had allowed him to come so far so fast. "You set the pattern and perhaps it was your fate to just be a little too soon, or maybe it required someone with the courage to do what you did with regard to campaigning on principles. I have tried to do the same and have found the people more receptive because they've had a chance to realize there is such a thing as truth." He told Goldwater to give him a call at some point, but made no mention of helping him campaign.[2] The omission was not forgetfulness. Distancing himself, at least in public, from controversial national figures like Goldwater, Reagan was determined to stand alone and attack the opposition for "bringing in the carpetbaggers."[3]

Wary of the Republican Right and eager to ensure party unity, in the aftermath of the June election Reagan moved quickly to patch up primary wounds, heal lingering Republican rifts, distance himself from high-profile conservatives, and recruit George Christopher moderates into his campaign. In his primary night victory speech, Reagan reminded the cheering throng at his Los Angeles headquarters that his number one priority in the period ahead was to "seek support of those who voted and campaigned for the other Republican candidates for Governor."[4] Discarding the hard-line anticommunism of the early sixties in favor of a more moderate, less strident conservatism focused on personal integrity, "progressive," "creative" leadership, and "sound common sense," Reagan began to reap the rewards of the previous year's work. The long-awaited transition from the primary to the general election was remarkably smooth.[5]

Building on the letters it had mailed before the primary to top Christopher people that announced Reagan's intention to support Christopher should he win the nomination, and unity pacts aides forged with many moderates, Reagan staffers in each county made follow-up phone calls to their counterparts in Christopher's campaign. The day after Reagan's victory, Tom Reed, Reagan's campaign manager in Northern California, called together top supporters in the north and said, "You call up the Christopher chairmen, and not only have lunch with them but put them on the executive committee."[6] Reagan too went out of his way to woo the enemy camp, making a flurry of phone calls immediately after the primary in which he invited Christopher aides to join his campaign, dangling before them offers of cochairmanships and roles in the Reagan administration.[7]

Stressing their opposition to Pat Brown and the importance of avoiding another bout of internecine warfare, Reagan's aides were able to recruit almost every key Republican. Tom Reed courted Caspar Weinberger, paying a visit to him at his office and urging, "Now we've got to win an election . . . we want you to get aboard and be chairman of the executive committee and when he gets to be governor, why you're gonna play a role in how this administration works."[8] Spencer and Roberts won over even Bill Bagley, among the most loyal of the Christopher diehards. A former Spencer-Roberts ally, Bagley admired their willingness to reach out to him; soon he agreed to come aboard.[9] "The longtime liberal Republicans of San Francisco," Reed remembered, "We went and pounded on the door and said, 'Ya, you now, I'm here."[10]

Not all conservatives were happy with such a strategy, of course. But they were, for the most part, willing to tolerate and even work with the liberals, so focused were they on winning the governorship. In the aftermath of Goldwater, ideological purity gave way to pragmatic politics.[11]

As he had been throughout, Reagan was instrumental in uniting the party. Though recruiting moderates was not his main focus

("Christopher wasn't on his screen," explained Reed), Reagan let it be known that aides and acolytes were to reach out to GOP liberals. As Robert Finch, that year's Republican candidate for lieutenant governor, recalled, Reagan "was very good about it. He followed almost every suggestion, and we had those sessions in Sacramento, and a good tone was set."[12] Reagan also proved adroit at winning over skeptics. When Reed was able to get potential supporters in the same room with Reagan, he was confident the candidate would soon secure their support. Reed said, "You meet him and you say, 'geez, here's a guy who really understands what he's talking about and has a set of principles . . . and I like him and he can win.' "[13]

Reagan's performance was so impressive that Republicans nationwide hailed his campaign as a model for their party. William Middendorf, treasurer of the Republican National Committee, praised Reagan for avoiding a Goldwater repeat. "The difference between the primaries of 1964 and your primary of 1966," he wrote Reagan, "is a study in contrasts. Barry . . . is a man of great personal courage, but tragically permitted himself to be miscast and to let his own words be thrown back at him. He became a study in mistake-clichés that the opposition could grab hold of. . . . You are not accident prone . . . you have not yet made a single mistake where a sometimes belligerent press can get a hook into you. In a word I am absolutely amazed at the performance so far, considering the big spotlight on you."[14]

Reagan's embrace was all encompassing. In the fall, Reagan asked John McCone, the former CIA director, to serve as a surrogate for him and apologize to Senator Thomas Kuchel, a longtime nemesis of California conservatives and an old Reagan foe, for past wrongs. Reagan admitted that he had made a mistake in supporting Kuchel's primary opponent, Loyd Wright, in 1962, and urged McCone to tell Kuchel that he had nothing to do with a scathing, anti-Kuchel smear sheet that had been distributed that year under Reagan's name. He also denied having anything to do with vicious, unfounded, right-wing-generated rumors about Kuchel's homosexuality, telling McCone to be sure to let the senator know that he "wouldn't touch it with a ten foot pole. . . . During the 1962 election I campaigned throughout the state for the entire Republican ticket including Senator Kuchel," Reagan reminded McCone. "I have long wanted to explain this to the Senator."[15]

Stalwarts like Kuchel and Christopher never came aboard, but it didn't matter—almost all their supporters already had. A scant few weeks after the primary, the Reagan and Christopher groups melded into one; top Northern California moderates like Leonard Firestone, Arch Monson, and Justin Dart, among others, joined Reagan's revamped executive committee, an organization that was now almost evenly divided between Christopher and Reagan supporters.[16]

Though there was room on Reagan's committees for everyone, the campaign was adamant about keeping Birchers and other right-wing radicals at arm's length. "Any people we knew who were Birchers or were real Birch sympathizers or even strongly conservative, we deliberately excluded from positions in the campaign," recalled Bill Roberts. "Later on some of them might have wound up on some little periphery things that didn't matter, but they were not in front." Reagan enthusiastically endorsed this tactic. "I agree with you 100 percent," he told Roberts. "I want a Reagan campaign and I want it to be identified as such. I want it to be mine."[17] Reagan also began taking a stronger stand against the society, contending that it was "an outside organization" that he had "no relationship with . . . whatsoever. I don't belong. I have no intention of joining. I've never sought its support, nor do I intend to seek its support."[18]

Reagan's aloofness did not always please his more right-wing backers. As Tom Reed explained, "They were not welcomed. They were sort of viewed as the dead hand of the cross. . . . The point was that there was no flashing big sign that '27 million people can't be wrong' and all that stuff."[19] Still, there was no mass right-wing defection during the campaign. Conservatives afforded Reagan a certain latitude that other politicians, Richard Nixon for example, had not enjoyed. They saw Reagan as a more electable, more genial Goldwater; if they had to endure a few slights, they would do so for the larger cause.

Richard Nixon praised Reagan for running such a deft primary campaign, and for following his earlier advice not to attack Christopher. Holding back, the former vice president predicted a day after the primary, "tremendously enhances your chances in November." Nixon urged Reagan to listen to his "well-intentioned advisors" and continue to "rely primarily on your obviously talented public relations team and on your own good judgment. This combination seems to have served you very well so far! The assault on you will reach massive proportions in the press and on TV as Brown and his cohorts realize that they are going to be thrown off the gravy train after eight pretty lush years. There is an old Mid-Western expression . . . which I would urge you to bear in mind as the going gets tougher. 'Just sit tight in the buggy!'"[20]

Reagan took heart from all the encouragement and support, and he let it be known that he was a conservative who did not want zealots tainting his candidacy. He told George Murphy that McCone and Call were on board, as were "all our old friends who happened to be on the other side in the primary. We do have the party glued together," Reagan wrote, "if only we can keep some of the kooks quiet."[21] Reed's experience is revealing on this point. Reluctant to confer with right-wing activists, whom he deemed more militant, Reed dealt only with conservative leaders whom he considered much more sane and pragmatic—"not crazy," but "hard-working believers," as he put it. Armed with a notebook containing a page for every county in Northern California, Reed identified the heads of prominent right-wing organizations, met with the leaders, and asked them for support, which they were only too happy to give.[22] As former Assemblyman Eugene Chappie recalled, Reed's grassroots efforts generated great enthusiasm for the campaign. "[Reagan] had a brigade of people throughout the state that would call and say, 'hey, I've got a little message here from Ronald Reagan. Got a few minutes? I'd like to have you listen to it.' They would come to your front room. They came to my front room. I mean, geez, all at once, . . . the flags are flying and you can hear John Philip Sousa coming down the road. It was effective as hell."[23] Even in the liberal north, George Christopher country, Reed was able to recruit hundreds of volunteers, organize virtually every county, and generate considerable support.

By the end of June, Reagan had almost every major Republican behind him. "Almost the total campaign structure of the other primary candidates has come aboard enthusiastically," Reagan boasted to a television interviewer around this time. "We just had a great organization. We invited Democrats in," Holmes Tuttle recalled. "We invited all the Christopher people. . . . The next morning [after the primary] . . . they were part of our campaign. . . . I have never seen such an effective campaign as we had in 1966." Lyn Nofziger concurred, noting, "The only person who remained upset was George Christopher, but all of his people came over. . . . They melted in very well. . . . It was the smoothest putting together of two campaigns I've ever seen."[24]

ON THE OTHER SIDE, unity was proving elusive. The Democratic primary had left Brown grasping tightly his familiar ground—only to discover that it was now to the left of most Californians. Nearly a million of them had voted for Yorty; few showed much inclination to support their governor. Over a year earlier, Brown had hopes of uniting party faithful around his candidacy; as he headed into the final contest with Reagan, those hopes seemed in tatters.

Yorty did not help things. On June 8, with the primary just ended, Yorty, as feisty as ever, announced that he would have beaten Brown had moderate Republicans been allowed to vote for him in the primary. The mayor declared that the election "demonstrated the fact that the discredited Brown machine has become an albatross around the neck of the Democratic party. With a strangle hold on the official party machinery and a left wing base in the anti-Johnson California Democratic Council, Brown and his supporters appear determined to hang on until they drag the Democratic party down to defeat. . . . I will make no decision at this time relative to what position, if any, I will take in the coming general election."[25]

Christopher was such a liberal Republican that he actually fell to the left of Yorty on the make-or-break issues that dominated the primary and the election. Yorty's supporters, Democrats all, were less likely to support Brown than were Christopher's. But most of George Christopher's supporters had quickly flocked to Reagan and Christopher himself was furious at the governor, whom he viewed as the architect of his downfall. Brown tried to make amends with the mayor, but he got nowhere. "I think I owe you an apology," the governor told Christopher soon after the primary.

"I know darn well you do," the mayor replied.

Brown asked Christopher to come to Sacramento so he could apologize in person. Christopher, still smarting, replied, "No, Pat, I'm not coming to Sacramento to have you apologize. . . . If you want to apologize you come down to my office in San Francisco."

When Brown arrived, he asked the mayor to accompany him outside, where a dozen or so television cameras were waiting to capture the apology on film. "Before we go," Christopher recalled saying to Brown, "I want to have a private conversation with you in my office. Pat, I've known you ever since I've gotten involved in politics. What you and Harry Lerner did is unconscionable. . . . This was not just a question of violating the milk laws, 'cause any time you mention violating the milk laws, the insinuation is that you must have adulterated milk," which, he told Brown, he never did.

Brown was deeply apologetic. "George, if I wasn't so serious I wouldn't have come all the way from Sacramento to be in your little private office and say how sorry I am for the whole thing, especially now that the truth is out."

The mayor replied, "Here's what we're gonna do. We'll go inside, the press is waiting, I'll accept your apology, but don't expect me to come out and campaign for you or say anything good about you during the campaign. I'm not gonna do it. The hurt has been too deep. Only for old time's sake, I'm accepting your apology so let's go out there and get it over with."[26]

On June 29, a few weeks later, Brown again tried to woo the mayor, telling him that he wanted "to express the high regard I have had for you over the past 30 years as a man of personal integrity and honor and as a public official who has made significant contributions to the welfare of our state. It is a source of personal regret to me that charges more than a quarter of a century old, relating to your milk company . . . were raised in the primary election." He also said that he agreed with the prosecutor who said the violations were technical and did not warrant criminal prosecution.[27] Brown's efforts were all for naught. In the end Christopher endorsed no one. Two of Christopher's campaign consultants, Herb Baus and William Ross, did decide to back Brown over Reagan because they had become so disillusioned while working for Goldwater in 1964. They tried to set up a Republicans for Brown organization—but it went nowhere.[28]

If almost no one to his right would support Brown, the governor had an even greater problem with the foundation on which he had built so much successful legislation—his party's liberal base. Brown watched helplessly as key Democratic friends, allies, and constituencies grew more militant. Many African-Americans were angry at Brown's handling of the Watts riots, and wanted a more far-reaching program of race reform that included civilian review boards for police and an admission that California society was still fundamentally racist and unjust.

Mexican-Americans also soured on the governor. In March 1966, on Easter Sunday, the United Farm Workers (UFW) sponsored a major march on the capitol to protest working conditions in California's agricultural fields. When Cesar Chavez, the popular head of the UFW, demanded a meeting with Brown, the governor refused, choosing instead to go on vacation in Palm Springs. *El Malcriado*, a Hispanic newspaper, captured the growing disillusionment among Mexican-Americans when it warned, "If you want to keep your job, Pat, you better not take us for granted. You better prove to us that you care about our problems. Because if we're going to have another four years with one enemy in Sacramento, we would rather have an honest enemy like Reagan. At least we would know where we stand."[29]

There was also, as an aide told the governor, "tension between Mexicans and Negroes in Los Angeles," a rift that Mayor Yorty had exacerbated with "some of the vilest race mongering I've heard of in this half of the 20th Century." The aide urged Brown to make amends with Chavez, flout the conventional wisdom that "Mexicans don't register and won't vote," and solicit their support.[30] But Brown, scrambling toward the center, did not make any major overtures either to blacks or to Mexican-Americans, lest he open himself to more attacks.

It was an equal-opportunity defection. Thousands of white liberals and Democratic activists, furious at Brown's support for the war in

Vietnam, left the party in droves. The governor was no great fan of the war, and harbored serious doubts about the wisdom of fighting a land war in a tiny nation thousands of miles away. But he was not about to go campaigning against it. Brown needed badly the support of the national party, and President Johnson had made it clear that politicians who wanted such backing had to toe the line on Vietnam. The governor believed reports coming out of Washington that the war was progressing apace.[31] As Fred Dutton explained, "When Vietnam came along, we didn't have that [antigovernment] attitude. We had presidential leadership, we had a party in whose judgment and experience we had a lot of confidence."[32]

Nineteen sixty-six was not a year for waffling, but Brown, as he had done with the Free Speech Movement, seemed unable to stop himself from reaching out. Andrew Glass, a correspondent for the *Washington Post* covering Brown's campaign, reported that the governor, despite trying to distance himself from noisy left-wing dissidents, harbored feelings for the protesters. Arriving in San Diego, Brown spotted a handful of antiwar activists who had turned out to picket the governor at the airport. One demonstrator told the governor, "We're sincere." The governor leaned across the rope that separated him from the demonstrators, until his face was almost touching the protester's. "I know you are very sincere," Brown whispered to the young woman. "You are all wonderful people."[33]

A conservative columnist, Ralph de Toledano, later wrote, "What, after all, is so 'wonderful' about the Vietniks?," the same "Vietniks who helped bring anarchy to the University of California campus[?]"[34] The columnist suggested that Reagan ask Brown to explain his statement. Antiwar activists took an equally dim view of Brown's conflicted feelings on the issue. In July, former Democratic State Chairman Roger Kent engaged in a series of debates about Vietnam with New Left activist Robert Scheer. Scheer was the peace candidate for Congress from Alameda County, who attracted to his cause left-wing leaders like Si Casady and Julian Bond, both of whom were trying to organize a National Conference of New Politics. Kent recalled the disastrous debates: "Boy, what a clobbering I took! This was just as the Vietnam dissent was really taking off. These guys were saying that there was no difference between Reagan and Brown." Kent tried to sway the activists by pointing out the stark differences between the candidates. "Don't just put blinders on and say there's one thing that you're interested in, which is this war," Kent beseeched them. "And furthermore, it's none of Brown's business and he hasn't got a damn thing to do with it."

"Well," an audience member growled, "why does he have to talk about it?"[35]

Fred Dutton captured the gravity of the situation for the Democrats when he told White House aide Bill Moyers that the Democrats were unraveling in large part because of Vietnam, which he said was "a fierce symbol and ulcer eating away at the local level support for moderate Democrats like Brown. . . . The strength of feeling over it . . . overrides any public issue or political tie in the state at present." The Left, he added, "feel[s] more intensely about this issue than anything since the mid-1930s and cannot be taken for granted or disregarded without lasting consequences."[36]

The war, the riots, the fight in the primaries, all had sown deep divisions within the Democratic party, leaving Brown in a poor position to take on any Republican challenger, let alone one who had a broad cross section of the GOP united behind him. To make matters worse, Brown's own campaign was bogged down in a series of debilitating feuds. Soon after the primary, it became apparent to aides in the Los Angeles headquarters that the campaign had fallen into disarray. Different advisors seemed to be in control on different days. Brown had only himself to blame; immediately after the primary, the governor, distraught by Yorty's showing, placed a call to his old campaign manager, Fred Dutton. Dutton had moved to Washington in 1961, when he went to work as cabinet secretary in the Kennedy administration. A sharp political tactician, Dutton embodied much of the can-do spirit of Brown's first years in Sacramento, and the governor called on him in the spring of 1966 in the hopes that he could somehow save him. Reaching Dutton at his home in Maryland, Brown urged his friend to return to California and take the reins of his campaign. You got me into this, said Brown, referring to 1958, now come help me get out.[37]

Dutton deeply admired the governor, and he felt bad for him as well. But he was reluctant to return, especially after being out of the California loop for so many years. Once you've left California politics, he thought, "you don't go back." Dutton knew Brown's other aides would resent his presence, and he realized that he was an outsider with no base of his own. Nonetheless, he came. He tried to maintain a low profile, but, highly critical of Brown's primary campaign, Dutton was eager to seize control of the operations. He believed in running a tight ship, where power was concentrated in a single individual.[38]

It did not take Dutton long to figure out that he had made a mistake. He arrived in Los Angeles, took up a room in a motel on Sunset Boulevard, and began surveying the political scene. He did not like what he saw. Brown, Dutton surmised, had become much too establishment and uncharacteristically subdued as well. In Dutton's eyes, Brown had grown accustomed to the trappings and the perks of power; he had been in office too long, Fred thought, had gotten too close to his wealthy campaign contributors, and had lost sight of key constituencies.[39]

"I like the game, the dynamics, the in-fighting and argument and relationships of politics," Dutton recalled. "In '66, I felt that basic priorities—identification with the people and the economy and life of the state—had been lost in preoccupation with running the governmental machinery. . . . The governor was ripe to be beaten. He was not entirely aware of it. Pat tended to run scared whenever he was up for election. But he thought in '66 that his situation would heal and go together, particularly after—and like—his surprise and admirable defeat of Richard Nixon in '62." Brown and his aides had focused too much on personalities; from the administration's perspective, "Yorty was an SOB, an opportunist. [The Brown people] were going to save California from him. Jesse Unruh was looked on as overly ambitious, avaricious, premature in his desire to move into the governorship, undercutting the governor. A lot of all that was true. But . . . they were focusing upon immediate personalities instead of what the real situation was. . . . They had sort of lost their immediate sensitivity and hunger towards the public."[40]

Dutton's arrival in California exacerbated tensions within the campaign. Brown's longtime political advisor, Don Bradley, had been in charge during the primary, and Hale Champion, the governor's closest confidant, had served as the key link between the administration and the campaign. Now, Brown seemed to be handing the reins over to Dutton, only the governor never stipulated that Dutton was in charge, leaving the two men to battle for control.

Dutton and Bradley were a study in contrasts. A fiery union supporter with a reputation as a street fighter, Bradley was the grizzled dean of California Democratic politics. Widely considered one of the state's savviest tacticians—a Democratic Spencer-Roberts—Bradley had engineered Brown's stunning come-from-behind campaign against Nixon, and was regularly referred to as a chain-smoking "political animal," a shrewd troubleshooter, and a tough negotiator, a politician who could bend people to his will and bring sides together. "I've seen him go into warring factions—and we've had plenty of them—talk to both sides and bring them together," Roger Kent said. Brown and Bradley were avid golfers, and they often discussed politics while playing. Brown had great trust in Bradley's judgment, telling a reporter at one point, "he gets results." Accustomed to pressure-filled campaign situations, Bradley was not, as he once boasted to a reporter, "inclined toward ulcers."[41]

The younger Dutton was also a steely tactician, but he was more cerebral, an exceedingly smart, aggressive advisor who plied the governor with multipage letters and memos—or "meemos," as Brown affectionately dubbed them—on a whole range of subjects. Many Brown aides found the hot-tempered Dutton imperious and overbearing. As campaign aide Joe Cerrell recalled, Dutton once stormed into Cerrell's office threatening to fire him over some minor incident. Cerrell calmed him down until Dutton admitted that he was overwrought and had overreacted. It was not an uncommon event.[42]

Hale Champion was still a third force, a man many considered a brilliant administrator but a poor tactician. Brown's director of finance and most trusted advisor, Champion tried to keep tensions between Bradley and Dutton to a minimum. It was not a job for which he was well suited. Kent, a Bradley loyalist, dismissed Hale as a man of poor political judgment and someone who "had participated in some of the most dismal and disastrous political decisions involving Senators and congressmen . . . that you could imagine. His judgment, to my mind, was totally faulty on these matters. He was not a good politician, and he was not going to be any good running the Brown campaign."[43] Dutton also thought that Champion lacked political savvy and was too governmental; he was too liberal, in other words, and had helped push Brown ahead of his constituency on thorny matters such as civil rights and crime. Dutton and Champion argued constantly about how to reconcile political and administrative needs, with meager results.

Champion, Bradley, and Dutton, in the words of Roger Kent, were the "perfect bastard troika." Some aides were loyal to Champion; others to Bradley. The machinery of the campaign belonged to Bradley, but Dutton had been elevated to a major advisory role. Brown had a difficult time resolving the festering "ego problems" and ideological rifts. Averse to conflict, the governor rarely imposed his will on the trio, instead letting them duke it out for control.[44]

Bradley and Dutton quickly grew to resent each other. Dutton revealed such tensions in a memo to his colleagues. Several key campaign people, he argued, were incompetent and unfit for their current jobs. "All are fine, loyal individuals," Dutton wrote. "But they just do not appear to be hard-driving, creative, heavyweight, flexible people for the tough predicament we face." The problem, Dutton explained, was that the old guard was hostile to new faces, including Dutton, Unruh, and Joe Wyatt, a powerful Democratic fund-raiser in Los Angeles. "The overall operation has to be upgraded, melded together, and made responsive to the changed concepts. . . . I don't want two 'camps.' . . . There seems to be some fighting over the steering wheel at present. . . . I frankly don't intend to have my original assignment changed by erosion."[45]

The Dutton-Bradley rift soon became painfully public, and it cost them one of the campaign's key allies. Carmen Warschaw, the heiress to the Harvey Aluminum Company fortune and a staunch Unruh supporter, was nicknamed the Dragon Lady for her acerbic wit and blunt-spoken ways. "The people with money don't have enough say in the Democratic party," Warschaw once complained. Up for election as Democratic party state chair, she lost narrowly after Brown's supporters threw their votes to her opponent, Charles Warren. Brown had promised to support Warschaw, but instead of a public endorsement, the governor voted by proxy and secret ballot and left the convention early. Bradley supported Warren, Dutton backed Warschaw. At one point during the convention, the two titans grew so angry with one another that they almost came to blows. Champion stepped between them, narrowly averting a brawl.[46]

Infuriated by the lack of support, Warschaw, who was also a Yorty ally, broke with Brown in October, announcing to the press that she had met with Reagan and that she approved of his "fresh new approach." Her husband, Louis, was later appointed by Reagan to the Airport Commission—something Roger Kent, for one, later speculated was a quid pro quo for the endorsement.[47]

With the Brown campaign in open disarray, aides stopped trying to maintain even the pretense of harmony. When asked who was in charge of the governor's reelection bid, Bradley told a reporter, "It just depends on whose day off it is." As Brown later admitted of the campaign, "It never went together."[48]

In spite of their differences, Bradley, Dutton, and even Champion realized they had lost the middle. Almost immediately after the primary, aides sent the governor a slew of memos on ways to recapture the center. Two suggestions stood out: First, advisors urged the governor to defuse the social issues that had done him so much damage. Though they did not exactly know how Brown would do so, the aides suggested that Brown marginalize the issues by arguing that race, the war, and the University were not fit topics for a political campaign. Second, the advisors told Brown that to compete with Reagan in the fall, he needed to develop a positive agenda for a third term, based on economic growth and on fresh approaches to the law-and-order issue.

Two days after the primary, on June 10, Fred Dutton sent Bill Moyers a letter analyzing the national implications of the California election. Dutton realized that the social upheavals in the state had precipitated a "major political-cultural watershed," and he suggested that the only way to hold the line was for Brown to take a more popular approach to these issues in the hopes of staving off a mass Democratic defection in the general election. Dutton urged the White House to make an off-the-record call to Yorty, whom he said "unquestionably got conservative Republican financing for his race. But he admires and has ample reason to respond to a Presidential call. No one within the state would have the slightest effect on Sam. If he takes on Brown this fall, the chance of the Democrats winning is 40–60 at best."

Race was also a crucial issue. "The racial backlash in the state is not latent but immediate, vocal and strong. It is far worse than in '64." Dutton wrote that ongoing flare-ups in Watts and Oakland only fed the "insecurity and hostility among much of the white majority." He said that fair housing had hurt Democrats, partly because the Republicans were deftly exploiting the issue and partly "because of an underlying and spontaneous welling up." And he argued that nothing was being done with Watts except for a few perfunctory press releases. Pleading for help, Dutton asked Moyers to pour money into Watts, not because the blacks needed assistance but because the governor did. "Help is needed not to get political credit in the area (in fact, Pat should let others take credit for what is done there) but to calm the Negro community for the next few months," a point he made to Sargent Shriver as well. Stressing the importance of "short-term results," Dutton concluded by saying that the time had come to dramatize Brown's accomplishments and to "draw up some approaches to problems . . . more public and politic—and not so damn 'governmental' all the time."[49]

In Dutton's view, Brown, Champion, and others had overstepped their mandate, moving too far, too fast, on issues such as civil rights, Berkeley, and welfare. Reagan was killing Brown on the social issues, Dutton said, and the campaign needed to come up with its own solutions, ones that they could contrast favorably to Reagan's. But what would these "new proposals" look like, and how would they bring voters back into the Democratic column?

Winslow Christian, Brown's executive secretary, had the answer. He urged Brown not to back off on some of his more controversial stances he had "taken because of principle," but he did say that Brown needed to find "new issues that have no strong left-right coloration, or have direct and personal economic pull of the kind that pulled so many basically conservative voters away from Goldwater," issues such as Social Security.

Christian observed that "the white majority" was "annoyed and fearful about the Negro rebellion and think you are too far out in front in this area. Here," he reassured the governor, "there are several substantively valid proposals that can re-identify you as a wise and progressive law enforcement officer rather than as a coddler of hoodlums and distributor of welfare checks." Voters were also "disaffected with us" over several thorny side issues, including welfare, taxes, cronyism, and farm workers' revolt. (Other voters, he said, were "simply bored and ready to let the 'outs' have their turn.")

The case for a third term, Christian and other aides agreed, rested on a program of tax cuts, welfare reform, new education programs (that could induce Reagan to attack parents, teachers, and the "educational establishment," as Nixon had done in 1962), and a transportation plan that would take some of the sting out of Reagan's attacks and at the same time show Brown at his Democratic best—a can-do chief executive with solid and responsible ideas for the future. Christian, like Dutton, urged Brown to think more politically and exploit public prejudices about welfare, race, and birth control. "People think that welfare is supporting hordes of illegitimate Negro children produced by women who probably welcome a new pregnancy as a chance to augment the welfare check," Christian wrote. "Rational argument will not put this idea down. We happen to have a good foundation for constructive and responsible action that would be both highly conspicuous and . . . gratifying to the prejudices I have mentioned." He suggested Brown appoint a commission to study the matter and then come out in support of family planning and birth control measures. Christian maintained that might reduce welfare babies while at the same time protecting "the individual's religious freedom and personal dignity."[50]

Other strategies were floated but they only revealed the campaign's defensive posture. Some friends suggested that Brown needed to improve his television image, and one made a serious offer to lend Brown his "exercycle." Another argued that Brown's appearances needed more drama and "staging," ("even the decorations should be planned"), and that every appearance should be designed "for maximum impact on the home television viewers who will be getting fleeting glimpses of the governor in action." More important, aides suggested that Brown start a war on white-collar crime and stake out positive positions on the so-called gut issues. Other aides argued that the social issues were political bombshells that Brown should avoid at all costs. Brown's instincts told him to stick to his program of liberal reform and defend the poor and the blacks from Reagan's seemingly vicious charges. The campaign was torn.[51]

No issue better illustrated Brown's dilemma than that of race. Democratic pollster Don Muchmore conducted a series of surveys for the Brown campaign that year on racial attitudes in California. The results left the administration shaken. In one poll, roughly 90 percent of black respondents said that Brown, more than Reagan, had done and would continue to do more for their interests. That figure was to be expected; Brown had been a staunch civil-rights supporter, and had passed liberal legislation favorable to African-Americans. The white response, however, surprised aides; roughly 50 percent said that *Reagan* would be a better governor for the blacks. Hale Champion, for one, understood the implication; as he explained years later, Governor Brown was strongly identified with black interests and yet many whites considered Brown a bumbler on race matters. "It was a very strong expression of racial feeling," Champion recalled. "The whites thought they knew what was good for blacks and Brown wasn't [it]. The point was that they didn't like what Brown was doing on behalf of the blacks and they thought that was bad for everybody including themselves."

Bowing to political realities, Brown tried to distance himself from black concerns by proposing the establishment of a blue-ribbon commission to examine ways to reform the wildly unpopular Rumford Act, which had recently been reinstated after the California Supreme Court declared Proposition 14 unconstitutional. The proposal, as Champion later admitted, was an attempt to allay white fears; but Brown refused to go any further, and in the end he pleased no one. Fair-housing advocates criticized Brown for backtracking on the issue and for playing to white prejudices, while Reagan attacked the governor for supporting a measure that infringed on individual property rights.

Brown announced that law enforcement, not racism, had become the "overriding issue" of the campaign. "People want the rule of law to be observed in this state," he said. "As Governor, I try my best to see it is." He argued that riots were a national problem, that a small handful of militant minorities were trying to start a revolution, and it was not an appropriate subject for a political campaign, "because it is the toughest domestic issue that we have had probably in the last 25 years."[52] Such convoluted logic, mixed with weak attempts to co-opt Reagan's lead on law and order, were doomed to fail.

Both candidates were striving toward an agreeable middle that in both spirit and rhetoric would be easier for Reagan to find. Indeed, the middle was rushing toward Reagan, and he had only to convince it that he was not a reactionary Republican but a bold-thinking conservative with fresh ideas and programs. To do this he reemphasized a campaign slogan, suggested to him by W. S. McBirnie, a right-wing preacher, that he had first utilized during the primary. The Creative Society, as McBirnie dubbed it, helped Reagan style himself as a kind of new-look conservative, a forward-looking right-wing Republican with a positive approach to the problems of modern society. The slogan also allowed Reagan to distance himself from the dour anticommunist ideology that he had championed just a few years earlier; and it gave him a way to match the soaring rhetoric emanating from the liberal camp. Though it never received as much attention as John Kennedy's New Frontier or Lyndon Johnson's Great Society, the slogan did lend a coherence to Reagan's campaign, blending his strident appeals for law and order with his emphasis on individual initiative.

By stressing self-help and the efficacy of private enterprise, McBirnie offered Reagan a way to couch conservative attacks on big government in a more positive light and a way to distance himself from the hackneyed ideas and antiquated programs of the American Right. Republicans, McBirnie said, "*could unite* on this concept. . . . I know in my heart something like this is the very thing needed to transform our campaign into a crusade! . . . It really could have *national* repercussions if it can be made to work in California."[53]

McBirnie's words were victory's fuel; the man himself was a liability. The host of a radio program that mixed pulpit preaching with the shrill rhetoric of the anticommunist Right, the reverend was a controversial figure. Though not a member of the John Birch Society, he incarnated the kind of conservative activist that had sent chills down the spines of Reagan's handlers. He was a danger in other ways as well. In June 1959, McBirnie had resigned as pastor of the Trinity Baptist Church in San Antonio, Texas, after confessing that he had slept with the wife of a former parishioner. "Satan has taken advantage of the Church's weakest link, me," McBirnie explained in his resignation speech, "but I can't even blame Satan. I can only blame myself." Following his admission, McBirnie divorced his wife of nineteen years and, a few days later, married his longtime lover.[54]

At least his Creative Society slogan was a winner. A Reagan campaign memo suggested the benefits of adopting McBirnie's program; the Creative Society, Reagan's aides argued, would convey to voters the message that

> There [was] no area of human need and no commonly shared problem which cannot be tackled and solved. The big question is not *whether* our national and state human problems shall be solved but *how*. Republicans have sometimes been caricatured as people who want to turn back the clock, to return to the status quo. But, on the contrary, our eyes are turned to the future for that is where we are going to live. . . . If the socialistic type of government is called the "Great Society," which it is mistakenly called, let us propose another, a better idea, a happy and constructive alternative: THE CREATIVE SOCIETY. The Premise of the "Creative Society" is that there is already or potentially present within the incredibly rich human resources of our state, the full solution to

> every problem which we face. . . . The "Creative Society" seeks to go beyond bleeding heart or bumbling "liberalism" . . . [and achieve] the ultimate in personal liberty consistent with law and order.[55]

Noting that the politicians of his generation had failed to solve society's most pressing problems, Reagan announced in a speech that the time had arrived for his new approach. The older generation, Reagan said, had fought hard for freedom, but "we are confused and we have confused you with a double standard of morality. We try to keep alive a moral code for our individual conduct, . . . but at the same time, we accept double-dealing at government levels, and we've lost our capacity to get angry when decisions are not based on moral truth, but on political expediency." Reagan declared that he was not a politician but an ordinary citizen "with a deep-seated belief that much of what troubles us has been brought about by politicians." It was time, he urged, for a government more in line with the ideas of the founding fathers—that individuals had the capacity for self-government, "the dignity and the ability and the God-given freedom to make our own decisions, to plan our own lives and to control our own destiny."

"Time to look to the future," Reagan exhorted. "Join me in a dream of a California whose government isn't characterized by political hacks and cronies and relatives—an administration that doesn't make its decisions based on political expediency but on moral truth. Together, let us find men to match our mountains. . . . This is a practical dream—it's a dream you can believe in—it's a dream worthy of your generation. Better yet, it's a dream that can come true and all we have to do is want it badly enough."[56]

It was a positive and unifying idea that captured well what Reagan stood for: simple values; hallmark American liberal traditions around which all Californians could unite. At a time when everything seemed so rotten, Reagan offered people something that seemed so good.

FINALLY, ALL THAT WAS LEFT for Brown was to go on the attack; to prove to voters that the wholesome image that Reagan was exploiting was nothing more than an intricate fraud. Almost every Democrat involved in the campaign agreed that attacking Reagan as a right-wing actor with no government experience could be Brown's escape hatch. As one aide recalled, "Only if you had voters feeling that Reagan was too far to the right, did you really have a chance of beating him by that time." Focused on Reagan's acting background and his right-wing credentials, the governor and aides believed that somewhere, somehow,

Reagan would slip up, reveal himself to be a kook, and sink his candidacy.[57]

On June 11, Fred Dutton said that the key to the campaign was to focus on one or two of Reagan's weaknesses and then exploit them mercilessly. "A sharp negative focus will require discipline on your part and a highly centralized campaign structure," Dutton told Brown. "Three hard-hitting 'heavies' should be selected and . . . scheduled on almost a continuous basis around the state, beginning in late August at the latest." A crash research job on Reagan was needed, Dutton added, so that the campaign could publicize Reagan's most incendiary statements from the past ten years. Don Bradley explained that the campaign did everything it could to tie Reagan to the Right. "We made a considerable effort to establish the right-wing connections Reagan had, and Reagan was making every effort to keep as far away from it as he could. That was the major battle."

Dutton suggested other lines of attack, namely, that Reagan was running for president or that he was "just an actor. . . . To a very considerable extent, Spencer-Roberts could even be made the real target of the campaign, ridiculing and satirizing both them and Reagan." Roger Kent explained Brown's strategy as a two-pronged approach that stressed Reagan's deficiencies and Brown's track record. "We'd just say, 'Well, he's just a damned actor. He's never run a business, he's never run a political office. And he's getting his money from these crooks!' That was the thrust of the negative campaign that we were pushing against Reagan."[58]

The campaign had started researching Reagan's background in early 1965, and by the fall of 1966, aides had several issues with which to pound; these included his position on Berkeley, "the menagerie of fanatics he would bring into the government," his presidential aspirations, and lack of knowledge on issues such as unemployment and disability insurance. "We can hang him on the specifics. Social security, right to work, all the rest," Patricia Sikes told Brown. "Note the statement by Reagan regarding Proposition 16," another Brown memo scoffed. "It is one of the most idiotic I've ever read. He is talking out of both sides of his mouth. . . . What kind of government leader can propose the adoption of a measure that is probably unconstitutional. . . . Someone could have some fun with this statement."[59]

Aides tapped Harry Lerner and Richard Kline to head up the negative campaign and to write a "detailed survey and plan of action." At the time, Lerner was retired and living in Palm Springs; but as Fred Dutton recalled, no one was better suited for the negative campaign than Lerner. "Harry is what we call in politics a 'carver,'" observed Dutton. "He's primarily a believer in highly-simplified, essentially-negative campaign: find one or two things to rip apart." Lerner and Kline were put in charge of a full-time, independent negative operation that had a direct line to the governor.[60]

With assistance from Democrats and liberals around the state, the campaign put together negative kits detailing Reagan's extremist ties and produced a fourteen-page pamphlet entitled, "Ronald Reagan, Extremist Collaborator, An Exposé." Birch bookstore bumper stickers advocating Earl Warren's impeachment and "phas[ing] out McNamara" were plastered across the title page, while Reagan was depicted as the "extremists' collaborator in California. He endorses their projects, promotes their policies, takes their money. He is their 'front man.'"

> IT IS TRUE THAT GENUINE CONSERVATIVES ALSO SUPPORT REAGAN. BUT THEY DO NOT CALL THE SHOTS. THEY BRING RESPECTABILITY TO A POLITICAL CAMPAIGN WHOSE TRUE NATURE, EXPOSED IN THIS DOCUMENT, WILL DISMAY MODERATES AND CONSERVATIVES OF BOTH POLITICAL PARTIES.

Chapters focused on salacious subjects such as "California 'Fright-Wing' Money Flows to Reagan" and "Reagan—Paramilitarists' Choice." The pamphlet informed voters that Reagan had helped raise money for the Birch-friendly magazine *Human Events* and had received substantial funding from right-wing anticommunist crazies. The sheet linked Reagan to anti-Semites and white supremacists (a few had endorsed his candidacy), and blasted Reagan for refusing to repudiate the support of such fringe figures.[61]

The Brown campaign, in fact, had a wealth of information on Reagan from several different sources. Aides compiled a list of incendiary Reagan statements on civil rights, education, and foreign policy. The American Jewish Committee (AJC) sent Brown material detailing the radical Right's involvement in the Reagan campaign. In a confidential memo to Brown, the AJC charted the connections between Reagan's wealthy backers, Walter Knott and Cy Rubel among others, and a host of ultraconservative figures and groups.[62]

In October, the governor, eager to link Reagan to the John Birch Society, taunted John Rousselot, the Birch public relations director, trying to get him to sue Brown for defaming the society, which Brown had compared to the Communist party in an address at the Commonwealth Club. "I hope you do sue—and promptly," Brown wrote. "I would welcome a court declaration on the subversive character of the John Birch Society. A suit would provide me with an opportunity to subpoena the secret records of the Birch Society to disclose the full extent of the penetration of Birchers into Ronald Reagan's campaign structure, and confirm the fact that Birch money is flowing into his campaign treasury." Brown had already identified 31 Birchers who were campaigning in some capacity for Reagan, and he believed a glimpse of the membership rolls would reveal many more.[63]

Brown's campaign employed other tactics as well. Aides suggested that someone should be put on full-time Reagan-watch and follow the candidate around the state, tape-record his talks, and relay any damaging information to press aides in Los Angeles. Aides also tried to convince reporters to run negative stories; as one Brown supporter suggested, "We should firmly plant with editors the fact that we will have a response to any substantive Reagan statement." The campaign began investigating whether Reagan had received $10,000 for a Goldwater speech in 1964. Aides retrieved transcripts from Reagan's news conferences in which he denied the charge and offered to make public his income tax return, and then forwarded them to a reporter at *Newsweek.* Brown aide John McDonald told Hale Champion that the campaign should continue investigating Reagan's income for "conflict of influence as a potential holder of public office and for any other goodies that might turn up."[64]

Trying not to sully Brown's reputation, the campaign employed liberal allies of the governor to hound Reagan. State Controller Alan Cranston began chasing Reagan around the state in the summer, hoping to confront the candidate in public about his right-wing connections. Cranston caught up with Reagan in August at the Sacramento airport. With cameras looking on, Cranston handed Reagan another pamphlet detailing Reagan's links to the Right, this one entitled "The John Birch Society: A Soiled Slip Is Showing." One of Cranston's staffers had spent months working on the piece.[65]

But Reagan, as he did with most of Brown's charges, simply shrugged off the attack, telling reporters that Brown was trying to divert attention from the real issues of the campaign. Reagan was largely immune to such charges. He had no scandal in his background, and the attempts to link him to the Right foundered on his genial personality. His campaign had worked hard in 1965 and early 1966 to defuse the Birch issue, and now that work was bearing fruit. Birchers had been excluded from the campaign, and right-wing activists in groups such as the United Republicans of California, the California Republican Assembly, the Young Republicans, and Young Americans for Freedom played only bit roles, leaving Brown's campaign with little fodder for the general election.[66]

Subterfuge was a part of Reagan's campaign, too. Bill Roberts, unafraid of hitting hard, and, below the belt if necessary, had placed a political spy in the Brown camp, who informed him one day of some bad news. Roberts came into Salvatori's office and said, "[M]y man tells me they are going to run a series of ads against Reagan besmirching his character involving some sexual misconduct, some female or whatever. I don't know exactly what it is, but they're going to do it."

Reagan's aides convened for an emergency meeting. Roberts argued that the campaign ought to put out some full-page newspaper ads, right away, warning the public of the attack to come and blasting the opposition for such devious scheming. Tuttle and Salvatori were more cautious. They pointed out first that Brown might never make such a charge, and even if he did they didn't know when or how he would do so. Second, they told Roberts, they shouldn't deny a smear before it occurred. Salvatori controlled the purse strings and thought the ads a waste of campaign coffers. He thought it his duty to prevent any unwise expenditures, and this was certainly one.

Tuttle and Salvatori decided to approach Reagan directly with the problem; perhaps he had information about this. Was this a rumor he had encountered before? Was it true? Might Brown have proof? About a half-dozen top aides met Reagan at his home. Someone broke the news: "Now, Ronnie, you understand that in politics you must tell us everything that has happened in your life." They explained what Roberts's spy had reported, and as they were doing so Nancy entered the room headed toward the front door. The men spotted her instantly and, growing apprehensive, clammed up.

Reagan recovered quickly, however. Sensing his aides were delving into some sensitive area, he tried to reassure his guests. "Fellows, I can tell from the way you stopped talking when Nancy appeared that you have something on your mind. Now, what exactly do you have in mind?"

They asked Reagan if he had had any affairs that the opposition might exploit.

"Look," he said, "since I have known Nancy I can assure you that there is nothing to any rumor of any kind of misbehavior on my part. You can be assured that there is nothing to worry about."

Yet Roberts, perhaps worried that the rumors would damage Reagan, still pressed for a preemptive strike. The next day Roberts contacted Reagan. It was a political decision, and Roberts was in charge of all political decisions, he told the candidate. Would you please instruct the Kitchen Cabinet of this? Roberts left and Reagan picked up the phone and called up Salvatori and Tuttle, who were downstairs. Would they come by his office?

Reagan was friendly when the men arrived, and he heard their side of the argument. He said he understood their view, adding that Roberts' position too had merit. He offered to split the difference. Run an ad, but change it in such a way as would be acceptable to you. Tuttle and Salvatori relented, and left impressed. Tuttle turned to Salvatori as the two left the office. "Well, we certainly won our point," he boasted. Salvatori replied, "Holmes, that was the most brilliant performance in how to reconcile differences between individuals. He pleased Roberts, who wasn't overruled, and he pleased us by agreeing to change the text of the ad." "I understood what he did, and I was very delighted," Salvatori explained.[67]

With the negative campaign falling flat, some Democrats grew disillusioned with Brown's tactics. Cranston's staff threatened to quit en masse over the smear campaign, according to one former aide. State Senator George Miller urged Brown to "run on your record and forget this Birch thing." And one Brown aide captured the ineffectiveness of the campaign when he admitted to a colleague that "The 1 point that has not gotten across about the John Birch Society is what is wrong with it. . . . People are pretty well convinced that Ronnie has some tie through his support with the John Birchers. But I sense no particular alarm except among the liberals."[68]

Frustrated by their inability to tie Reagan to the Right, Brown and aides began harping on Reagan's acting background. Miffed as to how "professional image makers can move thousands on thousands of citizens to support a man whose experience largely has been role playing, parroting the words of script writers and, for pay, carrying on a crusade for conservatism across the land," Brown tried to remind voters that Reagan was an actor with not a single day's experience in government, and certainly not someone fit to lead the largest state in the union.[69]

This strategy, even more than the extremist one, backfired; instead of revealing Reagan's lack of qualifications, it fed the growing impression, begun with the Christopher smear, that the governor was a scandalmonger running away from real problems of his own creation. In the closing days of the campaign, the Brown campaign unleashed hard-hitting television spots that showed voters scenes from Reagan's movies while a narrator intoned, "Ronald Reagan has played many roles. This year he wants to play Governor. Can you afford the price of admission?" Another advertisement opened with shots of Thomas Jefferson and Abraham Lincoln statues and a narrator saying, "Integrity, still a good word. Ronald Reagan has made it the foundation of his campaign. But how appropriate is it?" The camera then showed a movie set with a huge Reagan poster looming in the middle of it.[70]

Roger Kent, cochairman of the committee to reelect Brown, lampooned Reagan in the waning days of the race when he wrote in one newspaper that there would be "no 'retakes' if he's the real governor.

You will learn both that the governor must make hard, cold decisions and that a mind broadcasting 'contradictions' and 'fuzzy generalities' is not the equipment that a governor needs." A "nice but ignorant man," was how Kent described Reagan.[71]

The strategy proved wildly off the mark. George Murphy had made the transition from acting to politics when he won a Senate seat in 1964, proving that people did not have a problem voting for a one-time Hollywood star. Reagan, too, had already won his party's nomination and shown that he could handle himself effectively on the stump. And in Los Angeles, where many of the votes were, acting was one of the most important local industries.

Public reaction to a half-hour television documentary of Brown's life was telling. The film was produced by Charles Guggenheim, a Washington filmmaker and a pioneer in the field of political television advertising who had moved to California at the end of summer to head up Brown's television campaign. Working with Champion and others, Guggenheim decided that Brown's advertising should try to tear down the opposition and make Reagan and his candidacy look ludicrous. Guggenheim decided to produce a half-hour biography of Brown to balance some of his more negative advertisements. By all accounts, Guggenheim's film was a tender documentary that gave a moving chronicle of Brown's career. The campaign's most sophisticated television spot, it was, however, also the most self-destructive.

A few weeks before the election, Guggenheim screened the film for the entire campaign staff in a rented office next to campaign headquarters. Gene Wyman, Don Bradley, and almost everyone else who had worked closely with the governor over the past eight years attended. The film, as Guggenheim explained, "got inside [Brown]," showing the governor at his best—campaigning for office, speaking out on the issues, championing causes, and defending orphans, the old, and the infirm. Shots of an elderly woman, her bare feet shuffling along a hard floor, filled the screen. Then Brown appeared. Someone asked how he'd like to be remembered. "I'd like to have them say that he was a compassionate governor. I'd rather have them say that than anything."

When the film ended, there was only silence, except for a little coughing. A few people hurried out of the room. Guggenheim, thinking the film had bombed, fled to the bathroom. There he found several aides crying; they had been touched by the film, and realized that Brown's career was coming to a close. "I felt very good about it," Guggenheim later said of the reaction to the film.[72]

Aired in the final days of the campaign, the film touched off an unexpected firestorm of protest and criticism over one scene. In it Guggenheim showed Brown in an elementary school library standing before two smiling, smartly dressed black girls gazing up at the governor. Brown asked them if they had ever heard of "Governor Brown." The girls stared back in silence, crossing their arms and shaking their heads no.

"You never heard of Governor Brown?" Brown asked again, incredulous. The room, filled with students, teachers, and aides, erupted in laughter. "That's terrible," Brown said facetiously. Then, bending down, a serious look creeping across his face, the governor said to the girls, "I want to tell you something else. You know I'm running against an actor. Remember this, you know who shot Abraham Lincoln, don't you?"

Again the room burst into laughter. "An actor shot Lincoln," Brown said, and then smiled broadly and walked away.[73] The shot was unscripted, a moment captured while Guggenheim and his crew were following Brown on the campaign trail. Guggenheim thought the scene endearing, capturing Brown at his amiable, fun-loving, jocular best. Brown's aides, too, considered the line about the actor "good, fun stuff."[74]

But politicians and actors around the state found the line about Lincoln scurrilous. Reporters rushed to the airport to ask George Murphy, the former movie star, about the scene. "That's the kind of thing Pat Brown would do," the senator sniffed. "He would just shoot off his mouth. That's just the kind of thing they would do in this campaign." During a telethon for Brown, actor Jack Palance stormed off in protest when he learned of the scene. "Attack him if you wish for lack of experience," Palance said. "But don't go after him just because he's an actor."

As criticism escalated, Gene Wyman called Guggenheim and said, "Jesus, we're getting a lot of flak on this thing."

"Well, Gene, how far behind in the polls are we?"

"As far as I can see we're still about ten or twelve percentage points" behind. Guggenheim urged him to keep the spot on the air. "Look, we've only got this one chance. We've only got this film left. That's all we've got and everyone feels it's a very strong picture. If they generate a lot of press, people will want to see it, to see what's in it. Then they'll see they all made a lot out of nothing and they'll also get to see Brown as he hasn't been depicted before and it will be a plus."

As Guggenheim later realized, no matter how many voters saw the film, many more heard about it. And since the line about an actor shooting Lincoln "read terribly," as Guggenheim recalled, "word of mouth was horrible. It just didn't sound right."[75] On the screen, where it could be seen that Brown's remark was intended as a joke, it wouldn't look nearly as bad.

Reagan was speaking at San Francisco's Commonwealth Club when Brown's documentary first aired. Some reporters approached Lyn Nofziger and asked, "Have you heard about this statement Brown made, that it was an actor who shot Lincoln?" Nofziger said that he had not. Well, reporters wanted to know, what did the candidate think about it? "He hasn't heard about it," Nofziger replied. Nofziger made his way quickly to the head table, took Reagan aside, and said, "Brown apparently has said something to the effect that it was an actor who shot Lincoln. I think you ought to play it very cool. Don't get mad or be shocked about it."

Reagan told Nofziger not to worry. He then gave his speech. As he was leaving the stage a reporter asked him, "Have you heard that Pat Brown said it was an actor who shot Lincoln? What do you think?"

"Pat said that?" Reagan replied, affecting shock. "Why I couldn't believe that. Pat wouldn't say anything like that. I wouldn't want to comment on that until I heard further."

As Nofziger and Reagan walked out, Lyn joked, "Well, you at last won an Academy Award."

"Shush, reporters may be listening," replied Reagan.[76]

REAGAN DID NOT MAKE MANY MISTAKES, and, as the election drew close, was far enough in the lead that mudslinging would serve no purpose. In many respects, as countless others have argued, Reagan was a tailor-made television candidate, impressing voters with his good-guy charm, pleasant appearance, and genial demeanor. But Reagan's personality only partly explains his success. Tapping into voters' anxiety and frustration over the unraveling social structure, Reagan distanced himself from the less popular features of American conservatism and helped transform the Right into a more popular movement that promised to put a stop to widespread social upheaval. Jack Burby, Pat Brown's press secretary, knew that television would make Reagan a formidable candidate, but Burby also thought back to 1962, and the campaign against Nixon; the difference was as stark as night and day. Four years ago, he reflected, Brown had to figure out how to expand infrastructure and build things essential to a state experiencing an unprecedented population boom. In 1966 Brown had to try to figure out how to convince voters that he was a tough governor who would restore order to the state.[77] It was a near impossible task. As Richard Kline put it, events caught up to Brown. In 1962, Kline explained, it "was the pre-Kennedy assassination era, and there was great hope." But by 1966, "the nation had changed, perceptions had changed."[78]

In Reagan the Republicans had a candidate who understood the frustration and despair. He could point out the bad—and he could make it sound good. On September 9, 1966, on statewide television, Ronald Reagan offered a rousing attack on Pat Brown. Citing bloated budgets, high taxes, crime, and Berkeley, Reagan made it clear that his campaign would rest on a law-and-order platform that promised to protect California citizens from the dangers in their midst. He also understood the larger meaning of the election.

> There isn't anything we can't do, and that includes solving the one overriding issue of this campaign . . . the issue besetting not only California, but also the nation . . . the issue that over-shadows and colors all others. It is the issue of simple morality. Who among us doesn't feel concern for the deterioration of old standards, the abandonment of principles time-tested and proven in our climb from the swamp to the stars? Today voices are raised urging change for change's sake. Individuals have privilege, but no responsibility. While some young Americans fight and die for their country, others send blood and money to the enemy, and what is, in truth, treason, is called their right to freedom of expression. . . . Is this the way we want it to be? We can change it. We can start a prairie fire that will sweep the nation and prove we are number one in more than size and crime and taxes. If this is a dream, it's a good dream, as big and golden as California itself.[79]

Two days later, in a major appearance on *Meet the Press*, back-to-back with Pat Brown, Reagan showed what he could do with the Berkeley issue. He promised that he would get to the bottom of the Berkeley mess, and find those responsible "for what has been going on" and take appropriate action. Reagan said he was not opposed to free speech, but attacked the university for permitting dissent, and for forcing the other, law-abiding, decent students to listen to the filth on campus. He said there were violations of morality on the campus, and that the constitution of the state was being violated because Fred Dutton, a regent, was also Brown's campaign manager. Brown, in his appearance, called Reagan a dangerous figure who would bring to Sacramento people who had "an almost pathological fear of government."[80]

After *Meet the Press*, Brown didn't want any debates. Reagan had asked Caspar Weinberger to negotiate a format and terms with

Brown's team. Weinberger and Warren Christopher, Brown's representative, met to hammer out rules, but Christopher began issuing what Weinberger considered a series of crazy demands: no note cards allowed; the height of the rostrum had to be just so. Weinberger assented to all until Brown finally said he couldn't make it. Weinberger recalled, "We soon learned very early in the game that one thing the Brown representatives did not want was a debate with Reagan."[81]

As months became weeks, Brown could take some comfort, at least, in his newspaper support. His biggest backing came from his hometown *Chronicle and Examiner* and from the L.A. *Herald Examiner*. Reagan got some big hits, too: the *Los Angeles Times* and the *Oakland Tribune*. On the other side of the nation, the *New York Times* blindly editorialized, "On November 8, Californians will, we trust, understand where reality ends and fantasy begins." *Life* called Reagan "inexperienced except as a movie star," and Joseph Alsop in a widely read national column, wrote that "Ronald Reagan . . . resembles a carefully designed, elaborately customerized supermarket package, complete with the glossiest wrapping and the slickest sort of eye appeal. The Los Angeles advertising firm that is handling Reagan has brilliantly provided everything that can make their package sell—with the possible exception of any contents."[82]

One particular poll two weeks before the election showed Brown trailing Reagan by only 2 percent, but the narrow margin was the only straw left for Brown to grasp. Brown's big money contributors started giving to Reagan's campaign, just in case, and Brown was drawing small and sometimes hostile crowds. With a week to go in the campaign, Brown's allies were trying anything to drum up last-minute support for the governor. A few days before election day, Drew Pearson of all people made overtures to George Christopher, saying he would write "something about him and his milk business only if he came out for Pat Brown."[83] It was a surprisingly friendly exchange. Christopher said that would be fine but that he still wouldn't announce for Brown. So Pearson did not write the piece.

THEN, THE DAY ITSELF: On November 8, Reagan beat Brown by almost a million votes. He won fifty-five of California's fifty-eight counties. The governor took only three: San Francisco, Alameda, and Plumes counties.[84] It was a remarkable reversal from 1958, when Brown had trounced William Knowland by a similar margin. Brown's constituents had abandoned him for a conservative actor with no political experience, and ended his three-decade political career. As a politician Brown had his flaws: he wasn't terribly charismatic, he was not a man of powerful intelligence, he had been in office eight long years, and he looked bad on television. His campaign, too, could have been better run. But in 1966 he possessed one crippling defect: He was a liberal. And when Pat Brown went down, so did the philosophy that he had clung to throughout his adult life.

It has never really recovered.

# Epilogue

How did a right-wing actor win the most important governorship in the country and rise so far so fast in a field in which he had little experience? How did he become one of the most popular two-term presidents of his century? These are simple questions that defy easy answers. Democrats, casting Reagan as both evil reactionary and amiable dunce, argue that he rode to power on good looks, glib answers to complicated questions, and advice from handlers. Republicans take a much more benign view of Reagan, hailing him as a strong commander in chief with a vision that never flagged. Reagan, defenders argue, knew where he wanted to lead California and then the nation. He won the cold war, rolled back decades of liberal legislation, and restored pride to the nation in the wake of Vietnam and Watergate. Journalists and historians have embraced similar lines of argument, calling Reagan a manipulator of emotions and myths on the one hand and a stellar president and party leader on the other.

The debate over Reagan's prowess—brilliant tactician versus lucky bumbler; savvy statesman or smooth actor—is tightly focused on the strengths and weaknesses of the man himself and his immediate friends and supporters. The arguments leave the impression that Reagan was either a mediagenic personality armed with shrewd handlers or a man of uncommon talents and personal character with the strength of vision to become president.

Reagan was indeed a smart politician and a great communicator. He was quick with the quips and sound bites and adept at disarming hecklers and critics. He looked good on television. He gave confident answers to reporters' questions and enjoyed strong backing from wealthy conservatives and top political consultants. These advisors in turn helped him navigate the shoals of extremism, overcome the experience issue, and forge compelling positions on critical issues from foreign affairs and taxes to higher education, poverty, and crime.

Yet Reagan's success had less to do with personality and handlers than with larger political and social events. Reagan's stunning success was bound up with the fall of liberalism, the rise of the New Left, and the growth of a right-wing movement in response. Reagan benefited immensely from a liberalism that had moved too far too fast in a direction that most voters were unwilling to go. Democrats suffered as they struggled to recast their party in the wake of Watts, Detroit, Cleveland, the demonstrations in Chicago and at the Pentagon, the war in Vietnam, the Iran hostage crisis, and the economic woes of the Carter years. The Vietnam War, in particular, acted as a kind of political wrecking ball, obliterating the Democratic party's claim that it was best suited to win the fight against communism. The failure of the War on Poverty and the mixed successes of other social programs hurt liberals who had staked their domestic agenda on bold reforms. The party's identification with the civil rights movement and the New Left turned off voters increasingly concerned about order in the streets. And stagflation undercut the argument that Democrats were the keepers of the flame—the national guardians of prosperity.

Liberals during the Brown years had also become confident to the point of cocky, and the swagger led to a gross miscalculation about Reagan and his conservative supporters. Brown was the first politician to underestimate Reagan, but he was by no means the last. In the 1970s many Democrats continued to portray Reagan as an actor who simply could not win the White House. In truth, they were more out of touch with the voters than he was.

Liberal missteps created an opening for conservatives on domestic issues and foreign affairs, and Reagan seized it like no one else. Conservatives had long been identified with attacks on bedrock domestic programs like Medicare and Social Security and radical opinions about communism. Reagan helped change their prevailing image as kooks. He soft-pedaled the position on communism so that the movement was no longer synonymous with anticommunist crackpots and right-wing zealots. He helped turn riots, welfare, crime, student protests, and other issues into effective cudgels that could be used against liberals. He expressed the anger that voters felt toward a counterculture that seemed to flout traditional American values of hard work and economic success. And he blended these attacks with a message of soaring optimism. He promised to remake the nation into a City on the Hill and reclaim the values that had made it a democratic beacon for the world, and he aired Morning-in-America commercials that bore little resemblance to the doom documentaries produced by the Goldwater camp in 1964.

Some of Reagan's themes would change. His presidential races downplayed crime or law-and-order issues in favor of deregulation and a defense buildup. But his core identity never wavered. He remained rhetorically committed to smaller government and anticommunism, even when his presidency failed to reduce the size of government, managing at best to slow its rate of growth. His attacks on the welfare state would echo for years. His belief in a strong defense budget, which first arose in his freelance speeches in the '60s, continued for over two decades, right through the so-called Star Wars program. And he would help spearhead the revolt against taxes in the late 1970s, which, appropriately, began with the passage of Proposition 13 in California in 1978 and found its way into national policy with the Reagan tax cut of 1982.

Pat Brown, in the wake of his defeat, offered the most poignant expression of Reagan's political success. Brown remained a symbol of liberalism until his death in 1996. He continued to bash Reagan as a know-nothing movie actor and a reactionary who would rather crack down on students than solve serious problems. He wrote two books—*Reagan: The Political Chameleon* and *Reagan and Reality*, in which he castigated Reagan as a danger. He thought about challenging Reagan for reelection in 1970 (but he did not, partly because he didn't want to hurt his son Jerry, up for election that year), and continued to view government as an instrument of social reform and democratic progress. In 1978, the year of the tax revolt, Brown told an interviewer for a project on the Free Speech Movement that Proposition 13 was a disturbing measure that had just "cut the guts out of a great government." Brown explained he had "great faith" that Californians would elect enlightened leaders to run a progressive government, but he admitted that his "faith has been hurt terribly by what happened."[1] Two years later, that faith endured yet another blow when Reagan won the White House. Brown was loath to admit it, but Reagan and his supporters did the most to shatter his liberal shibboleths.

# *Afterword*

Writing in the heat of a governor's race that promised to change the face of California, reporters believed that the governor's mansion in Sacramento was no place for a novice politician, let alone a Hollywood actor. "There is something scary about the idea of actors in politics," editorialized the *Sacramento Bee*. Pundits similarly dismissed the idea of an actor running for governor of the Golden State. They scoffed at his lack of political experience and poked fun at his tendency to stumble on the stump. Politicians called him "shallow" and out of touch with ordinary citizens. Democrats especially made fun of his films, and some sent memos to their boss, the incumbent governor, promising to "hang [the actor] on the specifics." The Democrats also tried to attack the actor for infidelity, and aides to the candidate fretted that the allegations would damage his campaign.[1]

The neophyte politician faced another basic challenge—unity. In California's Republican ranks, the right wing despised the moderates, and the moderates believed that the zealots would lead them to ruin. The state's GOP comprised feuding personalities and ideological turf wars; Republicans were perennial losers in statewide elections. As the campaign continued, one Republican official told a high-dollar GOP fundraiser that the actor's candidacy stood to become "another throat-cutting operation."[2]

This scenario appears ripped from the headlines of 2003, when opponents of California's Democratic Governor Gray Davis forced a statewide vote on recalling him from office, and Arnold Schwarzenegger—then known as an action-film star and bodybuilder—emerged as the best bet to replace him. Yet the above scenes star Ronald Reagan in 1966 . . . not Arnold Schwarzenegger in 2003. Like Schwarzenegger, Reagan was consistently underrated not just because of his prepolitical career—but also because commentators underestimated the appeal of his powerful critique of bloated government.

The debates about an actor's suitability for high office were not the only echoes of 1966 heard in 2003. Schwarzenegger's candidacy also touched off a debate about the meaning of Reagan's legacy, in California and in national politics. Reagan's admirers argued that

Schwarzenegger came from the squishy, moderate wing of the Republican Party, while other Reagan supporters hailed Schwarzenegger as a viable candidate. Some Reagan defenders howled when Schwarzenegger hired Warren Buffet and other "liberals" to give him economic advice. They attacked the moderate former governor Pete Wilson, who, they said, was heavily involved in Arnold's campaign.

Schwarzenegger's conservative opponents also noted that in 1998 he had admitted that he felt embarrassed to be in their party when the Republicans in Congress impeached President Clinton. In 2002 Schwarzenegger championed a ballot initiative increasing financial support for California's after-school programs. Worst of all, from the conservative vantage point, he supported gay rights, abortion rights, and gun control. And, for good measure, he was married to the newscaster Maria Shriver, a Kennedy scion.[3]

Talk-radio kingpin Rush Limbaugh accused Schwarzenegger of "pandering to the majority." Lyn Nofziger, Reagan's first spokesman, argued that the differences between Reagan and Schwarzenegger "could hardly be greater." Stephen Moore, president of the Club for Growth antitax organization, questioned Arnold's commitment to Reagan's tax-cutting agenda. And the syndicated columnist, Cal Thomas, said that Schwarzenegger was "no Ronald Reagan."[4] In fact, many Reaganites initially refused to recognize any similarities between the two men, instead seeing Schwarzenegger as just another Republican in name only. The real Reaganite in the race, they argued, was state senator Tom McClintock.

But other Reagan loyalists argued that Schwarzenegger shared Reagan's all-important personal style. Both men had broad name identification, which they skillfully exploited. Both were optimists by nature, and both were quick on their feet in front of an audience. According to Martin Anderson, Reagan's former economic aide, Schwarzenegger possessed Reagan's charm and wit.[5]

Kenneth Duberstein, Reagan's former White House chief of staff, predicted that like Reagan, Arnold could unite California Republicans and win. Once the Reagan Republicans understood that Schwarzenegger was a winner, they would join the action hero's bandwagon. Even Reagan's biographers weighed in—citing Schwarzenegger's pragmatic disposition as evidence of his ties to Reagan's legacy.[6]

But the partisans missed the key point about Reagan's legacy. In their rush to Reagan's defense, these acolytes failed to capture the subtle but crucial ways in which Reagan's legacy influenced the wild 2003 recall election. Reagan supplied the broad structural framework that fueled California's distemper as well as the symbolism behind the "throw the rascals out" cry for new leadership. Reagan provided a model of an outsider politician that Arnold could copy.

THE FIRST WAY IN which Reagan helped Schwarzenegger was simple: Reagan gave Schwarzenegger a model of how to counter the charge that he was "just an actor." When Reagan threw his hat in the ring, he was green. The affable actor didn't know the intricacies of the state budget, and voters didn't know his positions on the environment, welfare, and other key issues. Reagan had a short fuse on the stump and a penchant for bromides that fired up the faithful but made his consultants cringe. Worse, he was prone to headline-grabbing gaffes. He muffed the location of the Eel River (one of the state's most important) and stormed out of a meeting in front of a large black audience. In response to questions about California's redwood forests, he said, "A tree is a tree—how many more do you need to look at?"[7]

Reagan adopted several strategies to counter the charge that he was a lightweight: he studied up, and he made himself available to the public, with no handlers in between. Reagan crammed like a freshman during exam week. He mastered enough specifics to dampen speculation that he would stumble in Sacramento. He used events to formulate a compelling vision for law and order that helped to offset the image of an actor reciting his lines. He cited reports on Berkeley student radicalism issued by the state senate, studied black binders stuffed with memos, and note cards packed with information about state issues.[8]

With this knowledge packed away, he took questions. In 1966 Reagan told his advisors that he wanted to hold question-and-answer sessions with reporters and Republican audiences to confront his critics head-on. Advisors fretted, but Reagan proved adroit at the give-and-take. He impressed moderates who had previously thought that the man didn't have a brain. Reporters like Jack S. McDowell of the *San Francisco Examiner* came away from events convinced that Reagan was, at the least, "not dumb." Also, Reagan had a knack for coming up with great one-liners. At Occidental College, students jeered him with placards that, mocking Reagan's sometime career as a detergent pitchman, asked, "Who Wants Boraxo in Sacramento?" Reagan looked them in the eye and said, "That may be only soap to you, but it was bread and butter to me." [9]

Reagan's performance during the Q & As reassured his supporters that he could win and showed skeptics that he was not going to self-destruct. The excitement of a first campaign—and of the candidate's poise and self-possession—proved infectious. Audiences loved it. One Republican official told Reagan in 1966, "I am absolutely amazed at the performance so far, considering the big spotlight on you."[10]

In 2003 Schwarzenegger also needed to convince the electorate that he was ready for prime time. Arnold didn't need to be a diehard policy wonk, but, like Reagan, he needed to demonstrate at least a passing familiarity with state issues.

The early going didn't bode well, as Schwarzenegger made numerous rookie mistakes. When in the early weeks of the campaign Warren Buffet told the *Wall Street Journal* that Proposition 13 was an obstacle to fiscal sanity, Schwarzenegger had to issue a statement defending the so-called third rail of California politics, deepening suspicions that he was a creature of his handlers. When asked to explain his ideas for eliminating California's multibillion dollar budget deficit, Schwarzenegger said weakly that "[budget] figures" didn't concern the average Californian.[11]

Schwarzenegger was also faulted for declining to join in the first two debates held during the recall race. To some, he looked as if he were running away from the likes of Peter Camejo, the Green Party candidate, and the charming but feisty pundit, Arianna Huffington, who was running as an Independent. As summer gave way to fall, Cruz Bustamante, the lieutenant governor, watched Arnold's poll numbers drop as his own ticked upward. In the 135-candidate free-for-all to replace Gray Davis, Mr. Universe came across as a lightweight.[12]

But in the fall, Schwarzenegger started looking decidedly Reaganesque. He convinced voters that he could stay calm, answer a question, and generate the brainpower needed to govern the nation's most populous state.

He began to take questions, and he participated in the election's third and final debate. In that face-off, he used humor to offset the charge that he had sexually harassed women.

He even managed some memorable one-liners. When Huffington knocked corporate tax loopholes as a contributing factor in California's budget woes, he looked her in the eye and accused her of having a tax "loophole . . . so big . . . I can drive my Hummer through it." Later in the debate, alluding to his demolition of a female villain in his current movie, *Terminator 3*, he promised her a key part in the next film.

Arnold gained confidence on the stump as the race continued. His speeches now hinted at how he intended to resolve the state's fiscal meltdown. While he attacked Davis's decision to increase the state's car tax, he also bemoaned the Davis-backed bill letting illegal immigrants obtain state driver's licenses. After the final debate, the vast majority of likely voters hailed Schwarzenegger's performance. The media coverage of his campaign also improved.[13]

In the second place, if Reagan showed Schwarzenegger how to master campaigning quickly, he also showed his heir how to unite a fractious Republican Party. Although on social issues Reagan and Schwarzenegger had planted themselves at near-opposite positions on the Republican political spectrum, both had to walk an ideological tightrope between the party's right-wing base and its moderates.

Reagan, in 1966, confronted this challenge head-on. He employed strategists from both wings of the Party, including the two most talented operatives at the time, Stu Spencer and Bill Roberts; moderates both, they helped him shed his image as an extremist.

Reagan also had to convince moderate Republicans (and reporters) that he was not close to the John Birch Society, a right-wing anticommunist organization with strong roots in California. With the help of his consultants, Reagan issued a shrewd one-page statement that said that anyone who supported him was accepting his philosophy—and not vice versa. The statement was a winner. At every opportunity, Spencer and Roberts delivered that message to the GOP's moderates, many of whom recalled the divisive debacle of Barry Goldwater's 1964 White House run and feared that Reagan would repeat the errors of the past.[14]

Then there were the fundraisers. While Spencer and Roberts sent a message to the middle, conservative power brokers made overtures to the GOP's right wing, shoring up Reagan's base and bringing the candidate one step closer to the elusive goal of unity in the GOP. Instead of relying on stalwarts in Young Americans for Freedom and the California Republican Assembly, Reagan hired a trio of consultants in their 30s who gave the campaign a shot in the arm. Part of a rising generation of fresh-faced conservatives, aides such as Lyn Nofziger could appeal to both wings of the GOP in 1966 because they had avoided a prominent role in the 1964 fiasco.[15]

Another important Reagan tactic was his "Creative Society" agenda, which moved beyond differences to pioneer a positive conservative politics. Shedding his image as a single-issue anticommunist, Reagan vowed to "clean up the mess at Berkeley" and to strike out in bold directions in Watts. He vowed to stop coddling antiwar demonstrators who, he said, were spreading panic at military bases in places like Oakland. Rejecting dour Goldwater politics, Reagan called attention to the failings in Sacramento's statehouse and said past GOP divisions must end under his leadership. Reagan ran as an optimist. He also embraced the Eleventh Commandment, in which he vowed to speak no "ill" about the moderate San Francisco Mayor George Christopher, who was opposing Reagan in the primary.[16]

In the 2003 recall race, Schwarzenegger also made a case to the party faithful that unity was essential if Republicans wanted to win the election. Schwarzenegger adopted several strategies reminiscent of Reagan. He hired consultants who represented the ideological composition of the state's Republican Party.

On the liberal-to-moderate side, he had financial guru Warren E. Buffett, former Secretary of State George P. Shultz (who successfully urged Reagan as president to negotiate with the Soviet Union), and Pete Wilson, who had served two terms in the office Schwarzenegger was fighting to win. But Schwarzenegger also showcased conservative supporters like Representatives Dana Rohrabacher (R-Ca.) and David Dreier (R-Ca.) to reach out to the wing that was not his natural constituency.

Schwarzenegger also emphasized his bedrock beliefs as a Reaganesque anticommunist. When he addressed the California Republican convention, he recounted tales of the evils of communism he'd witnessed in his native Austria. When he arrived in America, he said, he saw the Republican Party as the one political organization most fully committed to vanquishing this menace.

"I handed out leaflets for Republicans. I went door-to-door for Republicans. I couldn't wait to become a citizen so I could vote Republican," Schwarzenegger said. "I gave money to Republicans. And now I am running for governor as a Republican. . . ." Schwarzenegger also allied himself with the Republican faith in capitalism and the free market, and argued that communism was no longer a global force in 2003 due to the strength of stalwart conservatives.[17]

Finally, Schwarzenegger paid tribute directly to Reagan throughout the campaign. He repeatedly mentioned Reagan's name on the stump. He invoked Reagan's memory six times in his GOP keynote convention address. He put a Reagan bust on display in his office. He stressed that his connection with Reagan went beyond Hollywood. "I am a Republican because of what Ronald Reagan said—government bureaucrats can never substitute for millions of individuals working night and day to make their dreams come true."[18]

In the end, Schwarzenegger did well with both GOP moderates and conservatives. By sidestepping the divisive social issues—guns, gays, and abortion—where he differed from the Reagan right, Arnold was able to hit the fiscal themes that united all Republicans.

Third, and most significant, Reagan led the revolt against liberalism that paved the road for Schwarzenegger's gubernatorial win.[19] In 1966 Reagan evoked the notion of the "citizen politician," the outsider entering the fray to fix the professional politicians' failures. Politics were rotten, he argued; the government should get out of the business of seeking to eliminate social ills. Claiming that he "had just a citizen's resentment of certain things," Reagan ushered in the era of outsider politicians. He campaigned "with a deep-seated belief that much of what troubles us has been brought about by politicians."[20]

As governor, Reagan attacked government waste and promised to reduce the bloated bureaucracy. He cut financial assistance to California's mental hospitals. He excoriated the "welfare cheats" who, he implied, had never worked a day in their lives. In a memo to his staff, Reagan put "a heavy emphasis on the taxpayer as opposed to the taxtaker"; he wanted to cut the rising cost of what he called "the welfare monster."[21]

In 2003 Schwarzenegger stressed his background as an outsider—a weightlifter, actor, and business executive. He vowed to break the chokehold that career politicians and liberal interests had put on California. Arnold argued that the campaign pitted "us against them"—average citizens who wanted to take their government back versus the deeply entrenched Democrats who had failed to fulfill their promises. In 2003 voters, still angry at centralized government authority, bought into Schwarzenegger's message. His campaign theme song was "We're Not Gonna Take It."[22]

Reagan also paved the way for Schwarzenegger by stumping for tax cuts in the early 1970s. In doing so, Reagan sparked the fire that led to the passage of Proposition 13 in 1978—and the budget-busting politics to come. That initiative, which enacted a cap on property taxes, made California home to almost perpetual budget challenges with political leaders frequently scrambling to meet the needs of the country's most populous state and the world's fifth largest economy.

In 2003 polls revealed that voters felt distressed about California's struggling economy and viewed Davis's mishandling of the budget as a symbol of what the Democrats had gotten wrong. Schwarzenegger, like Reagan before him, pledged to cut the middle-class tax burden—and restore people's faith in government by unleashing people's native abilities to run their own lives.[23]

Reagan ran a race grounded in the growing desire in California for order in the streets and calm at the schools—as well as anger at the liberal activist government in Sacramento. Reagan never quite managed to articulate specific solutions to the uprisings in Watts and Berkeley, or to the rising rate of urban crime. He didn't need to. He effectively argued that things had fallen apart on the liberals' watch, and that he himself had a vision of leadership to restore the values that the middle-class held dear—freedom, opportunity, social stability. Instead of dwelling on the "socialist tide" allegedly lapping at America's shores, Reagan focused on taxes, crime, street riots, and student unrest.

Thirty-seven years later, Schwarzenegger duplicated this performance, combining the politics of angry populist protest with the allure of an agenda rooted in a faith for a better future. Schwarzenegger offered the electorate a clean break from the rotten politics of the past and a fresh hope for the days ahead.

Like Reagan, Schwarzenegger fueled the anger against his Democratic opponent and rode a revolt against a long-entrenched Democratic establishment. Schwarzenegger harped not on a social crisis but instead on statewide blackouts, a stalled economy, and a liberal political agenda that seemed distant and out of touch. In the haze of his long ride into the sunset, the ailing Reagan might have even smiled at Schwarzenegger's performance.

SCHWARZENEGGER WASN'T THE ONLY candidate forced to grapple with the legacy of Reagan's first victory. The recall's target, Gray Davis, had to stand in Pat Brown's shadow during the recall race. Davis and Brown shared a political fate. Like Brown, Davis had been touted early in his first term as presidential timber. Davis, initially, had dominated California politics just as Brown was the preeminent force in the state in 1959, his first year as governor. Then in 1962, Brown was reelected, and the Democratic Party won five of the seven statewide offices. Likewise, in 2002, Davis got reelected to a second term, and the Democrats won all seven statewide offices for the first time in 120 years.[24]

Both governors faced crises in each of their terms, and both struggled to maintain their popularity. Brown had to deal with the Free Speech Movement, the Watts riots, and the "fight in the fields" led by Cesar Chavez. Davis didn't have the same social issues on his plate, but he confronted an energy crisis and a rising budget deficit that dominated headlines and damaged his credibility. Davis admitted that his response to statewide blackouts was dilatory, while implicitly taking the blame for California's multibillion dollar deficit. Critics castigated Davis, as they had Brown, as being asleep at the switch while the state dissolved into crisis.[25]

In 2003 Davis signed a bill granting driver's licenses to illegal immigrants. In roiling the state's racial politics, he brought to mind the political difficulties that liberal interest groups posed for Brown in the mid-1960s, from civil rights organizations like CORE to labor unions such as the Chavez-led United Farm Workers. Davis raised taxes;

Brown too was tarred with the same tax-and-spend brush. Like Brown, Davis earned a reputation as a big-government Democrat, out of touch with the public and beholden to special interests.[26]

Another parallel is the extent to which the Democratic Party broke apart in both 1966 and 2003. True, Cruz Bustamante was a far cry from the white working-class, law-and-order protest politics that Los Angeles Mayor Sam Yorty mastered in 1966. But Davis, like Brown, inspired a great deal of animosity in diehard Democrats. Not only Bustamante but Huffington and Camejo offered themselves as alternatives to Davis, and another powerful Democrat, California Attorney General Bill Lockyer, wound up voting for Schwarzenegger. Lockyer gave voice to the dissent that animated thousands of disaffected Democrats who abandoned Davis on election day—many of them voted for Schwarzenegger.[27]

Working-class whites abandoned the New Deal when they abandoned Brown in 1966, but they also had someone to whom they could turn: Ronald Reagan. This phenomenon continued in the angry political climate in 2003. In the end, then, Reagan's legacy unleashed the recall election that forced Gray Davis into retirement and gave a burst of momentum to Schwarzenegger's fledgling political career. Reagan's influence also extended well beyond the Golden State in 2003.

President George W. Bush, Senator John McCain, and others in the GOP have also been claiming Reagan's pedigree in recent years. Throughout his presidential campaign and his presidency Bush insisted that he be seen not as the son of his actual father—who was disliked by conservatives for raising taxes to reduce the deficit—but as the son of Reagan. Bush "has been regularly invoking the 40th president in recent events, hailing Reagan's 'mandate for leadership' on Veterans Day, signing abortion legislation in the Ronald Reagan Building, and describing his Middle East policy as an extension of Reaganism in a major foreign policy speech on Nov. 6," wrote the *Washington Post*'s Dana Milbank in November 2003. The comparison was not just ideological. Bush's dramatic 2003 aircraft-carrier landing in which he declared the fighting in Iraq over stole a page from Reagan's White House image-making machine. Critics drew comparisons between Bush strategist Karl Rove and Reagan's public relations guru Michael Deaver.[28]

On Capitol Hill, McCain, a self-styled Republican outsider, took up Reagan's cry that government "pork" drained the nation's treasury. And by 2003, conservative Republican lawmakers were fighting to enact legislation authorizing a Reagan statue to be built on the National Mall—to enshrine Reagan in the presidential pantheon. Reagan's face will appear on the $10 bill if his powerful congressional champions succeed. One of Washington's airports has already been renamed "Reagan National."[29]

Reagan has also enjoyed broad support from beyond the nation's capital. When his admirers heard about a forthcoming CBS miniseries that depicted Reagan in unflattering terms, they launched a BoycottCBS.com site, which helped to force the media company to show the miniseries on a cable network instead. Two new volumes of Reagan's letters were published in September 2003, prompting fresh claims from his admirers that Reagan had intelligence, compassion, vision, and conviction.[30]

More broadly, Reagan's defenders argue that Reagan was a veritable god—ubiquitous, omniscient, and omnipotent. Reagan, accordingly, cut a bloated bureaucracy, reduced the middle-class tax burden, and rescued the United States from the radicalism and the counterculture that defined the decadent sixties-era society. In foreign affairs, Reagan also had ice in his veins, saving the world from communism and spreading liberal democratic ideals to one-time Cold War hotspots such as Grenada, Nicaragua, Poland, and Hungary. A persistent core of critics, however, contend that Reagan neglected the global HIV/AIDS pandemic, cut Aid to Families with Dependent Children, created a soaring federal budget deficit, and abused his presidential power in the Iran-Contra scandal.

The debate is so heated because the stakes are so high. Reagan's defenders see assaults on Reagan's reputation as part of a decades-long liberal push to discredit the modern conservative movement. When Reagan is under attack, so, too, are the ideals that the Reagan right cherishes, from tax cuts to smaller government. This isn't a debate just about Reagan per se. In fact, it's a struggle over the Republican Party's future and the nation's political direction.

While liberals are looking to tear Reagan down in order to build liberalism up, conservatives are striving to deepen Reagan's reputation as an iconic political figure. Reagan has become the Rosetta stone of modern American politics. Because he embodies the liberal-conservative struggle over the state's proper role in society, he will remain a fascinating and much-debated figure for years to come.

There is one final point for the partisans to grasp: the similarities between Schwarzenegger and Reagan will end when the focus moves beyond California politics. After 1966 Reagan reshaped the GOP at the national level in his image and, in the process, altered the nation's political direction. The right became the dominant force in the Republican Party in large part due to Reagan's leadership. His ideas, values, and vision for America became central features of American politics that endure today.

It's not clear that Schwarzenegger has such national ambitions—though his ambition has never been in short supply. The foreign-born Schwarzenegger is barred by the Constitution from running for president. While the Reagan revolution reshaped American political life, it is unlikely that Schwarzenegger—or anyone else in the near future—will have so dramatic an impact.

Even at the state level, California's thirty-eighth governor will have a tough time reshaping the party in his moderate image. As he seeks to cut the deficit, slash taxes, and restore people's faith in government, he will also have to contend with Reagan's legacy on hot-button social issues. Life could become difficult for Arnold. If he defies Reagan's supporters by seeking to depart from Reagan's legacy, he will face their wrath. The Reagan wing is still the most dominant force in California's Republican Party. Schwarzenegger will continue to hear Reagan's voice.

# *Notes*

*Periodicals and books are cited fully upon first use only. Archives, oral histories, and interviews are abbreviated as follows:*

## *ARCHIVES*

| | |
|---|---|
| EGB | Edmund G. Brown Papers (BANC MSS 68/90c), The Bancroft Library, University of California, Berkeley |
| EGBLBJ | Edmund Gerald "Pat" Brown Papers, Lyndon Baines Johnson Library, Austin |
| GRP | George Rochester Papers, Hoover Institution on War, Revolution, and Peace, Stanford, California |
| HCP | Hale Champion Papers, 1960–1966 (BANC MSS 67/98c), The Bancroft Library, University of California, Berkeley |
| HHHP | Hubert H. Humphrey Papers, Minnesota Historical Society |
| JLWR | Joseph L. Wyatt Collection of California Democratic Council Records, 1953–1967. Ms. Coll. 1082. Department of Special Collections, Charles E. Young Research Library, UCLA |
| NSP | Nancy Swadesh Papers (BANC MSS 88/182c), The Bancroft Library, University of California, Berkeley |
| PS1966 | Political Spots, California gubernatorial campaign, 1966, Ronald Reagan vs. Edmund G. Brown, Archive Research and Study Center of the UCLA Film and Television Archives |
| RKP | Roger Kent Papers (BANC MSS 74/160c), The Bancroft Library, University of California, Berkeley |
| RRGP | Ronald Reagan Gubernatorial Papers, Hoover Institution on War, Revolution, and Peace, Stanford, California |
| SYP | Samuel Yorty Papers, Los Angeles City Archives |
| TBCP | Tom B. Carvey Papers, 1948–1968. Ms. Coll. 1110. Department of Special Collections, Charles E. Young Research Library, UCLA |
| TSP | Thomas More Storke Papers (BANC MSS 73/72c), The Bancroft Library, University of California, Berkeley |
| WBRP | William Byron Rumford Papers (BANC MSS 73/112c), The Bancroft Library, University of California, Berkeley |

## *INTERVIEWS AND ORAL HISTORIES*

| | |
|---|---|
| AAOH | Alarcon, Arthur L. Interviewed 1988 by Carlos Vasquez. California State Archives State Government Oral History Program, Department of Special Collections, Oral History Program, Charles E. Young Research Library, UCLA. |

| | |
|---|---|
| AMI | Arch Monson. Interviewed by author. |
| API | Alexander Pope. Interviewed by author. |
| AROH | Albert Rodda. "Oral History Interview." Bancroft Regional Oral History Program, University of California, Berkeley. |
| ASOH | Alex Sherriffs. "Oral History Interview with Alex Sherriffs." Bancroft Regional Oral History Program, University of California, Berkeley. |
| BBOI | Bill Boyarsky. Interviewed by author. |
| BLBOH | Bernice Layne Brown. "Brown Family Portraits." Bancroft Regional Oral History Program, University of California, Berkeley. |
| CBOH | Carl Britschigi. "Oral History Interview." Bancroft Regional Oral History Program, University of California, Berkeley. |
| CGI | Charles Guggenheim. Interviewed by author. |
| CGOH | Charles Guggenheim. "Oral History Interview." Bancroft Regional Oral History Program, University of California, Berkeley. |
| CKFSM | Clark Kerr. Free Speech Movement Project Interview. Videorecording. Media Resource Center, University of California, Berkeley. |
| CKI | Clark Kerr. Interviewed by author. |
| CKOH | Clark Kerr. "Earl Warren Era History Project." Bancroft Regional Oral History Program, University of California, Berkeley. |
| CSWOH | Clement S. Whitaker. "Oral History Interview." Bancroft Regional Oral History Program, University of California, Berkeley. |
| CWBOH | Clair W. Burgener. "Oral History Interview." Bancroft Regional Oral History Program, University of California, Berkeley. |
| CWI | Caspar Weinberger. Interviewed by author. |
| CWOH | Caspar Weinberger. "San Francisco Republicans." Bancroft Regional Oral History Program, University of California, Berkeley. |
| DBOH | Don Bradley. "Managing Democratic Campaigns, 1954–1966." Bancroft Regional Oral History Program, University of California, Berkeley. |
| ECOH | Eugene Chappie. "Oral History Interview with Eugene Chappie." Bancroft Regional Oral History Program, University of California, Berkeley. |
| EDI | Elias P. Demetracopoulos. Interviewed by author, April 29, 1997. |
| EDOH | Earl Dunckel. "Ronald Reagan and the General Electric Theatre, 1954–1955," Ronald Reagan Gubernatorial Era Oral History Series. |
| EGBFSM | Edmund "Pat" Brown. Free Speech Movement Project Interview. Videorecording. Media Resource Center, University of California, Berkeley. |
| EGBLBJOH | Edmund "Pat" Brown. Oral History Interview, Lyndon Baines Johnson Library, Austin. |
| EGBOH | Edmund G. "Pat" Brown. "Years of Growth, 1939–1966; Law Enforcement, Politics, and the Governor's Office." Bancroft Regional Oral History Program, University of California, Berkeley. |
| EMI | Edwin Meese III. Interviewed by author. |
| EMOH | Edward Mills. "'The Kitchen Cabinet': Four California Citizen Advisors of Ronald Reagan." Oral History Program, California State University, Fullerton. |
| ERGOH | Elizabeth Rudel Gatov. "Grassroots Party Organizer to Treasurer of the U.S." Bancroft Regional Oral History Program, University of California, Berkeley. |
| ERSOH | Elizabeth Ring Storrs. "Republican Philosophy and Party Activism," 1984. Bancroft Regional Oral History Program, University of California, Berkeley. |
| ESOH | Elizabeth Snyder. "Oral History Interview with Elizabeth Snyder." |
| FCNI | Franklyn C. Nofziger. Interviewed by author, July 1, 1997. |

| | |
|---|---|
| FCNRGP | Franklyn C. Nofziger. "Press Secretary for Ronald Reagan, 1966," in Issues and Innovations in the 1966 Republican Gubernatorial Campaign. |
| FDI | Frederick Dutton. Interviewed by author. |
| FDOH | Frederick Dutton. "Democratic Campaigns and Controversies, 1954–1966." Bancroft Regional Oral History Program, University of California, Berkeley. |
| FMBOH | Francis M. Brown. "Brown Family Portraits." Bancroft Regional Oral History Program, University of California, Berkeley. |
| FMesOH | Frank Mesple. "The Governor's Office Under Edmund G. Brown, Sr." Bancroft Regional Oral History Program, University of California, Berkeley. |
| FMOH | Murphy, Franklin D. My UCLA chancellorship oral history transcript: an utterly candid view. Manuscript Collection 300/122. Department of Special Collections, Oral History Program, Charles E. Young Research Library, UCLA. |
| GCI | George Christopher. Interview with author. |
| GCOH | George Christopher. "Oral History Interview with George Christopher." |
| GPRRGE | Gaylord Parkinson. "Issues and Innovations in the 1966 Gubernatorial Campaign." Ronald Reagan Gubernatorial Era Series. |
| GWOH | Gordon Winton. "Oral History Interview with Gordon Winton." Bancroft Regional Oral History Program, University of California, Berkeley. |
| GZOH | George Zenovich. "Oral History Interview with George Zenovich." Bancroft Regional Oral History Program, University of California, Berkeley. |
| HBOH | Herbert Baus. "Oral History Interview with Herbert Baus." Bancroft Regional Oral History Program, University of California, Berkeley. |
| HBurOH | Hugh Burns. "California Legislative Leaders, Volume II," 1981. Bancroft Regional Oral History Program, University of California, Berkeley. |
| HCBOH | Harold C. Brown. "Brown Family Portraits." Bancroft Regional Oral History Program, University of California, Berkeley. |
| HCI | Hale Champion. Interview with author. |
| HCOH | Hale Champion. "Oral History Interview with Hale Champion." Bancroft Regional Oral History Program, University of California, Berkeley. |
| HPOH | Harold Powers. "On Prominent Issues, the Republican Party, and Political Campaigns." Bancroft Regional Oral History Program, University of California, Berkeley. |
| HRHOH | Haldeman, Harry R. Interviewed 1991 by Dale E. Treleven. California State Archives State Government Oral History Program, Department of Special Collections, Oral History Program, Charles E. Young Research Library, UCLA. |
| HSOH | Henry Salvatori. "'The Kitchen Cabinet': Four California Citizen Advisors of Ronald Reagan." California State University, Fullerton. |
| HTOH | Holmes Tuttle. "'The Kitchen Cabinet': Four California Citizen Advisors of Ronald Reagan." California State University, Fullerton. |
| JACOH | James A. Cobey. "Oral History Interview with James A. Cobey." Bancroft Regional Oral History Program, University of California, Berkeley. |
| JAHOH | James A. Hall. "Supporting Reagan: From Banks to Prisons." Ronald Reagan Gubernatorial Era Series. |
| JBOH | Burby, John. Interviewed 1987 by Carlos Vasquez. California State Archives State Government Oral History Program, Department of Special Collections, Oral History Program, Charles E. Young Research Library, UCLA. |

| | |
|---|---|
| JBurtOH | John Burton. "Oral History Interview with John Burton." Bancroft Regional Oral History Program, University of California, Berkeley. |
| JCI | Joe Cerrell. Interviewed by author. |
| JMOH | James Mills. "Oral History Interview with James Mills." Bancroft Regional Oral History Program, University of California, Berkeley. |
| JRCOH | Judy Royce Carter. "Oral History Interview." Bancroft Regional Oral History Program, University of California, Berkeley. |
| JROH | Joseph Rattigan. "Oral History Interview." Bancroft Regional Oral History Program, University of California, Berkeley. |
| JSMRRGE | Jack S. McDowell. "Republican Campaigns and Party Issues, 1964–1976." Ronald Reagan Gubernatorial Era Series. |
| JTOH | Tenney, Jack B. (Jack Breckinridge), 1898–1970, interviewee. Jack B. Tenney oral history transcript: California legislator. Manuscript Collection 300/56. Department of Special Collections, Oral History Program, Charles E. Young Research Library, UCLA. |
| JWOH | Jack Wrather. "Republican Philosophy and Party Activism," 1984. Bancroft Regional Oral History Program, University of California, Berkeley. |
| KFKOH | Kimiko Fujii Kitayama. Bancroft Regional Oral History Program, University of California, Berkeley. |
| KHRRGE | Kenneth Holden. "Issues and Innovations in the California Republican Gubernatorial Campaign, 1966." Ronald Reagan Gubernatorial Era Series. |
| LHI | Lucien C. Haas. Interviewed by author. |
| LHOH | Haas, Lucien C. Interviewed 1989 by Carlos Vasquez. California State Archives State Government Oral History Program, Department of Special Collections, Oral History Program, Charles E. Young Research Library, UCLA. |
| LMOH | Larry Margolis. "Larry Margolis, Oral History Interview." Bancroft Regional Oral History Program, University of California, Berkeley. |
| LNOH | Leland Nichols. "Oral History Interview with Leland Nichols." Bancroft Regional Oral History Program, University of California, Berkeley. |
| MBOH | Meredith Burch. "Pat Brown: Friends and Campaigners." Bancroft Regional Oral History Program, University of California, Berkeley. |
| MHOH | Holen, Marvin L. Interviewed 1990 by Carlos Vasquez. California State Archives State Government Oral History Program, Department of Special Collections, Oral History Program, Charles E. Young Research Library, UCLA. |
| NAI | Nita Ashcraft. Interviewed by author. |
| NEOH | Norman Elkington. "Pat Brown: Friends and Campaigners." Bancroft Regional Oral History Program, University of California, Berkeley. |
| NROH | Reagan, Neil. Private dimensions and public images oral history transcript: the early political campaigns of Ronald Reagan. Manuscript Collection 300/185. Department of Special Collections, Oral History Program, Charles E. Young Research Library, UCLA. |
| NSOH | Nancy Sloss. "Oral History Interview with Nancy Sloss." Bancroft Regional Oral History Program, University of California, Berkeley. |
| PHRRGE | Paul Haerle. "Appointments, Cabinet Management, and Policy Research for Governor Reagan, 1967–1974." Ronald Reagan Gubernatorial Era Series. |
| PLOH | Paul Lunardi. "Oral History Interview." Bancroft Regional Oral History Program, University of California, Berkeley. |
| RFOH | Robert Finch. Bancroft Regional Oral History Program, University of California, Berkeley. |
| RGOH | Roy Greenaway. Bancroft Regional Oral History Program, University of California, Berkeley. |

| | |
|---|---|
| RKentOH | Roger Kent. "Building the Democratic Party in California, 1954–1966." Bancroft Regional Oral History Program, University of California, Berkeley. |
| RKOH | Richard Kline. "The Governor's Office Under Edmund G. Brown, Sr." Bancroft Regional Oral History Program, University of California, Berkeley. |
| RMI | Ronald Moskowitz. Interviewed by author. |
| RMOH | Robert Moretti. "Legislative-Governor Relations in the Reagan Years: Five Views," 1983. Bancroft Regional Oral History Program, University of California, Berkeley. |
| RRI | Roy Ringer. Interview with author. |
| RRIOH | Ringer, Roy. Interviewed 1989 by Carlos Vasquez. California State Archives State Government Oral History Program, Department of Special Collections, Oral History Program, Charles E. Young Research Library, UCLA. |
| RRRRGE | Ronald Reagan. "Governor Reagan and His Cabinet: An Introduction." Ronald Reagan Gubernatorial Era Series. |
| RTMOH | Robert T. Monagan. "The Assembly, the State Senate, and the Governor's Office, 1958–1974." Bancroft Regional Oral History Program, University of California, Berkeley. |
| RWOH | Rus Walton. "Turning Political Ideas into Government Program." Bancroft Regional Oral History Program, University of California, Berkeley. |
| RWRRGE | Robert Walker. "Political Advertising and Advocacy for Ronald Reagan, 1965–1980." Ronald Reagan Gubernatorial Era Series. |
| SMI | Stanley Mosk. Interviewed by author. |
| SPRRGE | Plog, Stanley C. More than just an actor oral history transcript: the early campaigns of Ronald Reagan. Manuscript Collection 300/184. Department of Special Collections, Oral History Program, Charles E. Young Research Library, UCLA. |
| SSI | Stu Spencer. Interview with author. |
| SSOH | Stu Spencer. "Oral History Interview with Stu Spencer." Bancroft Regional Oral History Program, University of California, Berkeley. |
| SYI | Samuel Yorty. Interviewed by the author. |
| SYLBJ | Samuel Yorty. "Oral History Interview with Samuel Yorty." Lyndon Baines Johnson Library. |
| SYOH | Yorty, Samuel. Ask the mayor. Manuscript Collection 300/273. Department of Special Collections, Oral History Program, Charles E. Young Research Library, UCLA. |
| SZOH | Steve Zetterberg. "Oral History Interview with Steve Zetterberg." Bancroft Regional Oral History Program, University of California, Berkeley. |
| TBOH | Bradley, Thomas. The impossible dream. Manuscript Collection 300/230. Department of Special Collections, Oral History Program, Charles E. Young Research Library, UCLA. |
| TdJOH | Tirso del Junco. "California Republican Party Leadership and Success, 1966–1982." Bancroft Regional Oral History Program, University of California, Berkeley. |
| TLOH | Thomas Lynch. "A Career in Politics and the Attorney General's Office." Bancroft Regional Oral History Program, University of California, Berkeley. |
| TRI | Tom Reed. Interviewed by author. |
| TROH | Rees, Thomas M. Interviewed 1987 by Carlos Vasquez. California State Archives State Government Oral History Program, Department of Special Collections, Oral History Program, Charles E. Young Research Library, UCLA. |
| VJCOH | Vernon J. Cristina. "Republican Campaigns and Party Issues, 1964–1976." |

VOOH Verne Orr. "Governor Reagan and His Cabinet: An Introduction," 1986.

VSOH Vernon Sturgeon. "Legislative Issue Management and Advocacy, 1961–1974." Bancroft Regional Oral History Program, University of California, Berkeley.

VVOH Victor V. Veysey. "Oral History Interview." Bancroft Regional Oral History Program, University of California, Berkeley.

WAOH Wayne Amerson. "Northern California and Its Challenges to a Negro in the mid-1900s." Bancroft Regional Oral History Program, University of California, Berkeley.

WBagOH William Bagley. "Oral History Interview with William Bagley." Bancroft Regional Oral History Program, University of California, Berkeley.

WBI William Bagley. Interviewed by author.

WBOH William Becker. "The Governor's Office Under Edmund G. Brown, Sr." Bancroft Regional Oral History Program, University of California, Berkeley.

WChrOH Winslow Christian. "The Human Side of Public Administration." Bancroft Regional Oral History Program, University of California, Berkeley.

WCOH Warren Christopher. "Special Counsel to the Governor: Recalling the Pat Brown Years," in "The Governor's Office under Edmund G. Brown, Sr." Bancroft Regional Oral History Program, University of California, Berkeley.

WFOH Forbes, William E. Interviewed 1990 by Dale E. Treleven. California State Archives State Government Oral History Program, Department of Special Collections, Oral History Program, Charles E. Young Research Library, UCLA.

WFSRRGE William French Smith. "Evolution of the Kitchen Cabinet, 1965–1973." Ronald Reagan Gubernatorial Era Series.

WROH William Ross. "Oral History Interview with William Ross." Bancroft Regional Oral History Program, University of California, Berkeley.

WRRRGE William Roberts. "Issues and Innovations in the 1966 Republican Gubernatorial Campaign." Ronald Reagan Gubernatorial Era Series.

WTOH Trombley, William. Interviewed 1994 by Dale E. Treleven. California State Archives State Government Oral History Program, Department of Special Collections, Oral History Program, Charles E. Young Research Library, UCLA.

## *ONE*: The Giant Killer

1. Kevin Starr, *Endangered Dreams: The Great Depression in California* (New York: Oxford University Press, 1996), 115.

2. Roger Rappaport, *California Dreaming: The Political Odyssey of Pat & Jerry Brown* (Berkeley: Nolo Press, 1982), 24–25.

3. EGBOH, 217.

4. EGBOH, 18. RROH, 47.

5. EGBOH, 24–25. FMBOH, 7. HCBOH, 7. Rappaport, *California Dreaming*, 20–21.

6. EGBOH, 6, 24, 29.

7. EGBOH, 30–31, 37–39. Rappaport, *California Dreaming*, 22. Years later Brown's fraternity friends, many of whom had become successful businessmen, would provide crucial financial backing for Brown's political campaigns. Norton Simon, for example, contributed $100,000 to Brown's 1950 Attorney General race.

8. EGBOH, 44–46.

9. Rappaport, *California Dreaming*, 23. PS1966, director Charles Guggenheim, *Man against the Actor*, Pat Brown Campaign Advertisement (1966). EGBOH, 44–49, 54–55, 62, 66–67. "You know, Mr. Brown," Schmitt babbled at one point, "I'm like Jesus. I carry a cross like Jesus did. My cross is blindness." Schmitt told his protege that he was "going to make a million dollars for [him]. I'll make a million for myself and a million for you." Soon Schmitt was committed to a mental institution. BLBOH, 42.

10. Rappaport, *California Dreaming*, 28. BLBOH, 42.

11. EGBOH, 64. BLBOH, 38. NEOH, 5.

12. NEOH, 3, 8. EGBOH, 72, 75. HCBOH, 28. Rappaport, *California Dreaming*, 28–29.

13. EGBOH, 97–99, 120–25.

14. EGBOH, 9, 13–14, 77–79. Rappaport, *California Dreaming*, 29.

15. Brown also worked hard to cultivate his image as a friend of the working man. Afraid that his moralizing would alienate working-class voters, Brown let it be known that he hailed from a working-class family and subtly reminded voters that he had ties to organized gambling. He helped Edmund, Sr., register his gambling parlor as "a duly authorized corporation" that, Brown admitted, was "a facade for a gambling operation." Brown also took $500 a cousin had donated for campaign advertising, brought it to a bookie he knew, and placed a bet: Brown over Brady. The odds were five to one in Brady's favor, and Brown distributed his fifty $10 tickets to campaign workers. "If I win," he told them, "you get $60." The result, as Brown put it, was "fifty of the greatest campaign workers you'd ever seen." EGBOH, 93–95,124.

16. EGBOH, 100, 122. TLOH, 27–30.

17. Rappaport, *California Dreaming*, 33–34. EGBOH, 101–2.

18. Rappaport, *California Dreaming*, 49.

19. TLOH, 122–23.

20. RKOH, 124–25. Kent says Pat "made some noises" about running for Senate in 1956, but that he and his best friends thought that the incumbent, Thomas Kuchel, was "incredibly strong" and wanted Pat to run for governor instead (see Rappaport, *California Dreaming*, 10). For more information on Bernice's feelings, see FDOH, "Democratic Campaigns and Controversies, 1954–1966." On Jerry Brown, see Rappaport, *California Dreaming*, 10.

21. EGB ctn 1, Correspondence Folder, Letter, Dutton to James Keene, May 17, 1957. Letter Dutton to Jim (no last name), July 3, 1957.

22. EGB ctn 1, Letters Folder, Handwritten Note, Dutton to Brown, no date.

23. EGB ctn 44, Publicity Folder, "Pat Brown's 8-Point Program," campaign brochure. Party campaign activists longed for a more ideological campaign. See EGB ctn 1, Letters & Memos Folder, Memo, Dutton to Brown, Jan. 24, 1958.

24. EGBOH, 233. Rappaport, *California Dreaming*, 14. James Reichley, *States in Crisis: Politics in Ten American States, 1950–1962* (Chapel Hill: The University of North Carolina Press, 1964), 183.

25. EGB, "Inaugural Message to the California State Legislature," Jan. 5, 1959.

26. Ibid.

27. EGB ctn 14, Governor's Council Meeting Minutes Folder, Transcript, Governor's Council Meeting Minutes, 1959, 6–8.

28. EGBOH, 365.

29. EGB ctn 353, 1959 Legislation Folder, "A Tentative Over-All Appraisal," May 27, 1959.

30. EGB ctn 388, Governorship, June–September Folder, Memo, Dutton to Brown, "Specific Action Ahead," June 20, 1960. HCP ctn 1, Administrative Objectives of Brown Folder, Memo, Dutton to Brown, "Objectives of this Administration," May 3, 1960.

31. EGBOH, 284.

32. Rappaport, *California Dreaming*, 66–67.

33. EGB ctn 501, Politics and Government Folder, Memo, Burby to Brown, September 3, 1961.

34. HCP ctn 3, Memo Folder, Champion to Brown, Dec. 6, 1961.

35. RRIOH, 70–72. Ringer recalled the Engle quote.

36. EGB ctn 584, Politics and Government Folder, Memo, Lerner to Brown, March 15, 1962. EGB ctn 585, Politics/Nixon, Jan.–March, Memo, Jack Burby to Bradley, March 6, 1962.

37. EGB ctn 585, Politics and Government, Jan.–March Folder, Letter, Thomas Page to Brown, March 1, 1962.

38. Oliver Carlson, "'Pat' Brown: California's Most Expensive Governor," *Human Events*, September 8, 1962.

39. "The Case of the Mysterious Mailer," *CDC Bulletin*, March 1965, 15–16. TLOH, 100. EGB ctn 667, Democratic Central Committee Folder, 1962 Campaign Flier, "Pat Brown, The Nation's Leading Governor."

40. Christopher Matthews, "Former Governor Called Nixon 'Psycho,'" *San Francisco Examiner*, December 6, 1998.

## *TWO*: THE ANTICOMMUNIST

1. Matthew Dallek, "The Conservative 1960s," *The Atlantic Monthly*, December 1995, 130–35.

2. The two best works on the history of California's conservative movement are Lisa McGirr, *Suburban Warriors: Grassroots Conservatism in the 1960's* (Columbia University, Dissertation, 1995), and Kurt Schuparra, *Triumph of the Right: The Rise of the California Conservative Movement, 1945–1966* (Armonk, N.Y.: M.E. Sharpe, 1998).

3. Ibid.

4. RRGP Box 38, Pre-1966 Speeches Folder, "Losing Freedom by Installments," Speech to the Fargo Chamber of Commerce, Jan. 26, 1962.

5. Garry Wills, *Reagan's America* (New York: Penguin Books, 1988), 14–18. Ronald Reagan with Richard G. Hubler, *Where's the Rest of Me?* (New York: Best Books, 1965), 14. Lou Cannon, *Ronnie and Jesse: A Political Odyssey* (Garden City, N.Y.: Doubleday & Company, 1969), 4–5.

6. Wills, *Reagan's America*, 28.

7. Ibid., 22, 27, 38.

8. Ibid., Chapters 4 & 5.

9. Ibid., 73–75, 76. Anne Edwards, *Early Reagan* (New York: William Morrow and Company, 1987), 115.

10. Hubler, *Where's the Rest of Me?*, 78–79.

11. Ibid., 65, 67–68. Wills, *Reagan's America*, 136. Cannon, *Ronnie and Jesse*, 18–19.

12. Hubler, *Where's the Rest of Me?*, 8–9. Cannon, *Ronnie and Jesse*, 31–33.

13. Bill Boyarsky, *Ronald Reagan: His Life and Rise to the Presidency* (New York: Random House, 1981), 55.

14. Wills, *Reagan's America*, Chapters 17–24.

15. RRGP Box 1, Speeches & Writing, Pre-1966 Folder, Ronald Reagan Radio Advertisement, 1948.

16. Hubler, *Where's the Rest of Me?*, 262. Wills, *Reagan's America*, 266–67, 271, 273. Ronald Reagan, *An American Life* (New York: Simon and Schuster, 1990), 109, 272–73.

17. Hubler, *Where's the Rest of Me?*, 126.

18. NROH, 30–31.

19. Ibid. See also Wills, *Reagan's America*, Chapter 26.

20. Wills, *Reagan's America*, 295. Hubler, *Where's the Rest of Me?*, 187. Boyarsky, *Ronald Reagan*, 65.

21. Boyarsky, *Ronald Reagan*, 74–75.
22. Ibid., 74–75, 77.
23. RRGP Box 1, Speeches & Writings Pre-1966 Folder, "America the Beautiful," June 1952.
24. Ibid.
25. EDOH, 2.
26. Ibid., 9–10.
27. Hubler, *Where's the Rest of Me?*, 224.
28. Richard Nixon Pre-Presidential Papers Box 621, Reagan, R., series 320, Letter, Reagan to Nixon, July 15, 1960, National Archives and Records Administration, Laguna Niguel, Calif.
29. RRGP Box 38, Pre-1966 Speeches Folder, "Losing Freedom by Installments," January 26, 1962. Kitty Kelley, *Nancy Reagan: The Unauthorized Biography* (New York: Simon and Schuster, 1991), 125–26.
30. Lee Edwards, *Goldwater: The Man Who Made a Revolution* (Washington, D.C.: Regnery Publishing, 1995), 73. EGB ctn 688, Folder, "List of Reagan Activities from 1960–1965," in *L.A. Times*. Curt Gentry, *The Last Days of the Late, Great State of California* (Sausalito, Calif.: Comstock Editions, 1968), 40–43. Ronald Reagan, "Encroaching Government Controls," *Human Events*, July 21, 1961. Kelley, *Nancy Reagan*, 125–26.
31. Hubler, *Where's the Rest of Me?*, 240–42. Lee Edwards, *Ronald Reagan*, 72–74.
32. McGirr, *Suburban Warriors*, 148–50. RRGP Box 1, Speeches & Writings Pre-1966 Folder, "Republican Associates Luncheon at Biltmore Bowl," October 25, 1962. RRGP Box 1, Speeches & Writings Pre-1966 Folder, "Are Liberals Really Liberal?" circa 1962. RRGP Box 1, Speeches & Writings Pre-1966 Folder, "Transcribed from Ronald Reagan's Television Appearance," November 4, 1962, at 5, 15.
33. Patti Davis, *The Way I See It* (New York: Jove Books, 1993), 56–57.
34. Reagan, *An American Life*, 165–66.

## *THREE*: "ARE YOU NOW, OR HAVE YOU EVER BEEN A *LIBERAL*?"

1. EGB ctn 539, Gov. Office Organization Oct.–Dec. Folder, Memos, Fred Jordan to EGB, November 9, 1962. EGB ctn 536, Gov. Oct.–Dec. Folder, Letter, Fred Dutton to EGB, November 6, 1962. EGB ctn 569, Legis. Subjects 1963, Aug.–Nov. Folder, Memo, Sherrill D. Luke to EGB, November 9, 1962. EGB ctn 569, Legis. Subjects, Aug.–Nov. Folder, Patricia Sikes to EGB, November 17, 1962. HCP ctn 1, Br. Administration Folder, Fred Jordan to Arthur Alarcon, October 30, 1963. HCI.
2. Edmund G. Brown, "Inaugural Message to the California State Legislature," January 7, 1963.
3. Ibid.
4. HCP ctn 1, Gov. Edmund Brown Folder, Memo, Richard Kline to EGB, November 30, 1962.
5. EGBOH, 94–95.
6. Martin Schiesl, "The Struggle for Equality: Racial Reform and Party Politics in California, 1950–1966," in *California Politics & Policy* (Special Issue 1997), "The California of the Pat Brown Years: Creative Building for the 'Golden State's Future,'" Schiesl, Guest ed., 58. See U.S. Commissions on Civ. Rhts. HCP ctn 5, Housing Folder, Memo, Kline to Champion, "Position Paper on Housing," December 2, 1960.
7. For a discussion of Becker's record, see WBOH, 1–44. See also Coleman Blease, "Political Advocacy and Loyalty," oral history interview, 61.
8. TBCP Box 28, LF1, cover, "The liberal democrat," May 1963 picture of African-American holding up picket sign.
9. "Statement of Governor Edmund G. Brown on Human Rights," to a joint session of the Legislature, February 14, 1963. Thomas W. Casstevens, *Politics, Hous-*

*ing, and Race Relations: California's Rumford Act and Proposition 14* (Berkeley: Institute of Governmental Studies, University of California, Berkeley, 1964), 19–20.

10. Lawrence Crouchet, *William Byron Rumford, The Life and Public Services of a California Legislator* (El Cerrito, Calif.: Downey Place Publishing House, 1984), 56–58.

11. HburOH, 40. JROH, 37.

12. CBOH, 23. EGBOH, 493–94.

13. Casstevens, *Politics, Housing, and Race Relations*, 33–36. WBOH, 36.

14. CWBOH, 61–63. The meeting between Kennedy and Unruh is recounted by Leon D. Ralph, a former state assemblyman from Watts, 56. Former Assemblyman Paul Lunardi confirms that the Kennedy administration pressured Gibson into releasing the bill. "There was a lot of threat that if they didn't get the bill out and put it on the floor and at least have an opportunity . . . that they were going to do something about naval bases." PLOH, 202. WAOH, 79–81.

15. JROH, 38.

16. AROH, 107–9.

17. RKOH, 18–19. RROH, 41, 98. Ringer remembers clearly Gibson telling Brown's aides that they would regret Rumford as long as they lived.

18. RROH, 146–47. RKOH, 18–19. JBOH, 80. JROH, 36–41.

19. WBOH, 35–36, 38–39. "It solidified their concept of a kind of natural coalition," Becker said of labor and the minority opposition to right-to-work. EGBOH, 524–25, 527–28. Regan was appointed the following year. See AROH, 107–9, for a discussion of Regan's motives for supporting the bill.

20. EGB ctn 706, Housing Discrimination Folder, October. EGB ctn 706, Housing Discrimination Folder, "CREA News Release," November 5, 1963. WBRP ctn 1, January 1963–December 1963 Folder, Memo, L. H. Wilson to "All members, CREA," December 31, 1963.

21. WBRP ctn 2, Fair Housing Folder, "Our Friends Speak," a compilation of articles attacking Rumford, culled from various California newspapers, Dec. 1963. WBRP ctn 2, Fair Housing Folder, "Brown Press Release," September 19, 1963.

22. WBRP ctn 2, Fair Housing Folder, "Brown Press Release," September 19, 1963. Schiesl, "The Struggle for Equality," 61.

23. WBRP ctn 1, Fair Housing Jan. 63–Dec. 63 Folder, Letter, Brown to Wilson. RRGP Box 1, Fair Housing Jan. 63–Dec. 1963 Folder, "Real Estate Bulletin," Letter, Brown to "Real Estate Licensees." And article in same issue by Gordon entitled "Commissioner Speaks on Fair Housing Issue."

24. EGB ctn 602, Housing Div. July Folder, "What is the effect of the ca. fair housing act?" EGB ctn 602, Housing Div. July Folder, Letter, Becker to Rumford, November 26, 1963. EGB ctn 602, Housing div. July Folder, Letter, Becker to Harry Finks, Sec., Sacramento Labor Council, November 27, 1963. EGB ctn 685, FEPC Folder, Memo, Becker to Howden, January 3, 1964.

25. WBRP ctn 1, Fair Housing Jan. '63–Dec. '63 Folder, Summary of Meeting of Ca. Comm. For Fair Practices, November 2, 1963.

26. EGB ctn 601, FEPC Folder, Becker to EGB.

27. Crouchet, *William Byron Rumford*, 64–65.

28. WBagOH, 471.

29. EGB ctn 701, Memo, Becker to John Anson Ford, January 23, 1964. EGB ctn 706, Housing Disc., Feb. 15–28 Folder, Memo, Burby to Brown, "Counter-Initiative Organization" February 26, 1964. EGB ctn 701, Housing Division Feb. 1–14 Folder, Memo, Becker to Ford, January 23, 1964. HCP ctn 5, Housing Folder, Memo, Tom Sanders to Brown, April 22, 1964.

30. EGB ctn 706, Housing Disc. June 1–16 Folder, Letter, Becker to William A. Norris, "Cas. against prop. 14." EGB ctn 708, Housing Disc. June 18 Folder, Memo, Becker to Brown, June 24, 1964. WBRP ctn 7, Prop. 14 Folder. EGB ctn 2, Cnt. Prop. 14 Folder, "Housing Initiative, Background." EGB ctn 706, Housing Disc. Folder, Memo, "July Memo from Becker," July 22, 1964. EGB ctn 706, Housing Disc. March

25–31 Folder, Letter, Becker to Hawkins, March 30, 1964. EGB ctn 706, Housing Disc. Feb. 15–28 Folder, Letter, Robert Coate to Becker. EGB ctn 673, Civil Rights May 1–8 Folder, Memo, Becker to Ben McKesson, March 18, 1964.

31. EGBOH, 525–26, 539–40. WBRP ctn 11, Folder 6, Letter. EGB ctn 741, Rumford Folder, Form Letter, "Brown to Fellow Californian."

32. TBCP Box 21, Folder 3, "Governor Brown on Civil Rights," Address, May 27, 1964, in CDC Bulletin, Aug.–Sept. 1964, "Fair Housing Edition." See also EGB ctn 673, Civil Rights Aug. 13–31 Folder, Letter, EGB to Mr. Chairman, August 25, 1964.

33. EGB ctn 706, Housing Disc. August Folder, Letter, Harvey Schecter to Becker, March 25, 1964. EGB ctn 640, Legis. Civil Rights, May Folder, "Radio Script." EGB ctn 706, Housing Disc. April 15–30 Folder, Memo, Becker to Burby and Brown. EGB ctn 706, Housing Div. Feb. 1–14 Folder, Memo, Becker to Burby, February 4, 1964.

34. EGB ctn 707, Prop. 14, Sept. 18–30 Folder, Letter, Mrs. Stephen Brieger to EGB, August 30, 1964. EGB ctn 707, Prop. 14, Sept. 18–30 Folder, Memo, Jack Burby to Becker, September 22, 1964. EGB ctn 709, Prop. 14, Aug. 19 Folder, Letter, EGB to Otis Chandler, August 31, 1964.

35. Schuparra, *Triumph of the Right*, 104–6. Schiesl, "The Struggle for Racial Equality," 62. Wallace Turner, "Rightists in the West Fight Housing Act," *New York Times*, May 10, 1964.

36. EGB ctn 692, Prop. 14 Folder, Political Advertisement.

37. Thomas W. Casstevens, *Politics, Housing and Race Relations: California's Rumford Act and Proposition 14* (Berkeley, Calif.: Institute of Governmental Studies, 1967), 69, 77.

38. WBOH, 47. RKOH, 18–19. HCOH, 60.

39. LHOH, 71, 75, 134. LHI.

## *FOUR:* "RUN RONNIE RUN"

1. Robert Alan Goldberg, *Barry Goldwater* (New Haven: Yale University Press, 1995), 225, 231. For a discussion of Goldwater and 1964 see Goldberg, *Goldwater*, Chapter 8. See also RWOH, 16–21. Karl Hess, *In a Cause that Will Triumph: The Goldwater Campaign and the Future of Conservatism* (Garden City, N.Y.: Doubleday, 1967), 139–40.

2. Davis, *The Way I See It*, 44, 77–78. Edwards, *Early Reagan*, 482–83. RRRRGE, 1–2. Kurt Schuparra, "Barry Goldwater and Southern California Conservatism: Ideology, Image and Myth in the 1964 California Republican Presidential Primary," *Southern California Quarterly*, Vol. 74, Fall 1992, 287. RRRRGE, 2. HTOH, 113–14. Kelley, *Nancy Reagan*, 132. Harold Faber, ed., "The Road to the White House, The Story of the 1964 Election by the Staff of the New York Times," *New York Times*, 164.

3. Charles Mohr, "Attacks Provoke Goldwater Camp," *New York Times*, May 30, 1964. Joseph Lewis, *What Makes Reagan Run?* (New York: McGraw-Hill, 1968), 8–9.

4. Mohr, "Attacks Provoke Goldwater Camp." JAHOH, 1. See also Clifton White, with William J. Gill, *Why Reagan Won: A Narrative History of the Conservative Movement, 1964–1981* (Chicago: Regnery Gateway, 1981), 14–16.

5. JAHOH, 1.

6. White, *Why Reagan Won*, 14–15.

7. HTOH, 113–14. HSOH, 4–5. Reagan, *American Life*, 139–40. Davis, *The Way I See It*, 78. Edwards, *Goldwater*, 334–35. Cannon, *Ronnie and Jesse*, 71–72. Nancy Reagan, with William Novak, *My Turn: The Memoirs of Nancy Reagan* (New York: Random House, 1989), 130.

8. Wills, *Reagan's America*, 345–46. Joseph Lewis, *What Makes Reagan Run?*, 4. Edwards, *Early Reagan*, 484–85. NROH, 30.

9. Nicholas Lemann, "The Speech: Reagan's Break from the Past," *Washington Post*, A-1, February 22, 1981.

10. Reagan, *American Life*. RRGP Box 1, Pre-1966 Speeches Folder, "A Time for Choosing."

11. Reagan, *American Life*, 141–43. Reagan, *My Turn*, 131. HTOH, 114. White, *Why Reagan Won*, 24–25. Edwards, *Ronald Reagan*, 79.

12. Nicholas Lemann, "The Speech," *Washington Post*, February 22, 1981. David Broder and Stephen Hess, *The Republican Establishment: The Present and Future of the G.O.P.* (New York: Harper & Row, 1967), 253–54.

13. Goldberg, *Barry Goldwater*, 234–35.

14. Mervin Field, "GOP Race for Governorship," *San Francisco Chronicle*, February 11, 1965. Gladwin Hill, "Reagan Weighing a New Role in Gubernatorial Race on Coast," *New York Times*, January 23, 1965.

15. Lewis, *What Makes Reagan Run?*, 91–92. See also Edwards, *Early Reagan*, 488. Hill, "Reagan Weighing a New Role in Gubernatorial Race on Coast."

16. TdJOH, 12–13. George H. Smith, *Who Is Ronald Reagan?* (New York: Pyramid Books, 1968), 80. Gentry, *The Last Days*, 43–44. See also Joel Kotkin and Grabowicz, *California Inc.* (New York: Rawson, Wade, 1982), 71. VJCOH, 19–21.

17. JWOH, 4–5.

18. HTOH. Cannon, *Ronnie and Jesse*, 72.

19. JWOH, 4–5. Edwards, *Early Reagan*, 487–88. Reagan, *American Life*, 145. RRRRGE, 6. See also NROH, 23, 25. WFSRRGE, 7. EMOH, 68.

20. For the story of Mills' life, see EMOH, 53–55.

21. EMOH, 59.

22. HSOH, 1–9.

23. Kotkin, *California Inc.*, 50–51. HSOH, 1–4. Lewis, *What Makes Reagan Run?*, 11–12.

24. HTOH, 112.

25. HTOH, 109–13. See also "Auto Dealer Honored by 400," *The Valley News*, October 9, 1973.

26. ERSOH, 1–2. Kathy Davis, *But What's He Really Like?* (Menlo Park, Calif.: Pacific Coast Publishers, 1970), 19.

27. Cannon, *Ronnie and Jesse*, 74. HSOH, 5. See Kelley, *Nancy Reagan*, 138.

28. VJCOH, 19–21.

29. VSOH, 12. VVOH, 183–84. Nancy Reagan, *My Turn*, 131–32. ERSOH, 3.

30. Peter Kaye, "GOP Group Likes Reagan," *The San Diego Union*, April 11, 1965. Reagan, *American Life*, 147. McGirr, *Suburban Warriors*, 233, 236–37. See also *The Orange County Register*, March 28, 1965, March 30, 1965, and April 21, 1965. Earl C. Behrens, "A Boom for Goldwater and Reagan," *San Francisco Chronicle*, March 28, 1965. For poll results, see "Reagan Favorite of GOP," *San Francisco Chronicle*, April 23, 1965.

31. RRGP Box 19, B-C Folder, John W. Calvert to RR, February 22, 1965.

32. Cannon, *Ronnie and Jesse*, 74. Davis, *But What's He Really Like?*, 19. Davis writes, "No one, absolutely no one, could keep Mr. Reagan away from the letters he received during the early days of the campaign." WRRGE, 14–15. Edwards, *Ronald Reagan*, 84. Nancy Reagan, *My Turn*, 131. Reagan, *American Life*, 145–46. RRRRGE, 4. TRI. In a scorching autobiography Patti Davis, Reagan's daughter, writes, "I didn't sense . . . that there was any hesitancy about my father's plans—I could already envision the new bumper stickers," a reference to the Goldwater for President strips plastered on her father's Lincoln. Davis, *The Way I See It*, 79. Hill, "Reagan Weighing a New Role in Gubernatorial Race on Coast."

## *FIVE:* "YOU'VE GOT TO GET THOSE KIDS OUT OF THERE"

1. Gentry, *The Last Days*, 90–92. See also W. J. Rorabaugh, *Berkeley at War: The 1960s* (New York: Oxford University Press, 1989), 1–50. Seymour Martin Lipset and Sheldon S. Wolin, eds., *Berkeley Student Revolt: Facts and Interpretations* (Garden City, N.Y.: Doubleday, 1965), 234–37.

2. EGB ctn 675, Civ. Rights, Dec. Folder, Memo, Moskowitz to Christian, Dec. 2, 1964. CKI. EGBOH, FSM. CKFSM For Brown's opinions on the FMS, see also EGB, FSM Project. For letters encapsulating Brown's early opinions, see EGB ctn 673, Civil Rights Nov. Folder, EGB to Richard Schmorleits, October 28, 1964. EGB ctn 673, Civil Rights Nov. Folder, EGB to David Piper, October 23, 1964.

3. EGB ctn 742, Pol. Dem. Natl. Convention Aug. Folder, Letter, Mario Savio to EGB, July 24, 1964.

4. The story is recounted in Rappaport, *California Dreaming*, 82–83. EGBFSM.

5. EGBOH, 476–77.

6. EGBOH, 476–77. EMI. EGBFSM. A few months later Sproul, who had been abroad at the time of the takeover, returned to campus for a visit. Officials led Sproul to his office and said, "Look at that." Sproul looked around and said, "Looks just the way I left it." JBOH, 106–7.

7. ASOH, 35–37, 47–48.

8. FMOH, 248. EGBOH, 474–75.

9. EGBOH, 486. EGBFSM.

10. Steven Warshaw, *The Trouble in Berkeley* (Berkeley, Calif.: Diablo Press, 1965). Rappaport, *California Dreaming*, 83. EGBOH, 486.

11. EGB ctn 569, Legis. Subject 1963 Aug.–Nov. Folder, Letter, Kerr to EGB, June 12, 1962. WBRP ctn 4, Race Folder, "Charter Day Speech," May 5, 1964. For more on Kerr's views, see, EGB ctn 634, UC Mar.–Apr. Folder, Letter, Kerr to Lois Cshwarze, April 18, 1963.

12. For Brown's views on higher education, see John Aubrey Douglass, "Brokering the 1960 Master Plan: Pat Brown and the Promise of California Higher Education," in *California Politics and Policy, Special Issue*, 1997.

13. Kathleen Brown, "I Accept the Nomination," in *California Politics and Policy, Special Issue*, 1997. See also EGB ctn 667, Pol. Gov. July Folder, Letter, EGB to Charles Bugg, July 19, 1963. EGB ctn 502, Pol. Misc. Nov.–Dec. Folder, Letter, EGB to Ira Reifman, November 21, 1961. EGB ctn 543, Gov. Speech, March Folder, Letter, Stephen Shields to Richard Kline, February 19, 1962. RMI.

14. EGB ctn 415, Board of Regents June–Dec.1960 Folder, Letters, Hoover to Ed Pauley, February 8, 1960. EGB ctn 415, Board of Regents June–Dec. 1960 Folder, Letters, Chas. Johnson to Hoover, March 9, 1960. EGB ctn 415, Board of Regents, June–Dec. 1960 Folder, "Firing Line Newsletter," March 15, 1960. EGB ctn 634, UC Sept.–Oct. Folder, Letter, Mrs. John Kelly to EGB, July 16, 1963.

15. WBRP ctn 4, Civ. Rights Folder, Letter, Don Mulford to EGB, April 22, 1964.

16. W. J. Rorabaugh, *Berkeley at War*, 8–20. Brown described himself as a civil libertarian who read *The Nation* and *The New Republic.* He also said he never viewed the communists as a serious threat. EGBOH, 472–73. EGB ctn 465, Gov. Speeches Nov.–Dec. Folder, Memo, Sherrill Luke to Charles O'Brien, November 1, 1961.

17. EGB ctn 465, Gov. Speech July–Aug. Folder, Letter, Scott Newhall to EGB, August 3, 1961.

18. *California Dreaming*, 82–84. Warshaw, *The Trouble in Berkeley*, 76, 90.

19. EGB ctn 465, Gov. Speech July–Aug. Folder, Letter, Julian Foster to EGB, June 4, 1961.

20. SMI.

21. EGB ctn 752, Civ. Rights, March Folder, Letter, EGB to George Hardy, December 15, 1964.

22. Ibid.

23. Max Heirich, *The Spiral of Conflict: Berkeley, 1964* (New York: Columbia University Press, 1971), 75. James Benet, "4 Point Program To End UC Unrest," *San Francisco Chronicle*, December 19, 1964.

24. EGB ctn 752, Berkeley Civ. Rights, March Folder, Letter, EGB to George Hardy, December 15, 1964.

25. EGB ctn 675, Civ. Rights Berkeley, Dec. Folder, Memo, Judge Leonard Dieden (Through May Bonnell) to EGB, December 3, 1964. EGB ctn 675, Civ. Rights Berkeley, Dec. Folder, Memo, John McInerny to EGB, December 8, 1964. EGB ctn 675, Civ. Rights Berkeley, Dec. Folder, Letter, Carley Port to EGB, December 9, 1964.

26. EGB ctn 675, Berkeley Folder, Memo, Vivian Porter to Winslow Christian, December 10, 1964. EGB ctn 675, Civ. Rights Dec. Folder, Memo, Ron Moskowitz to EGB, December 23, 1964.

27. Heirich, *The Spiral of Conflict*, 280–84.

28. Ibid. EGB ctn 675, Civ. Rights 12-19-64 Folder, Resolution. EGB ctn 675, Berkeley Folder, Memo, Phyllis DeCroix to Ron Moskowitz, December 10, 1964.

29. "Governor Defends His Decision," *San Francisco Chronicle*, December 4, 1964. "UC Quarrel Unnecessary," *San Francisco Chronicle*, December 9, 1964. Robert Blanchard, "Governor Calls Dispute 'Unnecessary Quarrel,'" *L.A. Times*, December 9, 1964. For Brown's conflicting feelings about the protests, see also EGB ctn 752, Berkeley Civ. Rights Folder, Letter, EGB to George Hardy, December 15, 1964. EGB ctn 675, Berkeley Civ. Rights Folder, Letter, EGB to Mr. and Mrs. Kroll, December 18, 1964. EGB ctn 752, Berkeley Civ. Rights, Jan. 1–12, Letter, EGB to Norma Thomash, January 15, 1965. James Benet, "4 Point Program to End Unrest," *San Francisco Chronicle*, December 19, 1964.

30. EGB ctn 675, Civ. Rights, 12-19-64 Folder, Letter, Jack Burby to Abe Mellinkoff, December 21, 1964.

31. EGB ctn 752, Board of Regents Folder, Memo, Moskowitz to EGB, December 16, 1964.

32. Ibid.

33. EGB ctn 675, Civ. Rights Berkeley Dec. 3–31 Folder, Memo, Moskowitz to EGB, December 31, 1964. James Benet, "Faculty, Regents Tackle UC Crisis," *San Francisco Chronicle*, Dec. 18, 1964.

34. EGB ctn 931, 1966 Gov. Brown's Itineraries Riverside Folder, Memos, Moskowitz to EGB, January 13 & January 27, 1965.

35. Rorabaugh, *Berkeley at War*, 32–43. According to Kerr, Brown called Kerr and demanded Kerr put a stop to the agitation. CKI.

36. Matthew Dallek, "Liberalism Overthrown," *American Heritage*, October 1996, 50.

## *SIX:* "A Bunch of Kooks"

1. Bryan Stevens, *The John Birch Society in California Politics* (West Covina, Calif.: Publius Society, 1966), 5–6.

2. Ibid., 5–6, 49. Thomas Storke, *I Write for Freedom* (Fresno, Calif.: McNally & Lofton, 1962), 1–5.

3. McGirr, *Suburban Warriors*, 96–101. For a good discussion of the John Birch Society in California, see Schuparra, *Triumph of the Right*, 42–54. See also McGirr, *Suburban Warriors*, Chapter 2, and J. Allen Broyles, *The John Birch Society: Anatomy of a Protest* (Boston: Beacon Press, 1964), 24–25.

4. McGirr, *Suburban Warriors*, 98–100. Schuparra, *Triumph of the Right*, 86–87. Benjamin R. Epstein and Arnold Forster, *Report on the John Birch Society 1966* (New York: Vintage, 1966), 1–2. For a general discussion see Bryan Stevens, *The John Birch*

*Society in California Politics, 1966* (West Covina, Calif.: Publius Society, 1966); Barbara Stone, "The John Birch Society of California," Ph.D. Dissertation, University of Southern California, 1968.

5. Ibid.

6. Bruce Biossat, "Say It Again: We Are Right!," *Ventura Star Free Press*, September 4, 1965. RRGP Box 23, '66 Campaign Gov. Letters of Particular Importance Folder, Letter, John L. Harmer to Bill Roberts, July 12, 1965. RRGP Box 23, '66 Campaign Gov. Letters of Particular Importance Folder, Letter, Roberts to Harmer, July 15, 1965. RRGP Box 21, Bill Roberts Correspondence Folder, Letter, James T. Moriarty to RR, July 21, 1965. RRGP Box 21, Bill Roberts Correspondence Folder, Letter, Arthur Guy to RR, July 1, 1965. RRGP Box 21, Bill Roberts Correspondence Folder, Letter, Bill Roberts to Arthur Guy, July 15, 1965.

7. Ben H. Bagdikian, "In the Hearts of the Right, Goldwater Lives!," *New York Times Magazine*, July 18, 1965. Nancy Parr and Ruth McGrew, *The Real Ronald Reagan* (San Francisco: Reagan Book, Box B, Diamond Heights Station, 1968), 43–44. Gentry, *The Last Days*, 125–26. "Mr. Ruchel's Decision," *New York Times*, September 24, 1965.

8. McGirr, *Suburban Warriors*, 233, citing *The Register*, 4/21/65.

9. Gentry, *The Last Days*, 40–41.

10. "CDC's New Chief Lashes at Unruh," UPI; "Reagan is Ready to Run . . . If," *San Francisco Chronicle*, March 22, 1965. Lawrence Davies, "Reagan Assesses Political Future," *New York Times*, July 25, 1965.

11. RRGP Box 21, Bill Roberts Correspondence Folder, Letter, Harold Quinton to Cy Rubel, July 13, 1965. "Republicans Stage to Sacramento?," *Time*, July 20, 1965. RRGP Box 23, '66 Campaign Gov., Letters of Particular Importance Folder, Letter, John Harmer to Bill Roberts, July 12, 1965.

12. "Republicans: Stage to Sacramento?" *Time*, July 30, 1965.

13. RRGP Box 21, Bill Roberts Correspondence Folder, Memo, Cyril Stevenson to Reagan Campaign, July 14, 1965. RRGP Box 20, R-S Folder, Letter, Stevenson to Reagan, July 27, 1965. RRGP Box 19, B-C Folder, Letter, A.L. Bane to Fred Haffner, Letter, July 27, 1965.

14. Ibid.

15. Smith, *Who is Ronald Reagan?*, 10.

16. Ibid.

17. Ibid., 104–10.

18. RRGP Box 21, Bill Roberts Correspondents Folder, Letter, Kay to Ronnie and Nancy, September 4, 1965. RRGP Box 14 S Folder, Letter, RR to Allen J. Tenny, October 5, 1965.

19. "Furor Over Reagan's Birch Talk," *San Francisco Chronicle*, September 1, 1965. Laurence Davies, "Factions Trouble California G.O.P.," *New York Times*, September 5, 1965. RRGP Box 2, Correspondence Folder, News Clipping, "Ronald Reagan Exits Right," *Beverly Hills Courier.* Mike Young, Chairman of the Redwood City UROC, also confirmed Reagan's statement.

20. Kotkin, *California Inc.*, 55.

21. EGBOH, 499–500.

22. Storke, *I Write for Freedom*, 1–5. Stevens, *The John Birch Society*, vii. TSP Box 1, Allen, Roberts Letter Folder, Letter, Thomas Storke to Robert Allen, February 27, 1961.

23. TSP Box 19, Lyons, Louis Folder, Letter, Louis M. Lyons to John Holenberg, April 8, 1961. TSP Box 37, Warren, Earl Folder, Letter, Storke to Earl Warren, March 3, 1961. TSP Box 1, Robert Allen Folder, Letter, Robert Allen to Storke, March 10, 1961. TSP Box 3, Chandler, Otis Folder, Letter, Otis Chandler to Storke, April 6, 1961.

24. TSP Box 3, Brown, Edmund Gerald Folder, Letter, EGB to Storke, November 3, 1961. TSP Box 3, Brown, Edmund Gerald 1960–1970 Folder, Letter, EGB to

Storke, March 13, 1961. TSP Box 3, Edmund Gerald Brown 1960–1970 Folder, Letter, EGB to Storke February 16, 1962. TSP Box 3, Edmund Gerald Brown 1960–1970 Folder, Letter, EGB to Storke, No Date Indicated. TSP Box 3, Edmund Gerald Brown 1960–1970 Folder, Letter, Storke to EGB, May 16, 1962.

25. RKP Box 1, Memoranda 1 Folder, Letter, Stanley Mosk to Pat Brown, July 1, 1961.

26. Ibid.

27. Ibid. EGB ctn 502, Pol. Misc. June–Aug. Folder, Letter, Mrs. Ruth Havens to EGB, August 18, 1961. Mosk had called the rank-and-file a cadre of "wealthy businessmen, retired military officers and little old ladies in tennis shoes," and the picture of rabid elderly women trumpeting conspiracy theories appealed to liberals, suggesting the ridiculous leanings of the larger organization. RKP Box 11, Dutton, Fred Folder, Letter, Roger Kent to Fred Dutton, February 24, 1961.

28. EGB ctn 477, JBS Letters Folder, Letter, EGB to Jean Curter, December 13, 1961. EGB ctn 555, Atty. Gen., June 1–14 Folder, News Clippings, "Brown Deplores Attack on Ridge School Teachers," (No Date Indicated; Source Unknown). See also EGB ctn 465, Gov. Speech July–Aug. Folder, Letter, Julian Foster to EGB, June 4, 1961. EGB ctn 465, Gov. Speech May–June Folder, Warren Christopher to EGB, June 26, 1961.

29. TSP Box 3, EGB, 1960–1970 Folder, Storke to EGB, March 3, 1961. TSP Box 3, EGB, 1960–1970 Folder, Storke to EGB, May 16, 1962. EGB ctn 477, JB Letters, Marie Hall to EGB, November 20, 1961. EGB ctn 465, Gov. Speech July–Aug. Folder, Letter, Julian Foster to EGB, June 4, 1961. EGB ctn 465, Gov. Speech May–June Folder, Warren Christopher to EGB, June 26, 1961.

30. EGB ctn 477, JB Letters Folder, Letter, EGB to Mrs. M. B. Boyd, December 27, 1961.

31. EGB ctn 555, Atty. Gen., Jan. 1–15 Folder, Memo, Frank Mesple to Gov. Brown, January 15, 1962.

32. Ibid.

33. EGB ctn 555, JB Letters Folder, Memo, Canoy D. Crawford to Charles O'Brien, May 6, 1962.

34. TSP Box 9, Democ. Party, CA State Central Committee Folder, Roger Kent to Storke, September 29, 1964. EGB ctn 742, Pol. Goldwater Folder, Letter, EGB to Sam Creswell, November 2, 1964.

35. Ibid.

36. EGB ctn 787, JBS Letters Folder, William Becker to Frank Mesple, January 6, 1965.

37. EGB ctn 787, JBS Letters, "Report Sent to EGB, Notes on the Rally, Anonymous," January 28, 1965.

38. EGB ctn 787, Nazi Party Folder, Memo, Becker to Jack Burby and Winslow Christian, April 6, 1965.

39. RRGP Box 19, B-C Folder, Letter, A. L. Bane to Fred Haffner, July 27, 1965.

40. RRGP Box 2, Bill Roberts Correspondence Folder, Letter, Kay to "Ronnie and Nancy," September 4, 1965.

41. Ibid.

42. Ibid.

43. Ibid.

44. SSOH, 1–7, 22–25. WRRRGE, 4–8.

45. WRRRGE, 54–58, SSOH, 22–25.

46. HSOH, 5, 15. WRRRGE, 12–16.

47. SSOH, 26, 29. WRRRGE, 12–16.

48. Wills, *Reagan's America*, 347–48. See also Lewis, *What Makes Reagan Run?*, 107–8. Cannon, *Ronnie and Jesse*, 72.

49. SSOH, 26, 29. Lewis, *What Makes Reagan Run?*, 108. Edwards, *Ronald Reagan*, 86–87.

50. JSMRRGE, 8–9, 12.

51. RRGE Box 36, '66 Campaign, Staff Interoffice Memos Folder, Memo, Anonymous to Bill Roberts and "Kathy," May 19, 1965. RRGE Box 36, '66 Campaign, Staff Interoffice Memos Folder, Memo, Haffner to Kathy Davis, May 20, 1965.

52. Gentry, *The Last Days*, 70. "California: Will He Size Up?," June 7, 1965.

53. Hubler, *Where's the Rest of Me?*, 224.

54. Ibid.

55. For a discussion of Reagan and the Birchers, see SPRRGE, 11, and RRRRGE, 16.

56. RRGP Box 11, R Folder, Letter, RR to John Rousselot, September 16, 1965.

57. RRGP Box 18, Con-JBS Folder, Memo & Hached Draft of Statement, George Young to Bill Roberts.

58. RRGP Box 25, Vol. I & II Folder, "Statement of Ronald Reagan Regarding the 'John Birch Society,'" September 24, 1965.

59. RRGP, Box 18, Correspondences JBS Folder, Letter, R. R. Schlicter to RR, September 24, 1965.

60. RRGP Box 18, Correspondences JBS Folder, Letter, Frank Brophy to Mrs. Loyal Davis, September 28, 1965.

61. RRGP Box 18, Correspondences JBS Folder, Letter, Anonymous to RR, September 25, 1965.

62. RRGP Box 12, S Folder, Letter, Dudley Swim to RR, September 28, 1965. RRGP Box 12, S Folder, Letter, RR to Swim, October 5, 1965.

63. RRGP Box 3J, '66 Legislature: Withhold Folder Letter, John Schmitz to RR, September 24, 1965.

64. RRGP Box 12, Corr-Jbs. Folder, Letter, RR to Mr. and Mrs. Orville Jordet, October 26, 1965. RRGP Box 12, Corr-Jbs. Folder, Letter, RR to Schlicter, October 26, 1965.

65. RRGP Box 38, '66 Press/Media, Interviews with RR Folder, Transcript, Interview with Ronald Reagan, KPOL, September 27, 1965. Stevens, *The John Birch Society*, 26–27.

66. FCNI. See also TRI; NAI; FCNOH, 14; HRHOH, 304, 308–309.

## *SEVEN:* "CHARCOAL ALLEYS"

1. Gentry, *The Last Days*, 185, 199–219. "Violence in the City, an End or Beginning?," in *Governor's Commission on the Los Angeles Riots*, Los Angeles, December 2, 1965. Vol. II, 3–9.

2. Winslow Christian Testimony, "Transcripts and Depositions of Testimony Before the Governor's Commission on the Los Angeles Riots," *Governor's Commission*, Vol. V. William H. Parker Testimony, *Governor's Commission*, Vol. XI, 20–42, 84–85. Richard Kline Testimony, *Governor's Commission*, Vol. IX, 1–40.

3. Glenn Anderson Testimony, *Governor's Commission*, Vol. III, 10.

4. "Chronology," in *Governor's Commission*, Vol. II, 50–54.

5. Gentry, *The Last Days*, 199–217.

6. Christian Testimony, *Governor's Commission*, Vol. V, 20–42. Anderson Testimony, *Governor's Commission*, Vol. III, 10.

7. Richard Kline Testimony, *Governor's Commission*, Vol. IX, 1–10.

8. William H. Parker Testimony, *Governor's Commission*, Vol. XI, 84–85. Kline Testimony, *Governor's Commission*, Vol. IX, 3–4.

9. Kline Testimony, *Governor's Commission*, Vol. IX, 34–40.

10. Ibid., 11–34.

11. *Governor's Commission*, Vol. I, 85–126. WchrOH, 51–52, 56. Gerald Horne, *The Fire This Time* (Charlottesville: University Press of Virginia, 1995), 45–53, 158. Anderson Testimony, *Governor's Commission*, Vol. III, 100–107. HCOH, 47–48. The commission criticized Anderson for not deploying troops right away: "Violence in the City," 17–18. See also William Becker Testimony.

12. Hale Champion Testimony, *Governor's Commission*, Vol. V, 48–58. "Violence in the City," 134–35.

13. John Billett Testimony, *Governor's Commission*, Vol. III. For a description of Parker's agitated state, see TLOH, 222–23.

14. Anderson Testimony, *Governor's Commission*, Vol. III, 100. HCOH, 47–48. "Violence in the City," 138–39. Champion Testimony, *Governor's Commission*, Vol. V, 5.

15. Champion Testimony, *Governor's Commission*, Vol. V, 1–12. Edmund "Pat" Brown Testimony, *Governor's Commission*, Vol. IV, 1–10. EDI.

16. Champion Testimony, *Governor's Commission*, Vol. V, 26–30. "Violence in the City," 193.

17. Sal Perrotta, "Brown Here, Vows He'll Restore Law," Los Angeles *Herald-Examiner*, August 15, 1965. Spencer Crump, *Black Riot in Los Angeles: The Story of the Watts Tragedy* (Los Angeles: Trans-Anglo Books, 1966), 80–81. Champion Testimony, *Governor's Commission*, Vol. V, 26–30. Brown Testimony, *Governor's Commission*, Vol. VI, 33–39. Gentry, *The Last Days*, 228, 277–79.

18. "Meeting Metropolitan Problems," December 1960, Appendix A, "Governor's Charge to the Commission on Metropolitan Area Problems," March 26, 1959.

19. EGBOH, 320–23. HCOH, 60–61, 63–64.

20. WBOH, 43–44. JBOH, 115. EGBOH, 312–26. LHOH, 80–83. EGBLBJ, 3. Brown Testimony, *Governor's Commission*, Vol. VI, 66–67. HCOH, 124–25.

21. Horne, *The Fire This Time*, 31–42. Gentry, *The Last Days*, 200–201. Eldridge Cleaver, *Soul on Ice* (New York: Bantam Doubleday, 1968).

22. Brown Testimony, *Governor's Commission*, Vol. VI, 59–61.

23. EGB ctn 673, Civ. Rhts. Aug. 1–12 Folder, Memo, Becker to EGB, August 4, 1964. EGB ctn 673, Civ. Rhts. Sept. Folder, Letter, Becker to EGB, September 28, 1964.

24. "Summary of Phone Interview with Howard Jewel," September 21, 1965, *Governor's Commission*, Vol. XV, 65. EGB ctn 754, L.A. County Riots Sept. 4–30 Folder, Memo, Howard Jewel to Stanley Mosk, May 25, 1964.

25. Brown Testimony, *Governor's Commission*, Vol. IV, 54–59. Cohen, Jerry Cohen and William S. Murphy, *Burn Baby Burn: The Los Angeles Race Riot*, August, 1965 (New York: Dutton, 1966), 290–93.

26. In an exclusive interview, California Governor Brown declared to Ethnos: "U.S. must oppose dictatorships and discontinue aid to corrupt regimes." Text of interview, part of "unclassified" cable to U.S. State Department from H. Daniel Brewster, of the American Embassy in Athens. In author's possession.

27. Cohen and Murphy, *Burn Baby Burn*, 275–87.

28. Gentry, *The Last Days*, 199–217. Parker Testimony, *Governor's Commission*, Vol. XI, 24–28, 49–50, 58, 75–90, 100–101, 103, 113, 117, 141. Brown Testimony, *Governor's Commission*, Vol. IV, 1–26.

29. GWOH, 163–64.

30. Gentry, *The Last Days*, 185, 214. EGB ctn 754, Los Angeles Riot Aug.–Sept. 9 Folder, "Chief William Parker, Interview on Newsmakers," August 14, 1965. Parker Testimony, *Governor's Commission*, Vol. IX, 24–50, 58, 75–117, 141. Kline Testimony, *Governor's Commission*, Vol. IX, 30–38.

31. Gentry, *The Last Days*, 220–31. Ed Ainsworth, *Maverick Mayor: A Biography of Sam Yorty* (Garden City, N.Y.: Doubleday, 1966), 5.

32. RRI. Brown Testimony, *Governor's Commission*, Vol. IX, 33–39. Crump, *Black Riot*, 80–81. Gentry, *The Last Days*, 217, 228. Sal Perrotta, "Brown Vows He'll Restore Law," *L.A. Herald*, August 15, 1965.

33. Gentry, *The Last Days*, 225–29. EGB ctn 861, Publicity Nov. Folder, Letter, EGB to Robert Manning, November 14, 1966.

34. Robert Graham, "Slap by Brown at Chief Parker," *San Francisco Chronicle*, August 23, 1965.

35. EGB ctn 673, Memo, Becker to EGB, July 31, 1964. *Washington Post*, July 6, 1964, a2.

36. EGB ctn 754, LA County Riots Sept. 11–30 Folder, Memo, Jim Alexander to Winslow Christian, September 29, 1965.

37. EGB ctn 754, LA Riot Aug.–Sept. 9 Folder, Memo, Becker to Brown, August 30, 1965.

38. EGB ctn 768, Gov. Cabinet Folder, Memo, John McDonald to EGB, September 10, 1965. EGB ctn 754, LA Riot Material Folder, Memo, Paul O'Rourke to EGB, August 19, 1965.

39. Ibid. EGB ctn 754, LA Riot Folder, Memo, Winslow Christian to Department Heads, the Governor, and aides, November 1, 1965.

40. EGB ctn 880, McCone Comm. Jan. Folder, Letter, Christian to Dean Malcolm Stinson, January 5, 1966.

41. HCOH, 128–29.

42. Hale Champion confirmed that Christopher ran the commission and had been appointed as the governor's voice in an interview with the author.

43. Letter, Brown to John McCone, Aug. 24, 1965, in "Violence in the City, an End or a Beginning?"

44. "Violence in the City," 3–9.

45. EGB ctn 754, LA County Riots Dec. 1–15 Folder, Letter, EGB to George Murphy, December 10, 1965.

46. EGB ctn 880, McCone Comm. Feb. Folder, Letter, EGB to McCone, February 4, 1966.

47. Robert Blauner, "Whitewash Over Watts," *Trans-Action*, March/April 1966. Robert Fogelson, "White on Black: A Critique of the McCone Commission Report on the Los Angeles Riots," 118–20, 141–43. Bayard Rustin, "The Watts Manifesto—The McCone Report," 147–64. The last two articles are in Fogelson, ed., *The Los Angeles Riots, Mass Violence in America* (New York: Arno Press and The New York Times, 1969).

48. EGB ctn 754, LA County Riots Dec. 1–15 Folder, Letter, EGB to George Murphy, December 10, 1965. EGB ctn 880, LA Riot May Folder, Memo, Jim Alexander to Anonymous, May 26, 1966.

49. HCI.

50. "600 Negroes Riot Again in Watts," *San Francisco Chronicle*, March 16, 1966. Horne, *The Fire This Time*, 31–42. Gentry, *The Last Days*, 229–30.

## *EIGHT:* THE GEORGE WALLACE OF CALIFORNIA

1. EGB ctn 923, Politics-Government June 1–31 Folder, Letter, EGB to Hubert Humphrey, January 19, 1966; API. For a description of Brown's attitudes toward running for a third term, see HCOH, 77–79.

2. EGB ctn 36, Government Speeches Folder, Memo, Fred Dutton to Harry Firvetz, January 11, 1960.

3. NSP Box 1, CDC Org. Charts Folder, Memo, Marshall Wilmiller to March 20 Leadership Meeting, March 18, 1966; TBCP Box 17, Folder 3, Letter, Tom Carvey to Hale Champion, March 27, 1965.

4. Rappaport, *California Dreaming*, 85–90.

5. Ibid.

6. Ibid.

7. Ibid. Cannon, *Ronnie and Jesse*, 84–85. Gentry, *The Last Days*, 129–30.

8. LNOH, 81.
9. EGBOH, 469. FMesOH, 12–13.
10. EGBOH, 469–71, 495–96. LMOH, 116–27, 130–31.
11. EGBOH, 165, 504. In 1962, Unruh supported Brown for governor under the mistaken assumption that he would have Brown's endorsement for the same office in 1966. When it became apparent that he would not have it, relations between the two men became so frayed that Brown thought Unruh "simply was out to destroy him." FDOH, 85. FDI. LMOH, 130–31. Unruh's antagonism toward Brown and Brown's decision to deprive Unruh of the governorship were both recounted in JCI. RMOH, 152.
12. JCI. GZOH, 108. EGBLBJ, 17.
13. Cannon, *Ronnie and Jesse*, 171–73.
14. Ibid., 165–66.
15. LMOH, 123–44.
16. RKOH, 263–65.
17. SYLBJ, 14–15. David S. Broder, "Yorty and Shriver Dispute Over Riots," *New York Times*, August 18, 1965. Samuel Yorty Testimony, *Governor's Commission*, Vol. XIV, 87–88.
18. Yorty Testimony, *Governor's Commission*, Vol. XIV, 82–84.
19. RKOH, 262–64. SYLBJ, 14–15. Ainsworth, *Maverick Mayor*, viii. SYP Box C1005, 7/8/1965 Folder, Letter, Yorty to Clifton Carter, August 5, 1965.
20. Ainsworth, *Maverick Mayor*, 59–60. Letter, Yorty to father, quoted in Ainsworth.
21. Ainsworth, *Maverick Mayor*, 85–89. SYLBJ, 1–50.
22. Ainsworth, *Maverick Mayor*, 88–101. JTOH, 724, 782.
23. JTOH, 725. ESOH, 168. Ainsworth, *Maverick Mayor*, 101–104. For a description of Yorty's background, see *Time*, "Cities," September 2, 1966.
24. Ainsworth, *Maverick Mayor*, 124–26.
25. EGB ctn 586, Pol. View Folder, Memo, Richard Kline to EGB, January 31, 1962.
26. EGB ctn 539, Gov. Office Org. Oct.–Dec. Folder, Memo, Paul Ward to Sherrill Luke, December 19, 1962.
27. SYI.
28. EGB Testimony, *Governor's Commission*, Vol. IV, 1–26.
29. Ibid.
30. EGB ctn 742, Pol. Dem. Nat'l Convention Folder, Letter, Jim Bolger to EGB, February 18, 1964. John C. Bollens and Grant B. Geyer, *Yorty: Politics of a Constant Candidate* (Pacific Palisades, Calif.: Palisades Publishers, 1973), 142–48.
31. RRGP 38, '66 Press/Media Yorty Folder, Broadcast, KNXT-TV Morning News, Grant Holcomb, September 23, 1965. RRGP 38, '66 Press/Media Yorty Folder, Broadcast, KPOL Commentary, September 23, 1965.
32. DBOH, 96–99, 119–21. Bollens and Geyer, *Yorty*, 149–52.
33. SYP Box C1005, 7-65 Folder, Letter, Yorty to LBJ, July 28, 1965. TBOH, 96.
34. For the Communist issue, see SYP Box C1005, Report on Rev. H. H. Brookins, March 23, 1965. For the Parker-Yorty alliance, see SYP Box C1005, Memo, Erwin Piper to Yorty, August 16, 1965. SYP Box C1006, Memo, Yorty to William Parker, August 24, 1965. Horne, *Fire This Time*, 279–90. Ainsworth, *Maverick Mayor*, 5.
35. Yorty Testimony, *Governor's Commission*, Vol. XIV, 87–88.
36. David S. Broder, "Yorty and Shriver Dispute Over Riots," *New York Times*, August 18, 1965.
37. Ainsworth, *Maverick Mayor*, 5.
38. Bollens and Geyer, *Yorty*, 154–58.
39. RKOH, 107, 263. Yorty's idea of a good campaign, recalled Don Bradley, is one in which you collect more money than you spend. DBOH, 147.

40. Bollens and Geyer, *Yorty*, 154–58. SYP Box C1005, Sept. 1965 Folder, Letter, Yorty to Clift Carter, September 15, 1965. "Five GOP Hopefuls Favored Over Brown," *Los Angeles Times*, September 14, 1965.

41. EGB ctn 919, Dem. Campaign March Folder, Letter, John L. Horn to EGB.

42. EGB ctn 921, Dem. Central Comm. Folder, Memo, John Luce to Burby, Bradley, Kline, January 28, 1966.

43. ERGOH, 347–51.

44. Video Lab, Sacramento, Brown Press Conference, March 1966.

45. EGB ctn 928, Sam Yorty Folder, Letter, Poulson to EGB, March 8, 1966.

46. EGB ctn 931, 1966 Gov. Br's Interviews Folder, Memo, John McDonald to EGB, June 1, 1966. RKOH, 107.

47. SYP Box D12, Calif. Legis. 1966 Folder, Letter, Yorty to Brown, March 14, 1966.

48. SYP Box D22, Crime 1966 Folder, Letter, Rockwell Ames to Marvin Newman, June 13, 1966. SYP Box D22, Crime 1966 Folder, Letter, Marvin Newman to Yorty, December 17, 1965. Gene Blake, "Yorty Strikes Back at Criticism by Lawyer," *Los Angeles Times*, March 2, 1966.

49. SYP Box D25, General, U.S. Govt. 1966 Folder, Letters, Yorty to EGB May 31, 1966; John McInerny to Yorty, June 1, 1966. SYP Box D25, Gen US Govt., 1966 Folder, Press Release, Yorty, June 3, 1966.

50. RRGP Box 24, 7 Folder, Transcript of Yorty Press Conference, May 2, 1966. RRGP Box 24, 7 Folder, Press Release, Yorty Statement, April 29, 1966. FDOH, 136–37.

51. EGB ctn 923, Pol. Gov. June 9–15 Folder, Letter, Jim Bolger to EGB, April 22, 1966.

52. EGB ctn 928, Sam Yorty Folder, Letter, EGB to Hubert Humphrey, May 2, 1966.

53. EGB ctn 930, Corr. Comm. to Reelect EGB Folder, "White Paper: Why We Cannot Take Yorty."

54. EGB ctn 927, Pol. Press Release Folder, News Release, Rickershauser to Yorty, February 11, 1966.

55. Bollens and Geyer, *Yorty*, 155–60.

56. RRGP Box 5, Corr. G. Folder, Press Release, Yorty, June 8, 1966.

57. Letter, Brown to Yorty, July 13, 1966.

58. EGBOH, 331.

59. SYOH, 42–43.

## *NINE:* THE SEARCH FOR ORDER

1. RRGP Box 36, '66 Campaign Friends of RR, Memo, Bill Roberts to Steering Committee, October 8, 1965.

2. RRRRGE, 5–6.

3. Ibid., 10. RRGP Box 19, D–F Folder, Letter, Kay Daley to Bill Roberts, October 28, 1965. For more on Reagan's lack of knowledge, see, CWBOH, 37.

4. Parr, *The Real Ronald Reagan*, quoting *Sacramento Bee*, 52–53. Kelley, *Nancy Reagan*, 177–79.

5. Reagan, *An American Life*, 151–52.

6. RRGP Box 19, D–F Folder, Letter, William Roberts to Kay Daley, November 19, 1965.

7. JSMRRGE, 10.

8. SSOH, 28–31.

9. Boyarsky, *Ronald Reagan*, 91.

10. WRRRGE.

11. SSI.

12. RRRRGE, 8.

13. GPRRGE, 48–50.

14. For an excellent description of California party politics, see Cannon, *Ronnie and Jesse*.

15. GPRRGE, 48–50.

16. Ibid., 4–11.

17. Ibid., 20–21, 135.

18. Ibid., 20–21. SSOH, 14–15. RWRRGE. See also WRRRGE, 19.

19. UPI, "Ronald Reagan Will Enter GOP Governor Race," *St. Louis Post Dispatch*, January 1, 1966.

20. HTOH, 117.

21. RRGP Box 1, Pre-1966 Speeches Folder, Speech, "Roundtable Appearance," California Republican League Convention, December 4, 1965.

22. RRGP Box 19, B-C Folder, Letter, Alphonzo Bell to *Time* editors, no date indicated.

23. HPOH, 61. GCOH, 1–30. GCI.

24. Lawrence Davies, "Christopher Is Seeking California Governorship," *New York Times*, October 27, 1965.

25. GCOH, 13. RRGP Box 34, '66 Campaign, Christopher Folder, "Press Release," July 29, 1965.

26. GCOH, 39. RRGP Box 34, '66 Campaign, Christopher Folder, Tony Kent, KPOL, September 28, 1965. UPI, "Christopher Governor Bid Faces Right Wing Clash," *Sacramento Bee*, February 11, 1965.

27. GCOH, 42–43.

28. Ibid., 42–43, 48–49.

29. RRGP Box 34, '66 Campaign, Christopher Folder, Speech, "Christopher," June 1, 1966.

30. Jack McDowell, "Christopher-Reagan Pact," *San Francisco Examiner*, February 20, 1966. In author's possession, Letter, RR to Martha Scherf, March 9, 1966. Carl C. Behrens, "Brown Castigates the 'GOP Deal,'" *San Francisco Chronicle*, February 22, 1966. Henry Salvatori admitted that the two sides had met but said that they had done so only to discuss how to unite Republicans next fall.

31. RRGP Box 21, TUVWXYZ Folder, Letter, Parkinson to Russell Teasdale, February 22, 1966.

32. GPRRGE, 27.

33. Lewis, *What Makes Reagan Run?*, 113–14.

34. FCNRGP, 40–41.

35. RRGP Box 16, X-Y-Z Folder, Letter, RR to Charles Zweng, December 7, 1965. RRGP Box 12, S Folder, Letter, RR to Dudley Swim, December 14, 1965.

36. RRGP Box 14, S Folder, Letter, Reagan to Edith Turner, July 19, 1966.

37. GRP Box 1, Pol. 1966, "News Release," September 5, 1966.

38. Franklyn C. Nofziger, *Nofziger* (Washington, D.C.: Regnery Gateway, 1992), 30–35. HTOH, 125.

39. RRGP Box 25, Folder Vol. I, "Ronald Reagan Announcement Day Press Conference," January 4, 1966.

40. RRGP Box 37, '66 Legal Affairs, Watts Folder, "Ronald Reagan News Release," March 16, 1966.

41. Gentry, *The Last Days*, 184.

42. RRGP Box 12, R Folder, Letter, RR to Reverend Walter Robbie, July 25, 1966.

43. "Reagan Interview," *U.S. News & World Report*, November 21, 1966.

44. SPRRGE, 15. SSOH, 31. Firing Line Newsletter, March 15, 1960, "The FBI—The Prime Target of Attack by Pseudo-liberals and Other Left-Wing Ele-

ments." EGB ctn 634, UC, Sept.–Oct. Folder, Letter, Mrs. John Kelley to EGB, July 16, 1963.

45. David Lance Goines, *The Free Speech Movement* (Berkeley, California: Ten Speed Press, 1993), 70. Gentry, *The Last Days*, 93. Seymour Martin Lipset and Sheldon S. Wolin, eds., *Berkeley Student Revolt: Facts and Interpretations* (Garden City, N.Y.: Doubleday, 1965), 234–37. "When Students Try to Run a University," *U.S. News & World Report*, December 21, 1964. "You Don't Shoot Mice with Elephant Guns," *Life*, January 15, 1965.

46. RRGP Box 12, S Folder, Letter, Anonymous to RR, January 26, 1966. Rorabaugh, *Berkeley at War*, 23–27. SSOH, 31. SPRRGE, 15.

47. Dave Hope, "Reagan Critical of U.C. Officialdom," *Oakland Tribune*, October 22, 1965. RRGP Box 3, Corr. C Folder, Letter, RR to Warren Coates, August 31, 1965. SPRRGE, 11–12.

48. WFSRRGE, 53. SSOH, 30–40.

49. RRGP Box 15, W Folder, Letter, Caspar Weinberger to Philip Battaglia, August 9, 1966. HRHOH, 328–38.

50. RRGP Box 23, Vol. III Folder, Reagan Note Cards, "Education."

51. RRGP Box 21, TUVWXYZ Folder, "Charles Artman, Speaker UC Student Union," March 5, 1965, noon rally. RRGP Box 20, John Thomson Poem, "Spider," March 15, 1965. RRGP Box 22, "To Kill a Fuckingword."

52. RRGP Box 35, '66 Campaign Material Folder, Memo, Kenneth Holden to Campaign, March 31, 1966. HTOH, 128–29.

53. TSP Box 16, Kerr, Clark, 1954–1962 Folder, Letter, Storke to Clark Kerr, December 1, 1961. ASOH, 58, 65–66. CKOH, Earl Warren Series, 8–10. William H. Trombley "Oral History Interview," 75. HBurOH, 54–56, 62, 65–67, 78–79. Ron Fimrite, "UC Whirled into Political Arena," *Los Angeles Times*, May 13 1966; *San Francisco Chronicle*, May 8, 1966.

54. RRGP Box 36, '66 Campaign RR Committee Folder, "Reagan Roundup." Reagan Cow Palace Speech, KRON-TV Video Footage, *San Francisco Chronicle*, May 13, 1966.

55. EGB ctn 897, 56/66 Folder, Letter, J. F. Coakley to Mark Miller, May 18, 1966. EGB ctn 897, UC, Un-American Activities Report Folder, "Report Responding to the Burns Report," May 6, 1966. RRGP Box 13, S Folder, "Tribune Reported Facts."

56. UPI, "Ronald Reagan Will Enter GOP Governor Race," *St. Louis Post Dispatch*, January 1, 1966. Kelley, *Nancy Reagan*, 177–79.

57. Kathy Randall Davis, *But What's He Really Like?* (Menlo Park, Calif.: Pacific Coast Publishers, 1970), 4–5. Reagan's handwritten announcement speech is reprinted here. Boyarsky, *Ronald Reagan*, 92–93.

58. SPRRGE, 1–5. Boyarsky, *Ronald Reagan*, 93–96. Wills, *Reagan's America*, 350–53. KHRRGE.

59. SPRRGE, 6–13, 21. Kelley, *Nancy Reagan*, 140. Boyarsky, *Ronald Reagan*, 92–96. For more on Holden and Plog, see WRRRGE, 17–18. For Reagan's ignorance about government, see CWBOH, 37, and RRRRGE, 10–11.

60. Kelley, *Nancy Reagan*, 140. SPRRGE, 2–3, 6–7. Lewis, *What Makes Reagan Run?*, 111–13.

61. Susan Fraker, "The Backroom Boys," *Newsweek*, March 22, 1976. Boyarsky, *Ronald Reagan*, 93–96.

62. SPRRGE, 6–13, 21. Wills, *Reagan's America*, 350–52, 354. Boyarsky, *Ronald Reagan*, 108–10, 142–45, 148–50.

63. RRGP Box 37, '66 Exec. Appts. Folder, White Paper on Welfare, no date indicated. RRGP Box 2, Volume V Folder, Reagan's Note Cards, "Crime," "Public Welfare," "Brown and Brown's Appointments."

64. RRGP Box 24, C2 Folder, Letter, RR to John "Bud" Collier, February 24, 1966.

65. RRGP Box 14, S Folder, Letter, RR to Mary Toman, October 19, 1966.

66. RRGP Box 24, Volume V Folder, Reagan's Note Cards, "Crime," "Public Welfare," "Brown and Brown's Appointments."

67. RRGP Box 3, Corr. D1 Folder, Letter, RR to Frederick Duda, July 18, 1966.

68. RRGP Box 12, R Folder, Letter, RR to Mayor John Reading, July 28, 1966. RRGP Box 12, R Folder, Letter, RR to Reverend Walter Robbie, July 25, 1966.

69. NAI. Lewis, *What Makes Reagan Run?*, 114–15.

70. FCNRGP, 20–21. Lewis, *What Makes Reagan Run?*, 115–16. Nofziger, *Nofziger*, 38. Gentry, *The Last Days*, 131–33. Associated Press, "A Shouting Reagan Stalks Out," *San Francisco Chronicle*, March 7, 1966. Dave Hope, "Even Nice Guys Get Mad," *Oakland Tribune*, March 18, 1966.

71. Ibid.

72. Boyarsky, *Reagan*, 95–99. Cannon, *Ronnie and Jesse*, 84. Gentry, *The Last Days*, 131–33. Parr and McGrew, *The Real Ronald Reagan*, 40. RRGP Box 3, Corr. 2 Folder, Letter, RR to William Brehm, March 25, 1966. RRGP Box 11, P Folder, Letter, RR to Jack Rudder, May 9, 1966.

73. Cannon, *Ronnie and Jesse*, 82. Reagan, *American Life*, 150. Nofziger, *Nofziger*. RRGP Box 34, Letter Folder, News Release, Reagan's Campaign, March 6, 1966. Boyarsky, *Ronald Reagan*, 95–99.

74. JCI

75. Cannon, *Ronnie and Jesse*, 79–80.

76. NSOH, 15–16. See also RKOH, 29–30. Burt Henson Oral History, 72. PLOH, 179. JMOH, 64–65. Kelley, *Nancy Reagan*, 139.

77. JCI. For a discussion of the campaign's view of Reagan, see the following sources: RKentOH, 264–65. RRIOH, 107. WBagOH, 59. RKOH, 24–25. PLOH, 179.

78. Dick Nolan, "The City," *San Francisco Examiner*, Art, February 4, 1962. Letter, A. E. Bagshaw to George T. Davis, November 4, 1955, in WChrOH, 29–30.

79. Burton H. Wolfe, "The Real Christopher of San Francisco," *The Californian*, Summer 1962, vol. 1, no. 1. Letter, Christopher to George Dorsey, March 1, 1963.

80. HCOH, 58–59, 70–71.

81. WBagOH, 6–7. DBOH, 181. WBI. Cannon, *Ronnie and Jesse*, 78.

82. EGB ctn 861, Publicity March Folder, Letter, Haas to Pearson, April 15, 1966.

83. WBagOH, 14–15. WBI. Bagley accused Bradley of being behind the smear, even though Bradley denied as much in an oral history. RRGP Box 12, S Folder, Rowland Evans and Robert Novak, "Brown Forces Begin Hunting Skeleton in Reagan's Closet," n.d. Evans and Novak also wrote that Bradley had ordered the investigation into Christopher's background.

84. FDOH, 168–69. For more on Pearson and Lerner, see RRIOH, 76–78, 107. BBOI. WROH, 207–18. CSWOH, 51. EGB ctn 923, Pol. Gov. June 22, 1966 Folder, Letter, EGB to Carl Sugar, May 12, 1966.

85. TSP Box 25, Drew Pearson Folder, Pearson to Storke, May 16, 1966. Cannon, *Ronnie and Jesse*, 78–79.

86. AMI.

87. Assemblyman William Bagley also confirms the papers' reluctance to publish the article. WBagOH, 15. Drew Pearson, "Washington Merry-Go-Round," *Vallejo*, May 9, 1966. AMI.

88. RRGP Box 34, '66 Campaign Christopher Folder, Press Release, Reagan to George Christopher.

89. RRGP Box 15, V Folder, Letter, Reagan to Nick Venet, June 11, 1966. For another reaction to the smear, see WROH, 209–10. In an interview, Arch Monson later claimed, without citing evidence, that the Reagan campaign reprinted and redistributed the article like it was "candy on Halloween." AMI.

90. Matthew Dallek, "Liberalism Overthrown," *American Heritage*, 42. Cannon,

*Ronnie and Jesse*, 78–79. WBI.

91. Pearson release, EGB papers; Roy Ringer agreed that the Pearson smear was a "major mistake." "We bloodied Christopher up, always assuming that he was going to be running against him. . . . No one laid a glove on Reagan during the primary." RRIOH, 107.

92. RRGP Box 4, 1 Folder, "L.A.C." Says, "Brown attempting to Mend Fences," L. A. Collins, Sr., no date indicated. Roger Kent too believed the smear infuriated Christopher and many of his moderate backers, convincing them to choose Reagan over Brown in the general election. RKentOH, 266. For a good letter discussing the smear, see Kent Papers, Box 7, Comm. to Reelect Gov. Brown, Letter, Kent to Lerner, May 16, 1966.

93. HCOH, 58–59, 70–73. See also RKOH, 24–25.

94. TRI.

95. Earl Behrens, "Reagan Piles Up Huge Vote in the Conservative South," *Los Angeles Times*, June 8, 1966.

96. Spencer Williams Oral History, 13. For more on the unity efforts see the following sources: TRI. RRRRGE, 14. NAI. RFOH, 22. FCNI. WBI. CWI. RRGP Box 21, B Folder, Letter, RR to Frank Brophy, July 7, 1966.

97. California Analysis, "The Review of the News," June 22, 1966, 17–22.

## *TEN:* PRAIRIE FIRE

1. RRGP Box 21, G Folder, Letter, Goldwater to Reagan, June 2, 1966.
2. RRGP Box 21, G Folder, Letter, Reagan to Goldwater, June 11, 1966.
3. RRGP Box 21, A Folder, Letter, Reagan to Frederick Ayer, July 7, 1966.
4. Earl Behrens, "Reagan Piles Up Huge Vote in the Conservative South," *L.A. Times*, June 8, 1966.
5. RRGP Box 7, Corr. K Folder, Letter, Reagan to Kats Kunitsugu, November 1, 1966.
6. TRI.
7. FCNI.
8. TRI.
9. WBI.
10. TRI.
11. NAI.
12. RFOH, 22.
13. TRI.
14. RRGP Box 23, K Folder, Letter, William Middendorf to Reagan, August 19, 1966.
15. RRGP Box 9, M Folder, Letter, Reagan to McCone, October 3, 1966.
16. WFSRRGE, 12. TRI.
17. Cannon, *Ronnie and Jesse*, 81–82.
18. Ibid., 82.
19. TRI.
20. RRGP Box 10, N Folder, Letter, Nixon to Reagan, June 9, 1966.
21. RRGP Box 10, M Folder, Letter, Reagan to George Murphy, August 19, 1966.
22. NAI.
23. ECOH, 104.
24. HTOH, 128. FCNRGP, 12.
25. RRGP Box 34, '66 Campaign. EGB, "Post Election Statement of Mayor Yorty," June 8, 1966.

26. GCI. The story was recounted by George Christopher in an interview with the author.

27. EGB ctn 921, Pol. George Chris Folder, Letter, Brown to Christopher, June 29, 1966.

28. WROH, 158–66.

29. Gentry, *The Last Days*, 158.

30. EGB ctn 921, Pol. Ethnic Groups Folder, Memo, Fred Jordan to Winslow Christian, June 20, 1966.

31. Gentry, *The Last Days*, 128.

32. "Reagan's Lunch with Mayor Yorty," *San Francisco Chronicle*, June 24, 1966. FDI. FDOH. For Brown's view of Vietnam, also see HCOH, 66–67.

33. Ralph de Toledano, "Gov. Brown Reverts to Form," *King Feature Syndicate*, no date indicated.

34. RKentOH, 279–80.

35. RKentOH, 279–80. Letter, Dutton to Bill Moyers, 6/10/66, "Dem. party by state: ca. june–aug. 1966," Box 1057, Public Affairs File, Vice Presidential Files, HHH Papers.

36. JBOH, 108–10.

37. FDI. FDOH, 136–39.

38. Ibid.

39. Ibid.

40. Ibid.

41. Sydney Kossen, "Don Bradley," *The California Weekly People; San Francisco Examiner*, January 19, 1964. FDOH, 141. "Everybody was paddling his own canoe in the campaign," Dutton recalled.

42. RRIOH, 111–13. JCI. FDI.

43. RKOH, 267–68.

44. JCI. RKOH, 267–68. FDOH, 138. RRIOH, 111–13.

45. EGB ctn 939, F Correspondence Folder, Memo, Fred Dutton to Hale Champion and Don Bradley, no date indicated.

46. Cannon, *Ronnie and Jesse*, 85. JCI. HCOH, 74–75, 80–81. DBOH, 182. JBOH, 100, 108–10.

47. RKOH, 270–72.

48. FDOH, 138–39. JRCOH, 12–13. Also see JBOH, 108–10. Editorial, *Chico Enterprise Record*, October 18, 1966.

49. HHH Papers Box 1057, Public Archives File, Vice Presidential File, Folder, Letter, Dutton to Bill Moyers, June 10, 1966.

50. EGB ctn 919, Pol. Dem. Campaign, June 1–14 Folder, Memo, Christian to Brown, June 10, 1966.

51. EGB ctn 933, State Issues and Press Releases Folder, Memo, Jim Alexander to Winslow Christian, June 15, 1966. See also EGB ctn 933, State Issues and Press Releases Folder, Memo, Patricia Sikes to Champion, June 10, 1966. EGB ctn 933, State Issues and Press Releases Folder, Memo, Sikes to EGB, June 14, 1966. EGB ctn 914, Dem. Pol. Campaign July Folder, Memo, Dutton to Christan, July 1, 1966. For internal discussions of crime, see memos, Becker to Jim Alexander, July 19, 1966; John McInerny to Christian, July 27, 1966; EGB ctn 879, Law Enforcement July Folder.

52. HCOH, 64–69. EGB ctn 931, Notes and Info. Folder, Alan Cranston, "The JBS: A Soiled Slip Is Showing." GRP Box 1, Rumford Act Folder, Brown and the Rumford Act. Also see RRGP Box 37, Legal Affairs, Law Enforcement Folder, Press Release, August 26, 1966. EGB ctn 931, Campaign Info. Folder, Brown speech, Sept. 9, 1966.

53. RRGP Box 34, '66 Campaign, Creative Society Folder, Letter, McBirnie to RR, November 30, 1965.

54. RRGP Box 34, '66 Campaign, Creative Society Folder, Broadcast, "Sixth Hour News," Tom Brokaw, October 14, 1966.

55. RRGP Box 34, '66 Campaign, Creative Society Folder, "Outline of Speech on 'The Creative Society,'" no date.

56. RRGP Box 1, The Creative Society, USC, 4/19/66 Folder, Speech, "The Creative Society," April 19, 1966.

57. HCOH, 60–61, 64–69.

58. DBOH, 193–95. RKOH, 267. EGB ctn 939, Dutton Correspondence Folder, Memo, Dutton to Brown, June 11, 1966.

59. EGB ctn 927, Pol. Reagan Sept. Folder, Memo, John McInerny to Fred Dutton, September 16, 1966.

60. EGB ctn 933, State Issues and Press Releases Folder, Memo, Patricia Sikes to Brown, June 14, 1966. FDOH, 150–52.

61. RRGP Box 5 12 Folder, "Ronald Reagan, Extremist Collaborator, an expose."

62. JLWR Box 12, Folder 5, document, "Inside Ronald Reagan."

63. EGB ctn 922, Pol. Gov. Sept. 14–18 Folder, The American Jewish Committee, "Memo, Involvement of the Radical Right in the Ronald Reagan Campaign." EGB ctn 878, JBS Folder, Letter, EGB to Rousselot, October 22, 1966.

64. EGB ctn 926, Pol. Publicity June, Memo, John McDonald to Fred Dutton, June 28, 1966. EGB ctn 927, Pol. Reagan Folder, Memo, John McDonald to Hale Champion, June 21, 1966.

65. EGB ctn 931, Notes and Info. Folder, Alan Cranston, "The JBS: A Soiled Slip Is Showing." For more on Brown's attacks on Reagan, see EGB ctn 927, Pol. Reagan, Aug. 1–17 Folder, Memo, Champion to Dutton, et al., July 19, 1966. EGB ctn 919, Pol. Dem. Campaign, Aug. 1–8 Folder, Letter, EGB to George Brown, August 4, 1966. EGB ctn 919, Pol. Dem. Campaign Folder, Letter, Frank Mesple to George Zenovich, August 10, 1966. Earl C. Behrens, "Democrats' New 'Book' on Reagan," *San Francisco Chronicle*, August 12, 1966.

66. TRI. NAI. Cannon, *Ronnie and Jesse*, 80–81. Earl C. Behrens, "Reagan Walks into a Fight Here," *San Francisco Chronicle*, August 25, 1966.

67. HSOH, 15–16. There is no evidence that the Brown campaign ran such a spot.

68. Cannon, *Ronnie and Jesse*, 80–81. EGB ctn 878, JBS Nov. Folder, Memo, Jim Alexander to Dick Kline, September 22, 1966.

69. EGB ctn 919, Pol. Dem. Campaign, Sept. 14–19 Folder, Letter, Brown to Orville Freeman, Sec. of Agriculture, June 15, 1966.

70. Gentry, *The Last Days*, 278–81.

71. Letter to the Editor, *Chicago Enterprise Record*, October 18, 1966.

72. CGI. CGOH, 1–11.

73. PS1966, director Charles Guggenheim, *Man Against the Actor*. CGOH, 1–11.

74. LHI.

75. CGOH, 1–11.

76. FCNRGP, 41–42. For a discussion of the spot, see also WFSRRGE, 15; HTOH, 128; SSOH, 34; RRRRGE, 24.

77. JBOH, 100–105.

78. RKOH, 4–5.

79. RRGP Box 25, Vols. I & II, News Release, Transcript of RR Telecast, September 9, 1966.

80. RRGP Box 34, '66 Campaign: Debates, *Meet the Press*, September 11, 1966.

81. CWOH, 88. UPI, "Debate," September 16, 1966. Brown wanted a debate in which reporters peppered the candidates with questions. Reagan wanted a face-to-face confrontation.

82. Gentry, *The Last Days*, 185, 275–78.

83. TSP Box 25, Drew Pearson Folder, Letters, Pearson to Storke, Oct. 31 & Nov. 28, 1966.

84. Cannon, *Ronnie and Jesse*, 86–89.

*EPILOGUE*

1. EGBFSM.

*AFTERWORD*

1. Parr, *The Real Ronald Reagan*, quoting *Sacramento Bee*, 52–53. RRGP Box 21, Bill Roberts Correspondence Folder, Letter, Harold Quinton to Cy Rubel, July 13, 1965. RRGP Box 23, '66 Campaign Gov., Letters of Particular Importance Folder, Letter, John Harmer to Bill Roberts, July 12, 1965. EGB ctn 939, Dutton Correspondence Folder, Memo, Dutton to Brown, June 11, 1966. See HSOH, 15–16 for more information about the allegations.

2. RRGP Box 21, Bill Roberts Correspondence Folder, Letter, Harold Quinton to Cy Rubel, July 13, 1965.

3. For a good summary of the arguments that conservatives used to oppose Schwarzenegger's candidacy, see Cal Thomas, Commentary, "Defining the Differences," *Washington Times*, August 12, 2003. Also see Dean E. Murphy, "An Actor, Yes, but No Ronald Reagan," *New York Times*, August 10, 2003.

4. Ibid. Rush Limbaugh, "Schwarzenegger Not the Next Reagan," *The Rush Limbaugh Show*, August 8, 2003, RushLimbaugh.com. Lyn Nofziger, Editorial, "Why Arnold Schwarzenegger is no Ronald Reagan," *Sacramento Bee*, August 17, 2003. Donald Lambro, "Supply-siders wary of Schwarzenegger," *Washington Times*, August 18, 2003. Stephen Moore told the paper: "The Wilson crowd passed tax increases in 1991 that hurt the state a lot in the last recession. Wilson's record," he added, "is pretty poor on fiscal issues."

5. John Berlau, "Comparing Schwarzenegger and Reagan," *Insight*, October 6, 2003, www.insightmag.com.

6. Murphy, "An Actor, Yes, but No Ronald Reagan," *New York Times*, August 10, 2003. Lou Cannon, "Pity the Winner," *New York Times*, August 24, 2003. California Representative Dana Rohrabacher also argued that Reagan and Schwarzenegger had numerous personal traits in common: "Reagan was 56 years old when he left his acting career to run for governor of California, and that's the same with Arnold. And they're both about the same height, and Reagan didn't quite have the same build as Arnold, but he was just as strong and tough." Also see Erica Werner, "Different, but Schwarzenegger Follows Reagan's Path," StAugustine.com, September 1, 2003.

7. "Just an actor" line: EGB ctn 939, Dutton Correspondence Folder, Memo, Dutton to Brown, June 11, 1966. SSOH, 28–31. Lou Cannon, *Governor Reagan: His Rise to Power* (Public Affairs: New York, 2003), 177, 299–300. Also see Dallek, chapter 9, 184–85. For more information on Reagan's lack of state knowledge see CWBOH, 37.

8. SPRRGE, 6–13, 21. Boyarsky, *Ronald Reagan*, 93–96. Reagan Cow Palace Speech, KRON-TV Video Footage, *San Francisco Chronicle*, May 13, 1966.

9. Reagan, *An American Life*, 151–52. RRGP Box 19, D-F Folder, Letter, William Roberts to Kay Daley, November 19, 1965. For McDowell's quote, see JSM-RRGE, 10. For the Boraxo story, see SPRRGE, 11–12.

10. RRGP Box 23, K Folder, Letter, William Middendorf to Reagan, August 19, 1966.

11. "Editorial: Messing with a sacred cow; Prop. 13 changes best left to voters," *Ventura County Star*, November 9, 2003. Rachel Laskow, "Who will win?"

Teacher.Scholastic.com. Paul Krugman, "Conan the Deceiver," *New York Times*, August 22, 2003.

12. Bob Franken, "Schwarzenegger Won't Take Part in Gubernatorial Debate," CNN Live Today, September 1, 2003. "Actor holding off on specifics," *Associated Press* via *St. Petersburg Times*, August 8, 2003. Major Garrett, "Bustamante Leads Schwarzenegger in Polls," Fox News, September 9, 2003. The *Los Angeles Times* poll showed Bustamante with a 13 point lead over Schwarzenegger; the Field Poll showed that Bustamante had a five-point advantage.

13. Margaret Talev and Alexa H. Bluth, "Candidates Turn Heat on Schwarzenegger," *Sacramento Bee*, September 24, 2003. Michael Finnegan, "The Times Poll: Majority Now Favors Recall; Schwarzenegger Leads Rivals," Los Angeles Times, October 1, 2003. "Davis Concedes, Schwarzenegger Wins," CNN.com/Inside Politics, October 8, 2003.

14. RRGP, Box 25, Vol. I and II Folder, "Statement of Ronald Reagan Regarding the 'John Birch Society,'" September 24, 1965.

15. Cannon, *Governor Reagan*, 157. Also see Dallek, chapter 10, 212–16. The three aides who were put in key campaign posts were Lyn Nofziger, Thomas C. Reed, and Philip M. Battaglia.

16. Cannon, *Governor Reagan*, 157. RRGP Box 16, X-Y-Z Folder, Letter, RR to Charles Zweng, December 7, 1965. RRGP Box 12, S Folder, Letter, RR to Dudley Swim, December 14, 1965.

17. Arnold Schwarzenegger, "Remarks to the California Republican Party Convention," RecallCandidates.com, September 13, 2003.

18. Ibid. Murphy, "An Actor, Yes, but No Ronald Reagan," *New York Times*, August 10, 2003.

19. Matea Gold, "Many Democrats Vote Against Davis and for a Republican," *Los Angeles Times*, October 8, 2003.

20. RRRRGE, 5–6, 10. RRGP Box 1, The Creative Society, USC, 4/19/66 Folder, Speech, "The Creative Society," April 19, 1966. For a fuller discussion of the "citizen politician" concept, see Dallek, chapter 9, 175–76.

21. Cannon, *Governor Reagan*, 193, 349. Peter Schrag, *Paradise Lost: California's Experience, America's Future* (New York: The New Press, 1998), 125.

22. "Schwarzenegger, Twisted Sister Union No Accident," CBS2.com, October 6, 2003.

23. Cannon, *Governor Reagan*, 368–69.

24. "Statement of Vote for November 6, 1962 General Election," Compiled by Office of the California Secretary of State, pp. 4–8, 23. Murphy, "An Actor, Yes, but No Ronald Reagan," *New York Times*, August 10, 2003.

25. Thom Patterson, "Genesis of Recall Rooted in California Energy Crisis," CNN.com/Inside Politics, October 7, 2003. Laura Mecoy, "Davis Stands by His Record," *Sacramento Bee*, Aug. 20, 2003. *Los Angeles Times* political correspondent and CNN analyst Ronald Brownstein said that "the energy crisis created the image of vacillation and indecisiveness that began [Davis's] problems." Opponents tarred Brown with the same brush, denouncing him as a so-called "tower-of-Jello" who failed to act quickly enough in times of state crises.

26. See Dallek, chapter 3, 50, chapter 5, 91–102. CORE members occupied the State Capitol Building for three weeks as part of a 1963 protest in support of fair housing legislation. Brown sided with the activists saying that passage of such legislation was crucial. But he paid a political price when voters saw him as standing alongside the civil rights activists and the Berkeley Free Speech Movement protesters in 1964. Reagan capitalized on the impression that Brown was out of touch with the white middle class, and Schwarzenegger effectively argued that "this [Davis-driven] driver's license outrage" was a cave to Hispanic interest groups, and that the governor's decision undermined law-and-order in California.

27. California Attorney General Bill Lockyer, "Why I Voted for Arnold," *California Journal* (Vol. 34, No. 11), November 2003, p. 33.

28. Dana Milbank, *Washington Post*, "The Making of the President: The Nixon in Bush," November 25, 2003. Editorial, "Carping over 'Top Gun,'" *The Hill*, May 13, 2003.

29. Ray Suarez Interview with Sen. John McCain, *The NewsHour with Jim Lehrer*, February 21, 2000. Bill Adair, "Reagan, Reagan Everywhere," *St. Petersburg Times*, September 19, 2000. George Will, "DC Zealots," TownHall.com/Columnists/GeorgeWill, April 26, 2001; ironically, in 1986, Reagan himself signed a bill "stipulating that no individual will be honored on the Mall until 25 years after his or her death," wrote George Will. David Ruppe, "Monuments to the Gipper," ABCNEWS.com, March 30, 2001.

30. "CBS Denies Folding Over Reagan," News.BBC.co.uk, November 11, 2003. For a sampling of opinion about the Reagan letters' books, go to Amazon.com and look up *Reagan: A Life in Letters* (New York: Free Press, 2003) or *Dear Americans: Letters from the Desk of President Reagan* (New York: Doubleday, 2003).

# *Acknowledgments*

THIS BOOK took three and a half years. I had a lot of help. My first debt is to Nelson Polsby, the former director of the Institute of Governmental Studies (IGS) at the University of California, Berkeley. He gave me access to phones, faxes, computers, a carrel, a community of serious scholars and good people, and just about everything else a visiting graduate student needs to complete a project of this kind. I also thank the current director, Bruce Cain, and the head of publications, Jerry Lubenow, for taking an interest in my work and letting me stay at IGS until the book was nearly done. Mark Levin and the rest of the library staff helped me find books and articles; Sarah Kelsey, Karen Oto, and Eunice Park helped me secure parking passes and other items. And my colleagues in the carrels—Keena Lipsitz, John Sides, Meg Carne, Ray LaRaja, Eric McGhee, Allison Wegner, Mike Signer, Jon Cohen, Jonathan Koppell, and Jennifer Steen—offered conversation and friendship.

Three research assistants and a handful of librarians helped make this project possible. Chris Cappozolla worked on footnotes, Beth Glick transcribed interviews and found articles, and Michael Baratz tracked down documents and did an excellent job of filling in footnotes in the last months. At the Bancroft Library in Berkeley, Wayne Silka, Baiba Strads, and Franz Enciso processed my requests and supplied valuable information about the Pat Brown Papers. Carol Leadenham guided me in the Ronald Reagan Papers at Stanford University's Hoover Institution, Hynda Rudd answered questions about the Sam Yorty Papers at the Los Angeles City Archives, and Berkeley's Regional Oral History Office and UCLA's Special Collection Library provided useful information about their holdings.

More than two dozen people agreed to an interview for this book. They gave of their time and memories and added nuance to the portraits of Brown, Reagan, and California in the sixties. I also thank Lou Cannon for helping me track down interviews, Bill Boyarsky for doing the same, and Elias P. Demetracopoulos for sending me documents dealing with Brown's trip to Greece in 1965. Kurt Schuparra allowed me an advance look at his then forthcoming book about the rise of the California Right.

Old friends and new ones provided support of every kind. In the Bay Area, Evan McCulloch put me up at his apartment, introduced me to his volleyball league, and provided terrific friendship. Morgan Barbosa and Scot Listavich met me for dinner after work and were great friends. Alix Bockelman was a terrific friend and dinner companion. Jane Hong kept asking me if I had finished the book yet and did so with a smile and characteristic cheer. Lindsey Arent made me laugh even after I had spent twelve hours in the carrels staring at a Macintosh Classic filling in footnotes. My roommate Kim Blasberg let me set up my computer in the dining room of our apartment and still said kind things about the documents strewn across the table. Jesse Goldhammer provided excellent lunches at the sundry haunts on Berkeley's Telegraph Avenue and excellent friendship. And Jon Cohen, Mike Signer, Tina Sessa, Jon Schoenwald, and Jana Bruns provided insights into the trials of dissertation writing and terrific friendship.

In Los Angeles, friends let me stay in their homes, offered suggestions on research, and provided general support. Richard, Susan, and Daniel Weiss put me up in their home, and Jonathan Weiss shared thoughts about graduate school, dissertation writing, and countless other subjects. Minna and Lori Gossman offered me a place to stay; Dr. Joel and Madelynn Kopple put me up for several days and were exceedingly generous during my time in Los Angeles; and David Kopple was a terrific friend from start to finish. The following people suggested titles, listened to my stories about Pat Brown and Ronald Reagan, and provided support: Karen Hui, Craig Schuh, Ed Gackstetter, Nancy Albarran, Matthew Kuchta, Catherine Wang, David Grayson, Jamie Kerr, Peggy Vanderpool, Scott Sherman, Mario Vasquez, Eric Lauerwald, Christina B. Simon, Kevin Swope, Isabel Rosenthal, Vicki Porges, Mike Bender, Kay Friedman, Ariel Trost, Jane McKenna, Norvin Leong, Kate Volkman, Ashley Telles, Vivian Garay, Sam Lowenberg, Walter Hickel, Janice Hui, Dan Rohn, Elizabeth Valinoti, and Mike Balmoris.

Several scholars and journalists edited the manuscript and encouraged this project through kind words and tactful criticisms. Marie Arana published my reviews and encouraged my writing. Jack Beatty published an essay of mine in *The Atlantic* that led to a contract, and Richard Snow and Frederick Allen did the same in *American Heritage*. Tom Engelhardt and Deirdre English read a draft of the introduction and gave tips on style. Josh Freeman and Ira Katznelson commented on the project during a prospectus defense at Columbia University, and Elizabeth Blackmar, Mark Carnes, Kenneth Jackson, and Samuel Freedman served on my dissertation committee, commented on the manuscript, and helped sharpen the argument and refine the narrative.

Others helped bring the book to print. Irwin Gellman corrected errors in the manuscript, Vin Cannato edited the first chapters and provided friendship. Clare Wulker copyedited the book; Bill Molesky did the proofreading; and at The Free Press, Edith Lewis shepherded the book through copyediting while assistant editor Dan Freedberg helped edit the manuscript and fielded my questions with patience and helpful answers.

A few friends provided moral support and detailed comments on the manuscript. My agent John Wright helped me write a proposal and land a contract. He also edited chapters and provided excellent answers to questions.

Jeff Shesol was a terrific friend. He showed me how to organize my documents, shared insights into research and writing, encouraged this project through kind words, and even helped me find a job. Mark Brilliant read parts of this book more times than either of us probably cares to remember, but fortunately for me Mark had not just stamina but also a great eye and a deep understanding of California. He pointed out holes in the manuscript and offered suggestions on how to plug them. He was a strong voice of encouragement, and his own work on California history is but one part of a much larger friendship. I am also deeply indebted to David Greenberg. David line edited every chapter, offered excellent tips on writing, and pushed me to expand in places and cut others. He made a major difference in the prose and his larger comments improved the book dramatically. Editor, writer, historian, David is best of all a terrific friend.

My editor at The Free Press, Bruce Nichols, gave me a contract when there were only a few words on paper, provided an outline on how to turn the dissertation into a book, and did an excellent edit on the chapters. Patient, talented, and committed to this project, Bruce more than anyone in the last year helped bring the book to print. I also owe a large debt of gratitude to my advisor at Columbia University, Alan Brinkley. Professor Brinkley provided in-depth comments on the prospectus and dissertation; he pushed me to cut in places that needed cutting and flesh out points that needed to be developed. He was a source of advice, support, and encouragement from beginning to end. I could not have asked for a better advisor.

I also could not have asked for more support from my family. My grandmother Mildred Kronmal and great-aunt Edith Lasky took me to dinner in Los Angeles and provided love and support of every kind. My late grandfather David Kronmal was a friend and supporter; he is sorely missed. My sister Rebecca provided the kind of love, cheer, and encouragement that make her a wonderful sister and cherished friend. And my parents Robert and Geraldine offered the kind of encouragement, love, and support (as well as comments on the dissertation) that make a book like this possible.

# Index

Abortion issue, 198
Acheson, Dean, 116
Adam, Carl, 10
Adams, Frank, 119
Adams, John, 196
Ainsworth, Ed, 165
Alarcon, Arthur, 53–54, 60
Alexander, Jane, 110, 111, 119, 120, 124
Allen, Robert, 113
Alsop, Joseph, 238
American Federation of Labor, 33–35
American Federation of Labor-Congress of Industrial Organizations (AFL-CIO), 39
American Jewish Committee (AJC), 230
American Legion, 90, 189
American Medical Association (AMA), 39, 40
American Nazi Party, 56, 107
Anderson, Glenn, 130–134, 147, 158
Anticommunism
  John Birch Society and, 104, 114, 125
  Nixon and, 21–23
  Parker and, 141–142
  Reagan and, 27, 33–36, 38–41, 70
  Reagan's early backers and, 73–75
  Yorty and, 160, 161
Anti-Communism Voters League, 75
Anti-Defamation League, 57
Antiwar movement, 130–131, 152, 153, 159, 190, 219
Army Signal Corps, 31

Baez, Joan, 81, 83
Bagley, William, 205–206, 208, 213
Bagshaw, A.E., 204
Bane, A.L., 119
Barnett, Ross, 39
Baus, Herb, 218
Becker, William, 46, 49, 52–55, 58, 117, 118, 133, 138, 144, 145
Behavior Science Corporation of Van Nuys (BASICO), 196
Bell, Alphonzo, 108, 181
Berkeley. *See* University of California at Berkeley
Billett, John, 133–134
Birmingham, Alabama, 46, 52
Bliss, Ray, 186
Bond, Julian, 219
Boraxo, 190
Bradley, Clark, 49
Bradley, Don, 156, 205, 206, 208, 221–223, 229, 234
Bradley, Tom, 163
Brady, Matthew, 9–11
Brieger, Mrs. Stephen, 58
Broder, David, 68
Brophy, Frank Cullen, 125
Brown, Bernice Layne, 7, 10, 13, 128, 150, 154

Brown, Edmund Gerald "Pat"
anticommunism and, 111–112
as attorney general, 12, 45, 112, 162
becomes Democrat, 3, 8
Berkeley demonstrations and, 81, 83–88, 93–102, 192, 194, 199
birth of, 4
California Democratic Council (CDC) and, 151–155
Chessman case and, 19, 96
Christopher's candidacy, 203–209, 217–218
civil rights and race issue, 44–61, 136–137, 144–145, 225–226
commencement address at Santa Clara University (1961), 91–92, 99
as district attorney, 9–12, 45
documentary of life, 234–236
early jobs of, 5–6
education of, 6–7
extremism issue, 113–118, 167, 168
feud among staff, 220–223
gubernatorial campaign (1958), 12–15, 238
gubernatorial campaign (1962), 20–24, 42, 161, 221, 236
higher education and, 88–93
Hunter's Point riot and, 188–189
inaugural addresses, 1, 16–17, 43–44
law practice, 7, 10
marriage of, 7
negative campaign against Reagan, 228–233
nickname of, 6
parents of, 4–5, 248
political beliefs, 3–4, 8
Proposition 14 and, 54–61
religion and, 10
Republican party affiliation, 1–3, 7–8
results of 1966 gubernatorial campaign, 238
State Assembly campaign (1928), 7, 8
television style and, 20
Unruh and, 154–156, 261
urban reform and, 9, 11–12, 136–137, 146, 148–149
Vietnam War and, 151–154, 162, 169, 218–220
Watts riots and, 134–136, 138–140, 143–144, 146–149, 164–166, 187–188, 218
welfare system and, 198, 225
Yorty and, 156–159, 161–163, 166–172, 216–217
Brown, Edmund Joseph, 4–6, 10
Brown, Ida Shuckman, 4, 28
Brown, Jerry, 13, 23, 85, 86, 242
Brown, Ralph, 155
Bryan, William Jennings, 68, 159
Buckley, William, 40
Buggs, John, 129
Burby, Jack, 20, 50, 58, 98, 118, 236
Burke, Edmund, 196
Burns, Hugh, 48–50, 53, 117, 192–194

California Citizens for Goldwater-Miller, 66
California Democratic Council (CDC), 151–155, 159, 169
California Dynasty of Communism (CDC), 22–23
California Rangers, 106
California Real Estate Association (CREA), 51–53
California Republican Assembly (CRA), 62, 78, 103, 104, 106, 109, 110, 118, 119, 123, 231
California Republican League, 182–183
Cal Plan, The, 179
Canady, Charles, 94
Carvey, Tom, 152
Casady, Simon, 152–154, 219

Cerrell, Joe, 203–205, 222
Champion, Hale, 19, 60, 133–135, 137, 149, 205, 209–210, 221–224, 226, 231, 234
Chandler, Otis, 58, 113
Chappie, Eugene, 216
Chavez, Cesar, 218
Chessman, Cheryl, 19, 96
*Choice* (docudrama), 63
Chotiner, Murray, 120
Christian, Winslow, 98, 118, 131, 132, 134, 146, 224–225
Christian Anti-Communist Crusade, 38, 70, 75
Christopher, George, 20, 213–218, 238
  gubernatorial campaign (1966), 173, 175, 179, 181–185, 187, 195, 200–210
Christopher, Warren, 115, 146, 238
Church League of America, 39
Citizens for Constitutional Government (CCG), 106
Citizens League for Individual Freedom, 53
Civil Rights Act of 1964, 54, 188, 199, 200
Civil rights and race issue
  Brown and, 44–61, 136–137, 144–145, 225–226
  Reagan and, 188, 199–202
Cleaver, Eldridge, 138
Coakley, Frank, 194
Coate, Robert, 55, 195
Cohn, Mike, 158
Combs, Richard, 192
Committee for Fair Employment Practices, 46
Committee on Governmental Efficiency (GE), 48–49
*Commonweal*, 25
*Communism on the Map* (film), 114
Community Action Boards, 163
Congress of Racial Equality (CORE), 46, 47, 50, 82, 137, 151
Connors, Chuck, 193
*Conscience of a Conservative, The* (Goldwater), 63–64, 115
Conspiracy theories, 27, 104, 107, 125
Consumer protection, 18
Containment policy, 26, 111
Coolidge, Calvin, 2, 7, 62
COPE, 39
Cranston, Alan, 118, 152, 231
Creative Society slogan, 226–228
Cristina, Vern, 71, 77
Cuban missile crisis, 23

Dart, Justin, 75, 214
Davis, Jefferson, 55
Davis, Kathy, 79
Davis, Phil, 66
Death penalty, 19
*Death Valley Days* (TV series), 63, 70
Democratic National Convention (1960), 19
Dempster, Chas, 159
Dieden, Leonard, 95
Disciples of Christ, 28, 29
Disraeli, Benjamin, 196
Dixon, Illinois, 27
Dukmejian, George, 77
Dunckel, Earl, 36–37
Dutton, Fred, 13, 14, 18, 20, 114, 151, 206, 219, 220–225, 229–230, 237
Dylan, Bob, 81, 83

Ebsen, Buddy, 193
Economic Development Agency, 43
Education, 18–19, 43
Eisenhower, Dwight, 16, 74, 75, 101, 104, 107, 116, 125, 126, 165
Eleventh Commandment, 184, 185, 207, 210
Employment, 14, 17, 43, 45, 51, 52
Engh, Hans, 112

Engle, Claire, 21, 165
Evans, Rowland, 144
Experience issue, 174–176, 182, 197, 229, 233–234, 240
Extremism issue, 103, 105–111, 119–127, 182, 229–231, 233, 240

Fair Campaign Practices Committee, 179
Fair Employment Practices Act (FEPA), 17, 45
Fair Employment Practices Committee (FEPC), 14, 43, 51, 52
Fair housing issue, 48–61, 137, 210, 226
Farmer, James, 97
Farrell, Harry, 209
Faubus, Orville, 39
Federal Bureau of Investigation (FBI), 34, 90, 112, 125, 198, 208
Federal Emergency Relief Administration (FERA), 29
Federal Housing Authority (FHA), 48
Finch, Robert, 20, 120, 210, 214
Finn, Tom, 8
Firestone, Leonard, 214
Fleming, Karl, 123–124
Flournoy, Jim, 201
Fogelson, Robert, 148
Foreign policy, 26, 111
Freedom Democratic Party, 85
Freedom Summer, 81, 83, 85
Free Speech Movement (FSM), 83, 98, 151, 219
Friends of Reagan, 173, 184
Frye, Marquette, 128
Frye, Ronald, 128

Gaston, Robert, 58
General Electric, 36–37, 40
Gibson, Luther, 48–50, 53
Glass, Andrew, 219
Goldwater, Barry, 40, 78, 79, 120, 123–124, 180
  civil rights and, 200–201
  *The Conscience of a Conservative* by, 63–64, 115
  personality of, 64, 65
  presidential campaign (1964), 61–72, 76, 117, 121, 183, 195, 214
  Reagan and, 64, 71, 212
Goodman, Paul, 191
Great Depression, 1–2, 29
Great Society, 61, 137, 227
Gromala, John, 71
Gubernatorial campaign (1958), 12–15, 238
Gubernatorial campaign (1962), 20–24, 42, 161, 221, 236
Gubernatorial campaign (1966)
  abortion issue, 198
  Berkeley issue, 198–196, 237
  Christopher's candidacy, 173, 175, 179, 181–185, 187, 195, 200–210
  civil rights and race issue, 188, 199–202
  Creative Society slogan, 226–228
  experience issue, 174–176, 182, 197, 229, 233–234, 240
  extremism issue, 103, 105–111, 119–127, 182, 229–231, 233, 240
  Holden and Plog role in, 196–198
  law-and-order issue, 185–189, 197, 198, 237
  negative campaign against Reagan, 228–233
  Reagan's primary night victory speech, 213
  results of, 238
  welfare issue, 197–198
Guggenheim, Charles, 234–236

Haas, Lu, 54, 60–61, 205
Haffner, Fred, 120
Haldeman, H.R., 191
Hale, Nathan, 117
Hale, Prentiss, 183
Hall, James, 65
Hamilton, Alexander, 196
Harding, Warren, 2
Harris, Fred, 159
Harris, Lou, 210
Health care, 39, 40
Henry, Patrick, 6
Heyns, Roger, 194, 199
Hill, Gerald, 154
Hill, Gladwin, 70
Hill, Roderick, 132, 143
Hiss, Alger, 21
Hitler, Adolf, 38
Hoiles, Raymond, 26
Holden, Kenneth, 196–198, 201
Hollywood Independent Citizens Committee of the Arts, Sciences, and Professions (HICCASP), 33–34
Hoover, Herbert, 2, 8, 73
Hoover, J. Edgar, 90
Hopkins, Harry, 29
House Committee on Un-American Activities (HUAC), 34–35, 90, 159
Housing discrimination, 45–61
Howser, Fred, 12, 206
Hudson, Rock, 64
*Human Events* magazine, 22, 39, 230
Humphrey, Hubert, 32, 150, 169
Hunter's Point riot, 188–189
Huntley, Chet, 69
Hyer, Dick, 206

Initiative, by voters, 178
International Ladies Garment Workers Union (ILGWU), 32
International Workers of the World (Wobblies), 4

Jacobs, Paul, 96, 97
Japanese-Americans, 16
Jefferson, Thomas, 233
Jewel, Howard, 138–139, 141
Jewish Community Relations Council, 49
Jewish Labor Committee, 49
Jim Crow laws, 46
John Birch Society, 38, 101, 103–119, 121–127, 182, 215, 227, 230–231, 233
Johnson, Hiram, 4, 15, 16, 42, 177, 178
Johnson, Lyndon B., 49, 54, 61, 130, 163, 227
  1964 presidential campaign, 63, 69
  Vietnam War and, 152–154, 219

"Kay," 119
Kennedy, John F., 16, 19, 20, 23, 38, 42, 54, 55, 91, 166, 170, 227
Kennedy, Robert F., 158
Kent, Roger, 114, 117, 156, 165, 168, 171, 219, 221, 223, 229, 233–234
Kerr, Clark, 82–89, 91, 93, 94, 96, 100, 101, 190, 192–193
Khrushchev, Nikita, 21, 23
King, Martin Luther, Jr., 46, 164
*King's Row* (film), 31
Kline, Richard, 44, 45, 50, 54, 55, 60, 132, 205, 229, 230, 236–237
Knight, Goodwin "Goody," 12–15, 108, 202, 207
Knott, Walter, 26, 67, 230
Knowland, Evelyn, 14, 15
Knowland, William, 13–15, 21, 22, 23, 40, 105, 111, 238
*Knute Rockne* (film), 31
Kuchel, Thomas, 27, 39, 108, 167, 174, 181, 182, 214
Ku Klux Klan, 108, 117, 125

La Follette, Robert, 16
*Last Outpost, The* (film), 35
Lavis, Charlie, 119
Law-and-order issue, 185–189, 197, 198, 237
Layne, Arthur, 7
Leggett, John, 97
Lenin, V.I., 27
Lerner, Harry, 205, 206, 217, 229–230
Liberty Lobby, 39, 105
*Life* magazine, 190, 238
Lincoln, Abraham, 54, 55, 196, 233, 235, 236
Lippmann, Walter, 3, 10
London, Jack, 4
Los Angeles Dodgers, 23
*Los Angeles Times*, 58, 103, 106, 120, 161, 162, 166, 207, 238
*Louisa* (film), 35
Loyalty oaths, 112
Luke, Sherrill, 133
Lynch, Thomas, 11, 12
Lyons, Charlton, 39

MacArthur, Douglas, 104
Malcolm X, 149
Mardian, Robert, 202–203
Margolis, Larry, 155
Marx, Karl, 27, 38
Massey, Raymond, 64
Master Plan for Higher Education, 18–19, 89
McBirnie, W.S., 118–119, 226–227
McCarthy, Jack, 77
McCarthy, Joseph, 12, 104
McCone, John, 146, 148, 214, 215
McCone Commission, 146–148, 158, 164
McDonald, John, 231
McDowell, Jack, 122, 175
McInerny, John, 95
McWilliams, Carey, 92
Meese, Edwin, III, 86–88
*Meet the Press*, 237
Meiklejohn, Bill, 30
Mesple, Frank, 115–117
Mexican-Americans, 46, 218
Middendorf, William, 214
Miller, George, 233
Mills, Ed, 72–74
Minkus, Lee, 128
Monson, Arch, 183, 185, 206, 207, 214
Mosher, Clint, 21, 22
Mosk, Stanley, 114, 118, 139, 165
Moskowitz, Ronald, 87, 92–93, 98–100
Moyers, Bill, 220, 223, 224
Muchmore, Don, 225
Muckraking journalism, 112
Mulford, Don, 90
Murphy, Franklin, 87
Murphy, George, 61, 65, 149, 165, 204, 210, 234, 235

*Nation, The*, 25
National Association for the Advancement of Colored People (NAACP), 46, 47, 49, 151
National Guard, 130–135, 143, 188
*National Review*, 106
National States' Rights party, 58
Nazi Germany, 31
New Deal, 1, 3, 18, 29, 44, 73, 74, 76
New Frontier, 137, 227
New Guard, 9
New Order of Cincinnatus, 9
*New Republic, The*, 2
*Newsweek*, 109, 123
*New York Times*, 59, 65, 69, 70, 79, 107, 113, 164, 210–211, 238
*New York Times Magazine*, 106, 114
Nixon, Richard M., 27, 105, 111, 166, 177, 215
  anticommunism of, 21–23
  gubernatorial campaign (1962), 21–23, 42

personal characteristics of, 21–22
presidential campaign (1960), 20
as vice president, 21
Nofziger, Lyn, 126, 184–187, 201–203, 216, 236
Novak, Bob, 144
Nuclear weapons, 63

*Oakland Tribune*, 81, 194, 238
Olson, Culbert, 160
*Operation Abolition* (film), 90, 114, 189
*Orange County Register, The*, 26

Page, Thomas, 21–22
Palance, Jack, 235
Parker, William, 129–134, 137–145, 147, 148, 156–158, 163–165, 188
Parkinson, Gaylord, 177–179, 184, 185, 207
Pearson, Drew, 40, 205–209, 238
Peery, Ben, 200
Peterson, A.E., 118
Plog, Stanley, 196–198
Post, Manning J., 203–204
Potts, Ralph, 9
Poulson, Norris, 167–168
Presidential campaigns
1960, 20
1964, 61–72, 76, 117, 121, 183, 195, 214, 241
Pritchess, Peter, 138
Progressive Era, 112
Project Alert, 38
Project Prayer, 38
Proposition 13, 242
Proposition 14, 54–61, 137, 200, 226
Proposition 16, 74, 105, 229
Prussian, Karl, 118
Public Works Administration (PWA), 29
Putnam, George, 161

Rafferty, Max, 171
Rattigan, Joseph, 49–50
Reagan, Jack, 28, 29
Reagan, Nancy Davis, 35, 64, 76–79, 201, 232
Reagan, Neil, 29, 33–34, 186–187
Reagan, Nelle, 28
Reagan, Ronald
abortion issue, 198
anticommunism of, 27, 33–36, 38–41, 70
autobiography of, 33
becomes Republican, 41
Berkeley issue, 189–196, 237
Christopher's candidacy, 173, 175, 179, 181–185, 187, 195, 200–210
civil rights and race issue, 188, 199–202
Creative Society slogan, 226–228
as Democrat, 29, 32
early backers, 72–76
education of, 29
experience issue, 174–176, 182, 197, 229, 233–234, 240
extremism issue, 103, 105–111, 119–127, 182, 229–231, 233, 240
fan mail and, 76, 79, 80, 254
as General Electric spokesman, 36–37, 40
Goldwater and, 64, 71, 212
Goldwater presidential campaign and, 63–69
Holden and Plog role in campaign, 196–198
law-and-order issue, 185–189, 197, 198, 237
as lifeguard, 28–29
marriages of, 35
as movie and television actor, 30–32, 35, 63, 70
national television debut (The Speech), 67–69, 72, 186
negative campaign against, 228–233

Reagan, Ronald, *con't.*
Nofziger and, 186–187
official announcement of gubernatorial candidacy, 195–196
as orator, 66, 77
parents of, 28
party unity and, 212–216
personality of, 66, 72, 79, 236, 240
political beliefs of, 27–28, 37–38
political consultants of, 120–124
primary night victory speech, 213
as radio broadcaster, 29–30
religion and, 28
results of gubernatorial campaign, 238
Screen Actors Guild and, 32–33, 35
on Soviet Union, 27
as supporter of Roosevelt and the New Deal, 1
Vietnam War and, 186
Watts riots and, 186–188, 195
welfare issue, 71, 197–198
World War II and, 31
Yorty and, 185–186
*Reagan: The Political Chameleon* (Brown), 242
*Reagan and Reality* (Brown), 242
Recall, by voters, 178
Reed, Tom, 210, 213–216
Referendum, by voters, 178
Regan, Edward, 49–50
Republican Associates, 177
Republican Central Committee, 62
Republican National Convention (1960), 64
Reston, James, 69
Rickershauser, Charles, 170
Ringer, Roy, 50, 54
Roberts, Bill, 109, 120–124, 173–177, 179, 184, 189, 191, 196, 213, 215, 229, 231–233
Rockefeller, Nelson, 62, 65, 121, 123
Rogers, Will, 158–159
Roosevelt, Eleanor, 141
Roosevelt, Franklin D., 1, 3, 16, 18, 29, 44, 74
Roosevelt, James, 34, 163
Roosevelt, Theodore, 16
Ross, William, 218
Rousselot, John, 27, 38, 40, 41, 110, 111, 124–126, 230
Rubel, Cy, 72–73, 78, 108, 180, 183, 230
Rumford, Byron, 50–51
Rumford Fair Housing Act, 48–61, 137, 210, 226
Rusher, William, 106
Rustin, Bayard, 148

Salinger, Pierre, 61, 155, 204, 210
Salvatori, Henry, 66, 67, 72–76, 111, 183, 196, 202–203, 232–233
*San Diego Union*, 186
San Francisco Board of Supervisors, 9
*San Francisco Chronicle*, 149, 170, 207
San Francisco College of Law, 6
San Francisco Democratic Central Committee, 8
*Santa Barbara News-Press*, 112, 113
Savio, Mario, 83, 85–86, 88, 97, 98, 189, 190
Scheer, Robert, 219
Schmitt, Milton, 7
Schmitz, John, 126
School prayer, 38
Schwarz, Frederick, 38, 40, 75
Scranton, William, 76, 106
Screen Actors Guild (SAG), 32–35
Shearer, William K., 58
Shell, Joseph, 27, 41, 65, 77, 111, 174, 179–180
Shelley, John F., 188
Sheriffs, Alex, 87
Shriver, Sargent, 157, 163, 165, 224
Sikes, Patricia, 229
Sinclair, Upton, 8
Sloss, Nancy, 204

Social Security, 18, 63
*Soul on Ice* (Cleaver), 138
Soviet Union, 26, 27, 34, 36
Spencer, Stu, 109, 120–124, 174–177, 179, 185, 189, 191, 200, 202, 203, 213, 229
Sproul, Robert Gordon, 87
State Department, 34
Stevenson, Adlai, 152
Stevenson, Cyril, Jr., 109, 118–120, 123
Stevenson, Robert Louis, 4
Storke, Thomas, 112–113, 115, 192, 207
*Storm Warning* (film), 35
Storrs, Elizabeth, 78
Strikes, 32–33
Strong, Edward, 88, 100
Student Nonviolent Coordinating Committee (SNCC), 46, 82
Student protest, 81–90, 93–102, 130–131, 189–196, 199, 237
Students for a Democratic Society (SDS), 208
Sturgeon, Vern, 77
Swift, Wesley, 57

Thomson, John, 101
Thoreau, Henry, 191
*Time* magazine, 68, 69, 113, 205
Tobriner, Matthew, 2–3
*Tocsin* (weekly), 190
Toledano, Ralph de, 219
Truman, Harry, 32, 35
Tuttle, Holmes, 66–67, 72–73, 75–76, 173, 180, 191, 192, 196, 216, 232–233
Twain, Mark, 4

United Auto Workers (UAW), 15
United Farm Workers (UFW), 152, 218
United Republicans of California (UROC), 78, 109, 123, 231
U.S. Commission on Civil Rights, 48, 138, 148
U.S. Commission on Race and Housing, 48
*U.S. News & World Report*, 189
University of California at Berkeley, 81–90, 93–102, 130–131, 189–196, 199, 237
Unruh, Jesse, 49, 50, 53, 154–157, 166, 171, 203, 221, 222, 261
Unruh Civil Rights Act, 45
Urban League, 137
Urban reform, 9, 11–12, 136–137, 146, 148–149

Veterans Administration (VA), 48
Veterans Affairs Committee, 33
Veysey, Victor, 77
Vietnam Day Committee (VDC), 151–153, 191, 193
Vietnam War, 131, 151–154, 162, 169, 186, 218–220, 241
Voting Rights Act of 1965, 188

*Walden* (Thoreau), 191
Walker, Edwin, 115, 116
Walker, Robert, 177, 179
Wallace, George, 145, 158
Walton, Rus, 180
Ward, Paul, 161
Warner, Jack, 174
Warner Brothers, 30
War on Poverty, 137, 158, 163, 241
Warren, Charles, 223
Warren, Earl, 11, 12, 14–16, 26, 38, 42, 104–106, 112, 113, 150, 209, 230
Warschaw, Carmen, 166, 223
Warschaw, Louis, 223
*Washington Post*, 25, 68, 219
Waters, Laughlin, 174, 185
Watson, Marvin, 149
Watts riots, 128–149, 157, 164–166, 186–188, 195, 218

Wayne, John, 31, 32, 64
Wedeymeyer, Jack, 198
Weinberg, Jack, 82, 88
Weinberger, Caspar, 178–179, 191, 205, 213, 237–238
Welch, Robert, 104, 107, 110, 112, 114, 116, 122, 124–126
Welfare system, 18, 23, 27, 69, 71, 74, 197–198, 225
*Where's the Rest of Me?* (Reagan), 33
White, Clif, 66
Whitney, Peter, 87
Wills, Garry, 196
Wilson, L.H. "Spike," 51, 52
Wilson, Woodrow, 16, 159
Winton, Gordon, 141–142, 156
Women's Christian Temperance Union, 28
Works Progress Administration (WPA), 29
World War II, 10, 31
Wright, Loyd, 27, 39, 41, 214
Wyatt, Joe, 222
Wyman, Gene, 234, 235
Wyman, Jane, 35

Yearling Row, California, 40–41
Yorty, Sam, 137, 142, 185–186, 205, 223–224
  Brown and, 156–159, 161–163, 167, 169, 216–217
  gubernatorial campaign (1966), 158, 159, 163, 165–171
  Watts riots and, 132, 134, 143, 144, 147, 148, 157, 158, 164, 211
Young, Mike, 110
Young Americans for Freedom (YAF), 39, 106, 231
Young Republicans (YRs), 62, 104, 107, 109, 119, 120, 123, 177, 231